GROUP-BASED MANUAL FOR CHRISTCARE GROUP LEADERS

GROUP-BASED MANUAL
FOR CHRISTCARE
GROUP LEADERS

VOLUME 1
INITIAL TRAINING • SESSIONS 1–16

Group-Based Manual for ChristCare Group Leaders
ISBN: 1-930445-14-8

C: 02/01/2005   R:

13   11   09   07
 5   4   3   2

ChristCare Group Ministry

Stephen Ministries • St. Louis, Missouri • (314) 428-2600 • www.stephenministries.org

Dear ChristCare Group Leader Trainee:

Congratulations on your selection to train and become a ChristCare Group Leader!

First of all, your training will be a transforming journey. In fact, transformation—change, growth, morphing from a caterpillar to a butterfly—is what ChristCare is all about. ChristCare Groups are circles of care with Christ at the center. And you aren't likely to spend that much time with Jesus without his life penetrating yours and transforming you.

Personal transformation begins with what you will *learn* in training. You'll learn how to lead the four ChristCare Group activities—community building and care, Biblical Equipping, prayer and worship, and missional service—and how the Holy Spirit uses them to change lives. You'll learn both by listening and by doing—actually leading various role play and skill practice situations. You'll prepare prayer and worship experiences for the group and lead a group through your own Biblical Equipping session. You'll learn to be a great ChristCare Group Leader by practicing these activities in the safe and sympathetic company of fellow travelers. And through it all, Jesus will be calling you to follow him more closely and casting a vision for what your group is called to be and do.

In addition to what you learn, you and your Equippers will *be* a ChristCare Group. You'll build community and learn to trust one another on ever deeper levels. You'll hear the Word of God, meditate and live it out daily, and then share how God's Word is changing you. You'll work together on a missional service project to carry God's love outside your group. You'll deepen your life of prayer and worship. You'll experience being a circle of care with Christ at the center, and your experience will give you an ever clearer vision of the transformation possible in and through ChristCare Groups.

Then you'll carry that vision for transformation to others. God will use you to bring others in touch with Jesus. You'll tell your group members from your own experience about how God came to you in your ChristCare Group. Your life of faith and obedience will point them toward the transformation that Paul described to the Galatians: "I have been crucified with Christ and I no longer live, but Christ lives in me. The life I live in the body, I live by faith in the Son of God, who loved me and gave himself for me" (Galatians 2:20).

Can you be a ChristCare Group Leader? Certainly! You will be thoroughly trained and well supported by the Equippers in your congregation—and you will be led and empowered by the Holy Spirit. Prepare to be surprised by the changes God will make in you. "The one who calls you is faithful and he will do it" (1 Thessalonians 5:24).

Yours in Christ,

The ChristCare Team at Stephen Ministries

Table of Contents

And let us consider how we may spur one another on toward love and good deeds.

Hebrews 10:24

1. Welcome

FOCUS NOTE 1

1 Thessalonians 5:23–24

May God himself, the God of peace, sanctify you through and through. May your whole spirit, soul and body be kept blameless at the coming of our Lord Jesus Christ. The one who calls you is faithful and he will do it.

---

2. Community Building: Getting to Know One Another

3. *Beginnings: A ChristCare Group Experience*

A. L.I.F.E.—Learn It From Experience

1-OFN.pmd C: 01/06/2004 R: 11/16/2004

4. Biblical Equipping: Jesus Forms His Small Group (Luke 5:1–11)

FOCUS NOTE 2

Jesus Forms His Small Group (Luke 5:1–11)

[1]One day as Jesus was standing by the Lake of Gennesaret, with the people crowding around him and listening to the word of God, [2]he saw at the water's edge two boats, left there by the fishermen, who were washing their nets. [3]He got into one of the boats, the one belonging to Simon, and asked him to put out a little from shore. Then he sat down and taught the people from the boat.

[4]When he had finished speaking, he said to Simon, "Put out into deep water, and let down the nets for a catch."

[5]Simon answered, "Master, we've worked hard all night and haven't caught anything. But because you say so, I will let down the nets."

[6]When they had done so, they caught such a large number of fish that their nets began to break. [7]So they signaled their partners in the other boat to come and help them, and they came and filled both boats so full that they began to sink.

[8]When Simon Peter saw this, he fell at Jesus' knees and said, "Go away from me, Lord; I am a sinful man!" [9]For he and all his companions were astonished at the catch of fish they had taken, [10]and so were James and John, the sons of Zebedee, Simon's partners.

Then Jesus said to Simon, "Don't be afraid; from now on you will catch men." [11]So they pulled their boats up on shore, left everything and followed him.

[handwritten note, left margin: Liz = trust God, bit by bit, safe @ shore then deeper]

[handwritten note: ↱ stay in class, deep]

[handwritten note, bottom: Darin — scary, irresponsible, but trusting that her leap of faith will work]

FOCUS NOTE 3

Explore Questions

1. Knowing what you do about Jesus and his teachings, what do you think he may have been teaching about as he sat in Simon's boat and spoke to the crowd? *Trust me.*

2. What do you think Jesus was trying to teach Simon Peter by taking him out into the deep water and having him catch so many fish? *You can't just fish from shore - go further out, draw in.*

3. Do you think Simon Peter's understanding of the event in verse 8 was what Jesus was trying to teach? If not, then what?

4. What do you recall that Jesus' disciples did during the years they were together? *Ate. Taught. He was tough & to learn from experience.*

5. How was their small group like a ChristCare Group? *gentle; led group. See above. Small group; sent out for others*

6. Why do you think it was necessary for Jesus' disciples to leave everything behind in order to follow him? *God will provide - daily prayer, unencumbered.*

FOCUS NOTE 4

Connect Questions

1. How has God blessed you with <u>overflowing</u> <u>abundance</u>—as Jesus blessed Peter and his partners with the huge catch of fish? *Family, friends, connectedness, variety, more give = more get*

2. What do you think Jesus wants to teach the members of the ChristCare Group that you will lead? *nurturing, community, has value; faith where we meet God*

3. How is Jesus calling you to leave everything behind and follow him? *All the traits, things, comforts we love & yearn for are here.*

4. How might the ChristCare Group you lead be like Jesus' small group of disciples? How do you need God to help you lead your group to be like Jesus' group?

The other things that take up my time ($, job, house) don't inspire me as this path does.
Feel less burdened - peaceful.

Questions to Focus Sharing of Biblical Equipping Apart

- Share one insight that you've had as a result of your Biblical Equipping Apart this week.

- Describe one change in your life that you've made or committed to make as a result of your meditation on the Biblical Equipping passage this week.

- Tell about a time when you met God in a new way through Biblical Equipping Apart this week.

5. Creating a Covenant

A. L.I.F.E.: Learn It From Experience

B. The Benefits of a Covenant

A ChristCare Group Covenant Is Important

1. It is a tool for building group agreement and for helping the group learn to work together.
2. It is a tangible reminder of what the group has agreed to and says is important.
3. It encourages ongoing commitment.
4. It helps everyone agree to disciplines (such as confidentiality) that are necessary to the group's success.
5. It helps group members think through the practical ways they will live out their commitment to the group. They accept the requirements that go with ChristCare Group participation.
6. It establishes clear expectations for the group and helps avoid future disappointments and conflicts.

Focus Note 6 is continued on page 5.

7. It helps resolve conflicts that arise in the group.

8. It builds ownership of the group by all members and helps avoid a leader-centered group.

9. It spells out the group's purpose and helps hold the group accountable to that vision.

10. The covenant-building process allows group members to practice many skills they'll need in their future together.

11. The covenant-building process may help some group members discover that this group—at this time—may not be the right place for them.

12. A covenant helps keep group life focused and productive.

---

① Shared set of goals.
② Commitment to participate.
③ Sets a path for the future.

C. How to Create a Covenant

FOCUS NOTE 7

A Process for Making Group Decisions

Step 1: Identify Your Options

Brainstorm any options group members can think of. Write them where everyone can see them.

Step 2: Take a Pulse

Ask for a show of hands on each option to see if you already have consensus. If you have consensus, point out to the group that they agree and the decision is made. If you don't have consensus, move on to the next step.

You can take a pulse at different times as you work toward a decision. It is a way to see if the group has come to agreement on the decision.

Step 3: Narrow Your Options

Ask group members to vote for each option they favor. Write the number of votes where everyone can see. Eliminate any options that didn't receive any votes, or options that received so few votes that the group can agree to eliminate them.

Focus Note 7 is continued on page 6.

If you need to narrow the number of options further, ask each member to cast up to three votes, choosing the options they like best. Keep the top three vote-getters.

Step 4: Invite Comments

Invite group members to explain to the group why they favor one choice over another. Be sure everyone who wants to gets a chance to speak. Don't allow arguing or interruptions. Give people the chance to say what they wish without being challenged.

Step 5: Narrow Down to One Choice

Ask group members to vote for all but one of the remaining options. Continue to narrow down this way until a decision is reached.

FOCUS NOTE 8

What to Do If You Don't Have Consensus

A Process for Making Group Decisions

1. Compromise—see if the group can come up with an alternative that offers something to everyone and that enables all group members to feel comfortable.
2. Trial period—try it one way for an agreed-upon period of time; after that time, reassess the decision, changing it if necessary.
3. Wait—table the item if necessary; then in a week or two see if someone can suggest an acceptable alternative or if people's feelings have changed.

D. Create a Training Covenant

6. Prayer and Worship: Do Not Be Afraid, I Am with You

FOCUS NOTE 9

Do Not Be Afraid, I Am with You

Leader: God, you are our God. We trust in your great love for us.

All: Be with us as we begin this great venture in your name.

Leader: You have called us:

All: We are yours.

Leader: This is what the Lord says:

All: "'Fear not, for I have redeemed you;
I have summoned you by name; you are mine.

Men: When you pass through the waters,
I will be with you;

Women: and when you pass through the rivers,
they will not sweep over you.

All: When you walk through the fire,
you will not be burned;
the flames will not set you ablaze.

Leader: For I am the LORD your God,
the Holy One of Israel, your Savior; . . .

All: See, I am doing a new thing! . . .

Men: I am making a way in the desert
and streams in the wasteland.

Women: . . . I provide water in the desert
and streams in the wasteland,

All: to give drink to my people, my chosen,
the people I formed for myself'" (Isaiah 43:1b–3a, 19–21).

Take a moment now to feel God's
peace settle upon you.
— put concerns in a bubble & release to God
— prayers/needs
— praise

FOCUS NOTE 10

Prayer

All: "O LORD, I call to you; come quickly to me.
Hear my voice when I call to you.

May my prayer be set before you like incense;
may the lifting up of my hands be like the evening sacrifice."
(Psalm 141:1–2).

Leader: Lord God, we trust in your infinite wisdom and love.

All: We trust that what you have begun in us today you will bring to fulfillment in us.

Leader: You will never abandon us, Lord.

All: We know that you will be with us when the path is smooth and especially when the path is rough.

Appendix A

Covenant for ChristCare Group Leaders in Training

Put a check mark ☑ to indicate the items your training class agrees to. Cross out statements that do not apply to your training class. Write additional purposes, promises, and decisions in the space provided.

Our Class's Purpose

❑ We seek to answer God's call to serve as ChristCare Group Leaders and to live more fully as disciples of Jesus.

❑ We seek quality preparation to serve as ChristCare Group Leaders.

❑ We seek to know God better through Biblical Equipping, prayer, and living out Christ's love for one another.

❑ We seek to know one another better by listening, expressing feelings, accepting others' feelings, relating assertively, and accepting one another (and ourselves) unconditionally.

❑ We seek to equip one another to reach out with Christ's love to ChristCare Group members, to visitors, to our ChristCare Groups, and to those outside the groups we lead.

Other purposes (write them below):

Promises We Make to One Another

In order to achieve this purpose, we will:

❑ Keep confidential whatever other trainees share with us, both during meetings and outside of meetings.

❑ Attend training sessions faithfully, missing only when it is unavoidable and notifying an Equipper ahead of time when an absence is necessary.

❑ Begin and end our training sessions on time.

❑ Understand that because this is a training class, we will not be able to invite visitors, prospective group members, or prospective ChristCare Group Leaders to any training session or to accept new trainees during the course of this training class.

❑ Complete necessary reading assignments prior to each training session in order to make each in-class experience the best it can be.

❑ Hold one another accountable for these promises.

Other promises (write them below):

Decisions about Training Sessions

In order to work together most effectively as a training class, we agree to the following:

❑ Our meeting time will be (day, time, length of meeting)_____

❑ Our meeting place(s) will be_____

❑ When we must be absent or late, we will

_____

❑ Concerning refreshments, we will_____

❑ We will participate in_____retreats together on_____

Other decisions (write them below):

With God's help, we will abide by this covenant.

Date _____

Signatures_____

_____

_____

_____

_____

_____

_____

_____

_____

_____

Appendix B

ChristCare Group Covenant

Put a check mark ☑ to indicate the items your group agrees to. Cross out statements that do not apply to your group. Write additional purposes, promises, and decisions in the space provided.

Our Group's Purpose

❏ This group's members seek to know God better through Biblical Equipping, prayer, and living out Christ's love for one another.

❏ This group's members seek to know one another better by listening, expressing feelings, accepting others' feelings, relating assertively, and accepting one another (and ourselves) unconditionally.

❏ This group seeks to equip group members to reach out with Christ's love to visitors, new group members, and others outside the group.

Other purposes (write them below):

Promises We Make to One Another

In order to meet these goals, we will:

❏ Remain a distinctively Christian group, looking to God in Scripture and through prayer for guidance and spiritual growth and seeking to share Jesus' love with one another and with others outside our group.

❏ Care for one another by accepting one another unconditionally and by being available to one another during times of crisis.

❏ Keep confidential whatever group members share, both during meetings and outside of meetings.

❏ Attend group meetings faithfully, missing only when it is unavoidable.

❏ Begin and end our meetings on time.

❏ Stay evangelistic and missional by welcoming visitors and new members at any meeting.

❏ Complete reading assignments.

Other promises (write them below):

Decisions about Group Meetings

In order to work together most effectively as a group, we agree to the following:

❏ Our meeting time will be (day, time, length of meeting)_____

❏ Our meeting place(s) will be_____

❏ When we must be absent or late, we will
_____

❏ Concerning refreshments, we will _____

❏ We will continue to meet together as a group until
_____

Other decisions: (Issues to consider might include choice of Bible translation, completing assignments, practicing spiritual disciplines such as daily prayer or Bible reading, arrangements for child care, or smoking during meetings)

With God's help, we will abide by this covenant.

Date _____

Signatures _____

_____

_____

_____

_____

_____

_____

_____

_____

_____

Building Community in Your ChristCare Group

Preclass Reading

Dear friends, let us love one another, for love comes from God.
Everyone who loves has been born of God and knows God.

1 John 4:7

PRECLASS READING OUTLINE

I. What Is Community?

What do you think of when you hear the word *community*? The neighborhood where you live? Your church family? The people you work with? In ChristCare Groups, community has a special meaning. In this section you'll learn what Christian community is and how to create it in your group.

A. *Koinonia*

The Greek word *koinonia* describes what we mean by Christian community. Read Luke's description of koinonia in the early church:

FOCUS BOX 1

They devoted themselves to the apostles' teaching and fellowship, to the breaking of bread and the prayers. Awe came upon everyone, because many wonders and signs were being done by the apostles. All who believed were together and had all things in common; they would sell their possessions and goods and distribute the proceeds to all, as any had need. Day by day, as they spent much time together in the temple, they broke bread at home and ate their food with glad and generous hearts, praising God and having the goodwill of all the people. And day by day the Lord added to their number those who were being saved (Acts 2:42–47 NRSV).

Many people translate the word *koinonia* as *fellowship*. But it also includes these ideas: to hold something in common, to be in partnership with, to be connected with, to participate in something together, and to share.

2-PRE.pmd C: 12/16/1993 R: 01/24/2005

Take another look at the Scripture verses from Acts with all these meanings of koinonia in mind. Focus Box 2 lists the ways in which Christians in the early church had koinonia.

FOCUS BOX 2

Examples of Koinonia in the Early Church

- Learning together
- Eating together
- Praying together
- Witnessing to God's greatness
- Sharing material goods
- Providing for others' needs
- Meeting together regularly
- Sharing the Lord's Supper
- Praising God
- Reaching out to others with Christ's love

As you can see, Christians in the early church shared time, resources, care, and their love for God. They didn't try to be "lone-wolf" Christians. They knew they needed one another to be God's people and truly to love. They knew that Jesus was with them in the person of their sisters and brothers in Christ.

Today, ChristCare Groups can offer the same kind of koinonia to members.

Application

Have you ever experienced koinonia? If so, briefly describe the group and how it felt to be part of it. Write your thoughts in the space below.

Why Koinonia Was Important Then and Is Important Now

Life was tough in Luke's day. People faced crime, hunger, illness, poverty, and injustice. They proclaimed Jesus as the Son of God—a dangerous stand to take. This could get them in trouble with religious and political leaders.

To survive, these Christians stuck together. They discovered koinonia. They shared a bond as the children of God, which united them in times of joy and of sorrow.[1] Koinonia, or Christian community, made it possible for the early church to survive and flourish.

Koinonia is still important. Towns and cities all over the world still can be perilous places to live. They are filled with people who are poor, hungry, lonely, and facing crises, who need to hear God's Word. Many of these people are not part of a caring community. They need koinonia, the life-tie that bonds people with one another and with God.

Koinonia Is People-to-People and People-to-God

Community can occur in many different kinds of groups, including groups at work, neighborhood groups, or among friends. Biblical koinonia, or Christian community, goes beyond this. In addition to their caring relationships with one another, Christians together experience koinonia with God. Biblical koinonia provides a life-tie to people and a life-tie to God.

Here's how the Bible describes Christian community:

- "fellowship with his Son, Jesus Christ" (1 Corinthians 1:9)
- "the fellowship of the Holy Spirit" (2 Corinthians 13:14)
- "We proclaim to you what we have seen and heard, so that you also may have fellowship with us. And our fellowship is with the Father and with his Son, Jesus Christ." (1 John 1:3)

Koinonia and ChristCare Group Vision

Looking back over history, it's incredible to see what koinonia has achieved. Christ's church started out as a small band of devoted followers. They met together in small groups and enjoyed the Spirit's gift of koinonia—Christian community. These communities grew and birthed new communities. Today Christ's followers can be found all over the world.

Koinonia is powerful, and your ChristCare Group can tap into that power through community building.

B. How Community Works

The following description of a community in action is adapted from one developed by the Pittsburgh Groups.[2] As you read through the list, keep in mind a small group you've been a part of, if any. In front of each item, circle the letter that best describes your group.

A = Always true for my group.

B = Sometimes true for my group.

C = Never true for my group.

Twelve Critical Ingredients of a ChristCare Group

A B C 1. We accept one another as we are.

A B C 2. We share as much as we like from our own struggles and successes, victories and failures, joys and pains.

A B C 3. We are honest with ourselves and others, telling it like it is.

A B C 4. We listen to one another to hear what people say and what they mean.

A B C 5. We don't criticize or condemn what others share, but instead we affirm the positive things we see in others.

A B C 6. We don't give advice unless others ask for it.

A B C 7. We gather to care and to be cared for—and not to cure. If we care for one another, God will do the curing.

A B C 8. We share our own experience of faith in our words, not someone else's experience in his or her words.

A B C 9. We grow in trust for one another, knowing that what we share will remain within the group.

A B C 10. We give ourselves and others the freedom to be silent.

A B C 11. We spend our group time discussing important personal issues in an informal, natural way.

A B C 12. We encourage one another to serve in and beyond the group.

As a ChristCare Group Leader, remember that the preceding description is your goal—something you'll work toward one step at a time. It doesn't happen easily or automatically.

II. Building Community Means Building Individuals

A healthy group supports and affirms members as *individuals.* This affirmation of individuality doesn't separate group members. Instead, it unites them as confident members of a community.

A. Keeping People from Getting Lost in a Group

Have you ever been part of a group in which the group members began to act alike, talk alike, and even dress alike? In a healthy group, this overidentification is usually just a passing phase. But when it keeps happening, it's time for the ChristCare Group Leader to intervene.

What's Wrong with Everyone Being Alike?

Bad things can happen when group members lose their individuality.

- Group members may suppress their own needs and desires in order to fit in. But this can cause them to feel frustrated and they may quit.

- When group members put a lid on "unacceptable" feelings like anger, hurt, or fear, those emotions can break out in other ways that hurt the group and the person.

- Group members share only what's safe to show—the parts of themselves that will be accepted by the group. They never experience having someone see them as they really are and love them anyway.

- When group members hide their individuality, the group loses a chance to model God's love—love that is freely given, no matter how a person talks, acts, or feels.

- Growth is much less likely to occur in a group where everybody's busy trying to be like everybody else.

- Group members can develop a "herd mentality," going along with decisions or actions just because the rest of the group does.

How to Tell If People Are Getting Lost in Your Group

If you as a ChristCare Group Leader begin to wonder if your group is emphasizing group needs so much that it ignores individual needs, ask yourself these questions:

- Is it difficult—almost impossible—to get the group to focus on one individual group member's needs?
- If someone does manage to express a need, does the group seem disapproving, as if that's a problem that the group member should already know how to deal with?
- Does the group give quick-fix, pat answers to questions, dilemmas, or problems that are brought up?
- Does the group affirm only those members who go along with the group's way of doing things?
- Does it seem as if there's only one way to be Christian in your group—and individual differences are discouraged?
- Do all or a few of the group members see themselves as the "in-crowd"?

B. Helping People Find Themselves in a Group

ChristCare Group Leaders work to ensure that group members are loved *as they are*. This gives members a taste of what God's unconditional love is like. Group members who are loved as they are can better accept themselves, understand that God loves them, and grow as followers of Jesus.

A group that values its members' individuality can be called a *community of individuals.* In this community, individual gifts and differences don't just disappear; instead, they enhance the community.

What's Right about Caring for and Affirming Individuals?

When group members feel free to be themselves:

- Group members discover they can be loved as they are—they don't have to change or conform to some standard. Often, this freedom *not to change* frees people *to change!*
- Group members discover their gifts and know that the group appreciates them.
- Group members admit their questions and doubts about God, work through them, and come out with stronger faith.
- Group members feel safe enough to share and work through problems.

- Group members aren't embarrassed to admit they don't know something—they realize everyone is still growing, personally and spiritually.
- Group members realize that no one in the group is perfect, but that each person is an individual, valuable creation of God.
- Group members set their own goals—goals that are appropriate for their own lives.
- Group members grow in their understanding of Christ by seeing how his love and values are interpreted differently by his followers.

How to Tell If Your ChristCare Group Is a Community of Individuals

If you wonder whether your ChristCare Group is a place where group members feel free to be themselves, ask yourself these questions:

- Do group members completely accept one another?

   When someone expresses a belief that others in your group would call "wrong," watch what happens. If group members accept one another, they'll express their opinions in a way that says, "I disagree with what you say, but I value your right to say it, and I value you as a person. Let's talk about it." As a result, the speaker is much more likely to listen to what the group members have to say.

- Would a non-Christian or a new Christian feel comfortable in your ChristCare Group?

   In a healthy group, members want to learn about others' ideas and beliefs. They also feel free to express their own beliefs. Group members look for opportunities to affirm the visitor and make him or her comfortable.

- Are people cared for as individuals in your ChristCare Group?

   Do group members try to find out what's really going on in others' lives so they can support and pray for them? Do they follow up between meetings with a call or a card when someone is bearing a heavy burden?

- Are individuals more important than the group's regular agenda?

   When someone is facing a crisis, do group members willingly give extra attention and care? Do they agree to leave the regular agenda and focus on this hurting person?

- Do group members feel free to bring any need to the ChristCare Group?

In a community where people know they are valued as individuals, they feel safe enough to ask for help at any time and in any circumstance.

C. Individual Growth Means Group Growth

As group members are nurtured and encouraged in their ChristCare Group, they will grow in many ways. They will become more:

- honest;
- friendly;
- communicative;
- accepting;
- caring;
- trustworthy;
- assertive;
- understanding;
- active;
- trusting;
- aware of personal limitations and gifts.

As group members grow personally, they will in turn create a more mature and accepting group. Following is a list of some characteristics of a mature group.

Characteristics of a Mature Group

- Inclusive—Group members welcome other group members and visitors (in open groups).
- Missional—The group exists to serve those outside the group and finds ways to serve that use group members' gifts and that group members enjoy.
- Open—Group members don't have hidden agendas. When they have comments or concerns, they voice them.
- Safe—Group members protect one another by practicing confidentiality and acceptance.
- Authentic—Each group member is comfortable being who he or she really is.
- Dynamic—The group is energetic, it gets things done, and all members actively participate.
- Decisive—Group members cooperatively and efficiently make decisions.
- Interconnected—Every group member relates to every other group member and to the whole group.
- Free from prejudice and preconceptions—Each group member values the others as individuals, with unique backgrounds and challenges.

A group that values individuality begins a positive cycle that can be described this way: Members nurture and value one another as individuals. As they receive this nurture from one another, they grow in their ability to sacrifice their needs for others. That in turn leads them to nurture and value one another even more effectively. This cycle of individual and group growth continues.

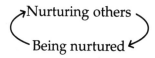

Through this cycle you are building Christian community—koinonia—that helps members grow as disciples and reach out with Christ's love to others.

III. Community Grows in Stages

ChristCare Groups pass through several stages of development on their way to maturity. As groups go through these stages, the group members grow individually, learn to trust one another more, and start working together. Christian community develops. Developmental stages and community building go hand in hand.

As an adult, you have passed through several stages of development in your life, including infancy, childhood, adolescence, and adulthood. Looking back, you might wish you had skipped one of those stages, perhaps a difficult childhood or a turbulent adolescence. But developing children can't be rushed. If a child is forced to skip an important stage, he or she may not function well as an adult.

Knowing about child development helps parents and teachers guide children more effectively through stages of growth. They know what stage the child is in and what kind of growth to expect. They also see what stages are coming up and encourage the child to grow in those directions.

ChristCare Groups also go through definite stages of development as they mature. Although it's the group's job to move through the stages, it's the ChristCare Group Leader's job to prepare and guide the group. The more you know about stages of group development, the better you can guide your group to maturity.

A. Stages of Group Development

Authors and other experts have described the stages of group development in a variety of ways. In this module, you will learn about six stages of group growth.

The acronym "MATURE" will help you remember the stages' names:

M	A	T	U	R	E
Meet	Ask	Test	Undertake	Realize	Extend

The following information describes each stage of group development. Notice how Christian community deepens with each stage, as members grow in their ability to risk, trust, and accomplish. (You'll find a quick-reference summary of these stages on page 17.)

Meet
A new ChristCare Group has a lot of growing to do. Like an infant, it has to learn many different skills. Group members heavily depend on the ChristCare Group Leader during the "Meet" stage. They're unsure of themselves and need guidance as they take their first wobbly steps.

Because this is the first time members have met as a group, they are also careful to be on their best behavior. They don't want to be embarrassed or alienate another group member. They are polite but don't reveal much about themselves.

Ask
ChristCare Group members in the second stage of group development use words like "why," "what," "who," "where," and "when." They begin questioning all kinds of things—the format, the agenda, the actions of other group members, and—of course—the ChristCare Group Leader's leadership.

This happens because group members are dropping their facades of politeness and preparing to get down to business. Individuals begin to reveal their true selves, and the group starts to take on a unique personality.

Test
Groups in this third stage of group development spend their time testing one another: How far can I push before you push back? If I take a risk in sharing, how will you respond? Are you going to let me have my way?

Members also test the ChristCare Group Leader: How much control can we have? Does she really know what she's doing? How does he handle conflict? Whose agenda is this?

Some sparks can fly during this stage, and you, as ChristCare Group Leader, will have to be on your toes. But during this valuable stage, group members learn about one another. They work through power struggles, build relationships, and begin to admit their brokenness. Working through this stage bonds your group into a supportive, productive Christian community.

Undertake
In this stage, group members try out various roles to learn how they will serve and work together. In this fourth stage of group development, groups ask themselves, What shall we do? and How shall we do it? As a ChristCare Group Leader, you don't need to answer these questions for group members. They can—and will—discover the answers themselves.

Some groups decide to focus on discipleship or outreach. Others will take on a project, giving themselves to others outside the group. Many groups will do several kinds of service as they grow and mature.

Realize
Group members in this stage are comfortable with themselves and with one another. They've learned to trust and be trusted. They know how to work with each other, and they've identified important work to do, often missional in nature. These group members know how to make decisions, set goals, and plan the strategies that get their work done.

Extend
A small group in the sixth stage of development shows growth and a pattern of accomplishments. They aren't bored.

A mature small group asks, What's next? They've learned a lot in their time together, and they'd like to share it with others.

At this stage, some group members will go on to become ChristCare Group Leaders. Others will develop other ministries, applying the skills they learned in their ChristCare Group. Still others will become members of new ChristCare Groups, using their expertise to help new groups grow through the stages of development and build Christian community.

B. Leadership Styles That Help Build Community
Knowing the stages of group development will help you as a ChristCare Group Leader. You also need to know how to use different leadership styles to move your ChristCare Group through those stages.

Stages Small Groups Pass Through as They . . .

M	A	T	U	R	E
MEET	**ASK**	**TEST**	**UNDERTAKE**	**REALIZE**	**EXTEND**
In this initial stage, group members get acquainted. They are polite to each other as they form their first impressions of individuals and of the group as a whole.	In this stage, group members ask questions, including: Why are we here? What are we doing? Who are these other people, anyway? What makes this leader so special?	Group members in this stage experience conflict. Group members test one another and the leader to figure out just where each individual stands in terms of power, important issues, and ideas about what the group is going to do.	Group members are now ready to get to work carrying out their small group's vision. They decide how they're going to operate and what they will accomplish, and then they do it.	Groups in this stage are finally realizing their goals as they work well together.	Group members are ready to share what they've learned. They love and appreciate one another and are pleased with their personal growth and accomplishments. Energized by their achievements, group members want to facilitate this same kind of growth in other groups.
As group members near the end of this stage, they become impatient with the superficiality that characterizes it.	Questioning helps group members break through the facade of politeness and prepare to work.	During this stormy stage, group members lay the groundwork for future cooperation.	Group members spend less time trying to figure out who is in charge and more time trying to work together smoothly.	Group members are growing personally, and the group as a whole is efficiently doing important work. Group members make decisions, set goals, plan actions, and carry them out.	
Leadership styles most often used in this stage are: • Giving Direction • Receptive to Input	Leadership styles most often used in this stage are: • Giving Direction • Receptive to Input	Leadership styles most often used in this stage are: • Receptive to Input • Offering Opportunities for Leadership	Leadership styles most often used in this stage are: • Receptive to Input • Offering Opportunities for Leadership	Leadership styles most often used in this stage are: • Offering Opportunities for Leadership • Welcoming Independence • There When Needed	Leadership styles most often used in this stage are: • Welcoming Independence • There When Needed

The acronym "GROWTH" can help you remember the five different leadership styles that help ChristCare Group Leaders move their groups toward maturity:

G	**R**	**O**	**W**	**TH**
Giving Direction	Receptive to Input	Offering Opportunities for Leadership	Welcoming Independence	There When Needed

The following section describes each leadership style. Notice that the styles become progressively more participatory. (You'll find a quick-reference summary of these styles on page 19.)

Giving Direction
In this leadership style, a ChristCare Group Leader takes charge. He or she decides what's going to happen and tells the group how to make it happen. Here are some times when you might use this style:

- In the "meet" stage of group development. A ChristCare Group needs plenty of structure and guidance when they first meet together. The ChristCare Group Leader gives direction by making the meeting arrangements and by setting the group's agenda and format. He or she also leads the group in making a covenant.

- As needed during any other stage of group development. Whenever a crisis such as a heart attack, a tornado warning, or an emergency phone call occurs, the ChristCare Group Leader needs to use this style. Giving direction is also necessary when a group member brings an overwhelming need to the group, requiring a complete change in agenda.

Receptive to Input
In this style, a ChristCare Group Leader invites the group to help make decisions. For example, he or she might say:

- "There are a number of different ways the group could handle child care. Let's list them together."

- "I've identified several options for a Bible study topic. I'll describe them, and then tell me what you think."

- "I'll be out of town on the next meeting date. Our group could handle my absence in a couple of different ways. Which do you prefer?"

After offering opinions, the ChristCare Group Leader invites group discussion and helps the group make its decision.

Offering Opportunities for Leadership
In this style, the ChristCare Group Leader doesn't present choices, but asks group members to come up with their own ideas from scratch. For example, the leader might ask open-ended questions such as these:

- "What do you want to do about this?"
- "How shall we handle this?"
- "What shall we study next?"

The ChristCare Group Leader may even step aside and let another group member take over leadership of the discussion and the decision making. This allows group members to try out their ideas and exercise more and more leadership.

Welcoming Independence
In this style, a ChristCare Group Leader gradually turns leadership of a nearly mature group over to group members. This allows group members to practice their leadership skills in preparation for future leadership roles. For example:

- A ChristCare Group Leader might ask an Apprentice Leader to regularly take over part of the agenda, such as Biblical Equipping or sharing.

- A leader affirms group members when they show skill and sensitivity in listening and caring for one another.

There When Needed
In this style, the ChristCare Group Leader is available but no longer on center stage.

Usually, the group has reached the "Extend" stage. Group members are in charge most of the time and are ready to move on to leadership roles in the congregation, community, or other groups. This leadership style is best defined as participatory leadership—the ChristCare Group Leader is one participating leader among many. A ChristCare Group Leader would use this style when:

- Group members rarely slip up in communicating and interacting with one another. If someone does slip, other group members catch it in an affirming way.

- Group members are leading most group activities and taking most responsibilities.

- Group members are actively seeking new ways to grow and minister, either inside or outside the group.

Leadership Styles That Facilitate . . .

G R O W TH

GIVING DIRECTION	RECEPTIVE TO INPUT	OFFERING OPPORTUNITIES FOR LEADERSHIP	WELCOMING INDEPENDENCE	THERE WHEN NEEDED
In this style, a ChristCare Group Leader decides where the group is going and how it's going to get there. This leader takes charge.	In this style, a ChristCare Group Leader solicits input on process, content, and direction. This leader leads democratically.	In this style, a ChristCare Group Leader encourages group members to come up with and try out their own ideas. This leader is providing a safe place for future leaders to test their wings.	In this style, a ChristCare Group Leader lets group members lead, but still works to help them grow and lead effectively. This leader is focusing on helping others become effective leaders.	In this style, a ChristCare Group Leader acts, when needed, as a resource for the group. This leader is serving the group by becoming a fellow member.
A leader might use this style when:	A leader might use this style when:	A leader might use this style when:	A leader might use this style when:	A leader might use this style when:
• Helping a new group get started, when group members don't know what to do and haven't learned to work together; • Communicating the congregation's vision to a new group; • Directing group members to jettison their agenda and focus on caring for a hurting group member; • Confronting a group that refuses to deal with some important issues.	• Helping group members develop their covenant; • Selecting a program or topic for the group; • Setting the agenda for meetings, planning social events, or choosing mission projects.	• Individuals in the group have experienced personal growth and might be ready to demonstrate it; • Group members are ready to explore their own leadership potential.	• He or she has identified one or more group members as apprentice ChristCare Group Leaders; • Group members are taking more and more responsibility for care, instruction, and other types of leadership; • The group is ready to subdivide and birth a new group.	• It's clear that a group has matured enough to operate most of the time without the leader's guidance; • Group members are consistently and effectively handling leadership responsibilities.

C. Combining Group Development Stages and Leadership Styles

Remember that stages of development don't always happen as neatly in real life as they do on paper. Children, for instance, can show surprising wisdom and maturity at times. Conversely, adults sometimes act like children. Don't be surprised if your small group's development is a little different from the MATURE pattern.

For example, you might expect that your group will complete the "Meet" stage and move directly to "Ask." But it's not that simple. Your group might jump from one stage to another, get stuck on a stage for a while, or regress to a stage they've already gone through. This doesn't make a ChristCare Group Leader's job any easier—but that's the way it is!

You'll need to switch leadership styles, using different styles in different stages or even different styles in one stage. The diagrams on pages 21 and 22 can help you understand this interplay of styles and stages. Take a few minutes now to look at them.

D. A Special Challenge—The Ask and Test Stages

Let's take a closer look at ways to handle the Ask and Test stages of development.

The Ask and Test stages can be frustrating for ChristCare Group Leaders and members alike. But if you understand what's going on and why it's important to the group's later development, you'll find it easier to cope with these stages.

What Happens in Ask and Test

In the Ask stage of group development, group members gradually stop being polite and superficial. They begin to let their real feelings show to you and to other group members. They start thinking seriously about "why we're here." The Ask stage is a little bit like thunderclouds forming on a sunny day. When you see the clouds, you know that a storm is coming!

If the Ask stage is the thundercloud, Test is the lightning, thunder, and downpour. As a group moves into the Test stage, the expression of individual differences becomes more pronounced. It's almost as if group members wear their uniqueness, their individuality, as a badge.

Group members assert their uniqueness in many ways. For instance, they may try to decide what the group is going to study or complain about the current format.

Being unique isn't bad. In fact, individuality is something to affirm in people. But during the Ask and Test stages, group members try to impose their own needs and wants on the group. It's as if they are saying, "Do it this way. My way is the right way."

When 10 or 12 people in a group are all saying, "Do it my way," a power struggle ensues. Whose way will win out? The struggle escalates as group members stubbornly cling to their own "right way." The group may even turn on you, saying you're not a good ChristCare Group Leader—just look at the mess the group is in!

The strife that can occur during the Ask and Test stages makes most ChristCare Group Leaders feel like taking tight control and steering the group back on course. Unfortunately, that would only postpone the problem's solution. You can't fix the group's problem. The group members must face it and fix it for themselves.

How to Recognize the Ask and Test Stages

When you see several of these signs, your group is probably in the Ask or Test stage:

- group members openly express their differences;
- group members try to get others to agree with their positions or opinions;
- group members tell others how to solve their problems;
- group members resist help from others;
- there's plenty of unproductive interaction among group members;
- no one is having much fun;
- group members accuse the leader of doing a bad job.

Your group probably won't show all these signs at once. Also, different groups will experience these signs at different levels of intensity and for differing lengths of time.

When Group Members Get Tired of Ask and Test

Group members in the Ask and Test stages aren't enjoying themselves. They get tired of the power struggles and look for ways out. Here are some solutions they might try:

- Group members may try to organize their way out of difficulties they're in. However, they don't deal with the root problem—the conflict between individuals who haven't yet learned how to make room for one another's uniqueness.

Diagram 1: ChristCare Group Growth

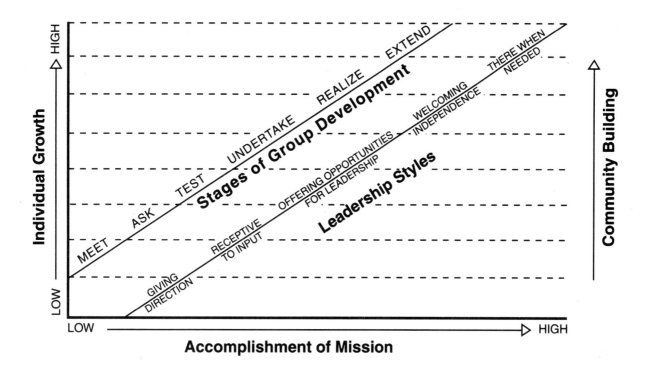

As a ChristCare Group experiences growth, these things occur:

- The group progresses through stages of development.
- The leader uses more participatory leadership styles.
- Individual growth increases.
- The group becomes a community.
- The group accomplishes its mission.

Diagram 2: Growth Is Not Orderly or Completely Predictable

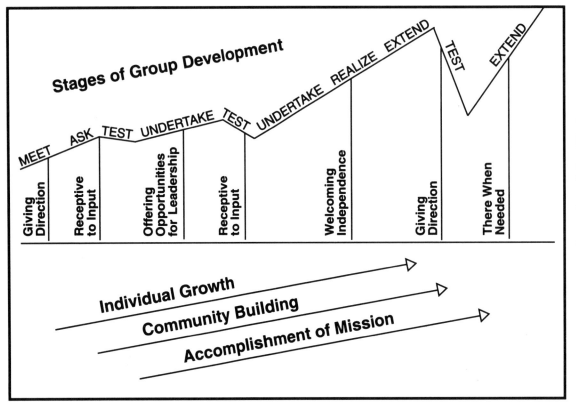

Diagram 1 might lead you to believe that a group's progress to maturity is orderly and predictable. It's not. Groups bounce between stages, hit plateaus, skip stages, and regress. Healthy, growing groups, however, keep moving in the general direction of personal growth, community building, and accomplishment of the group's mission.

An effective leader uses each of the leadership styles whenever it is needed. For example, a ChristCare Group that has reached the "Extend" stage may inexplicably begin ignoring a group member's obvious need. Even at this late stage of group development, the ChristCare Group Leader still needs to be ready to give direction to the group. In this case, a single intervention is usually enough to get the group back on track.

Because group members are ignoring the basic problem, their efforts at organization won't work. The problems will come back.

- New leaders might try to take your place. A group member might say, "We haven't been doing so well. Why don't we try . . ." If this happens, try not to become defensive; realize that this is a normal, although frustrating, stage. Retain your leadership by making room for the would-be leader to try out his or her ideas (and, likely, fail).

An Example of Handling the Test Stage
A ChristCare Group is struggling with how to handle hosting responsibilities. The ChristCare Group Leader is moderating the discussion, heading off personal attacks, but mostly displaying a wait-and-see attitude.

In the middle of one meeting, Marcia decides she's tired of waiting for the leader to take charge. She says, "Let's stop this nonsense. Here's a sign-up sheet. Just pass it around, and we'll all take turns hosting the meetings from now on."

The ChristCare Group Leader says, "What do the rest of you think about trying this plan?"

The leader's assertive action has these advantages:

1. She retains leadership by speaking up and referring the question to the rest of the group—not ignoring it.
2. She avoids personal conflict with the would-be leader by referring judgment to the entire group.
3. If the group likes the idea, she can show she has retained leadership by saying, "That was a great idea, Marcia."
4. If the group doesn't like the idea (and members probably won't, since one person has imposed it on them), she has still put the problem back where it belongs—in the group's lap. The group continues to work through the Test stage.

How Group Members Get Out of Ask and Test
The only way group members move out of these difficult stages is by changing their attitudes about their individuality. Rather than, "My individuality makes me right," group members begin to say, "My individuality makes me me, and yours makes you you." This happens gradually.

Here are some signs that ChristCare Group members are growing out of the Ask and Test stages:

- group members begin communicating honestly;
- they drop barriers to communication, including
  - preconceived ideas: "Mine is the only way to feel (or act)"
  - prejudices: "She's old, so she doesn't have anything to offer me"
  - narrow-mindedness: "I can't stand people like that"
  - the need to fix others and their problems
  - the need to control others;
- group members begin to talk about their brokenness, their cares, and their failures rather than only their successes, their achievements, and their solutions.

What You Can Do during Ask and Test
The most difficult—and the most important—thing for you as a ChristCare Group Leader to do is to maintain your leadership without taking control of the group. The group has to work its own way out of these stages.

It is appropriate to use Giving Direction, but use it sparingly and in these ways:

- Point out what's going on. "It looks as if each of us has our own ideas about what to do here." "Trying to fix one another's problems doesn't seem to be working."
- Explain the Ask and Test stages to the group. It won't hurt them to know about the stages; they will still go through them anyway.
- Explain community to the group. Ask the group how they could create community.
- Ask group members what they think is getting in the way of creating community.
- Affirm group members when you see them beginning to express honest feelings of frustration.
- Affirm group members when they begin to admit their weaknesses, fears, and brokenness.
- Let the group know when they're heading in the right direction.

Hang In There!
When your group goes through Ask and Test, talk about it in your SEA Group. Get some support and ideas from other ChristCare Group Leaders. Re-read this information. It can be a challenging time, but the rewards for working through it are great.

IV. How to Build Christian Community in a ChristCare Group

Christian community doesn't just happen in ChristCare Groups. It's something that group members continue building throughout the group's life.

A. Basic Principles of Community Building

The basic principles of community building are listed below:

- Lay a foundation of trust
- Build supporting walls of affirmation
- Install windows of authenticity
- Cover with a roof of confidentiality

Trust

Some dictionary definitions of "to trust" include:

- to depend on;
- to be confident in;
- to place in another's care or keeping;
- to rely on the truthfulness of.

You can't build community without the foundation of trust. Look for every opportunity to model trust by trusting others and by being trustworthy yourself. Structure opportunities for group members to trust one another and to demonstrate their trustworthiness. Build trust by asking group members to take small risks, then move on to larger risks. Watch for these signs that trust is growing in your ChristCare Group:

- group members follow your lead in taking risks;
- group members begin to drop their masks and pretenses and feel free to be themselves;
- group members grow in their ability to love and accept themselves and others;
- group members begin to take more and more significant risks;
- group members share deeply and honestly about themselves and their lives;
- group members volunteer to take risks before they're asked.

In the early weeks of your ChristCare Group, you may need to move carefully with sharing activities if you believe some of your group members don't know how to trust or how to be trustworthy. Supplement A of this training module provides trust-building activities appropriate for different stages of group development.

As trust grows among group members, you'll notice the beginnings of community building and maturity.

Affirmation

Walls of affirmation are an important part of demonstrating care for others. Notice what a simple act of affirmation can accomplish:

Act of Affirmation	What It Can Communicate
"I appreciate you."	"You are a valuable and worthwhile person."
"Thank you."	"You've made a valuable contribution."
"That's right."	"Your ideas are sound; you have good insight."
"Good idea."	"Your input is helpful."
"I admire your ability to . . ."	"Your good qualities are noticeable."

Affirming people sends a message that they are worthwhile and important. It also makes it much more likely that they will repeat the action or attitude you affirmed.

As ChristCare Group Leader, affirm people when you see them moving toward greater growth and maturity. When you affirm others, you are setting a good example. Soon group members will begin to affirm others, too. Affirmation helps build trust, and trust builds community.

Christ affirmed and accepted tax collectors, rulers, prostitutes, soldiers, Gentiles, and thieves. Later, he pointed out how they could grow into the people God meant them to be. But first he accepted them—affirmed them—as they were.

Authenticity

When people begin to trust and when they receive affirmation for who they are, they are ready to risk opening windows of authenticity. Being authentic means being your real, genuine self—not hiding behind a mask. It means knowing these things:

- I don't have to pretend I'm perfect; I can just be me.
- Others here aren't perfect; it's normal to have struggles.
- I might choose a different solution to my problem than someone else; my solution only has to work for me.
- My struggles might be different from other group members', but we all have struggles.

- The other people in my group are okay; I'm like them in many ways and different in others; I'm okay too.
- My differences make me unique and worthwhile.
- I know who I am; I appreciate the good things about me; I'm working on the rest.
- Others in this group see me as I am and care about me.
- God sees me as I am and loves me.

Confidentiality

Houses need roofs to keep out the storms. Confidentiality is the roof that can keep your ChristCare Group safe from outside storms.

Confidentiality means that everything that's shared in the group stays in the group. No one talks without permission—even to a spouse—about what other group members say, do, share or feel. Confidentiality is part of the group covenant. (You will learn much more about confidentiality in a later module.)

B. Community Building Is a Process

Your group won't achieve total trust first, and only then move on to affirmation, authenticity, and confidentiality. Your group will grow in all of these areas from the beginning. These elements depend on one another. Affirmation builds trust. Confidentiality is essential if people are going to risk being authentic. As each element grows, so will your group's overall community.

V. Getting Ready for the In-Class Session

After completing this Preclass Reading, you've learned about:

- what community is;

- the importance of maintaining individuality within a community;
- how stages of group development relate to community building;
- how leadership styles fit different stages of development;
- how to build community in your ChristCare Group.

You've also had opportunities to apply this information in some personal and practical ways. In the in-class training session, you'll experience some aspects of community building firsthand.

Here are several things you can do to help apply what you've learned in this Preclass Reading and to prepare yourself for the in-class training session:

- think about the role trust plays in your relationships with your family, friends, and co-workers;
- as you participate in various communities—your family, your neighborhood, your church, your workplace—notice what you enjoy about them. Also think about how those communities could be strengthened. Could you play a role in building up those communities?

ENDNOTES

1. Colin Brown, general editor, *The New International Dictionary of New Testament Theology* (Grand Rapids: Zondervan Publishing House, 1975). Many of the concepts in the section on koinonia came from this source.

2. The Pittsburgh Groups, Pittsburgh, Pennsylvania.

Supplement A: *Community-Building Activities*

Part One
Part One activities require group members to share facts about their histories and backgrounds. They are appropriate for the beginning stages of community building.

Truth, Truth, Surprise
Ask each group member to share any two truths about himself or herself. These would probably be the basics, such as, "I've lived in Kentucky all my life, and I'm a civil engineer." After the two truths, the group member shares one more truth, but this time it should be something that might surprise others, such as, "I once sang the national anthem at a World Series baseball game." Others may ask for more details about the surprise statement. As leader, encourage other group members to ask for more information by modeling—"When was that, Bob?"—or extending—"Anyone want to know more about that?"

May I Introduce You?
Break the small group into pairs. Explain that they will have a total of four minutes. During the first two-minute period, one partner tells the other about him- or herself—whatever that person wants to share. The partners switch roles during the second two-minute period. Then everyone comes back to the group and each partner introduces the other, telling the group as much as he or she can remember.

Dates of the Decades
Explain to the group that you're going to go back in time by decades, and ask each group member to share one important personal date from each decade. The date should stand for an important event in his or her life. Depending on the ages and size of your group, go back at least three or four decades.

History of Homes
As in "Dates of the Decades," go back in time decade by decade. This time, ask each group member briefly to describe a home he or she lived in during each of those decades.

How Did You Get Your Name?
There are often interesting stories behind the names people have. Ask each group member to share how or why his or her name was chosen.

Questions
Use any of these questions to help group members share facts about their personal backgrounds.

- When you were ten years old, where were you living? What was your house like? Who was in your family? What was your favorite thing to do? (You can use these questions again for different ages, such as five, 15, 25, etc.)
- When I say "hometown," what place do you think of and why?
- Who were the members of your family when you were growing up?
- What did you like to do for fun as a child?
- What was your favorite food as a child?

Part Two
Part Two activities move a little deeper into community building. They require group members to share feelings about their backgrounds. A ChristCare Group Leader would be most likely to use these activities during the "Ask" or "Test" stage of group development.

Childhood Table
(Use one, several, or all of these questions.) Picture sitting at the dinner table at home when you were ten (or five, or 15, etc.) years old.

- What was talked about at this table?
- Who was there?
- Who was a "warm" person at this table?
- How were problems dealt with at this table?
- If you could have changed something about this table, what would it have been?

Safety in Numbers
As in the "Dates of the Decades" activity, go back in time by decades. This time ask the group members to describe a place where they felt happy at some time during each decade.

VIPs
Ask group members to describe how one Very Important Person influenced them in their lives. You could give them a time frame for this, such as childhood, adolescence, adulthood. Or you could simply let them share about whoever comes to mind.

Nicknames

Ask group members to share nicknames they've had in the past, to explain where the nicknames came from, and to share how they felt about having the nicknames.

Through a Mirror Dimly

Invite group members to share about the earliest time they were aware of God.

Questions

Use any of these questions to help group members share feelings about their personal backgrounds.

- What is something you really liked about growing up?
- What is something you would have changed about growing up?
- What was something you did that you were proud of during childhood? Adolescence? Early adulthood?
- What was your most embarrassing experience as a child? Teenager? Adult?
- What childhood event evokes warm memories?

Part Three

Part Three activities require group members to share facts and feelings about their past and present circumstances. They are appropriate for deep levels of community building. A ChristCare Group Leader would be most likely to use these activities during the "Undertake," "Realize," and "Extend" stages of group development.

The Movies

Ask each group member to think of a movie title that would best describe his or her life to this point and to explain why the title fits.

Name That Feeling

Ask each group member to put an adjective in front of his or her name that describes how he or she feels right now—for example, Stressed-out Susan, Worried Dan, or Peaceful Tim. Variation: Use an adjective that describes how he or she would like to feel.

Trust Walk

Break the group into pairs, then explain that they will have three minutes. One partner should close his or her eyes, and the other partner will take him

or her on a "blind" tour of the house or room. After three minutes, call time and ask the partners to switch roles and repeat the exercise. Bring group members back together and lead a discussion, asking questions such as

- "What did your partner do to help you feel safe?"
- "Was it difficult or easy to trust your partner for your safety? Why?"
- "What was something that surprised you about this activity?"
- "What have you learned about trust?"
- "What have you learned about yourself?"

Successes/Failures

Ask group members to share three successes they are most proud of and why. Then ask them to share one failure and explain why they saw it as a failure and how it helped them grow as persons.

Faith to Have Faith

Ask group members to describe an experience when they had serious doubts about their faith in God. Invite them to explain how they got through the experience.

Questions

Use any of these questions to help group members share facts and deep feelings about themselves.

- What is something that you're afraid of?
- What would you like to change about yourself?
- What is your greatest joy in life?
- What would you still like to achieve in life?
- If you are unoccupied for a moment, what are you likely to think about?
- What makes you angry?
- What makes you sad?
- What are your greatest strengths? What are your greatest weaknesses?
- What do you most often pray about?
- When is God most real to you?
- What makes you really laugh?
- What's the biggest hurdle you've had to overcome in your life?
- When have you felt really cared for?
- What would you most like to be remembered for?

Supplement B: *Other Resources for Community Building*

Coleman, Lyman. *Serendipity Youth Ministry Encyclopedia.* Littleton: Serendipity House, 1985.

Hart, Lois B. *Saying Goodbye.* King of Prussia, Pennsylvania: Organization Design and Development, Inc., 1989, Second Edition.

Hart, Lois B. *Saying Hello.* King of Prussia, Pennsylvania: Organization Design and Development, Inc., 1989, Second Edition.

Scannell, Edward E., and John W. Newstrom. *Still More Games Trainers Play.* New York: McGraw-Hill, Inc., 1991.

Sheely, Steve. *Ice-Breakers and Heart-Warmers.* Littleton: Serendipity House, 1994.

Building Community in Your ChristCare Group

Outline and Focus Notes

Dear friends, let us love one another, for love comes from God.
Everyone who loves has been born of God and knows God.

1 John 4:7

1. Worship: Finding a Home

FOCUS NOTE 1

Psalm 84

How lovely is your dwelling place,
　　O Lord Almighty!
My soul yearns, even faints,
　　for the courts of the Lord;
my heart and my flesh cry out
　　for the living God.

Even the sparrow has found a home,
　　and the swallow a nest for herself,
　　where she may have her young—
a place near your altar,
　　O Lord Almighty, my King and my God.
Blessed are those who dwell in your house;
　　they are ever praising you.

Blessed are those whose strength is in you,
　　who have set their hearts on pilgrimage.
As they pass through the Valley of Baca,
　　they make it a place of springs;
　　the autumn rains also cover it with pools.
They go from strength to strength,
　　till each appears before God in Zion.

Hear my prayer, O Lord God Almighty;
　　listen to me, O God of Jacob.
Look upon our shield, O God;
　　look with favor on your anointed one.

Better is one day in your courts
　　than a thousand elsewhere;

Focus Note 1 is continued on page 30.

29

2-OFN.pmd C: 01/27/2004 R: 01/24/2005

I would rather be a doorkeeper in the house of my God
  than dwell in the tents of the wicked.
For the LORD God is a sun and shield;
  the LORD bestows favor and honor;
no good thing does he withhold
  from those whose walk is blameless.
O LORD Almighty,
  blessed is the man who trusts in you.

---

2. Community Building: Establishing Bonds of Trust

FOCUS NOTE 2

The Interrelationship of Trust, Maturity, and Community in ChristCare Groups

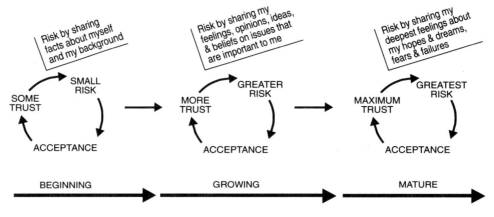

Levels of Community Building

3. Biblical Equipping: What Does Christian Community Look Like? (Colossians 3:11–17)

FOCUS NOTE 3

Questions to Focus Sharing of Biblical Equipping Apart

• Share one insight that you've had as a result of your Biblical Equipping Apart this week.

• Describe one change in your life that you've committed to make as a result of your meditation on the Biblical Equipping passage this week.

• Tell about a time when you've met God in a new way through Biblical Equipping Apart this week.

FOCUS NOTE 4

What Does Christian Community Look Like? (Colossians 3:11–17)

[11] Here there is no Greek or Jew, circumcised or uncircumcised, barbarian, Scythian, slave or free, but Christ is all, and is in all.

[12] Therefore, as God's chosen people, holy and dearly loved, clothe yourselves with compassion, kindness, humility, gentleness and patience. [13] Bear with each other and forgive whatever grievances you may have against one another. Forgive as the Lord forgave you. [14] And over all these virtues put on love, which binds them all together in perfect unity.

[15] Let the peace of Christ rule in your hearts, since as members of one body you were called to peace. And be thankful. [16] Let the word of Christ dwell in you richly as you teach and admonish one another with all wisdom, and as you sing psalms, hymns and spiritual songs with gratitude in your hearts to God. [17] And whatever you do, whether in word or deed, do it all in the name of the Lord Jesus, giving thanks to God the Father through him.

FOCUS NOTE 5

Explore Questions

1. How would you summarize the way that Paul says Christians are to live together?

2. What internal changes does Paul seem to find necessary for Christians to live together in this way?

3. What does Paul tell the Colossians to do in order to help bring those changes about?

4. Based on the first and last verses of this passage, what does Paul believe is most important in making Christian community happen?

FOCUS NOTE 6

Connect Questions

1. What signs do you see—in our group, our congregation, our community, or our world—of people living in community where "Christ is all, and is in all"?

2. What can prevent us from experiencing the kind of Christian community that Paul describes?

3. What could we do in this class to increase our experience of the community that Paul describes?

4. How do you need to grow in order to be able to lead others into the community that Paul describes?

4. Stages and Styles—and Building Trust

A. Stages of Group Development

FOCUS NOTE 7

Stages of Group Development

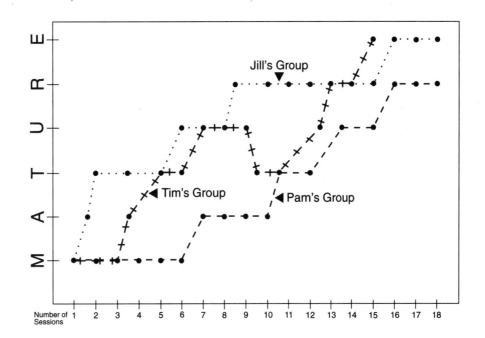

B. Leadership Styles

FOCUS NOTE 8

Your Comfort Level with Leadership Styles

How comfortable are you with using the different leadership styles? Circle the number on the right that best fits for you.

	Never Comfortable			Always Comfortable	
Giving Direction	1	2	3	4	5
Receptive to Input	1	2	3	4	5
Offering Opportunities for Leadership	1	2	3	4	5
Welcoming Independence	1	2	3	4	5
There When Needed	1	2	3	4	5

C. Building Trust

FOCUS NOTE 9

How to Build Trust in Your ChristCare Group

1. Trust others

Risk being more vulnerable than the others in your ChristCare Group. When others see your trust, they will gain confidence to trust also.

2. Be trustworthy

Show that you are trustworthy. For example, offer to pray for someone, then do it, and let him or her know you did it. Promise to check into something, do so, and then report your findings to the group. As you show that you are trustworthy, group members will begin to place their trust in you and in one another.

Focus Note 9 is continued on page 35.

3. *Make the group a trustworthy place*

Help your group establish a covenant in which you agree to maintain confidentiality, to care for one another, and to allow each member to proceed at his or her own pace. Challenge group members to risk and grow, but always give them the chance to pass if an activity makes them uncomfortable. Model good listening and show others how to make your group a safe place where trust can grow.

4. *Deal openly with broken trust*

No one (except Christ) is trustworthy all the time. At some point, someone in your ChristCare Group—perhaps even you—will break a trust. If you break trust, deal openly with it, admit the mistake, apologize, and then move on. If someone else breaks trust, talk with him or her privately to see if he or she can bring it into the open and deal with it.

5. *Structure trust-building opportunities*

When you're planning discussions, worship, study, and prayer times, consider how you can use these activities—for example, by modeling or sharing your own experiences—to help ChristCare Group members learn to trust one another more.

5. Prayer: Share Prayer Concerns and Pray in a Circle

Appendix A

Four Exercises

Exercise One—Don't Leave Home without It

**EXERCISE
GOAL**
To use humor to help put group members at ease while they share something about themselves.

LEADER
The directions you'll give your ChristCare Group members are indicated by the word Say. Everything else, indicated by the word Leader, is background information for you. In this exercise, you are a participating leader—you both lead and participate in the exercise.

SAY
I'd like you to take out your wallet, purse, hip-pack, backpack, or whatever you have with you that comes close to that.

LEADER
If a group member doesn't have any of these things, a Bible might work if the individual stashes items in it, such as old church bulletins. If this doesn't work, ask the group member to imagine having his or her wallet there for the exercise.

SAY
Now take a minute to look through your wallet or purse and find the most *useless* thing you have in there.

LEADER
Wait about 30 seconds.

SAY
Now let's take turns sharing what your useless item is and why in the world you carry it around with you.

LEADER
Give everyone a chance to share.

SAY
Okay, let's put this useless stuff away and wait for further directions!

Exercise Two—This Is What I Think about That

EXERCISE GOAL To offer group members the opportunity to share their thoughts, feelings, beliefs, and opinions about a topic.

LEADER Here is the quotation you will discuss:

> *It's fine to level with people if you don't level them in the process.*
> —Walter St. John

The directions you need to give the ChristCare Group members are indicated by the word *Say*. Everything else, indicated by the word *Leader*, is background information for you. In this exercise, you are a participating leader—you both lead and participate in the exercise.

Ask these questions one at a time, and ask group members to share their answers.

SAY Has everyone had a chance to read the quotation up on the board? I'd like to know what you think of it.

- Do you think the statement is true or false? Why?

- Why do you think people level others in the process of leveling with them?

- What is the one most important thing you can do when leveling with someone to keep from leveling him or her?

LEADER If no one wants to start the discussion, you go first. Remember not to worry about silence. Group members may need a minute to think about their response to the quotation.

If the discussion is fairly superficial, you can take it deeper by saying something like, "I can remember a time when I got leveled . . ." Or ask the group, "Have you ever been leveled by someone? How did it make you feel? What did you do after you got leveled?"

Announce the one-minute warning, and then end the exercise with the following question.

SAY Does anyone have something to add before we end our discussion?

LEADER If someone hasn't contributed to the discussion yet,

SAY *[Name]*, would you like to share some thoughts before our time runs out?

Exercise Three—Sentence Starters, Part One

EXERCISE GOAL   To offer group members the opportunity to share something personal about their history.

LEADER   **The directions you need to give the ChristCare Group members are indicated by the word *Say*. Everything else, indicated by the word *Leader*, is background information for you. In this exercise, you are a participating leader—you both lead and participate in the exercise.**

SAY   For our first sharing activity, I'd like for each of you to finish the sentence, "One of my fondest childhood memories is . . ."

LEADER   **Start the discussion by asking, "Who would like to begin?" If no one responds for a while, say, "Why don't I go first?" and do so. If your group finishes early and wants to extend the exercise, continue with one of these sentences:**

- **One of my fondest memories from my teen years is . . .**
- **One of my fondest memories as an adult is . . .**

After everyone has shared, conclude the exercise by saying the following.

SAY   It's really interesting to hear a little bit about your backgrounds. I think it's helped us all to learn a bit more about one another.

Exercise Four—Sentence Starters, Part Two

EXERCISE GOAL To offer group members the opportunity to share at increasingly deeper levels.

LEADER **The directions you need to give the ChristCare Group members are indicated by the word *Say*. Everything else, indicated by the word *Leader*, is background information for you. In this exercise, you are a participating leader—you both lead and participate in the exercise.**

SAY In this next exercise, we're going to complete two sentences that go a little deeper and require a bit more risk in what we share.

We're going to complete a sentence about ourselves just as we did last time. We're also going to work on responding to one another. That means that after someone shares, each of us will respond by saying, "When you said that, I felt, or I wondered"—whatever expresses your reaction to what the person shared. If anyone feels uncomfortable completing either of these sentences, that's absolutely fine. Just say, "Pass."

The first sentence to complete is, "A time I can remember being lonely is . . ."

Who would like to begin?

LEADER **If no one responds for a while, you share first. After each person completes the sentence, go around the group asking others to respond to him or her. Again, if group members have trouble getting started responding, you go first.**

If you finish early and want to extend the exercise, use one of these statements as a second sentence starter:

- **A time when I've been afraid is . . .**
- **A time when I've been worried is . . .**

After everyone has completed a sentence, close with the following words.

SAY Thank you for participating so honestly in this exercise. Even in this short time together, I think that we all know one another a little better and have begun to build some trust.

(handwritten notes)
① Read by Tues 5/24
40 - 51
② fill out Role UP on TRI-FOLD

"My command is this: Love each other as I have loved you."

John 15:12

PRECLASS READING OUTLINE

I. Introduction: The Nature of Care in Groups

   A. An Example of Typical ChristCare Group Care

   B. The Scope of ChristCare Group Care

   C. The Scope of This Module

II. How Jesus Cared

III. A Simple Definition of Care

IV. What Kinds of Needs for Care Do People Have?

   A. Emotional Needs

   B. Physical Needs

   C. Social Needs

   D. Intellectual Needs

   E. Spiritual Needs

   F. Needs Are All Mixed Together

V. How Do ChristCare Groups Meet People's Needs for Care?

   A. Presence

   B. Empathy

   C. Listening

   D. Prayer

   E. Tangible Care

   F. Challenge and Encouragement

   G. Cultivation

   H. Evangelization

VI. Snapshots of Caring in and through ChristCare Groups

   A. Caring *in* ChristCare Groups

   B. Caring *through* ChristCare Groups

VII. The ChristCare Group Leader's Roles in Group Caregiving

   A. Facilitator

   B. Caregiver

   C. Teacher

   D. Organizer

   E. Referrer

VIII. Getting Ready for the In-Class Session

I. Introduction: The Nature of Care in Groups

A. An Example of Typical ChristCare Group Care

After prayer and worship the ChristCare Group settled into their regular time of community building and care.

Brenda said, "I can't tell you what a relief it is to be here with all of you. This has been the week-from-you-know-where, and it is so nice to be with people I know care about me."

Claire, the group leader, replied, "Tell us more."

Brenda said, "Work has been a nightmare. We are two weeks away from a very difficult deadline, and I'm asking the people I work with to step it up a couple of notches. If they have to stay an extra hour or come in earlier to get their part of the project done, then that's what they need to do. Everyone is counting on everyone else.

"But there are a couple of people who are making trouble for everyone else—especially me. They moan and complain every chance they get. They interrupt others' work in order to draw them into these complaining conversations. When I ask them to get back to work, they glare at me. They seem to be deliberately working more slowly—doing what they can to sabotage the whole team. They are making my life miserable."

Frances said, "I'm sorry this is so difficult for you. I know you've been excited about your project at work for months. It must be disappointing to deal with such petty behavior."

"I was looking forward to coming to the group meeting," Brenda said. "It is great knowing that I'll be listened to and understood."

George said, "I wonder if it might help to pray for the two people making life difficult for you."

Brenda sighed. "I know that's what Jesus wants me to do. Maybe praying will help me love them like Jesus does—I certainly can't do it by myself. By myself I don't even want to."

Group members laughed and Brenda joined in. Then Claire said, "Let's pray."

B. The Scope of ChristCare Group Care

The care that ChristCare Groups provide inside and outside the group is important and needed, a blessing to those who receive it. In order for ChristCare Groups to care well, however, it is important to know what kinds of care ChristCare Groups do well and what kinds of care ChristCare Groups are not qualified to provide.

The care that ChristCare Groups are qualified to provide is the nurturing, supportive care that people need as they experience the stress and challenge of daily life. The example above shows this kind of care. Group members also provide a caring presence for one another during emergencies and times of crisis. You'll read examples of this kind of care later in this Preclass Reading.

The care that ChristCare Groups give, however, is limited in scope. ChristCare Group Leaders are not trained to be counselors, therapists, pastors, or other professional caregivers. ChristCare Groups are not qualified to provide all the care that people with major needs require. There may be times when a ChristCare Group member requires additional care from a Stephen Minister or other lay caregiver, a pastor, a counselor or psychotherapist, or some other professional.

ChristCare Groups care best when they understand that they can't provide all the care some people need, and when they rely on others to help care for members with more extensive needs.

C. The Scope of This Module

This module introduces care. There are many modules in ChristCare Group Leader training that fill in a lot more detail about how to care. They include:

- Session 4, Listening Skills for ChristCare Group Leaders;
- Session 5, Confidentiality in ChristCare Groups;
- Session 6, When and How to Make Referrals for Additional Care;
- Session 7, Prayer and Worship in ChristCare Groups;
- Session 8, Missional Service by ChristCare Groups;
- Session 11, Being a Process-Oriented Leader;
- Sessions 18 and 19, Assertiveness Skills for ChristCare Group Leaders;
- Session 22, Evangelism in and through ChristCare Groups; and
- Session 23, Dealing with Strong Feelings in ChristCare Groups.

II. How Jesus Cared

As Christians we strive to care as Jesus did. We can build our understanding of how we can care in ChristCare Groups by looking at how Jesus cared for others.

There are many passages in the Gospels that show Jesus caring for people. Read the passages listed in Focus Box 1 below.

FOCUS BOX 1

Biblical Examples of Jesus' Care

- *Matthew 9:2–7*
  Jesus forgives a paralyzed person's sins (and also heals him)

- *Matthew 14:13–21*
  Jesus feeds 5,000 hungry people

- *Matthew 14:25–27*
  Jesus calms fearful disciples

- *Luke 5:12–13*
  Jesus touches a leper

- *Luke 23:33–34*
  Jesus obtains forgiveness for us

- *Luke 23:39–43*
  Jesus promises paradise to a condemned criminal

- *John 3:1–15*
  Jesus explains himself to Nicodemus

- *John 11:20–36*
  Jesus comforts Lazarus' sisters

- *John 19:25–27*
  Jesus provides a family for his mother

Jesus understood others' needs and met their needs with God's healing power and love. He didn't limit his care to what people might define as "spiritual" needs, but cared for people with all kinds of needs. He cared courageously when he touched people afflicted with leprosy. He sacrificed himself to meet humanity's greatest need—alienation from God brought about by our sin—with God's gifts of forgiveness and new life.

III. A Simple Definition of Care

The intent of the following simple definition of care is to give you a practical understanding of what it means to care in and through your ChristCare Group.

> *Care is responding to people's needs with God's love and with ours.*

This module will equip you with a better understanding about how to determine people's needs and respond to them with love. As Christian caregivers, we can be sure that God is at work in and through our caring, and that the love we give to others is in fact God's love.

IV. What Kinds of Needs for Care Do People Have?

God has created people with five broad types of needs for care:

- emotional;
- physical;
- social;
- intellectual; and
- spiritual.

A. Emotional Needs

God created people with feelings, which can be wonderful or deeply painful. Grief, anger, despair, and fear are examples of difficult feelings that often require care. It is also caring to share another person's very positive feelings, such as celebrating another's happiness at the birth of a child or a grandchild.

You read some examples of Jesus caring for people's emotional needs when he calmed his disciples' fears and grieved along with Mary and Martha at Lazarus' death. Jesus understood others' feelings, shared them, and spoke to them with words of comfort and hope.

B. Physical Needs

Jesus clearly showed that care involves helping meet people's physical needs. Physical needs include:

- hunger and thirst;
- health;
- safety;
- shelter and clothing;
- other needs, such as help with child care for a single parent or car repair for a person experiencing financial difficulties.

C. Social Needs

Jesus cared for people's social needs. He knew his mother needed family, and he instructed his disciple to take her into his care. When he healed lepers, he instructed them to go to the temple for rites of cleansing so they could reenter society.

Caring for people with social needs might mean providing respite care by staying with a homebound person so the group member who customarily has that responsibility can get away for a while. Care for social needs may involve helping a widowed or divorced person find the courage to make new friends.

D. Intellectual Needs

Nicodemus had such burning questions that he had to talk to Jesus, even though he had to come at night to keep the visit secret. Jesus cared for Nicodemus on an intellectual level. He took Nicodemus' questions seriously and treated Nicodemus with respect.

People with intellectual needs might include mothers of young children who rarely get to talk with other adults. Older persons who are no longer employed may yearn for the challenging conversations they used to have at work.

Intellectual needs can also include the lack of necessary information. If a person with financial difficulties doesn't know how to make a budget, he or she has an intellectual need that group members can help meet, either by providing assistance themselves or by finding someone else who can.

E. Spiritual Needs

Jesus knew the paralyzed man needed forgiveness even more than he craved healing. When Martha's world seemed to be coming apart, she needed to know that her brother Lazarus would live again and that God was still in charge. The robber crucified next to Jesus needed to know that he would live on in God's love, even as he was about to die. When Jesus said, "Father, forgive them . . ." he cared not only for those present at his crucifixion, but for all of us who are lost without his sacrifice for our sin.

ChristCare Group members respond to people's spiritual needs by connecting them with God's love. If a person is deeply afraid, it may be helpful to pray with him or her. Those wondering about their life's meaning may receive hope and encouragement from Scripture. People suffering guilt may benefit from confessing their guilt and receiving assurance of God's forgiveness.

F. Needs Are All Mixed Together

None of these five kinds of needs is likely to exist in isolation. A person in need of forgiveness (spiritual need) may suffer very painful feelings (emotional need) as he or she regrets the effects of his or her sin on a very important relationship (social need). A poverty-stricken person may be very cold and hungry (physical needs) and not know what to do to get out of that situation (intellectual need); he or she may be unable to act on his or her own behalf because of depression (emotional need).

When ChristCare Group members or Leaders try to understand others' needs in order to care for them, it is important to realize that people will always have a cluster of interrelated needs. Those who give care will look for several kinds of needs in order to fully understand how to care for a hurting person.

Given all these needs, what concrete activities can ChristCare Group members do to care for one another and for others outside the group? How can Christians address others' needs with God's love and with their own?

V. How Do ChristCare Groups Meet People's Needs for Care?

Sometimes the care exhibited in a given situation seems instinctive. When a young child cries out in pain, many parents know that holding or stroking the child will be comforting.

Often, however, effective caring does not come naturally. Effective caregivers learn ways of responding that have been proven over time to communicate love to people in need. Following are descriptions of eight ways ChristCare Group Leaders, members, or anyone else can respond with care for others.

A. Presence

Sometimes the most powerful thing a ChristCare Group member or Leader can do is just to be present with a hurting person. Your presence says to the other person that he or she does not have to suffer alone. You care enough to be there with that person, even if it hurts you to do so.

The ministry of presence means just being there. It means giving others the gift of your time. That can be very difficult for action-oriented people who want to quickly diagnose and solve every problem. Such quiet presence can be, however, exactly the kind of love a hurting person needs. Often hurting people aren't ready to solve their problems and appreciate caring friends who are willing to be there with them as they go at their own pace. The presence of a faithful friend can help a person in need find the courage to work out his or her own solutions to difficult problems.

Presence conveys God's love. Jesus' incarnation (becoming a human being and sharing what it is like to live as one of us) was a ministry of presence. It is as if God said to humankind, "I love you so much that I will become one of you. I will be there with you in the worst of your pain. You can be certain that you will never have to suffer alone."

Sometimes, at a ChristCare Group meeting, someone may share a deep need or pain. Group members may be tempted to jump right in and suggest ways to solve the problem. A group with the insight to be quietly present for the hurting person will powerfully express their love and God's. Later they will undoubtedly care in other ways—perhaps listening, praying, and sharing words of hope and encouragement.

There may be times when a group member is in the hospital or has a family member who is hospitalized. There may be nothing others in the group can do to change the situation, but the hurting person needs someone to be there. Belonging to a ChristCare Group means that person doesn't have to bear such times alone.

B. Empathy

Empathy is a special kind of presence. It means understanding the other person so well that you know what he or she is going through. In *Giving and Taking Help*, Alan Keith-Lucas writes, "Empathy is the ability to know, or to imagine, what another person is feeling and, as it were, feel it with him (or her) without becoming caught in that feeling and losing one's own perspective."[1]

Empathy is caring for another person's feelings. If caregivers don't understand what another person is feeling, they are unlikely to understand the other person's needs or know how to respond to them. On the other hand, if the caregivers become so caught up in the other person's feelings that they are just as needy as the care receiver, they will not be able to give much care.

If a person is crying, the empathic response is to feel that person's sadness, but not to be overwhelmed by the other person's feelings. If group members don't understand the crying person's sadness and don't share those feelings, they will seem detached and uncaring. If, on the other hand, the group members feel overwhelmed by the care receiver's feelings of sadness and also start crying, then they may be so caught up in their own feelings they aren't able to care for the care receiver.

Empathy means accepting another's feelings as real and valid. Empathetic group members don't condemn another's feelings—they try to understand them. For care receivers it is comforting to be understood, to know that someone else knows what they are feeling and still cares for them and accepts them.

The author of Hebrews tells how Jesus has empathy for us, and how we benefit. "For we do not have a high priest who is unable to sympathize with our weaknesses, but we have one who in every respect has been tested as we are, yet without sin. Let us therefore approach the throne of grace with boldness, so that we may receive mercy and find grace to help in time of need" (Hebrews 4:15–16 NRSV).

There is much more information about empathy and feelings in session 23, Dealing with Strong Feelings in ChristCare Groups.

C. Listening

Listening is a powerful way to respond to another's needs with love. When people experience difficulty, they just need people who will listen while they talk about it. Careful listeners make it possible for others to "talk it out," "get it off their shoulders," "spill their guts." Getting their feelings out in the open can produce a great sense of relief. In the act of telling a caring listener about a problem, it is possible to discover a solution. Caring listeners can help others understand their circumstances and recognize their feelings about a difficult situation.

God is a caring listener. He hears us when we pray. Paul encouraged the Thessalonians to "pray without ceasing" (1 Thessalonians 5:17). God is such a wonderful listener that he hears every word, no matter how much we pray.

There is much to learn about listening therapeutically. Session 4, Listening Skills for ChristCare Group Leaders, goes into much more detail about how to exercise listening as a caring tool.

D. Prayer

When Jesus came down from his transfiguration, he found a child who was possessed by an evil spirit. Jesus' disciples had tried to cast the spirit out, but they could not. The Gospel account says, "But Jesus took him by the hand and lifted him up, and he was able to stand. When he had entered the house, his disciples asked him privately, 'Why could we not cast it out?' He said to them, 'This kind can come out only through prayer'" (Mark 9:27–29 NRSV).

Prayer is at the heart of Christian care. People have needs that only God can meet, and so they seek God's care for others through prayer. In the book of James it says, "Are any among you sick? They should call for the elders of the church and have them pray over them, anointing them with oil in the name of the Lord. The prayer of faith will save the sick, and the Lord will raise them up; and anyone who has committed sins will be forgiven. Therefore confess your sins to one another, and pray for one another, so that you may be healed. The prayer of the righteous is powerful and effective" (James 5:14–16 NRSV).

Prayer is a central part of ChristCare Group meetings. Group members share about their lives and their needs. The normal response is to bring those needs to God in prayer. Group members pray for one another between group meetings. As

ChristCare Group Leaders, you pray for members of your groups between meetings.

It can be very comforting for hurting people to know that others are praying for them. It helps them know that God is caring for them and renews their hope that God will be with them throughout their time of need and deliver them from their pain and unhappiness.

You will learn much more about the part prayer plays in ChristCare Group meetings in session 7, Prayer and Worship in ChristCare Groups.

E. Tangible Care

To say that something is tangible means that you can touch it; it is concrete rather than theoretical, it is practical. Sometimes people have needs that require very tangible care. Jesus cared tangibly when he fed 5,000 hungry people. Focus Box 2 contains some additional examples of tangible care.

FOCUS BOX 2

Examples of Tangible Care

Some examples of tangible care are when ChristCare Group members:

- open their home to a group member whose house has burned;
- offer rides to someone who cannot drive;
- take care of a group member's children while he or she goes to a job interview;
- bring meals to a family just home from the hospital with a new baby;
- fill sandbags to protect another's home from a flood;
- go as a group to help at a homeless shelter;
- adopt a needy family for the holidays; or
- fix a person's car when he or she cannot afford repairs.

Group members care for one another in tangible ways. If a group member has an emergency need, he or she may feel comfortable calling another group member and asking for help. When group members are in crisis, the rest of the group will rally around them and do all they can to bring the power of God's love to meet the needs of the person in crisis.

Group members may also offer tangible care to those outside the group. Your ChristCare Group

Leader training includes session 8, Missional Service by ChristCare Groups.

F. Challenge and Encouragement

There are times when the loving response to another's need is to challenge him or her to try something new, to take the next step in growth, or to abandon harmful ways of thinking and acting. Jesus' message to the man—to sell all he owned and follow—was not what the man wanted to hear, but it was what he needed to hear. The author of Hebrews writes about this kind of care: "And let us consider how to provoke one another to love and good deeds, not neglecting to meet together, as is the habit of some, but encouraging one another, and all the more as you see the Day approaching" (Hebrews 10:24–25 NRSV).

There may be times when a group member needs to be challenged to practice spiritual disciplines in order to grow in faith, which is something he or she desires to do. A group member may complain to the group about the same problem, week after week. He or she may know what to do to solve the problem, but never act. In such a circumstance, the caring thing for the group to do might be to challenge the group member to act to solve his or her problem.

A group member once told a story about how his group helped him renew his relationship with his father. He had been estranged from his father for many years and had shared with the group about that relationship. As he told the group about his father, he became convinced that he should write his father a letter, and he told the group about this conviction. Over the weeks and months that followed, group members asked the man whether he had written the letter and encouraged him to do so. Finally, he wrote the letter, mostly because of the group's persistent encouragement. The letter eventually led to a renewed relationship with his father, and the man credited his group with challenging him to take that first step.

Challenging care always takes place in an atmosphere of support and encouragement. The Hebrews passage clearly places the "provoking" (stimulating, spurring on, urging) in a context of community and encouragement. Note how Mark writes that, "Jesus looked at him and loved him" (Mark 10:21). David Augsburger, in his book *Caring Enough to Confront*, tells how confrontation can be a caring act if it is framed in a loving relationship.[2] Challenging another is a caring act only if it is bathed in love, and if the one doing the challenging has previously cared enough to establish a relationship with the one being challenged.

Be careful with this kind of care. It can easily turn into results-oriented attempts to fix others' problems. With all kinds of care, but especially with challenging, the caring group members need to ask themselves, "Whose needs are we trying to meet?" If the honest answer to that question is that the challenge is for the sake of the other person, then it can be a caring act.

Such an act can also be uncaring. A challenge is not caring if it is made to get the other person to conform to the caregiver's standards, to make the caregiver feel more comfortable, or to exercise control over the other person.

You will learn more about how to challenge and encourage effectively when you read the book *Speaking the Truth in Love* and study sessions 18 and 19, Assertiveness Skills for ChristCare Group Leaders.

G. Cultivation

In his book *Care of the Soul*, Thomas Moore writes, "Care can also mean cultivation, watching, and participating as the seed of soul unfolds into the vast creation we call character or personality."[3] In the parable of the sower Jesus compares God's Word to a seed that grows inside people and results in faith and good works. One of the ways groups care is to cultivate the seed of faith that the Holy Spirit has placed in every group member.

Cultivating care occurs over time. Group members pay attention to the faith that is growing in one another. They "water" the seed regularly as they gather at group meetings and share the joy of God's love. Sometimes they "feed" the seed with stories of their own experiences of receiving God's love and following Jesus, or by reminding one another of biblical truths about God's love and care. They shelter one another's "seeds" from the heat of painful crises by sharing one another's pain. They encourage maturity by working together to serve others.

Everyone needs help growing as Jesus' disciple. No one can do it alone. Patient, long-term cultivation is a way group members meet this need with God's love.

H. Evangelization

To evangelize others is to "good news" them, to share with them the wonderful truth of God's love for us, which comes through most clearly in Jesus' life, death, and resurrection. Evangelization traditionally means sharing the good news of Jesus' love with those who don't yet believe in Jesus. That is certainly the first meaning of evangelization, but it is not only that.

Christian people also need to hear regularly the good news of Jesus' continuing love for them. When ChristCare Group members respond to this need by assuring one another of Christ's promises, they are evangelizing—good newsing—one another. They are inviting one another to believe Jesus' promises and to live their lives joyfully remembering that they are God's beloved children because of Jesus.

This doesn't mean that those evangelized are not Christians—by God's grace they are. It also doesn't mean that Christians shouldn't experience challenging times or difficult feelings. Day-to-day experience shows how unrealistic that notion is. It does mean that all Christians need to hear the Gospel again and again. No one ever outgrows the need to be reminded that God cares deeply for them, because of Jesus.

You'll learn more about evangelizing—outside the group and within the group—when you read *Me, an Evangelist? Every Christian's Guide to Caring Evangelism* and study session 22, Evangelism in and through ChristCare Groups.

VI. Snapshots of Caring in and through ChristCare Groups

You've read about types of needs for care and what ChristCare Group members can do to meet them. Now look at some "snapshots" that show how care takes place *in* ChristCare Groups and *through* ChristCare Groups for people outside the group.

A. Caring *in* ChristCare Groups

Community Building and Care

Arlene's group's meetings always started with a brief prayer, and then group members took turns sharing what was going on in their lives.

This evening, Fred shared first. "I'm really excited to report that God has answered our prayers, and my daughter's husband has found a good job."

Group members responded with comments like, "Thank God," "That's wonderful," and "Tell us about it."

Fred described the new job. Then he said, "Our daughter is so relieved. She was having trouble sleeping, she was so worried. Last week they even mentioned moving in with us, so I guess you could say everyone is relieved."

The group laughed, and then Arlene said, "Let's thank God for his goodness." She led the group in a brief prayer.

Fred's wife, Susan, shared next. "I have something I suppose I want to confess to all of you. This incident with our daughter has caused me to rethink some of my opinions. All my life I have scoffed at people who reported that God had answered their prayers about concerns from their everyday lives—like our concerns about Sally and her family. I have always thought that God expects us to take care of such things ourselves and to save our prayers for very big concerns.

"But I discovered that I was not able to solve Sally's problems, even though I tried very hard to do so. It was so frustrating for me.

"Every week, however, you listened to Fred, and to me, as we poured out our concerns. You didn't try to fix our problems, you just listened. You also prayed, every week. Some of you even called me during the week and assured me of your daily prayers.

"Now that Sally's family is back on track, I have gained an entirely new appreciation of the power of prayer. I don't know how else to attribute this good fortune, except to God's intervention. I am certainly going to begin praying about many more concerns than I did before. I thank God, and I thank all of you, for helping me to see God in this new way."

The group was quiet for a few moments as members thought about what Susan had said. Then Arlene invited Jake to share about his week.

Emergency Care
Gloria was involved in a serious auto accident. She suffered a broken arm and some cuts and bruises. Gloria was a single mother of two children in grade school.

The Group's Response
- Gloria called Jo, her group leader, and told her about the accident. Jo called Felix and Maria, who went to the hospital as soon as they heard. They drove Gloria home when she was released from the hospital.
- Jo called the pastor to make sure she knew about Gloria's situation.

- Jo called Nancy, who went to pick up Gloria's children at school and stayed with them until Gloria came home from the hospital.
- Nancy, Steve, and Maxine took turns providing evening meals until Gloria was able to take that responsibility back.
- Nancy came over every morning to get Gloria's children ready for school until Gloria was able to take over.
- Arturo lent Gloria a car to use until hers was repaired.
- Jo had several long phone calls with Gloria in the few months after the accident. Gloria was still upset by the accident—she was haunted by wondering what would have happened to her children had they been in the car with her at the time of the accident. She had become scared of driving. Jo listened a lot as Gloria talked through her fears and settled them.

A Long-Term Need
Irene and her husband, Bob, had been members of their ChristCare Group for a year when Bob died. Soon afterward, Irene had a stroke and ended up mostly confined to her home. Irene was afraid she would have to quit the ChristCare Group because she couldn't get to meetings.

Her ChristCare Group provided care during Irene's crises. Group members stayed with her when Bob died, and regularly visited her in the hospital as she recovered from her stroke. Once Irene was able to return home, the group decided to meet at her house so she could continue to attend meetings. One group member went over in the afternoons before the meetings and helped Irene straighten up so she would feel good about having people over.

Irene's grief and adjustment to her new life circumstances were difficult for her, but she was able to handle the changes with the group's help. Over the months the group listened as Irene talked about her losses and quietly prayed for her when she cried. Other group members also shared about their lives and cared for one another, but the group always made time for Irene.

When the group grew too big for Irene's home, it divided into two new groups, one of which kept meeting at Irene's home. About a year after her stroke, Irene said to her group, "All of you give me a reason to keep on living. You are like family to me. I would be so lonely if you didn't meet here. Different ones of you call during the week, and it is so nice to have someone to talk to. You send cards and notes that brighten my days. I want all of you to know that I pray for each of you every day. I thank God for you, and I also pray that God will help with the problems you share at group meetings. Thank you so much for being part of my life."

B. Caring *through* ChristCare Groups

The Guest

Ray's ChristCare Group met at his home every week. Group members had decided always to meet at the same location and to meet every week so that guests would never have to guess about the time or location of the next group meeting. The five members of Ray's group were all committed to inviting new people into the group.

Walter and Stu worked in the same laboratory. Walter attended a group meeting on Stu's invitation. Several weeks later, Walter attended again, and thereafter was a regular guest.

Walter was a quiet person; his manner was very reserved. Whenever he spoke, he would pause to think about what he was saying; he seemed to be trying to get his words just right. Walter would listen to the group's discussions about the book of Luke and sit silently during group prayers. His occasional questions made it clear that he thought a lot about what went on in the group.

When the group studied the Christmas story in Luke, Walter asked, "Where are the wise men?" When he learned that the Christmas story he had grown up with was a combination of Matthew's and Luke's accounts, he asked where he could find the Christmas story in Matthew and studied it on his own.

The account of Jesus' temptations led Walter to ask group members whether they believed there really is a devil. That discussion led to the group's talking about why there is evil in the world. Walter was an interested participant in these discussions. He mostly asked questions and listened as others suggested answers.

One evening, when Walter had been a guest at group meetings for about half a year, he shared with the group what he had been thinking. "I grew up in a family that insisted on clear thinking and rejected religion because it was full of emotion and unsupported claims to eternal truth. I've never been sure my family was right in their rejection of God, but the few times I looked into Christianity, I ran into people who couldn't think or speak clearly about their religion, and seemed afraid of me when I asked them to do so.

"When Stu invited me to visit your group, I had been talking with friends about the scientific assumption that the entire universe is one big accident. That thinking seemed fuzzier to me than some of the religious explanations I'd heard. I decided to accept Stu's invitation, hoping I might find some Christians with whom to discuss these ideas.

"We haven't discussed creation here, but I have enjoyed your willingness to tackle difficult questions, even when you weren't sure of the answers. Your openness encouraged me to read the New Testament to see what it is that Christians claim to believe."

The Natural Disaster

Don and Stephanie's neighbor, Larry, lived near the creek. When the creek started flooding, Stephanie saw Larry's family trying to dig a trench to divert the rising waters. She showed her husband, Don, and said, "You go down to help. I'll call Martin and see if anyone from the group can help."

An hour later Martin and five other members of the ChristCare Group were at Larry's house helping fill sandbags and stacking them against the rising water. Peter and Ron suggested carrying furniture and other valuables upstairs. When Larry agreed, Peter and Ron took responsibility for doing it. When it got dark, Cindy invited Larry's wife, Edna, and their two young children to spend the night. Soon thereafter another group member, Tom, showed up with pizzas for everyone.

By midnight the water had begun subsiding, and Larry's house had escaped damage. He and the members of the ChristCare Group sat down to rest, exhausted but happy. Martin asked Larry, "Do you mind if we take a moment and thank God for sparing your home?" Larry said, "No, that's fine."

After they prayed, Larry said, "I don't know how I can thank all of you. I guess I never expected neighbors to help like this these days. And most of you aren't even my neighbors." Stephanie said, "God has loved us so much. It's a privilege to be able to share his love with somebody else."

The Friend

"I'd appreciate your prayers for a friend of mine at work. I'll call him Frank, even though that isn't his real name," Cedric shared with his ChristCare Group. "Frank has a kid in the hospital and he's really going through a tough time." The group listened as Cedric told a bit more about his efforts to care for Frank. Then they prayed for both Frank and Cedric.

"I really appreciate you letting me tell you about the situation with Frank," Cedric said. "I've told Frank about all of you and how you're praying for him. He seemed surprised that someone would be praying for him, but he also seemed happy. I told him I wasn't using his real name. He said it would be okay if I did, but I feel more comfortable just calling him Frank.

"Frank is hurting so badly, and it's not always easy for me to be there for him. His child is going to need surgery, and his wife is having a tough time dealing with it. Some days all she can do is sit and cry. Of course, that makes things really tough on Frank. He's trying to be understanding and keep the family functioning, in addition to holding down a job. I listened to him for the entire lunch hour today, and then I suggested that Frank's wife might need to get some help. He said that was a good idea. By the end of lunch, I was exhausted. I think Frank was too."

"I went with Frank to the hospital this afternoon after work," Cedric reported. "His son came through the surgery with no problems, but now they face several more weeks in the hospital and months of rehabilitation. Frank's wife was there, and she was looking a lot better. I guess she has found ways to cope—Frank hasn't said much. The biggest problem now is financial. The insurance company is fighting them on every claim and the bills are really piling up."

"Is there anything we could do to help?" asked Harriet, the ChristCare Group Leader.

"Your prayers help."

"Could we help them with a food basket, or something?"

"No, I don't think things have reached that point yet. Let's just wait and see."

"Frank's son finally got out of the hospital today. Frank took the day off to be with his family. It was a relief for me that he wasn't there. I care a lot for Frank, but it certainly is draining talking with him. All he can talk about is his troubles."

Harriet asked, "Is there anything we can do for you, Cedric, to support you as you support Frank?"

"All of you have been a rock for me," Cedric said. "You let me talk about Frank every time we get together. You pray for us. I've thought several times that you are caring for Frank as much as I am."

"Cedric, have you ever prayed with Frank, or talked with him about God's love?" Rita asked, after Cedric had told about his week with Frank.

"I wonder about that, but I don't want to push religion. I don't want Frank to think that I'm caring for him just to get something from him."

"Has he ever said anything that would make you think he's interested in hearing more about God or in praying?" asked Mark.

"When you sent the Christmas gifts for the children, Frank was really touched. He wanted to find a way to thank you, and he looked like he didn't know why you had done this for him and his family."

Harriet said, "Maybe that could have been a time to just mention that we love him because of Jesus. Then see what he said."

"Maybe you could look for another opportunity like that," Mark said. "Telling Frank about Jesus is caring for him also."

"It's hard for me to do," Cedric said, "but I think you're right. I should try to do that."

"I'd like you to meet Frank—actually his name is Keith Sarter, and this is Keith's wife, Amanda." Members of the ChristCare Group greeted Keith and Amanda warmly.

"I always told Keith what we had talked about in group meetings, and he said he doesn't mind your knowing about what has happened."

"You have all proved that you can be trusted," Keith said. Amanda nodded.

"We wanted to meet all of you," Amanda said. "Actually we'd like to get to know you. From what Cedric has told us, your group has something very special. We were so happy when Cedric invited us to attend."

"We've been praying for you for so long," Harriet said. "Now it will be nice to pray with you."

"We'd like that, I think," said Keith.

VII. The ChristCare Group Leader's Roles in Group Caregiving

You have seen how ChristCare Groups provide care in several different circumstances. Part of the ChristCare Group Leader's job is to make sure needed care takes place. Group leaders certainly don't do all the caring themselves, but they fill several important roles to make sure that people receive the care they need. These roles are facilitator, caregiver, teacher, organizer, and referrer.

A. Facilitator

You will learn about your role as facilitator for your ChristCare Group in session 12, ChristCare Group Facilitation Skills. When you exercise those skills, you can help group members care for one another.

One of the four main activities of ChristCare Groups is community building and care. You've learned about building community in your ChristCare Group. Such community creates the trust that allows group members to share about their needs and to care for one another.

As group members share about their lives and their faith, the rest of the group will learn about needs for care that they have. Group members can then listen, empathize, and do for one another the kinds of caring actions described in this Preclass Reading.

Your job is to:

- make sure everyone has a chance to share;

- respond with care to others' needs, modeling a caring response for the rest of the group;

- encourage group members to care for one another;

- help group members understand how to respond in caring ways to others' expressions of need; and

- make sure that the group's responses are indeed caring.

A ChristCare Group where this community building and care takes place can become a haven for group members, a place where they can be supported and nurtured so they can deal with the stresses and challenges of everyday life. Such a ChristCare Group can also support group members and encourage them to reach out to others with the same kind of care that they have received.

B. Caregiver

There will be times when members of the group have needs that they want to share with you. Since you will be the ChristCare Group Leader, some will naturally look to you when they need someone to talk to. You will have opportunities to be there for group members, to listen, and to pray with and for them.

There may be times when you meet with other members between group meetings. You may have lunch together, or sit and talk for a while in the evening. You may also care over the telephone, listening and empathizing as you would in person.

Your role as caregiver will be a limited one. If a group member needs regular one-to-one care, you will help him or her find a caregiver more suited to that task (you'll read more about this below). Also realize that you will not be the only caregiver in the group. Ideally everyone in the group will be available to care for one another.

C. Teacher

In order for group members to care for one another and for others outside the group, some may need to learn more about how to care. There are several ways you may be able to help.

You can summarize and pass on some of what you have learned in this and other ChristCare Group Leader training modules. While your ChristCare Group is not a class, and you don't have to be a trained teacher to lead a ChristCare Group, there will be times when a five- or ten-minute summary of what you have learned in your training will be of great help to group members.

You might encourage group members who want to learn more to read a book about caregiving. Two good ones are *Christian Caregiving—a Way of Life* by Kenneth C. Haugk and *Me, an Evangelist? Every Christian's Guide to Caring Evangelism* by William J. McKay. (*Me, an Evangelist?* is the Preclass Reading for session 22, Evangelism in and through ChristCare Groups.) Both are available from Stephen Ministries. You, your teachers, or your pastor may know of other good books to recommend.

Your congregation may offer classes that deal with caregiving. If so, encourage group members to participate. Both of the books listed above are parts of larger courses: The *Christian Caregiving—a Way of Life* Course and the *Caring Evangelism* Course. Be on the lookout for these or other courses to recommend to group members to help build their caring skills.

D. Organizer

There will be times when a member of your group, or someone outside your group, experiences a crisis. Your group will want to respond with many kinds of care. In order for the group's care to be most effective, it needs to be organized.

As an example, consider how the group might care if a member was hospitalized with a heart attack. Group members might:

- be with him or her in the hospital;

- be with his or her spouse;
- help take care of his or her children;
- bring meals to the family;
- enlist others to pray for the family;
- help find information about living a healthier lifestyle.

If everyone shows up at the hospital at the same time to be with the person, that may be actually somewhat uncaring. Likewise, you wouldn't want three people to show up with a casserole one night, and then no one bring anything for the rest of the week.

Organizing is simple. It means calling group members and coordinating their care—deciding who will care for the children which day and who will be with the spouse and when. This is certainly a task you could delegate to another group member. Your responsibility is to make sure it gets done.

You may also help your group organize missional service activities. These will be times when your group works together to intentionally care for others outside the group. The subject of missional service is covered in depth in session 8, Missional Service by ChristCare Groups.

E. Referrer
There may be times when a group member requires more care than the group can provide. The ChristCare Group will be good at caring for one another at group meetings and at being there for one another during crises. When someone requires regular one-to-one care, however, it is time to look for another caregiver. ChristCare Group Leader training does not qualify you to be a long-term one-to-one caregiver, nor is your group qualified to provide that level of care.

If the group tries to meet all the needs of a person who requires regular one-to-one care, two undesirable things may happen:

1. The person will not receive all the care he or she needs.

2. The group will so focus on one member that other group members will have little or no time to share about their lives, and the group will begin to fall apart because everyone's needs are not being addressed.

It is better all around for the person to receive care from a more appropriate caregiver.

This isn't to say that a ChristCare Group will not focus all its caring energy on one member for a few weeks. That may certainly happen and it is appropriate. If one person needs all the group's energy for more than a few weeks, however, you should help that person find additional care.

This also doesn't mean that the group won't continue to care for a person who is receiving additional care from someone else. The group will continue to be there for that person and to care for him or her. It's just that the additional care he or she receives will provide what the group is not able to provide because they aren't trained and may not have the time.

You will learn much more about helping people find the additional care they need in session 6, When and How to Make Referrals for Additional Care.

VIII. Getting Ready for the In-Class Session
This Preclass Reading has begun your training in caring in and through ChristCare Groups. Your training will continue with the in-class session, and all the additional training sessions that deal with caring topics. With God's help and guidance, your ChristCare Group will be a very caring place.

In preparation for the in-class session, think about a concept or idea from this Preclass Reading that you might teach to ChristCare Group members to help them care more effectively.

ENDNOTES

1. Alan Keith-Lucas, *Giving and Taking Help* (Chapel Hill: University of North Carolina Press, 1972), pages 79–80.

2. David Augsburger, *Caring Enough to Confront* (Ventura: Regal Books, 1981).

3. Thomas Moore, *Care of the Soul* (New York: Harper-Collins, 1992), page xvii.

Caring in and through ChristCare Groups

Outline and Focus Notes

"My command is this: Love each other as I have loved you."

John 15:12

1. Worship: Coming into God's Presence

FOCUS NOTE 1

Psalm 121

A Song of Ascents

I lift up my eyes to the hills—
    where does my help come from?
My help comes from the LORD,
    the Maker of heaven and earth.

He will not let your foot slip—
    he who watches over you will not slumber;
indeed, he who watches over Israel
    will neither slumber nor sleep.

The LORD watches over you—
    the LORD is your shade at your right hand;
the sun will not harm you by day,
    nor the moon by night.

The LORD will keep you from all harm—
    he will watch over your life;
the LORD will watch over your coming and going
    both now and forevermore.

3-OFN.pmd C: 02/10/2004 R: 12/10/2004

2. Biblical Equipping: Love One Another
(1 John 4:7-21)

FOCUS NOTE 2

Questions to Focus Sharing of Biblical Equipping Apart

• Share one insight that you've had as a result of your Biblical Equipping Apart this week.

• Describe one change in your life that you've committed to make as a result of your meditation on the Biblical Equipping passage this week.

• Tell about a time when you've met God in a new way through Biblical Equipping Apart this week.

FOCUS NOTE 3

Love One Another (1 John 4:7–21)

[7] Dear friends, let us love one another, for love comes from God. Everyone who loves has been born of God and knows God. [8] Whoever does not love does not know God, because God is love. [9] This is how God showed his love among us: He sent his one and only Son into the world that we might live through him. [10] This is love: not that we loved God, but that he loved us and sent his Son as an atoning sacrifice for our sins. [11] Dear friends, since God so loved us, we also ought to love one another. [12] No one has ever seen God; but if we love one another, God lives in us and his love is made complete in us.

[13] We know that we live in him and he in us, because he has given us of his Spirit. [14] And we have seen and testify that the Father has sent his Son to be the Savior of the world. [15] If anyone acknowledges that Jesus is the Son of God, God lives in him and he in God. [16] And so we know and rely on the love God has for us.

God is love. Whoever lives in love lives in God, and God in him. [17] In this way, love is made complete among us so that we will have confidence on the day of judgment, because in this world we are like him. [18] There is no fear in love. But perfect love drives out fear, because fear has to do with punishment. The one who fears is not made perfect in love.

Focus Note 3 is continued on page 54.

---

[19] We love because he first loved us. [20] If anyone says, "I love God," yet hates his brother, he is a liar. For anyone who does not love his brother, whom he has seen, cannot love God, whom he has not seen. [21] And he has given us this command: Whoever loves God must also love his brother.

FOCUS NOTE 4

Explore Questions

1. What does John say is the primary evidence of God's love for us?
   Sent his son & his spirit

2. How did Jesus love and care for others? Share what you remember from other parts of the Bible. *Compassion, healing touch fed physically & spiritually, calms*

3. What do you think John meant when he wrote "God is love"?

4. What does John say are the relationships between God's love for us and our love for others?
   Can't have one w/o other

FOCUS NOTE 5

Connect Questions

1. What are specific ways in which we at this congregation love as Jesus did? What are other ways that we might add to what we already do?

2. How might fear keep us from caring for others? How is God's love a solution for our fear? *Trust*

3. How can we get better at loving?

4. What might be some ways in which group leaders could lead ChristCare Group members into more Christlike loving of others?

Show love by being caring & considerate whenever given the chance — don't let it pass.
Compassion

3. The Nature of Care in ChristCare Groups

A. The Relationship between Community Building and Care

B. ChristCare Groups Give Nurturing Care

C. Care That Goes beyond ChristCare Groups

1. Kinds of Care That Go beyond ChristCare Groups

2. Why Some Care Goes beyond ChristCare Groups

4. Kinds of Needs and Types of Care

A. Kinds of Needs

FOCUS NOTE 6

Five Kinds of Needs

1. Emotional
2. Physical
3. Social
4. Intellectual
5. Spiritual

B. Types of Care

FOCUS NOTE 7

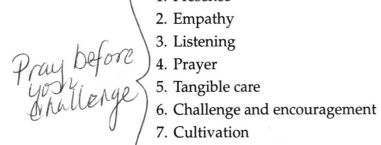

Pray before your challenge

Eight Ways to Care

1. Presence
2. Empathy
3. Listening
4. Prayer
5. Tangible care
6. Challenge and encouragement
7. Cultivation
8. Evangelization

C. Determining Kinds of Needs and Types of Care

FOCUS NOTE 8

Exercise Instructions

1. Quickly read all these instructions to yourself.
2. Choose one member of your group to write down all the needs and ways to care that your group identifies for each situation.
3. Choose one of the situations from Focus Note 9 and have someone read it aloud.
4. Brainstorm all the needs for care you think the person in this situation has.

Focus Note 8 is continued on page 57.

5. Brainstorm all the ways you can think of that a ChristCare Group might care for the person in this situation.

6. Move on to another situation in Focus Note 9 and discuss the same questions for the person in that situation.

7. Complete as many of the situations as you have time for. There is no need to complete them all, so take your time.

FOCUS NOTE 9

Exercise Situations

1. This afternoon Steve had a terrible argument with his 17-year-old son, Clayton. Clayton had stayed out two hours past his curfew the previous night, and Steve was very angry. Clayton got angry also and yelled at Steve. Steve threatened to take away Clayton's car keys. Clayton went to his car, drove off, and hadn't returned by the time Steve left for his ChristCare Group meeting.

2. Máire's car broke down on the way to the group meeting. She left the car on the side of the road and walked the rest of the way to the group meeting. This is the third time the car has broken down in the past month. Máire is angry with the mechanic who has been unable to repair it. She is also worried about being able to afford more car repairs.

3. Shirley is a single parent with a daughter in fourth grade. She holds down a full-time job and is also going to college on weekends to earn a graduate degree. Shirley has said she may have to quit the ChristCare Group because she has so many demands on her time.

4. Bonito just found out that his father has been diagnosed with Alzheimer's disease and will have to move into a care facility. Bonito's mother died many years ago, and he is the only child who lives in the same city as his father. His father is angry and confused. Bonito is sad, confused about what his father faces with this disease, and scared of the responsibility of taking care of his father. He feels guilty about his feelings.

5. Ngoc's sister has started going to the Buddhist temple with her fiancé. She had been coming to church with Ngoc for about a year. Ngoc is very concerned about his sister's relationship with God. He wonders if she is committing an unforgivable sin by worshipping at the temple. He is afraid other members of his family might leave the church and follow his sister's example of going to the temple.

Handwritten margin notes:
- Listen
- Ask Q, find soln
- How can we be helpful
- Help him come to conclusions
- Referrals → Mechanic
- listen
- Rides Loan car
- Listen   Tangible help
- Empathy
- Prayer
- Comfort   Shared experience
- Support
- Validate feelings
- Networking
- Referral
- Support groups

5. Community Building and Care

Jenny — sadness lift, enjoy accompl.
SOLOEYEWEAR.COM

referral Morgan — peace, balance, not spread
Daria — guidance re: internship, thin
& enrichment program, VBS

6. Prayer and Worship: Praying for One Another July 25-29

Patti — family coming home, share time
relief, Linda — son grad, Eagle Scout, peace
decision   affirm working mom, Berkeley
Liz — connection to family   transition
            marriage   Empty Nest
Kim —
Mary — good place

Listening Skills for ChristCare Group Leaders

Preclass Reading

"Listen carefully to my words; let this be the consolation you give me."

Job 21:2

PRECLASS READING OUTLINE

I. The Importance of Listening

   A. Leading Involves Listening

   B. Caring Involves Listening

II. The Three Parts of Listening

   A. Hear the Speaker's Message

   B. Think about the Speaker's Message

   C. Respond to the Speaker's Message

III. Active Listening—Putting Theory into Practice

   A. Pay Attention

   B. Ask Questions

   C. Reflect What Was Said

IV. Listening Skills with ChristCare Groups

   A. Involving Group Members as Listeners

   B. Developing Listening Skills in Group Members

V. Getting Ready for the In-Class Session

I. The Importance of Listening

Just as a jockey needs to know how to ride a horse, a ChristCare Group Leader needs to know how to listen. It's that simple—listening is fundamental to your effectiveness as a ChristCare Group Leader.

A. Leading Involves Listening

Leading isn't taking people where you want them to go, it is helping them get where they want and need to go. The following quotation, posted on a youth minister's office door, offers a humorous look at a leader who forgot this important concept:

> Have you seen them?
>
> Which way did they go?
>
> I must find them. I am their leader.

Listening is the primary way that you can avoid "losing" your group! Listening will enable you to stay in close contact with group members and learn what's going on in their lives. You'll find out about their joys and worries, their hopes and fears, their dreams and disappointments. The only way to do this is to listen.

Listening is also a way you earn the right to lead. Just holding the position of ChristCare Group Leader doesn't mean the people in your group will automatically or enthusiastically follow you. As you demonstrate your commitment to group members by taking the time to listen to them, they'll become more willing to follow your leadership.

B. Caring Involves Listening

As a ChristCare Group Leader, you have many opportunities to care. You will lead the group in caring responses to members' hurts and challenges. Outside group meetings, you sometimes will care for group members through phone calls or personal visits. You won't be the only person who cares for group members in these ways, but you probably will do so more than anyone else in the group.

Listening is your most effective caring tool. You'll learn that your job in caring is to remain process oriented and leave the curing to God. Listening is a great way to stay process oriented. As you listen, you help bear another's burdens for a while—maybe long enough for the person to be free to discover some of his or her own solutions. As you listen, you show the other person that he or she is worthy of your complete and undivided attention.

Such listening is not easy. It requires an act of will. Willingness to listen enables you to care. Without that willingness, caring is impossible.

II. The Three Parts of Listening

Listening—like many important skills—isn't quite as simple as it sounds. In fact, three separate activities take place when you listen effectively. The following diagram shows these three activities and the order in which they occur.

The Listening Cycle

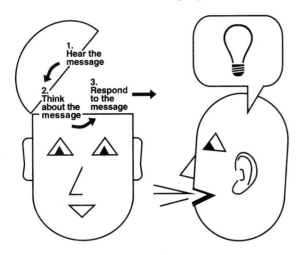

Hearing the message that the speaker is sending is essential to listening. It's our first encounter with what the speaker is saying. In the following section, you'll learn about different ways people communicate, and about how you need to use your eyes, as well as your ears, to "hear" everything others are saying.

Thinking about the message is something you probably do without even realizing it. Section B

will give you some strategies that will help you be a better listener by more consciously thinking about the information you receive from a speaker.

Responding to the message is the third step in listening. Anyone can respond, or speak back, to a speaker. A good listener will respond in ways that are most helpful to the speaker. In addition, a good listener will respond in ways that steer the conversation back to the start of the listening cycle so that further communication can occur. Section C will help you learn how to do this.

A. Hear the Speaker's Message

Has anyone ever said to you, "You're not listening to me"? You know from your own experience that much can get in the way of active listening. Hearing the speaker's message isn't always easy, as the following examples show:

- You're having a disagreement with your spouse or a close friend. He or she has just said, "I can't believe you did that again!" But instead of really listening to the message about what's causing the argument, you're getting ready to fire back your response.

- Your supervisor has just told you about some big changes in your job. You don't know why the changes are necessary, or if they'll be good or bad for you. But instead of really listening to learn what's going on, you're trying to control your feelings of surprise and insecurity.

- You're a ChristCare Group Leader. One of the group members often tells long stories. You've just said, "Who has an idea about that?" The storyteller says, "Well, I think …" You really don't feel like hearing what she or he has to say.

Listen to the Speaker's Words

A listener should pay close attention to the words a speaker is saying. But that's not always easy, as you saw in the examples above. Even good listeners must be aware of their own feelings, outside distractions, and many other things that can get in the way of listening.

The list in Focus Box 1 on page 61 gives you some rules you can follow to help yourself really listen to others. As you read through this list, place a check in the box under the column that best describes your ability in this area. Work through the list on the next page now.

Simple Rules for Hearing Others

	I usually do this when I listen	It's difficult for me to do this when I listen
1. Prepare in advance a good setting for listening to occur, a private place with no distractions. Modify the setting if necessary. For example, close the door or ask someone to turn off a radio or television.	❑	❑
2. Keep your attention focused on the speaker.	❑	❑
3. Help the speaker relax by being relaxed yourself. If you are anxious about the situation, remind yourself that God's Spirit is with you and will help you be a good listener.	❑	❑
4. Use nonverbal messages to show the speaker you are listening. Make eye contact, lean toward the speaker, nod your head, make "listening noises" ("Uh huh," "Ah," "Mm hmm"), and don't fidget.	❑	❑
5. During your conversations, listen more than you talk.	❑	❑
6. Welcome expressions of feelings such as tears, laughter, and talking about feelings.	❑	❑
7. Allow silence—don't try to fill it up with words. Let the speaker be quiet when he or she wants to.	❑	❑
8. Avoid interrupting the speaker.	❑	❑

How *Not* to Hear a Speaker's Message[1]

Here are some behaviors to *avoid* in order to become a better listener.

Mind-Reading

If you mind-read, you decide for yourself what a speaker is trying to say. For instance, a speaker might say, "I can hardly stand to have my teenager live with me anymore." If you're mind-reading, you might jump to the conclusion that the speaker means, "I want my teenager to live with his father, not with me." But the speaker might really mean, "I need to talk about this and let off some steam so I can go home and deal with my teenager better."

Rehearsing

If you are busy rehearsing what to say, your mind will be going a mile a minute, planning what to say next. You won't be able to focus on the speaker's message.

Dreaming

You might start out really listening to a speaker, but something the speaker says starts you thinking about your own concerns instead of listening to what the speaker is saying. For instance, while listening to the speaker's problems at work, you might start thinking about your own job and begin making a mental to-do list instead of listening. When this happens, your attention is turned inward—to what you are thinking—rather than outward—to what the other person is saying.

Listen beyond the Words

When you listen to another person, you listen to his or her words, of course. But you can also listen beyond the words. You can listen to the person's voice and notice the person's body language.

Vocal Cues

When a person speaks, you hear *how* a person says the words. Is the person speaking loudly? softly?

quickly? slowly? These vocal cues in speech are an important part of the content of what a person says. Vocal cues help the listener better understand what the speaker is saying. Sometimes a speaker's vocal cues contradict his or her words. For instance, a speaker might say, "I'm not angry about that!" in a loud, harsh voice with clipped words. Is the speaker angry? Yes—her vocal cues show her true feelings.

Notice how these aspects of vocal communication can give you clues to a speaker's real message or feelings.

- Pitch—How high or low is the speaker's voice?

  Tightened vocal cords cause the pitch of a voice to rise. Intense feelings of joy, fear, anger, or excitement make the pitch go up. Children squeal with excitement, and some people speak in a squeaky voice when they're trying not to cry.

  On the other hand, relaxed vocal cords cause the pitch of a voice to go down. Someone who is tired, sad, or depressed might speak in a low-pitched voice.

  Generally, the more intense the emotion, the more extreme—either high or low—the pitch of the voice becomes.

- Articulation—How carefully does the speaker pronounce the words?

  Does she slur the words or give them sharp edges? Does he run the words together or say each one distinctly? Sharply articulated words can show stress or anger. Words slurred together can communicate sadness, fatigue, or depression.

- Tempo—How fast does the speaker talk?

  Rapid speech can convey a wide range of emotions, including fear, excitement, happiness, nervousness, or insecurity. Slow or hesitant speech might show that the speaker feels indifferent, sincere, unsure, or thoughtful.

  The rate of a person's speech can also depend on where he or she grew up, in the country or in the city, in New York or in Atlanta.

- Volume—How loudly does the person speak?

  Loud speech can mean anger or excitement, exaggeration or confidence. It can convey dominance over someone.

  Soft speech can indicate caring or trust. It can also show a feeling of inferiority, sadness, awe, or fear.

- Rhythm and emphasis—What words does the speaker emphasize?

  Rhythm and emphasis can give a variety of meanings to the same statement. Notice how many different ways this three-word statement can be said, each with a different meaning:

  I'm not going. (You might be going, but I'm not.)

  I'm *not* going. (You might want me to go, but I'm not.)

  I'm not *going.* (I'm not leaving; I'm staying.)

As you can see, vocal cues won't give you a complete picture. In each situation you must consider these cues along with the words that are said, as well as the speaker's nonverbal cues. Here are three questions you can ask yourself about a speaker's vocal cues to learn more about what the speaker is saying.

1. Does the speaker's voice help you understand the message better? ("I'm so upset that I can't even go to work" said in a slow, deep voice with slurred words could mean this person is struggling with depression.)

2. Does the speaker's voice match or conflict with the words he or she is saying? ("So she's moved out, and it suits me fine!" said in a loud voice with clipped words really means something else.)

3. What additional information does the speaker's voice give you about the situation? ("Nothing's wrong" said in a high-pitched, loud voice means that something is wrong.)

Nonverbal Cues

A person doesn't have to speak in order to communicate. In fact, a person can't help communicating when in the presence of another person. If you and another person were in a room together and were told not to speak to each other, you would quickly sense the other person's thoughts and feelings through his or her body language. For instance, a giggle might say, "This is silly, isn't it?" Or rolling the eyes might mean, "Can you believe this?" Standing silently apart from the other person and not making eye contact might mean, "I don't want to have any part of this."

You may not be aware of it, but you already understand body language. Almost everyone who lives with other people learns body language right along with spoken language. In the diagram on the next page, notice what a minor part words play in a message when compared to vocal cues and body language.[2]

How the Whole Message Is Communicated

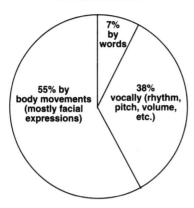

7% by words

55% by body movements (mostly facial expressions)

38% vocally (rhythm, pitch, volume, etc.)

Amazing, isn't it? You can see why it's important to pay attention to body language, to "listen" with your eyes.

Five Main Kinds of Nonverbal Cues

Long books and lengthy lists have been written about body language and what it means. Instead of going into great technical detail here, this section will provide you with five main kinds of nonverbal cues to notice.

Body Movements

Walking with a swagger, bowing, shaking hands, motioning "come here," nodding agreement—these are all body movements people learn by growing up in a particular culture or family. Most body language is learned in this way, and it varies from culture to culture and family to family.

Body movements serve two main communication purposes. First, they illustrate what a person says. Pointing or nodding helps a person get the message across. Second, a listener's body movements give messages to the speaker while he or she is talking. If you raise your eyebrows or look away while someone speaks, you are telling them what you think of what they're saying.

Facial Expressions

A person's face is the most expressive part of his or her body. When you listen to others, watch for these facial expressions:

- Skin color—is it flushed or pale?
- Eyebrows—are they wrinkled, raised, or lowered?
- Forehead—is it wrinkled or smooth?
- Eyes—are they looking at you, looking down, intently focused, or staring into space?

- Chin—is it sagging or jutting out?

Arm and Hand Gestures

Here are some arm and hand gestures with their usual meanings:

Gesture	Meaning
Scratching head	"I don't know" or "I'm not sure"
Rubbing neck	"I'm tired," "I'm frustrated," "I'm tense"
Placing hands on knees, palms down, elbows out	"I'm ready to go"
Clenching fists	"I'm angry"
Holding arms out with palms up, and shrugging shoulders	"So what," "I don't know," "I don't care"

Legs and Feet

Here are some leg and feet gestures with their usual meanings:

Gesture	Meaning
Legs uncrossed, feet apart	Openness
Legs crossed, foot swinging	Boredom, anger, frustration
Ankles crossed	Resistance
Legs and feet pointing in one direction	The person's interest lies there

Posture and Breathing

Think about your own posture and breathing for a moment. How do you feel when you:

- Slump
- Sit or stand very erect
- Lean forward
- Lean away
- Sit or stand tensely
- Breathe rapidly
- Sigh
- Hold your breath, then take gasps of air
- Breathe shallowly
- Breathe deeply

As you have learned, each part of listening is important. The speaker's body language cannot be separated from the vocal cues and words. When you notice all these things, you are best able truly to listen to and understand the speaker.

B. Think about the Speaker's Message

When you listen to someone, you naturally think about what he or she is saying. You think about what was said or not said. You consider your own thoughts and ideas about what the other person is communicating, and you experience some feelings because of what is said. Much of this thinking, or processing, happens without your even knowing about it. Sometimes all you're aware of is that you want to say or do something in response to what you've heard.

As a caring listener, you'll want to work on the skill of deliberately thinking about and assessing your responses to what the other person is communicating.

The authors of a book called *Messages: The Communication Book*[3] explain that a listener can process, or think about, what he or she hears in four different ways.

FOCUS BOX 2

Four Ways to Think about a Message

- Observe—what do you notice about what the speaker says and how he or she says it? Is the message a sad or happy one? Is the speaker nervous or relieved, happy or sad, tired or excited?

- Draw conclusions—what can you learn from what the speaker says? Has the speaker made some decisions, or is the speaker at a loss for what to do? Is this a new or old problem for the speaker?

- Feel—what feelings does the message bring up in you? What is your emotional response to the speaker? Do you feel angry, happy, sad, or sympathetic? What other feelings do you have?

- Identify needs—what else do you need to know to continue the communication? Would it help to find out more facts, feelings, ideas, or thoughts?

The following example shows how a ChristCare Group Leader might use these four ways of processing information to think about what a group member shares.

An Example: Dave's Grief

Dave is grieving the recent death of his father. He comes to a group meeting and sits resting his forehead against his hand. The ChristCare Group Leader asks Dave how he's feeling. He looks up with tears in his eyes. His voice catches as he says, "I'm so angry . . . I guess with myself. Or maybe with my dad. I'm angry that our relationship wasn't better. Look at all the years we could have been close but weren't. I feel guilty about that, as if it were my fault. And I'm scared my relationship will be the same with my children when they grow up. Maybe I'm making the same mistakes my dad made with me."

Observe: What do your senses tell you?

- Dave is sitting with his head down.
- Dave has tears in his eyes.
- Dave's voice catches.

Did you observe anything else in this example?

Draw conclusions: What did you learn from what the speaker said?

- Dave is grieving the loss of a person, as well as an imperfect past.
- Dave fears similar losses in the future.
- Dave is allowing himself to grieve, even though it's difficult.

Did you draw any other conclusions from this example?

Feel: What emotions do you feel in response to what Dave said?

- It upsets me to see Dave in so much pain.
- I have some of the same worries about my children.
- I'm afraid of dealing with the death of my aging parents.

Did you feel any other emotions while reading this example?

Identify needs: What else do you need to know?

- I need to know how I can share Dave's pain.
- I need to know if Dave's needs are so great that I should refer him to a caregiver, such as the pastor or a therapist.

What else would you need to know in this example?

How *Not* to Think about a Speaker's Message[4]

Comparing

If you're busy comparing the speaker's situation with your own, you won't be free to think about the message. If you're trying to decide whose situation is worse, who is suffering more, or whose kids are in the most trouble, you won't be able to respond to the speaker's feelings.

Filtering

Filtering is listening selectively to what a speaker says. For instance, you might listen closely enough to tell that the speaker isn't angry with you or that the speaker is going to talk about the same old problem again. Then you might decide the situation doesn't warrant your full attention. So your mind wanders to what you have to do after the meeting or to the disagreement you had with your spouse today. You filter out the input coming from the speaker.

One reason people sometimes filter when they listen is that certain subjects can be painful. Some people simply remove themselves mentally and emotionally from a conversation when painful subjects come up in order to protect themselves from hurting.

Judging

Have you ever formed a strong and immediate opinion of someone? Perhaps it was her accent, his way of dressing, or the car she drove that led you to categorize someone instantly. As a ChristCare Group Leader and caring listener, it's especially important to guard against forming instant judgments about people. They get in the way of listening, understanding, and relating to others.

Identifying

When you relate everything a speaker says to your own experience, you are identifying. For example, if a person tells you about problems with his children and you start thinking and talking about your problems with your own children, you are identifying. Avoid responding to input about a person's divorce with a story about your own divorce. Avoid responding to someone with money worries with a story about your own financial concerns. Instead, focus on what the speaker is saying, not on a matching situation in your life.

C. Respond to the Speaker's Message

After you have heard and thought about a speaker's message, you'll want to respond to the speaker. You can respond in a number of different ways. In any given situation, there is no clear right or wrong response. But there are some skills you can develop to respond in the most caring way possible.

It's important to remember that you respond to a speaker in many different ways, just as you take in information in many different ways. In addition to your words, pay attention to your own vocal and nonverbal cues as you respond. Focus Box 3 contains a list of some behaviors to be aware of as you respond to a speaker. As you read through this list, place a check in the box under the column that best describes your ability in this area.

FOCUS BOX 3

Skills for Responding to Input

Skills	I usually do this when I listen	It's difficult for me to do this when I listen
1. Take responsibility for your own communication. Don't imagine the listener knows your thoughts, questions, and feelings. Go ahead and put them into words.	❑	❑
2. Try to speak clearly. Don't use confusing terms or jargon. Be sure of the message you want to give, then say it as simply as possible.	❑	❑
3. Be congruent. Avoid giving mixed messages in which your body language doesn't match your tone of voice or words (smiling while you tell the speaker you're angry).	❑	❑

Responding with Verbal and Nonverbal Cues

- Does the pitch of your voice match the feelings you want to communicate?

- Do you articulate your words in a way that shows you are thinking carefully about what you're saying?

- Does the speed of your speech match your feelings?

- Does the volume of your speech match the message you want to get across?

- Do your body movements show that you are paying close attention to the speaker?

- Do your facial expressions convey your feelings of attention and concern?

- Do the gestures of your arms, hands, legs, and feet enhance your responses to what the speaker is saying?

- Do your posture and breathing reflect your attitude of close attention and caring?

Listening is a complicated skill. Good listening takes a lot of effort on the listener's part. Does this mean that if you can't remember and recite all the suggestions and rules in this Preclass Reading that you can't be a good listener? No! But it is clear everyone can continue to grow as a listener. You can grow by learning how to understand others more clearly. You can grow by becoming more self-aware about how you think about others' messages. You can also grow by learning to respond more congruently to others so that all the messages you are sending, verbally and nonverbally, clearly communicate the same message.

How *Not* to Respond to a Speaker's Message[5]

Just as in receiving input and processing input, there are also a few pitfalls to avoid in responding to input.

1. Advising

Always remember that you are a listener. You don't have to solve the speaker's problems. In fact, you can't. Only the speaker, with God's help, can work through his or her problem.

2. Sparring

If you argue or debate with the speaker, the speaker won't feel heard. If you sincerely disagree with the speaker on something you believe is very important, use an I-message (When you . . . I feel . . . because . . . I would like . . .).

3. Needing to Prove You're Right

When you are busy proving you have the right answer or that you aren't wrong, you block all three parts of good listening—hearing the message, thinking about the message, and responding to the message in a helpful way.

4. Derailing

Have you ever talked to someone who responds to what you say by changing the subject, telling a joke, or making a sarcastic comment? If you as a ChristCare Group Leader find yourself derailing a speaker, first stop doing it. Then ask yourself what was so uncomfortable that you had to avoid honest communication.

5. Placating

When someone is upset, it's tempting to say, "It's going to be all right ... Don't worry ... It will all work out ... You can do it." These messages indicate that you don't want to listen to the speaker. You're not tuning in, perhaps because you're fully preoccupied, you don't want the speaker to feel so upset, or it's difficult for you to handle what's going on.

III. Active Listening—Putting Theory into Practice

As the diagram below shows, everything you have just learned about the theory of listening can be put into practice with active listening.

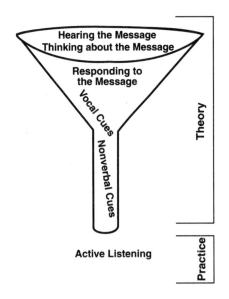

Active listening is a way of fully understanding what others are communicating and also helping others understand themselves better.[6] It is the act of listening fully—with your eyes, ears, intuition, and intelligence. Active listening means making sure you understand correctly what the speaker is trying to communicate. It is using everything you know about listening to encourage the speaker to express his or her feelings and thoughts completely. An active listener serves as a kind of mirror, helping speakers see themselves through another's eyes.

There are three main parts of active listening: paying attention, asking questions, and reflecting.

A. Pay Attention

You've read how important it is to pay attention, to really hear what the other person is saying. You can't understand others, or help them understand themselves, unless you pay attention.

There is another good reason for paying attention to others. It helps them feel valued. It helps them know that there's a person who cares for them so much that he or she is willing to put aside everything else and focus only on them. Regrettably, it is uncommon to have someone pay that much attention to you. When someone does, you know he or she cares.

The care you show by paying attention helps others trust you. That trust enables them to tell you about thoughts, feelings, fears, joys, and hopes that are very personal, that they don't entrust to everyone. When they share these personal issues with another person, they can find some freedom. They can move past some of the ideas or feelings that have paralyzed them in the past.

Here are some practical suggestions for helping yourself pay attention when someone is speaking, and for helping them know that you are doing so.

- Make eye contact.
- Use your posture to show that you are listening (lean forward slightly, face the speaker, nod your head).
- Avoid looking at your watch, doodling, or other activities that show your mind is elsewhere.
- After an interruption, summarize what the speaker was saying before the interruption; for example, "Before we were interrupted, you said you had called your mother and . . ." This helps get the conversation back on track, shows you were paying attention, and helps the conversation keep rolling.

B. Ask Questions

One way to understand another person better is to ask questions. Two types of questions are especially useful.

Open-Ended Questions

If you ask a question that can be answered with a "yes" or "no," or with a one- or two-word response, you won't get much new information. You'll find out a lot more if you ask a question that requires sentences or paragraphs to answer. Questions that can be answered with a "yes" or "no," or with a simple, short statement of fact, are **closed-ended questions**. Questions that require an "essay-type" response, that ask for more than the bare facts, that call for interpretation and elaboration, are **open-ended questions**.

Here are some examples of closed- and open-ended questions. Notice how much more information can be learned from the open-ended questions.

Closed	Open
Did that make you angry?	How were you feeling when that happened?
Did you like the Sunday school class?	What did you think of the Sunday school class?
How many children do you have?	What can you tell me about your children?
Are you going to quit work?	What do you plan to do about your job?
Did you feel as if that was an honor?	Wow! How did that make you feel?

One of the goals of active listening is to encourage others to continue talking about their interests or concerns. The more they share, the more you understand. Telling you about their concerns can also help them understand themselves better. You can see that open-ended questions will achieve that goal much better than closed-ended questions.

Clarifying Questions

Clarifying questions can help you understand better what the person means. If someone says to you, "I can't stand my job another day," you could ask, "What's going on at work?" You might find out that the speaker wants to change careers, that the speaker's having serious problems with a coworker, or any number of other things.

Phrase clarifying questions in a way that shows your care and concern. Say "Can you explain to me again how that happened?" instead of "What did you do that for?" When your questions are gentle and kindly inquisitive, the speaker probably will tell you more. If your questions are aggressive and confrontational, the speaker may feel defensive or end the conversation.

What—Not Why—Questions

Questions that begin with the word *why* can put a speaker on the defensive—she or he may feel a need to explain, justify, defend, or give reasons for feelings or behaviors. People who feel defensive are not likely to trust.[7] Instead of asking *why*, try asking *what* most of the time. *What* questions ask for specifics about the situation and help you and the speaker get a clearer idea of what is going on. *What* also focuses on how a problem can be solved or a situation improved.

C. Reflect What Was Said

Reflecting means listening to a portion of what others say, then summarizing it in your own words and saying it back to them. Reflecting does not mean simply parroting back others' exact words. It means saying back what others say *as you have understood it,* which adds a new layer of information.

Here's an example.

Speaker:
I don't know what's wrong with my sister. If I call her, she doesn't want to talk to me. If I don't call her, she writes and complains that I don't care about her.

Listener:
You're confused about how your sister is treating you.

You might be wondering why you should reflect, or restate, what a speaker says. There are many good reasons. One is that reflecting helps you know how well you understood what the speaker was trying to say. For example, if you continue the conversation above, the speaker might say:

Speaker:
That's right. I just don't know what she wants from me . . .

On the other hand, the speaker could say:

Speaker:
No, I'm not confused about it! She's treating me badly, and I don't like it!

By reflecting, the listener can understand more clearly how the speaker feels. In this case, it could be either hurt or anger. In addition, the speaker learns that the listener cares enough to make sure he or she understands correctly.

Reflecting responses can also serve to invite others to tell you more. They show that you are interested in what others are saying and would be willing to continue hearing about it. A reflecting response is a gentle invitation, not a demanding one. Others are free to take you up on your invitation and continue discussing the subject, or they are free to choose to talk about something else or to end the conversation.

Another benefit of reflecting is that the speaker gets a chance to hear his or her words, ideas, and feelings repeated. This can lead the speaker to greater self-awareness and self-understanding. After stopping to think, "Yes, that's what I mean," or "No, it's not quite like that," the speaker clarifies for you, and for himself or herself, what is really meant. You've given the speaker a gift—a chance to understand more clearly the situation and his or her feelings about it.

When you first begin to make reflective responses, you might feel a bit awkward. Don't worry—it will soon start to feel more natural. Avoid parroting the speaker with mechanical, memorized responses. Instead, focus on saying back what you have understood, and the responses will come to you naturally.

If you are uncomfortable with making reflective responses, it may be that you haven't had a good model for this skill. For instance, you might have heard someone repeat the same phrase over and over, never varying it. Or you might have heard a response that sounded like psychological jargon, such as, "I hear you saying that . . ." But there are many different ways to make reflective responses. You can vary the words you use or ask a clarifying question instead of making a statement. Notice the many different types of reflecting responses on the next page. See if you can add any responses to the end of this list.

Reflecting Responses

"It sounds to me like you're wondering if . . ."

"It seems as if you're feeling . . ."

"From what you're saying, I get the idea that . . ."

"As I understand it, you're planning to . . ."

"Let's see if I have it right. You've decided to . . ."

"If I understand what's going on, the situation is . . ."

"I think what you're telling me is . . ."

"So it seems to you that . . ."

Add a few reflective responses you can think of:

Three Kinds of Information You Might Reflect

There are three kinds of information you can reflect back to the speaker: content, feelings, and spiritual concerns.

Content

Content includes the who, what, why, when, where, and how of what the speaker said. When you reflect content, you encourage the speaker to tell you more. Here are some kinds of content, followed by statements that reflect content:

- Thoughts

  "It sounds as if you're thinking this would be a good time to change jobs."

- Beliefs

  "Am I right in saying that you don't agree with what she did?"

- Plans

  "So your family is planning to move next spring?"

- Evaluations

  "It seems to me that you really don't like what's going on at work."

- Ideas

  "You're thinking that the best thing to do now might be to quit."

- Attitudes

  "I can see that you'd like things to be different."

- Dreams

  "So your idea of where you'd like to be in five years is …"

- Opinions

  "It's clear to me that you don't approve of hypocrites."

- Expectations

  "You thought marriage would be different from this."

- Judgments

  "You've decided it's time to do something about this."

- Hopes

  "It's not hard to see that you want things to be better."

- Values

  "That seems like a waste of time to you."

- Wishes

  "It sounds as if you'd like things to be different."

Feelings

Feelings are the internal reactions people have to other people, events, and experiences. When you reflect a speaker's feelings, you encourage the speaker to talk more about those feelings, even if they are painful or difficult to talk about. Offering this opportunity to someone is a caring thing to do; many times, people don't have others who invite them to share their feelings. The following words describe different kinds of feelings. The first five words are followed by examples of statements that reflect feelings.

- Sad

  "You're feeling sad about your mother's death."

- Unconcerned

  "It seems as if you aren't worried about what's going to happen."

- Excited

  "I can tell you're excited about the possibilities."

- Angry

  "That's something that really made you angry."

- Pleased

  "If I'm reading you right, you're really pleased with how it turned out."
- Joyful
- Afraid
- Amazed
- Anxious
- Happy
- Relaxed
- Furious
- Glad
- Nervous
- Frustrated

Take a few minutes right now to write a reflective statement for three of the feelings listed above.

1.

2.

3.

Spiritual Concerns

Sometimes a speaker shares spiritual concerns with a listener whom he or she has learned to trust. Spiritual concerns are people's hopes, fears, questions, concerns, or joys that at root have to do with their relationship with God.

Sometimes speakers will know that their thoughts and feelings are spiritual concerns. They will talk about how they need God's help, or about how God has come through for them.

Other times, people won't realize that only God can fully meet their concerns. They talk about intense feelings and difficult life issues, and they are confused because they don't know that they need to turn to God for help.

Regardless of whether the other person knows his or her concerns have to do with a need for Jesus, you can still summarize and repeat those concerns. When you reflect spiritual concerns, you encourage speakers to talk more about their relationship with God. You may or may not actually mention God in the conversation, but you know that the needs you are discussing are ones that only God can meet.

The following list gives some examples of spiritual concerns that could come up in a ChristCare Group or in a one-to-one conversation. The first

five concerns are followed by statements that reflect them.

- Identity

  "It sounds to me as if you have some questions about who you are and who God might want you to be."
- Self-Esteem

  "Am I right that you don't feel so great about yourself right now?"
- Meaning

  "Sometimes it's difficult for you to see why life is worth living."
- Hope and Despair

  "Right now you're dreading what lies ahead, when you'd rather have hope that things will be okay."
- Evil

  "You're wondering why God allows so much evil in the world."
- Failure
- Loneliness/Separation from God
- Guilt
- Aging, Pain, Suffering
- Purpose in Life
- Forgiveness
- Regrets
- Doubts about Self and God
- Death

Spiritual concerns can be risky to talk about, for both the speaker and the listener. Don't try to solve the spiritual concerns others bring up. In fact, you can't solve them. You *can* listen and care and struggle along with others. You can pray with and for them. You can also trust that God is at work in others' lives through you and the other group members.

IV. Listening Skills with ChristCare Groups

While it is true that you can listen only to one person at a time, a ChristCare Group setting requires you to consider the needs and circumstances of everyone present while one person speaks. ChristCare Groups require some special applications of the skill of listening.

A. Involving Group Members as Listeners

Imagine that your ChristCare Group is engaged in community building and care. Pat is talking about some problems she's having at work. You as the ChristCare Group Leader are using the skills you've learned in this module to listen closely and caringly to Pat as she speaks. But Pat is only one member of your ChristCare Group. You'd like to make sure all group members are actively involved in what's going on. In addition, you sense that the discussion is causing other group members to feel some emotions and come up with some observations and thoughts they would like to share.

In a situation like this—one you will encounter in almost every ChristCare Group meeting you lead—there are some strategies you can use to tune in to what's going on with the group as a whole and help them listen to the one who is speaking.

- Stay in the here and now.

  Keep your attention focused on both the speaker and the group. Don't let your mind wander or become sidetracked with thoughts that can make you less than 100 percent present.

- Invite others to become an active part of the listening process.

  Like you, the other listeners are receiving input, responding to input, and noticing verbal and nonverbal cues as the speaker is talking. Invite them to share their observations, thoughts, and feelings. Phrase the invitations in a personal way and link them to the speaker. For instance, you can say, "Tom, I know you've gone through something like this; would you like to share some feelings about what Pat is saying?" or "Michelle, I can tell you really care about what's going on with Pat; would you like to say anything to Pat about that?"

- Model good listening.

  Group members will watch how you listen to the speaker and will quite often follow your lead—especially if they have learned the basics of good listening.

- Express the reactions you notice in the group.

  Let group members know you're aware of their presence and feelings—as well as aware of the speaker—by making observations such as, "It seems as if what you've shared really hits home for some people here, Pat," then make eye contact with group members and back to Pat. Or say, "The silence of the group tells me we're having some deep feelings about this." One or more group members will probably follow up such a comment with a supportive statement, showing Pat that the group is "with her" in her struggle.

The preceding strategies enhance listening in your ChristCare Group in three ways:

1. They help you as a ChristCare Group Leader focus on the speaker as an individual.

2. They help you let the other group members know that you haven't forgotten they're there.

3. They provide ways in which you can include group members as caring listeners, helping them meet the speaker's needs even as you model and teach listening skills.

B. Developing Listening Skills in Group Members

One of the ways group members will grow is through their relationships with one another. And one of the signs of good relationships is that people listen to one another. As a ChristCare Group Leader, you can help group members learn to listen in five main ways:

1. Openly address the subject of listening.

   Teach about listening, starting with the listening session in *Beginnings*. Talk about listening and point out when you see good listening occur in the group. Listening isn't a secret skill. It's best learned when it's talked about openly.

2. Model good listening.

   Put the skills you've learned in this module into practice. Show that you are paying attention. Demonstrate how to use clarifying questions effectively or how to say a reflecting response.

3. Invite others to be actively involved in listening.

   Sometimes, in listening, "four ears are better than two." In the case of small groups, you've got 10 or 16 or more ears listening to a speaker! When every group member knows how to listen, the speaker stands a better chance of really being heard. For instance, if you don't pick up on a vocal cue, or if you miss a body-language signal, someone else in the group might notice it.

   Tell your group that you are counting on the whole group to be a listening team. If they hear something that you have missed, you want to hear about it. Make sure they know everyone has the responsibility to listen.

4. Affirm good listening skills.

You've heard the expression "Catch someone doing something right." In your ChristCare Group, catch someone being a good listener. Then praise him or her! Say, "Marcia, you noticed something I didn't catch—you were really listening to Tom" or "Peter, thank you for showing you care by really listening to Todd." When someone in the group listens to you, tell them how it makes you feel. Say something like "Patricia, thank you for listening to me. I needed someone to understand what's going on."

5. Draw attention to inattention or poor listening.

Don't let poor listening by group members slip by. If you notice attention wandering, say something like "Let's be sure to pay attention to Charlotte. She's sharing something very personal and needs to know that we care." When group members begin paying attention, affirm them for their change in behavior.

In addition, realize that even you will slip up from time to time. You'll be tired, get sidetracked, forget to focus on the listener … that's okay! Those are good opportunities to say, "Mike, I'm sorry. I've got a lot on my mind tonight, and I missed what you said. Would you repeat that, and I'll listen more closely this time." When you repeat back to a speaker what you thought you heard, the speaker might say, "No, that's not what I meant." You can say, "Oh, then could you explain it again, and I'll try to listen more closely."

V. Getting Ready for the In-Class Session

In the in-class training session for this module, you'll have a chance to practice good listening skills. Until then, try these activities to apply what you've learned in this Preclass Reading and to prepare yourself for the in-class training session.

- When someone at home or work sits down to talk with you, consciously apply what you've learned about hearing the message: focus your attention, be patient, let the speaker know you're listening, and avoid interrupting.

- If someone tells you about a problem this week, apply some skills you've learned for responding to the message: active listening, speaking clearly, using body language when you speak, asking "what" rather than "why" questions, and avoiding solving the problem for the speaker.

- Try this activity[8] to practice your awareness of vocal and nonverbal cues. Spend a few minutes in a shopping center, library, or other place where you're likely to see quite a few people. Focusing on one person at a time, see what you can find out by noticing how each person:

  o walks (fast or slow?)

  o talks (loudly or quietly?)

  o uses facial expressions (animated or controlled?)

  o uses tone of voice (happy, sad, high-pitched, low-pitched?)

  o uses posture (relaxed or rigid?)

  o makes eye contact (direct or nondirect?)

  o uses body gestures (many or few, exaggerated or minimized?)

  o reacts to other people (outgoing or restrained?)

ENDNOTES

1. Matthew McKay, Ph.D., Martha David, Ph.D., and Patrick Fanning, *Messages: The Communication Book* (Oakland: New Harbinger Publications, 1983). Much information in several sections of this module was adapted from this source.

2. Bob Philips, *The Delicate Art of Dancing with Porcupines: Learning to Appreciate the Finer Points of Others* (Ventura: Regal Books, 1989), page 19.

3. McKay, David, Fanning, *Messages: The Communication Book.*

4. McKay, David, Fanning, *Messages: The Communication Book.*

5. McKay, David, Fanning, *Messages: The Communication Book.*

6. McKay, David, Fanning, *Messages: The Communication Book.*

7. William J. McKay, *Me, an Evangelist? Every Christian's Guide to Caring Evangelism* (St. Louis: Stephen Ministries, 1992). Much information in the section on active listening was adapted from this source.

8. Philips, *The Delicate Art of Dancing with Porcupines: Learning to Appreciate the Finer Points of Others*, page 25.

Group-Based Manual for ChristCare Group Leaders
Listening Skills for ChristCare Group Leaders

Outline and Focus Notes

"Listen carefully to my words; let this be the consolation you give me."

Job 21:12

1. Introduction

FOCUS NOTE 1

Listening = Caring

The principal form that the work of love takes is attention. . . . When we attend to someone we are caring for that person. The act of attending requires that we make the effort to set aside our existing preoccupations . . . Attention is an act of will . . . By far the most common and important way in which we can exercise our attention is by listening.

—M. Scott Peck, *The Road Less Traveled*[1]

[handwritten notes:]

Listening

#1
irritation
invalidated
dismissed
frustrated
judged

#2
supported
heard
understood
cared for
TMI ?

2. Active Listening—Getting the Facts Straight

---

1 M. Scott Peck, M.D., *The Road Less Traveled: A New Psychology of Love, Traditional Values, and Spiritual Growth* (New York: Simon and Shuster, 1978), pp. 120–121.

4-OFN.pmd C: 02/18/2004 R: 01/24/2005

3. Active Listening—One to One

FOCUS NOTE 2

Sharing Situations

1. Tell about what you did on your last vacation (content).

2. Tell about the most frustrating thing that's happened to you recently (feelings).

3. Tell about something that's difficult for you in trying to live a Christian life (spiritual concerns).

FOCUS NOTE 3

How to Listen Well

1. Hear the message. Listen to the person's words, voice, and body language.

2. Think about the message.

   a. Observe: What do your senses tell you?

   b. Draw conclusions: What did you learn from what the speaker said?

   c. Feel: What emotions do you feel in response to what the speaker said?

   d. Identify needs: What else do you need to know to continue the communication?

3. Respond to the message.

   a. Pay attention: Really hear what the speaker is saying. Make him or her feel valued.

   b. Ask questions.

      i. Use open-ended or "what" questions that require more thought and response than one or two words.

      ii. Use clarifying questions to better understand what the speaker says. Make them gentle and kindly inquisitive so the speaker will tell you more.

   c. Reflect what was said:

      i. as content—the who, what, why, when, where

      ii. as feelings—internal reactions to others

      iii. as spiritual concerns—hopes, questions, fears, concerns, or joys that are rooted in the speaker's relationship with God

---

Discussion Questions

1. What were some instances in which the listener reflected well?

2. Were there any instances in which the listener could have reflected even better?

4. Active Listening in a ChristCare Group

FOCUS NOTE 5

Sharing Situations

1. Tell about a time in the last few months when you felt very happy.

2. Tell about a time when you really felt as if you needed God's presence and help.

FOCUS NOTE 6

Job Descriptions

Speaker—Talk about the sharing situation you chose.

ChristCare Group Leader—Involve others in the group in listening and responding, and also listen and respond yourself. Make sure the speaker is heard and understood.

ChristCare Group members—Practice your active listening skills; reflect content, feelings, and spiritual concerns where appropriate; ask open-ended questions and clarifying questions; help the sharer say as much as he or she wants to say.

FOCUS NOTE 7

Discussion Questions

Speaker—Did you feel as if the group listened to you and heard what you were saying? What could they have done to listen to you even more?

ChristCare Group members—How did you help the speaker feel listened to and cared for?

ChristCare Group Leader—What did you do to help the group listen well?

All—What could either the group members or ChristCare Group Leader have done to improve active listening in the group?

5. Biblical Equipping: Jesus on Prayer (Luke 11:1–13)

FOCUS NOTE 8

Questions to Focus Sharing of Biblical Equipping Apart

- Share one insight that you've had as a result of your Biblical Equipping Apart this week.

- Describe one change in your life that you've committed to make as a result of your meditation on the Biblical Equipping passage this week.

- Tell about a time when you've met God in a new way through Biblical Equipping Apart this week.

Jesus on Prayer (Luke 11:1–13)

[1] One day Jesus was praying in a certain place. When he finished, one of his disciples said to him, "Lord, teach us to pray, just as John taught his disciples."

[2] He said to them, "When you pray, say:

"'Father,
hallowed be your name,
your kingdom come.
[3] Give us each day our daily bread.
[4] Forgive us our sins,
for we also forgive everyone who sins against us.
And lead us not into temptation.'"

— Honoring God
For heaven on Earth
Daily provisions
Forgive
Strength to wx journey righteous+ good

[5] Then he said to them, "Suppose one of you has a friend, and he goes to him at midnight and says, 'Friend, lend me three loaves of bread, [6] because a friend of mine on a journey has come to me, and I have nothing to set before him.'

[7] "Then the one inside answers, 'Don't bother me. The door is already locked, and my children are with me in bed. I can't get up and give you anything.' [8] I tell you, though he will not get up and give him the bread because he is his friend, yet because of the man's boldness he will get up and give him as much as he needs.

[9] "So I say to you: Ask and it will be given to you; seek and you will find; knock and the door will be opened to you. [10] For everyone who asks receives; he who seeks finds; and to him who knocks, the door will be opened.

[11] "Which of you fathers, if your son asks for a fish, will give him a snake instead? [12] Or if he asks for an egg, will give him a scorpion? [13] If you then, though you are evil, know how to give good gifts to your children, how much more will your Father in heaven give the Holy Spirit to those who ask him!"

Luke 11:9
Ask
Seek
Knock

FOCUS NOTE 10

Explore Questions

1. What does Jesus say that we should pray for?

2. What does Jesus' teaching about prayer tell us about what God is like? *wants to give*

3. What is the role of persistence in prayer? Given that God knows what we need and want, why do you think Jesus recommends such persistence? *2 way street*

4. Do you think Jesus prayed with the persistence he recommends to us? What do you think he was asking God for?

• evolving prayer v.
• change
be where you are
• give me what I need TODAY

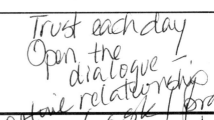

Trust each day
Open the dialogue
actual relationship of ask / prayer, rec'v.

FOCUS NOTE 11

Connect Questions

1. What are you asking, seeking, and knocking for in your prayers these days?

2. How is your life of prayer like Jesus' life of prayer? How is it different?

3. What does praying teach you about God? *2 way street feedback*

4. What effect would it have on a person's life if he or she consistently prayed as Jesus taught us to pray?

6. Prayer and Worship: Listening to God

Psalm 95 Let us make a joyful noise.

Appendix A: Active Listening Quiz Questions

Directions: Circle the most correct answer.

1. Which of these behaviors shows that you are paying attention to a speaker?

   a. Biting your fingernails and checking your watch

   b. Leaning forward slightly and making eye contact

   c. Finishing the speaker's sentences for him or her

   d. All the above

2. What's an example of an open-ended question?

   a. You're not *that* old, are you?

   b. Did you have a bad day?

   c. What are you going to do next?

3. Which of the following questions is the better choice? For what reason?

   a. What are your choices in this situation?

   b. Why would you choose to do that?

4. You're talking with a friend. The friend says, "You wouldn't believe what happened to me today." You respond with a clarifying question. Which of the following would be best?

   a. Do you want to go to the movies?

   b. What happened?

   c. You spilled food on your tie again. Is that it?

5. When might you ask a clarifying question?

   a. When you aren't sure you understood the speaker correctly

   b. When you want to find out more about what was said

   c. When you want the speaker to feel free to keep talking

   d. All the above

Active Listening Quiz Answers

1. Which of these behaviors shows that you are paying attention to a speaker?

   Answer: *b. Leaning forward slightly and making eye contact.*

   Follow-up Question: *What are other ways to show you're paying attention?*

2. What's an example of an open-ended question?

   Answer: *c. What are you going to do next?*

   Follow-up Question: *What kind of response might you get to questions "a" and "b"?*

3. Which of the following questions is the better choice? For what reason?

   Answer: *a. What are your choices in this situation?*

   Follow-up Question: *What is better about asking a what-question? Why do you think why-questions tend to put people on the defensive?*

4. You're talking with a friend. The friend says, "You wouldn't believe what happened to me today." You respond with a clarifying question. Which of the following would be best?

   Answer: *b. What happened?*

   Follow-up Question: *Why is "b" a clarifying question?*

5. When might you ask a clarifying question?

   Answer: *d. All the above*

   Follow-up Question: *How can you make sure clarifying questions don't come across as pushy or intrusive?*

Active Listening Quiz Questions (continued)

6. Why would you reflect back what a person has said to you?
   a. You want the speaker to know you were listening
   b. You want to let the speaker hear back what he or she is saying
   c. You want to encourage the speaker to keep talking
   d. You want to see if you understood the speaker correctly
   e. You can't think of anything else to say
   f. You forgot all the other parts of active listening
   g. All the above
   h. All the above except "e," "f," and "g"

7. What would be a good reflective response to the following statement: "Almost all my ancestors died in their fifties. I'm turning fifty next week"?
   a. Have you made out your will yet?
   b. When I turned fifty my family gave me a black birthday cake.
   c. Sounds like you're a little apprehensive about turning fifty.
   d. As far as I'm concerned, life begins at fifty.

8. Which of the following statements expresses a spiritual concern? That is, which could lead to a discussion of the speaker's relationship with God?
   a. How could God do this to me?
   b. I never thought I'd outlive my child.
   c. Life is so wonderful. How did I ever deserve such happiness?
   d. All the above.

9. If you said, "It seems to me as if caring for your mother is hard work," what would you be reflecting to the speaker?
   a. Content
   b. Feelings

10. A friend has just told you she's angry about something you've done. Which response appropriately reflects her feelings?
    a. You're angry about that silly little thing?
    b. Gosh, I guess that made you pretty angry.
    c. You're angry? Yeah, well so am I!

Active Listening Quiz Answers (continued)

6. Why would you reflect back what a person has said to you?

   Answer: *h. All the above except "e," "f," and "g"*

   Follow-up Question: *How does it help a speaker to hear someone else reflect what he or she said?*

7. What would be a good reflective response to the following statement: "Almost all my ancestors died in their fifties. I'm turning fifty next week"?

   Answer: *c. Sounds like you're a little apprehensive about turning fifty.*

   Follow-up Question: *What is really wrong with responses "a," "b," and "d"?*

8. Which of the following statements expresses a spiritual concern? That is, which could lead to a discussion of the speaker's relationship with God?

   Answer: *d. All the above.*

   Follow-up Question: *What spiritual concerns could each statement lead to?*

9. If you said, "It seems to me as if caring for your mother is hard work," what would you be reflecting to the speaker?

   Answer: *a. Content*

   Follow-up Question: *What would be a response that reflects feelings?*

10. A friend has just told you she's angry about something you've done. Which response appropriately reflects her feelings?

    Answer: *b. Gosh, I guess that made you pretty angry.*

    Follow-up Question: *What's wrong with answers "a" and "c"?*

There is a time for everything, and a season for every activity under heaven: . . . a time to be silent and a time to speak.

Ecclesiastes 3:1, 7b

PRECLASS READING OUTLINE

I. What Is Confidentiality?

Confidentiality is the act of keeping information private. According to the dictionary, when something is confidential, it is:

"Marked by intimacy or willingness to confide; private, secret; entrusted with confidences."[1]

Has a friend ever said to you, "Please don't tell anyone else"? Or has someone ever shared such deeply personal information that you simply knew you shouldn't pass it on? If this has happened to you, you already have some personal understanding of the issue and importance of confidentiality.

You've probably dealt with the issue of professional confidentiality too. If you've ever met with an attorney, counselor, or medical doctor about a private matter, you have benefited from that professional's pledge to keep your information confidential.

As a ChristCare Group Leader, you'll encounter many situations in which you'll need to understand the concept of confidentiality and how it applies to your interactions with group members. Focus Box 1 gives you an idea of some of the situations you may have to assess in terms of how you handle confidentiality.

FOCUS BOX 1

Confidentiality Challenges

How would you handle these situations that deal with confidentiality?

1. A member of a small group you led several years ago once shared a moving personal story.

5-PRE.pmd C: 04/06/1994 R: 01/24/2005

- Would you repeat this story to a friend in another city who doesn't know the group member?

- Would you use it as an illustration in a Sunday school lesson after the group member moved away?

- Would you use it as a way of comforting a friend who is going through similar circumstances?

2. A group member shared in a ChristCare Group meeting something that is upsetting her. What she shared has upset you, too. You're not sure how to support her or how to resolve your own feelings.

- Would you talk this over with your spouse (who is not a member of your ChristCare Group)?

- Would you bring this up in your SEA Group—taking care not to reveal the person's identity?

- Would you talk with your sister, who is a social worker, so she can help you better understand what's going on?

- Would you pray aloud for the group member by name in a prayer time during a Wednesday evening church service?

- Would you tell someone else about the situation if you are concerned the group member might hurt herself?

- Would you tell someone else about the situation if you are concerned the group member might hurt someone else?

- Would you tell someone who is not a member of your ChristCare Group about what's going on?

These are difficult questions. They show how important it is for you to understand confidentiality. This module will help you know how to deal with personal information that group members share. You'll learn when to speak, when to be silent, and what to say when it's time to speak.

Confidentiality Pertains to Private Knowledge

Must everything that happens in a ChristCare Group or with group members be kept confidential? No. For example, if your group is studying the Gospel of Mark, that isn't a secret. Nor is it usually a matter of confidentiality if a group member breaks an ankle while participating in a softball game at a picnic.

In confidentiality, there is a distinction between public knowledge and private knowledge. *Public knowledge* is information that people have a good chance of already knowing. It would do no harm if it were publicly broadcast. It is either intended for the public (such as information about your group's meeting time and place) or it is information that the speaker would not mind having repeated to the world. Public knowledge also includes events and information that are already well known to the outside world—for example, the fact that someone's spouse has just died.

Private knowledge is knowledge that you have only because you are a trusted group member or leader. Examples of information that are often private knowledge include:

- the fact that someone is struggling with a particular temptation;

- marriage or family problems;

- a past history of chemical dependence or eating disorder;

- mental illness;

- a criminal record;

- the fact that someone was once the victim of rape, incest, or child abuse;

- job plans or struggles that are not generally known;

- many medical problems;

- any other information that a person asks be kept confidential. Such a request is all it takes to make the information confidential.

Occasionally you may be unsure whether a particular issue is private or public. For example, one couple who is undergoing treatment for infertility may be comfortable having everyone know that and may be happy for you to put them on the congregation prayer list. In that case, the infertility can be considered public knowledge. Another couple in the same situation may be uncomfortable having anyone but group members know about their difficulties. In that case it's private knowledge. *If you aren't absolutely sure, ask permission from the person before you tell others inside or outside the group.*

What about instances where something that is usually considered private knowledge has nevertheless become public? For example, what if a prominent group member files for bankruptcy and this becomes public knowledge in the congregation? In such a situation, the best rule is to avoid giving any information that isn't already known. The fact of the bankruptcy is known, so you needn't pretend not to know about it. However, the fact that the bankruptcy resulted from a relative's dishonest management is not generally known, and you should still treat this detail as private knowledge. In general, avoid adding more fuel to the fire. Don't gossip even after the broad outlines are publicly known. Instead, try to steer people who ask toward care and prayer.

Confidentiality Applies to Word and Deed

Usually people think of confidentiality in terms of something that's said. In ChristCare Group leadership, though, confidentiality also extends to impressions, observations, and written records.

For instance, what if a group member doesn't speak during a group discussion about divorce, yet seems upset? You might wonder about something in that person's marriage or background, but under the guidelines of ChristCare Group confidentiality, you must not discuss your observations or impressions with others.

Confidentiality Is Intentional

Many people think of confidentiality as *not* doing or saying something—they think of it as a passive act. In reality, keeping information confidential is an active and intentional behavior. People who actively decide to keep a confidence have a much-reduced risk of breaking that confidence, either intentionally or by accident.

People who assertively keep a confidence are prepared with answers for curious others. They've thought through their responses to inquirers. They are especially viligant when they're in a situation that could bring up a confidence.

Confidentiality as a Professional Issue

When the word *confidentiality* is mentioned, people often think of a few particular professions, including ministers, psychologists, attorneys, and medical doctors. People in these professions are compelled, usually by law, to keep most kinds of client information confidential.

The earliest example of confidentiality in the helping professions is the Hippocratic oath, which includes this pledge:

"Whatever, in connection with my profession, or not in connection with it, I may see or hear in the lives of men which ought not to be spoken abroad I will not divulge as reckoning that all should be kept secret."[2]

A specific application of this pledge's content is contained in the following excerpt from the "Ethical Principles of Psychologists." This document has been adopted by the American Psychological Association and applies to psychologists, students of psychology, and others who work under the supervision of a psychologist.

"Psychologists have a primary obligation and take reasonable precautions to respect the confidentiality rights of those with whom they work or consult . . ."[3]

Another example of a professional statement about confidentiality is from the American Medical Association:

"The information disclosed to a physician during the course of the relationship between physician and patient is confidential to the greatest possible degree. The patient should feel free to make a full disclosure of information to the physician in order that the physician may most effectively provide needed services. The patient should be able to make this disclosure with the knowledge that the physician will respect the confidential nature of the communication. The physician should not reveal confidential communications or information without the express consent of the patient, unless required by law."[4]

Confidentiality as an attorney-client privilege is spelled out in this way:

"Where legal advice of any kind is sought from a professional legal advisor in his capacity as such, the communications relating to that purpose, made in confidence by the client, are at his instance permanently protected from disclosure by himself or by the legal adviser, except the protection be waived."[5]

Pastors are also bound to confidentiality, but guidelines vary from denomination to denomination. Episcopal priests, for example, follow this directive:

"The content of a confession is not normally a matter of subsequent discussion. The secrecy of a confession is morally absolute for a confessor, and must under no circumstances be broken."[6]

In addition to the helping professions listed above, other professions also carry expectations of confidentiality. Secretaries and administrative assistants must keep particular types of information confidential. People who work in the area of personnel or human resources keep confidential some kinds of information about past, present, and possible future employees of their companies.

Have you ever asked for a fellow employee's home phone number and been told, "I'm sorry, I'm not allowed to give that out"? Or have you ever signed an insurance form that permitted your physician to divulge medical information to your insurance company? Instances like these remind us that confidentiality is an important responsibility in many professions.

Confidentiality as a Personal Issue

It's quite clear that confidentiality is expected of certain professionals. But the issue of confidentiality as a personal responsibility is often less clear. You may have found yourself in situations like these:

- You tell one friend something another friend has told you, then say to yourself, "Hmm. I wonder if I should have said that."

- You ask a friend not to repeat something you've said, but you feel uneasy because you aren't sure that your friend will indeed keep it confidential.

- A friend tells you something he or she has heard about you; you're surprised to hear something repeated that you have said in confidence to another friend.

- You pause as you dial your congregation's prayer chain to ask for prayers for a friend who left town on a family emergency. It crosses your mind that the friend might not want others—even people on the prayer chain—to know about the situation.

What situations can you think of in which you would have or have had a question about confidentiality?

You can see that the issue of confidentiality raises some difficult questions. When difficult questions arise in any area of life, the Bible is a good place to go for guidance.

Confidentiality as a Christian Issue

You won't find the word *confidentiality* in a biblical concordance. You *will* find Scripture references that offer advice about when it's appropriate to talk about other people and what it's appropriate to say. Some verses are listed in Focus Box 2.

FOCUS BOX 2

Scripture	Message
"You shall not give false testimony against your neighbor." *Deuteronomy 5:20*	Avoid saying anything that's not true.
Keep your tongue from evil and your lips from speaking lies. *Psalm 34:13*	Avoid saying anything that will bring sorrow, distress, calamity, suffering, or misfortune. Avoid saying anything that is disloyal, untrue, insincere, or misrepresentative.
Reckless words pierce like a sword, but the tongue of the wise brings healing. *Proverbs 12:18*	Avoid speaking carelessly—you might hurt someone. Speak with good judgment, sound understanding, and keen discernment so your words can help someone.

The Scriptures make it clear that the tongue is a powerful tool capable of causing both harm and healing. This is especially noticeable in groups because of the personal and private information shared there. That's why it's so important for ChristCare Group Leaders and members to understand when it's time to be silent.

II. The Two Exceptions to Maintaining Confidentiality

There are two important exceptions to maintaining confidentiality that every ChristCare Group Leader and member should know about:

- when there's a chance that a person might hurt himself or herself;

- when there's a chance that a person might hurt someone else.

If a group member is talking about killing himself or herself, it's time to suspend confidentiality and get some additional help. When an individual's life is at risk, get immediate advice or assistance from an Equipper, a pastor, or an appropriate mental health professional.

Likewise, if a group member talks about hurting someone else, it's also time to suspend confidentiality and get some help. This includes threats of murder, child abuse (including sexual abuse), spouse abuse, elder abuse, and any other threats of harm to another person. As in the previously mentioned situation, get immediate advice or assistance from an Equipper, a pastor, or another appropriate professional, such as a counselor or law enforcement officer, depending on the immediacy of the situation. Your state may require you to report situations involving child or elder abuse (you'll find out more about this in the in-class session).

III. Why Confidentiality Is Important in ChristCare Groups

A. Trust

ChristCare Group Leader training session 2, Building Community in Your ChristCare Group, covers the importance of trust in ChristCare Groups. Without trust, members can't form the close relationships that are necessary for growth to occur. Just as growth isn't possible without trust, trust isn't possible without confidentiality.

Group members must know without a doubt that others will not share information outside the group without permission. If group members are not assured of this confidentiality, they will not share openly. If they do share, they may eventually regret their openness.

B. Witness

ChristCare Groups offer a unique opportunity for Christians to "be Christ" to one another. New Christians may learn for the first time about real caring. Maturing Christians will grow in Christ as they grow in their relationships with other group members. A break in confidentiality can abruptly stop the growth of both new and maturing Christians within a group.

For instance, imagine that a new, non-Christian group member takes a risk and shares something personal with the group. What if this person then discovers the more mature Christians in the group treat this information without the confidentiality—and respect—that it deserves? The non-Christian's view of Christ and Christianity could suffer tremendously. In the worst case, this person might even think, "Christians don't care about me any more than anyone else does. I've had it with this."

On the other hand, what if a group member shares something personal, then finds that others *do* handle it confidentially? That group member receives wonderful gifts, including love, support, and a better idea of what God's love is like.

Confidentiality truly can mean the difference between life and death. Small hurts that come from small disappointments about broken confidentiality can cause "little deaths," including loss of trust and disillusionment with Christianity. Big hurts that come from extremely painful disappointments about broken confidentiality could offend a non-Christian group member so much that he or she could reject Christ because of it.

Breaking confidentiality can hurt individual group members, the ChristCare Group as a whole, a congregation's ChristCare Group Ministry, and even the congregation as a whole. Confidentiality is that important.

As the ChristCare Group Leader, you are pivotal to your group's understanding and practice of confidentiality.

IV. How You and Your Group Members Can Maintain Confidentiality in Your ChristCare Group

Because confidentiality is such an important issue to your ChristCare Group, it is something you'll want to bring up more than once and in several different ways, including:

- building confidentiality into your covenant;
- explaining exactly what confidentiality is;
- teaching about confidentiality;
- reminding group members about confidentiality;
- informing new members and visitors about confidentiality;
- modeling confidentiality;
- affirming confidentiality.

A. Build Confidentiality into Your Covenant

You saw the ChristCare Group Covenant in the *Beginnings* course you read before your first ChristCare Group Leader training session. You learned that building a covenant is important for many reasons, including giving you the positive opportunity to talk about the issue of confidentiality.

Take a minute now to locate the ChristCare Group Covenant at the end of your Outline and Focus Notes for session 1, How to Get Your ChristCare Group Off to a Great Start. Read through the covenant, finding the third item under the "Promises We Make to One Another" section. This item says, "Keep confidential whatever group members share, both during meetings and outside of meetings."

Including confidentiality in the covenant is critical to maintaining confidentiality over the long haul. Mentioning it helps your group set operating standards.

Putting confidentiality into the covenant also encourages group members to recognize its importance and helps them enforce it with one another. In his book *Making Groups Effective*,[7] Alvin Zander says that the more important a standard (like confidentiality) is to a group, the more pressure members exert on one another to live up to the standard. Help group members see that you can't have a trusting, nurturing ChristCare Group without confidentiality. Then they will take ownership for making sure it is observed.

B. Explain Exactly What Confidentiality Is

In order for group members truly to understand what it means to keep something confidential, you want to be able to explain confidentiality and its importance clearly. Focus Box 3, adapted from *Pragmatic Group Leadership*,[8] provides an example of how to explain confidentiality concisely.

FOCUS BOX 3

How to Explain Confidentiality to Your ChristCare Group

What goes on in this ChristCare Group belongs only to us, as ChristCare Group members. It's our business and no one else's. If a group member shares personal information, revealing such information can result in harmful consequences. If any one of us believes that what is revealed here will leave this room, none of us will feel safe enough to talk about personal concerns. Does everyone understand this? Is there anyone in the group who cannot subscribe to this, who feels she or he won't be able to respect this idea and live by it?

You might want to go farther and spell out in detail the behaviors it takes to keep information confidential. Focus Box 4 includes specific behaviors expected of group members who maintain confidentiality within their ChristCare Groups. You can present this list to your ChristCare Group and invite discussion or lead the group in brainstorming a similar list.

FOCUS BOX 4

Specific Ways to Maintain Confidentiality

To keep information shared in this group confidential, I will:

- not share personal information that I've heard from, or observed in, other group members with anyone outside the group, including my spouse and close friends;

- always ask permission before I share confidential information outside the group, even if I'm asking others for prayer, care, or another kind of support;

- ask permission to share information with others if I am not sure whether the information is public or private knowledge;

- refrain from discussing group members and their life issues with other group members outside group meetings; instead, I will recommend that we all bring these discussions to the group session or that group members talk *with* one another, not *about* one another;

- break confidentiality if necessary to get immediate help for a group member who is in danger of hurting himself, herself, or another person.

C. Teach Confidentiality

You can reinforce the concept of confidentiality by teaching it. You may choose to do this if you think your group members need more information or might be especially prone to breaking confidentiality. It's also a good idea to mention confidentiality, on occasion, as a general reminder of how important it is.

It is up to you to determine if and when to teach confidentiality. You might want to do it early in your group's life, later on as a reminder, or after one or more new members join the group.

In preparing a lesson on confidentiality, you can use the information in this Preclass Reading, notes from this module's in-class session, or additional information you find as you research the subject. Focus Box 5 gives you an idea of what you might want to include in a sample lesson plan.

Teaching about Confidentiality—Sample Lesson Plan

1. Define confidentiality for the group

2. Tell why confidentiality is important—five minutes

   A. Group members share their ideas on why confidentiality is important, using personal examples of times when keeping a confidence has been important or when breaking a confidence has caused hurt.

   B. ChristCare Group Leader sums up discussion, emphasizing that confidentiality is essential to trust, and trust is essential to building and maintaining a safe environment in the ChristCare Group.

3. Biblical direction regarding confidentiality—15 minutes

   A. Group members take turns reading and explaining Bible passages included in this Preclass Reading on page 86.

   B. Group members apply Scripture to real life by discussing how they would handle the Confidentiality Challenges posed in Focus Box 1 of this Preclass Reading.

4. Committing to Confidentiality—two minutes

   ChristCare Group Leader reads out loud "How to Explain Confidentiality to Your ChristCare Group" in Focus Box 3.

5. Tying up loose ends—ten minutes

   ChristCare Group Leader and group members answer and discuss questions group members have about confidentiality.

You'll want to be careful teaching confidentiality if it has been broken in your ChristCare Group. Before you decide to teach on this subject in that situation, be sure to review section VI on pages 91–93, "What to Do If Confidentiality Is Broken."

D. Remind Group Members about Confidentiality

Throughout your ChristCare Group's life, you'll want to remind members at appropriate times about confidentiality.

For instance, if someone has just shared information that could be especially damaging if it were revealed outside the group, say something like, "Mae has just shown us that she trusts us enough to share something deeply personal and important to her. As part of our caring response, let's be especially aware of keeping this information confidential."

Or at the beginning of your ChristCare Group's check-in time, you might once in a while say something like, "Before we begin sharing what's going on in our lives, I'd just like to say again that we have all promised to keep confidential whatever is shared here."

You might feel led to include the issue of confidentiality in a prayer from time to time. For example, your prayer might say something like this: "Thank you, God, for the sharing that has occurred here. Please help each of us uphold our responsibilities to one another—to lend support where we can and always to keep confidential what we've heard."

E. Inform New Members and Visitors about Confidentiality

When someone attends your ChristCare Group for the first time, either as a new member or a guest, you need to inform him or her about your group's commitment to confidentiality. Preface each session at which guests or new members are present by saying, "I'd like to take a minute to remind all of us about our commitment to confidentiality. Anything said in this group stays in the group. We don't tell anyone about the personal information we learn in group meetings. That's the only way we can be a group. Does everyone here still agree with that?" This allows you to communicate group expectations to members and visitors alike.

F. Model Confidentiality

As a ChristCare Group Leader, you are the group members' best example of how to maintain confidentiality, so you'll have to be especially careful in this area.

If a ChristCare Group member tries to engage you in a lengthy discussion about another group member outside of a group meeting, use the opportunity to say something like, "You know, this is the kind of thing we need to talk about in our group sessions. Let's do that instead of going on with this conversation."

When you assertively act to avoid breaking confidentiality, let the group members know. Say something like, "Last week, a well-meaning person asked about someone in our group. I was so glad for our promise to maintain confidentiality because I could just say, 'You know, our group has made a promise not to share information about group members outside the group because that can really cause trouble for people. I appreciate your concern, but you can talk directly to that person about it.'"

G. Affirm Confidentiality

When you know that group members have maintained confidentiality, praise them for it. Invite them to share about times they've been tempted to break confidentiality and didn't. Let them share about how they've handled situations with well-meaning—or even not-so-well-meaning—inquirers.

When a ChristCare Group member shares something personal, then he or she or someone else might remind the group that it's confidential. Affirm the group member for the reminder. Say something like, "Larry, I'm so glad you added that. It's a reminder we all can use from time to time, especially on something so important."

If a group member takes a risk in sharing, compliment the group on the trust it has built. Say, "The fact that we have all agreed to keep what's said in the group confidential has helped us trust one another so deeply."

V. How Confidentiality Fits In with SEA Groups

As a ChristCare Group Leader, you will be part of a Support, Encouragement, and Accountability (SEA) Group. During SEA Group sessions, you will talk about what's going on in your ChristCare Group. You may need to get rather specific about particular problems or issues. Even so, it is possible to maintain confidentiality and still get the help you need.

A. Inform Your ChristCare Group

Your ChristCare Group needs to be aware that you are involved in a SEA Group, and that occasionally you will be reporting to that group about things that happen in ChristCare Group meetings. Reassure your group members that no names are used, and that everyone involved also is committed to confidentiality. Help them understand that the SEA Group is not a gossip group; it is a group that provides support and accountability to ensure that ChristCare Groups get the best possible leadership. (You may also wish to tell them that SEA Group

attendance is mandatory for all ChristCare Group Leaders and helps you to be a better leader.)

Near the beginning of your group's life, you need to make group members aware of your participation in a SEA Group. It's not necessary to make a big issue about this. Simply communicate it positively, as a guarantee that they're getting the best possible leadership from you.

B. The SEA Group's Commitment to Confidentiality

In your SEA Group, you will regularly report what is going on in your ChristCare Group and challenges or problems you may face. As you do this, you will want to take certain precautions to protect confidentiality.

Don't Use Names

First of all, don't use names when talking about group members. If it is easier for you to talk about a situation by using a name, make one up. "John" or "Jane" are time-honored pseudonyms.

Don't Share Unnecessary Details

Avoid mentioning identifying details when you're talking about your ChristCare Group. For example, if you're discussing the interaction between group members and one of them happens to use a wheelchair, don't bring up that fact unless it's absolutely critical to the SEA Group's understanding and ability to help you lead most effectively. It's likely that only a small number of people in your congregation use wheelchairs regularly. Including this detail makes it easy for other SEA Group members to identify the person about whom you're talking.

Maintain the Balance between Too Much Detail and Not Enough

What if you were having major problems finding places for your group to meet because none of the members had wheelchair-accessible homes? When you tell your SEA Group about what's happening in your ChristCare Group, you need to keep a delicate balance between being too vague and too specific. Obviously, if you need the SEA Group's ideas about how to solve the meeting place problem, they need to know why it is a problem. In that case you would diminish the SEA Group's effectiveness if you didn't share the important detail about the wheelchair.

Here's another example. If a couple is having marriage problems and this is seriously affecting the rest of the group, you should not go into all the unhappy details. It is unnecessary and can easily lead to breaking confidentiality. Yet it's not helpful, either, for you only to say, "A married couple in my group is having trouble, and it's affecting the group" and then refuse to say more. To provide adequate supervision and accountability, your peers in your SEA Group need to know a little more. For example, are the couple's problems affecting the group because one or both members are using the meeting as a battleground? Or is it because they are sitting in hostile silence? Or is it because they are trying to get the group to take sides? Or is it because they are the hosting couple for your group meetings?

Some detail is necessary. It is *not* necessary to reveal the identities of the couple having marriage problems, nor to tell details that will make their identity obvious to everyone. There will be times when you have to make your best judgment about how much to share, knowing SEA Group members will keep any information they hear confidential.

If You Figure Out Who Is Being Talked about, Keep It to Yourself

It is possible that at some time during a SEA Group session you will recognize the person about whom another SEA Group member is speaking. Don't get upset with the SEA Group member for breaking confidentiality. You may have been able to identify the member because you have specific knowledge others don't have. Instead, honor confidentiality yourself by keeping quiet what you've guessed.

Get Individual Supervision When Necessary

In certain rare situations, you may be dealing with a group problem that is so sensitive you can't talk about it even in a SEA Group. For example, it could be that one of the congregation's lay leaders, who is in your ChristCare Group, has just learned that he has been accused of a crime. If you think the subject matter is just too painful and potentially damaging to risk talking about in your SEA Group, bring it up with your SEA Group Facilitator. Together you can decide if the issue is really that sensitive. If it is, your SEA Group Facilitator will put you in touch with the SEA Group Coordinator, who will see that you receive individual supervision for as long as necessary.

VI. What to Do If Confidentiality Is Broken

As a ChristCare Group Leader, you will work extremely hard to help your small group understand the importance of confidentiality. And group members will work hard to maintain confidentiality. Even so, it may happen that someone in your ChristCare Group will break confidentiality at some time.

Experiencing a break in confidentiality is, of course, something you hope and pray will never happen. If it does, though, you must deal with it quickly and effectively, no matter how painful it is.

If a break in confidentiality occurs in your ChristCare Group, there are six actions you need to take.

One: Find Out Exactly What Happened

You may find out about broken confidentiality in a number of ways:

- The person who broke confidentiality may tell you.

- A group member who was hurt by a break in confidentiality may tell you.

- Someone outside your group may tell you about a broken confidence in your group.

- You could hear something that's confidential in your ChristCare Group "through the grapevine," thus learning that you have a confidentiality leak among group members.

No matter how you find out about a break in confidentiality, the first thing you need to do is gather information. At this point, don't be judgmental; just do your best to discover what happened. Stay objective. First make sure that the confidential information was indeed revealed by a member of your group and not through some other source (a neighbor or relative of the person involved or a witness to the event). Once you've established that the confidential information came out of your group, you'll need to gather all the facts before deciding what further action to take.

If you know who broke confidentiality, go to that person and find out what happened. Explain the importance of your need to know so that you, the person, and the ChristCare Group can deal effectively with the incident.

If you don't know who broke confidentiality, go to your ChristCare Group as a whole and explain that you know confidentiality has been broken. It is often sufficient simply to inform the group that this has happened—you may not need to find out exactly who broke confidentiality. In such a case, just bringing up the issue usually will be enough to prevent it from happening again. You could, of course, invite the offender to talk about what happened with the group, with the individual who has been hurt, or with you privately. Depending on the situation, this may be helpful to heal the hurt that has been caused. Just be sure you don't seem to be forcing the person to come forward.

Two: Treat This Situation with Confidentiality

If you find yourself in the middle of a situation in which someone has broken confidentiality, be very careful to keep this "situation within a situation" confidential. It involves deeply personal information and has the potential to do great harm to many people and even to your congregation's ChristCare Group Ministry as a whole.

By treating the person who broke confidentiality with respect, you are helping that person learn firsthand how important it is to know that deeply personal information is "safe" with another person (you).

The person who broke confidentiality may decide to make the situation or parts of it public. But that is not your decision or your responsibility. The person whose confidence was broken may also decide to make the matter public.

Three: Support the Person Who Broke Confidentiality in Making Amends

If you know who broke confidentiality, you can talk with that person about what amends could or should be made in order to repair damage done or prevent further harm. For instance, you could suggest that the person talk with those who received confidential information, explaining the mistake that was made and asking those people not to repeat the information and compound the problem. If the information has spread to more than one or two individuals, you need a bigger plan for damage control; see the following section.

If you don't know who broke confidentiality, you could talk with your entire group about what could be done to make amends. Group members, especially the one whose confidential information was shared, will probably have some ideas. Even if the person who broke confidentiality chooses to remain anonymous, he or she will receive some input on what can be done to help right the wrong.

Four: Address the Issues of Confession and Forgiveness

After the person who broke confidentiality has shared the whole story with you, and after he or she has done what is possible to make amends, talk about confession and forgiveness as appropriate next steps to take. You will probably want to recommend to the person who broke confidence that he or she:

- acknowledge the mistake and ask God for forgiveness;
- confess the mistake to the person or people who were hurt and ask for forgiveness;
- confess the mistake to the ChristCare Group as a whole and ask for group members' forgiveness. Depending on the situation, this is usually the choice of the person who broke confidentiality, unless the entire group has been damaged by the situation. Such an action can result in growth for everyone in the ChristCare Group as well as be an effective reminder of what can happen when confidentiality is broken.

As a ChristCare Group Leader and caring friend, do what you can to support both the person who broke confidentiality and the person or people who were hurt while the above steps are taking place. Chances are, everyone involved will have feelings of sadness, hurt, and anger about what has happened.

A person who breaks confidentiality, once he or she realizes the consequences, may believe he or she should quit the group. Do all you can to keep the person in the group. He or she is forgiven. Exceptions, in very difficult situations, are discussed below.

Five: Take Steps to Make Sure This Doesn't Happen Again

There are several factors you need to take into account here:

- Has this happened before in your ChristCare Group?

   If it has, you'll want to make sure your ChristCare Group more clearly understands the issue of confidentiality and its importance. Talk about it, teach about it, find out why keeping confidentiality is a problem in your particular group, listen to what group members have to say. If your small group simply doesn't "get it," ask for advice from your SEA Group or from the Equippers in your congregation. In the meantime, call a halt to deeply personal sharing in your ChristCare Group until you are confident that group members can handle confidentiality.

- Has this individual broken confidentiality before?

    If not, make sure the person who broke confidentiality understands why it was wrong, takes responsibility for his or her action, and acknowledges the damage it has caused. This person then needs to promise not to break confidentiality again. Don't browbeat the person, don't make him or her feel condemned (God knows we all make mistakes, and Christ died to forgive them), but do make sure this person understands the seriousness of what has happened.

    If the person has broken confidentiality before, you have a very difficult situation with which to deal. The individual has established a pattern of being unable to keep others' personal information to himself or herself. In such a situation you have a limited number of options.

    You may want to ask your pastor to talk with the individual, sharing the importance of maintaining confidentiality and assessing if the person's inability to maintain confidentiality points to a need for further care. If so, work with your pastor to help the person find and take advantage of additional care.

    In the most difficult situations you may need to ask the person to leave your ChristCare Group. Doing so may be the only way to preserve your ChristCare Group's ministry and your congregation's overall ChristCare Group Ministry. The person who broke confidentiality is a forgiven sinner, just like the rest of us. But if he or she refuses to admit wrongdoing, or if the person has proved incapable of keeping information confidential, his or her continued group membership is not possible. Group members would find it impossible to trust the group enough to share about themselves.

    For the sake of the ministry, you may need to make a difficult decision and take tough actions. You should make such a decision with the help of your SEA Group Facilitator. If you need to inform the person that he or she is no longer welcome in your ChristCare Group, you may want to have an Equipper present to lend authority to your announcement (and support you as you make it).

If you have to ask a person to withdraw from your group, you should offer some other means of ongoing nurture, if possible.

Six: Do What You Can to Repair Damage with the Group

When someone in your ChristCare Group breaks confidentiality, you will need to help group members talk about their feelings and build trust again. Spend time listening to group members' feelings as they talk about what happened. Ask them what they think it will take to learn to trust each other again. If you decide it is necessary to ask the person who broke confidentiality to leave the group, give group members many opportunities to talk about that also. Open conversation about such a difficult issue will be the best way to help group members learn from it and move on.

A breach in confidentiality can cause serious damage beyond an individual ChristCare Group. If word gets out to the members of your congregation or community about a break in confidentiality, people will be less likely to participate in ChristCare Groups and less likely to trust others if they do participate.

In situations such as this, don't try to address the problem by yourself. Report it to your SEA Group and to your Equippers Team (remembering to keep confidentiality as you report the situation). Let these leaders deal with repercussions that have far-reaching effects.

VII. Preparing for the In-Class Session

Focus Box 1 is repeated here, with suggested responses to the situations. Read the responses and make comments or write questions in the space provided. You may refer to these comments and questions during the in-class session.

FOCUS BOX 1

Confidentiality Challenges

How would you handle these situations that deal with confidentiality?

1. A member of a small group you led several years ago once shared a moving personal story.

    - Would you repeat this story to a friend in another city who doesn't know the group member?

Only if the group member gave you or your group members permission to talk about it outside the group.

- Would you use it as an illustration in a Sunday school lesson after the group member moved away?

  Not without getting the person's permission.

- Would you use it as a way of comforting a friend who is going through similar circumstances?

  Only if you had permission to talk about it outside the group.

2. A group member shared in a ChristCare Group meeting something that is upsetting her. What she shared has upset you, too. You're not sure how to support her or how to resolve your own feelings.

- Would you talk this over with your spouse (who is not a member of your ChristCare Group)?

  No.

- Would you bring this up in your SEA Group—taking care not to reveal the person's identity?

  Yes. That is what SEA Groups are for.

- Would you talk with your sister, who is a social worker, so she can help you better understand what's going on?

  No.

- Would you pray aloud for the group member by name in a prayer time during a Wednesday evening church service?

  No.

- Would you tell someone else about the situation if you are concerned the group member might hurt herself?

  Yes—tell an appropriate individual, such as an Equipper, your pastor, a counselor, or even a law enforcement officer, depending on the immediacy of the danger.

- Would you tell someone else about the situation if you are concerned the group member might hurt someone else?

  Yes—tell an appropriate individual, such as an Equipper, your pastor, a counselor, or even a law enforcement officer, depending on the immediacy of the danger.

- Would you tell someone who is not a member of your ChristCare Group about what's going on?

  No.

Do you have questions or comments about any of these situations or responses? What other comments or questions about confidentiality do you have? Write them here:

ENDNOTES

1. *Merriam Webster's Collegiate Dictionary,* 11th ed. (Springfield, MA: Merriam-Webster Inc., 2003), s.v. "confidentiality."

2. "Privacy and Confidentiality in Psychotherapy," *American Psychologist,* September 1980, page 829.

3. American Psychological Association, *Ethical Principles of Psychologists and Code of Conduct* (Washington: American Psychological Association, 1992), page 10.

4. American Medical Association Council on Ethical and Judicial Affairs, *Code of Medical Ethics* (Chicago: American Medical Association, 1994), page 71.

5. Jonathan S. Lynton and Terri Mick Lyndall, *Legal Ethics and Professional Responsibility* (Albany: Delmar Publishers Inc., and Lawyers Cooperative Publishing, 1994).

6. William W. Rankin, *Confidentiality and Clergy: Churches, Ethics, and the Law* (Harrisburg: Morehouse Publishing, 1990).

7. Alvin Zander, *Making Groups Effective* (San Francisco: Jossey-Bass Inc., Publishers, 1982).

8. Jeffrey A. Kottler, *Pragmatic Group Leadership* (Belmont: Brooks/Cole Publishing Company, 1983).

There is a time for everything, and a season for every activity under heaven: . . . a time to be silent and a time to speak.

Ecclesiastes 3:1, 7b

1. Prayer and Worship: Confession and Forgiveness

2. Public versus Private Information

FOCUS NOTE 1

Being Transferred

Eric found out two weeks ago that his company is considering transferring him to another part of the country. Eric, a member of his church council, informed the council at their meeting last week, since they may have to find a replacement. Eric's wife, Laura, also mentioned the move to her women's group. Their two teenage daughters are very upset about the possibility because they don't want to leave their friends. In your ChristCare Group, Eric confides that he doesn't know what to do. He doesn't want to upset his family. He thinks this is a very difficult time for his family to pick up and move. He has talked with someone from another company about perhaps switching jobs so he can continue to work in town, but he really doesn't want to because he likes the company he's working for now.

Are the following facts public or private knowledge, and why?

1. Eric might be transferred.
2. Eric's daughters are very upset.
3. Eric is thinking about changing jobs.

95

5-OFN.pmd C: 02/24/2004 R: 01/24/2005

Caring for a Friend

Sharon has told your ChristCare Group that she recently found out a good friend has AIDS. The friend lives in a distant city, and Sharon wants to travel there to support and spend time with her friend. Sharon has a lot of questions about the disease—how fast it progresses, what's the latest treatment, which cities have especially good treatment programs, and so on. Since Sharon is a single mother with two children, she has asked for the group's help in caring for her children when she makes the trip out of town.

Are the following facts private or public knowledge, and why?

1. Sharon has a friend who has AIDS.

2. Sharon wants to know more about AIDS so she can better understand and support her friend.

3. Members of your ChristCare Group are caring for Sharon's children while she visits her friend.

Marital Difficulties

Arturo has asked the ChristCare Group for prayers because his wife, who isn't a member of the group or the church, has moved out of their home and is taking steps toward divorce. Arturo doesn't want a divorce and is trying to talk his wife into seeing a counselor with him.

Are the following facts private or public knowledge, and why?

1. Arturo's wife has moved out.

2. Arturo's wife is initiating divorce proceedings.

3. Arturo wants his wife to see a marriage counselor with him.

3. Questions and Answers

4. Preserving Confidentiality

FOCUS NOTE 4

Confidentiality Role-Play Roles

A. ChristCare Group Leader

B. Person Asking for Confidential Information

C. Observer

FOCUS NOTE 5

Role-Play Discussion Questions

A. *ChristCare Group Leader*

Describe how it was to respond to the inquiry. What surprised you? What was difficult? What could you have done differently or better?

B. *Person Asking for Confidential Information*

Describe how you felt when you didn't get an answer to your question. Did you understand why you didn't get a response? What did the ChristCare Group Leader do well in handling your request? Is there any way in which the ChristCare Group Leader could have handled your request better?

C. *Observer*

What did you notice about the interchange between the two participants? What did they do well? What could they have done differently or better?

---

5. Biblical Equipping: Why Pray? (Psalm 86:1–17)

FOCUS NOTE 6

Questions to Focus Sharing of Biblical Equipping Apart

- Share one insight that you've had as a result of your Biblical Equipping Apart this week.

- Describe one change in your life that you've committed to make as a result of your meditation on the Biblical Equipping passage this week.

- Tell about a time when you've met God in a new way through Biblical Equipping Apart this week.

FOCUS NOTE 7

Why Pray? (Psalm 86:1–17)

A Prayer of David

¹ Hear, O LORD, and answer me,
    for I am poor and needy.
² Guard my life, for I am devoted to you.
    You are my God; save your servant
    who trusts in you.
³ Have mercy on me, O Lord,
    for I call to you all day long.
⁴ Bring joy to your servant,
    for to you, O Lord,
    I lift up my soul.

⁵ You are forgiving and good, O Lord,
    abounding in love to all who call to you.
⁶ Hear my prayer, O LORD;
    listen to my cry for mercy.

Focus Note 7 is continued on page 99.

⁷ In the day of my trouble I will call to you,
    for you will answer me.

⁸ Among the gods there is none like you, O Lord;
    no deeds can compare with yours.
⁹ All the nations you have made
    will come and worship before you, O Lord;
    they will bring glory to your name.
¹⁰ For you are great and do marvelous deeds;
    you alone are God.

¹¹ Teach me your way, O Lord,
    and I will walk in your truth;
  give me an undivided heart,
    that I may fear your name.
¹² I will praise you, O Lord my God, with all my heart;
    I will glorify your name forever.
¹³ For great is your love toward me;
    you have delivered me from the depths of the grave.

¹⁴ The arrogant are attacking me, O God;
    a band of ruthless men seeks my life—
    men without regard for you.
¹⁵ But you, O Lord, are a compassionate and gracious God,
    slow to anger, abounding in love and faithfulness.
¹⁶ Turn to me and have mercy on me;
    grant your strength to your servant
    and save the son of your maidservant.
¹⁷ Give me a sign of your goodness,
    that my enemies may see it and be put to shame,
    for you, O Lord, have helped me and comforted me.

FOCUS NOTE 8

Explore Questions

1. There are many kinds of prayer, including praising God, asking for God's help, making requests of God, and confessing sins to God. What kinds of prayer do you see in this psalm?

2. Prayer reveals what is going on deep inside a person. What does David's prayer tell you about the kind of person he is?

3. Why does David need to pray? Is David's only reason for prayer to get God to do something for him? If not, then what other reasons does he have?

4. How would you describe David's relationship with God, based on what you read in this prayer?

FOCUS NOTE 9

Connect Questions

1. How can prayer affect a Christian's relationship with God?

2. What kinds of prayer do you typically pray? What kinds of prayer would you like to learn to pray more?

3. How could your life of prayer change and grow in order to transform you into even more of the person God wants you to be?

4. What might you do to help make prayer a transformational activity in your ChristCare Group?

6. Missional Service: Research Referral Resources

7. Closing Prayer

When and How to Make Referrals for Additional Care

Preclass Reading

"When you pass through the waters, I will be with you; and when you pass through the rivers, they will not sweep over you. When you walk through the fire, you will not be burned; the flames will not set you ablaze."

Isaiah 43:2

PRECLASS READING OUTLINE

I. Introduction

II. Determine That a Person Needs Additional Care

    A. Why Additional Care Is Sometimes Needed

    B. How to Tell When Additional Care Is Needed

    C. Consulting with Your SEA Group or SEA Group Facilitator

III. Identify Possible Sources of Additional Care

    A. Types of Additional Care

    B. Identifying Sources of Additional Care

IV. Recommend Additional Care

    A. Bring Up the Subject

    B. Recommend One or More Specific Resources

    C. What to Do When a Group Member Refuses a Referral

V. Follow Up After Making a Referral

    A. Follow Up with the Person You Referred

    B. Lead Your ChristCare Group in Continuing to Care

VI. Maintain Confidentiality When Making Referrals for Additional Care

    A. Who Needs to Know?

    B. Follow Good Rules of Confidentiality

    C. In Extremely Sensitive Situations, Get Permission to Find Out about Additional Care

VII. Getting Ready for the In-Class Session

Supplement A: Signs That Can Indicate the Need for Additional Care

Supplement B: ChristCare Series Guide to Community Resources

I. Introduction

It's impossible for anyone to get through life without having to "pass through the waters," as phrased in the verse that begins this module. We all face challenges and problems in life.

ChristCare Groups can meet only *some* needs for care. Other needs are simply beyond a ChristCare Group's caring ability.

Focus Box 1 contains descriptions of five different situations that may require additional care. Read through each description in Focus Box 1 and ask yourself if this situation requires additional care. If it does, think about how you might help the person get the necessary care.

FOCUS BOX 1

Is Additional Care Needed Here?

Situation 1

Stan and Connie have been members of your ChristCare Group for two years. From the first, this couple shared openly their intense desire to have a child. Your group has supported them through a miscarriage and then through a successful pregnancy. A few months after their baby's birth, however, the baby was diagnosed with cystic fibrosis.

Situation 2

Sandra is a member of your ChristCare Group, which consists of single people in their thirties and forties. Sandra often seems to be sad, even depressed, when she arrives at ChristCare Group meetings. She is usually cheerier by the time the meetings are over.

Situation 3

Julia and Dave are in their fifties and have two college-age children and one teenager. They are concerned about their teen's behavior and are dismayed that he is so different from his older siblings, who were "model" kids. At last week's meeting, Julia shared that her aging father had been hospitalized in another city and now needed to be moved to a nursing home. In addition, Dave learned that his company was downsizing, and his job would be eliminated within the next six months.

Situation 4

Your ChristCare Group meets during lunch on Wednesdays. Charlie, one of the members, has a stressful job that requires long hours away from home. He has said several times in the past that his wife's support and understanding really help him withstand the stress from work. When your group met today, though, Charlie said that his wife announced over the weekend that she has fallen in love with one of her coworkers and wants a divorce.

Situation 5

Mary Jo confided in your ChristCare Group that her 26-year-old brother has AIDS. He has asked her for help in telling their parents.

You probably aren't sure what you would do in the above situations. This Preclass Reading and the upcoming in-class session will help you know exactly what to do in situations like these. You'll learn how to work with your SEA Group or SEA Group Facilitator to carry out the four steps in making a referral for additional care. These steps are shown in Focus Box 2.

FOCUS BOX 2

Four Steps in Making a Referral for Additional Care

1. Determine that a person needs additional care.
2. Identify possible sources of additional care.
3. Recommend that the person receive additional care.
4. Follow up to make sure the person is receiving the care he or she needs.

II. Determine That a Person Needs Additional Care

The first step in making a referral for additional care is to determine that the care is needed.

A. Why Additional Care Is Sometimes Needed

People don't need additional care for every challenge they face in life. Most people can cope with the bumps and bruises of daily life on their own or with the support of family, friends, and their ChristCare Group. So what makes a challenge severe enough to warrant additional care? It is usually a combination of the nature of the challenge and the person's ability to cope.

The Nature of the Challenge

Factors that make a challenge severe enough to require additional care include:

- intensity;
- duration;
- the consequences or results; and
- how many challenges the person is facing at one time.

Any of these factors, separately or together, may point to a need for more care than the ChristCare Group can give.

Intensity

Some challenges demand full attention and prevent the affected person from focusing on anything else. Examples of intense challenges are: death of a loved one, divorce, a life-threatening illness or accident, and being the victim of a crime. The more intense the challenge, the more likely it is to require additional care.

Duration

Short-lived challenges usually are easier to cope with than long-term ones. For example, a few days of aches and pains following strenuous exercise is much easier to cope with than years of pain from arthritis. Chronic conditions can require additional care because, over time, they wear down a person's energy and willpower.

Consequences

The same challenge can have different consequences for different people. If a person who becomes unemployed has been providing the family's sole financial support, the consequences are often much more severe than if a person's spouse is working. If a person is in a car accident but has no long-term injuries or financial consequences, he or she may cope more easily than one who is severely injured or has caused others severe injuries.

Accumulated or Simultaneous Challenges
Many people can handle one or two challenges at a time, but sometimes challenges pile up on people:

- A group member's spouse has a heart attack, the group member changes jobs, and then their child becomes seriously ill.

- A family relocates to a new city, an elderly relative moves in with them, and two of the four children begin having trouble in school.

- A single person in your group goes through a broken engagement, receives notice that his rent is going up dramatically, and has just been passed over for a promotion at work.

In the 1960s, Thomas H. Holmes and Richard H. Rahe developed a Social Readjustment Rating Scale[1] to reflect the difficulty one might have adjusting to life changes. They assigned each event a value to represent its relative difficulty as a life challenge. Rahe recently updated the scale to reflect changes in attitudes and values since the 1960s. This updated scale, found in Focus Box 3,[2] assigns a measurement called the Life Change Unit (LCU) to events that can cause stress.

Additional research determined that if enough changes listed in Focus Box 3 occur within one year, with values that add up to more than 450, a serious illness, accident, or emotional upset is significantly more likely to occur. A person experiencing many challenges at once is more likely to need additional care.

The Person's Capacity to Handle Challenges
Some people seem better equipped than others to handle life's challenges. We all vary in how well we handle challenges and how many challenges we can handle at once. Two important factors can influence a person's capacity to handle challenges: the person's *history and experiences* and the *amount of support* the person receives.

History and Experience
Some people have a naturally positive outlook on life. They see the good in bad situations. They're more hopeful. When a challenge hits, they don't crumble; they confidently muster their own personal forces to confront the problem. If the problems pile up, they bounce back; they seem to be more resilient than other folks.

FOCUS BOX 3

Dr. Rahe's Life Changes Stress Test

Life Event	LCU
Health	
An illness or injury that was: Very serious	74
Moderately severe	44
Less serious than above	20
Work	
Change to a new type of work	51
Change in your work conditions	35
Change in your work responsibilities	41
Taking courses to help you	18
Troubles at work	32
Major business readjustment	60
Loss of your job	74
Retirement	52
Home and Family	
Change in residence	40
Major change in living conditions	42
Change in family get-togethers	25
Major change in health or behavior of family member	55
Marriage	50
Pregnancy	67
Miscarriage or abortion	65
Birth (or adoption) of a child	66
Spouse begins or stops work	46
Change in arguments with spouse	50
Problems with relatives or in-laws	38
Parents divorce	59
A parent remarries	50
Separation from spouse due to work/marital difficulties	79
Child leaves home	42
Relative moves in with you	59
Divorce	96
Birth of a grandchild	43
Death of a spouse	119
Death of a child	123
Death of parent or sibling	101
Personal and Social	
Change in personal habits	26
Beginning or ending school	38
Change of school or college	35
Change in political beliefs	24
Change in religious beliefs	29
Change in social activities	27
Vacation	24
New, close, personal relationship	37
Engagement to marry	45
Personal relationship problems	39
Sexual difficulties	44
An accident	48
Minor violation of the law	20
Being held in jail	75
Major decision about your future	51
Major personal achievement	36
Death of a close friend	70
Financial	
Major loss of income	60
Major increase in income	38
Loss/damage to personal property	43
Major purchase	37
Minor purchase	20
Credit difficulties	56

If resiliency were a magic potion you could bottle up and sell, you'd be rich! But there is no magic formula. Most people who cope well with many challenges have learned to do so through their past experiences. For example:

- Some people have learned from past experiences to trust God to see them through difficult times.
- Some people have gone through enough challenges to know that they can overcome them. They've developed a certain toughness, a history of facing crises successfully. They have decided not to be afraid of challenges when they come.
- Some people have received additional care in the past and the caregiver has taught them specific coping skills.
- Some people had good role models as children. Parents, teachers, or friends helped them overcome challenges and develop habits for dealing with difficulties.

On the other hand, some people's life experiences have lessened their coping ability. For example:

- Some people don't believe God loves them enough to care for them during difficult times.
- Some people have faced especially difficult challenges that have left them emotionally scarred or injured.
- Some people have had unreliable or inadequate caregivers and have come to distrust the care others give in times of crisis.
- Some people have not had opportunities to learn from parents, teachers, friends, or other mentors methods for effectively facing challenges.
- Some people have had to face challenges before they reached a point of emotional or spiritual maturity that would have enabled them to cope well.

The Support Received from Others
Just about everyone can handle a certain amount of challenge. Everyone may also, however, reach the point where life's challenges mount and others' care and support become necessary. People's "support systems" vary widely.

Some people have a strong family as a support system. Others may have a loyal, loving group of friends who are always available to help. The church is a support system for some. ChristCare Groups can also serve this function. Fortunate people have several, or even all, of these support systems in place. Others may not have any of them. The stronger a person's personal support systems and the more groups he or she has to provide support, the more likely he or she is to be able to cope with challenges without needing additional care. Focus Box 4 illustrates how additional challenges demand additional capacity to cope.

FOCUS BOX 4

Mounting Challenges Require Better Coping Skills

1. People's internal capacity to face life's challenges often balances the amount of challenge.

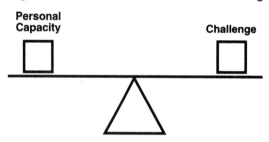

2. Life's challenges increase regularly, and people need additional help from their support systems (for example, family, friends, church, or ChristCare Group) to balance life's demands.

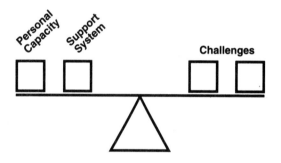

3. Occasionally people face challenges so great that their normal resources can't match the demands. At such times people need additional care in order to balance the weighty challenges they face.

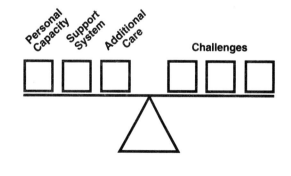

B. How to Tell When Additional Care Is Needed

There are several ways of determining that someone may need additional care. The person may talk with you privately, or with the whole ChristCare Group. One group member may tell you about another group member's extraordinary needs. You may notice that the person is taking up a lot of the group's time talking about his or her dissatisfaction with life.

When you notice that a person is going through a difficult time, look for indications that additional care might be needed. Some indications might be:

- major changes in the group member's behavior during ChristCare Group meetings;
- signs that the group member's present challenge is causing difficulties in other parts of his or her life;
- one or more signs listed in Supplement A, "Signs That Can Indicate the Need for Additional Care."

Signs That Can Indicate the Need for Additional Care

Supplement A on pages 117–120 contains lists of many different signs that could indicate a need for additional care. As you read through these signs, please remember two important facts:

- If a sign is on one of the lists, it doesn't always mean that additional care is needed. It is simply a sign that indicates that you as ChristCare Group Leader should be aware that additional care *might* be appropriate.
- The lists are not exhaustive. You may see other signs in group members that also indicate the possible need for additional care. If you see another behavior or characteristic in a group member that concerns you, follow up as you would in any situation that might need additional care.

Take time now to read through Supplement A. As you lead your ChristCare Group, occasionally refer to this list to remind yourself of signs to look for. Or use it to check when you believe that someone in your group might need additional care. It's one more way to add some objectivity to your judgment in an area that by nature is fairly subjective.

Major Changes in the Group Member's Behavior during ChristCare Group Meetings

When a group member is facing challenges that require additional care, you are likely to notice behavioral changes. These changes include:

- irregular attendance;
- a dramatic change in the group member's normal demeanor (quiet to talkative, friendly to withdrawn, cheerful to depressed);
- a tendency for the group member to monopolize the group's time by sharing at length about what's going on;
- talk about the challenge that suggests that the group member is becoming more overwhelmed, not coping with it;
- a sudden announcement that "everything's okay again," suggesting that the group member is glossing over a difficult challenge;
- inappropriate responses to the challenge, such as falling apart over something relatively minor or ignoring something serious;
- frequent outbursts of anger, crying, laughing, or other emotions that seem nearly out of control.

Signs That a Challenge Is Affecting How a Group Member Handles Other Aspects of Life

Sometimes dealing with a challenge is so all-consuming that it affects people's capacity to cope with other aspects of life. For instance, going through a divorce often affects a person's parenting ability or effectiveness at work. Experiencing a child's death might make it difficult to be productive at home or at the office. Retirement can turn long-anticipated free time into depressing, empty hours that never seem to end.

When you notice that a challenge is contaminating other parts of a person's life, it's an indication of the possible need for additional care. Watch for this "spill-over" effect when group members are facing difficult or accumulated challenges.

C. Consulting with Your SEA Group or SEA Group Facilitator

When you suspect that a group member needs additional care, let your SEA Group Facilitator know that you'd like to take some time in your next meeting to talk about this.

In the SEA Group meeting, explain the need as you understand it. Maintain confidentiality. With the other SEA Group members, decide if it is appropriate to recommend additional care. Question five in Focus Questions for SEA Groups Set F—Focus on ChristCare Group Members' Caring for One Another (session 15)—will help you discern the need for additional care.

Sometimes a situation or need is so urgent that you can't wait until the next SEA Group meeting to recommend care (for example, a group member's teenage son has run away from home and the group member is consumed with worry, or the utility service to a group member's home has been shut off). In emergencies like these, contact your SEA Group Facilitator right away and explain the situation, including why you can't wait until the next SEA Group meeting to talk about it. With the SEA Group Facilitator, decide if a referral for additional care is appropriate.

III. Identify Possible Sources of Additional Care

When you have determined that a group member needs a referral for additional care, you'll want to find some sources of care to suggest to that person. Different situations call for different types of care.

A. Types of Additional Care

On the next full page in this Preclass Reading, you'll find a chart titled "Types of Additional Care." This chart gives you a quick-reference summary of the types of care you'll want to know about for making referrals to group members. The rest of section III gives you additional information on the types of care shown on the chart.

Urgent Care

If the problem a group member is facing involves the possibility of abuse, homicide, or suicide, urgent care is *required*. Caregivers might include a physician, a psychiatrist, a social worker or other counselor, or the police.

This category of urgent care also includes acute physical needs, such as obtaining treatment for heart attack, seizure, unconsciousness, severe pain, or any other immediate and critical physical need.

Professional Care

Some needs aren't emergencies but still require a professional's help.

Mental health professionals include psychiatrists, psychologists, counselors, marriage and family therapists, and psychiatric social workers, among others. People often need the help of mental health professionals when they are deeply depressed, having a difficult time grieving the death of a loved one, or otherwise experiencing emotional difficulties that substantially diminish their quality of life.

Occasionally, someone in your ChristCare Group might benefit from the assistance of other professionals. These include medical specialists, physical therapists, educational or vocational counselors, attorneys, and financial counselors.

Special Needs Small Groups

Sometimes people benefit from being in a group with others who share similar needs. It helps to hear how others have dealt with the same challenge. Such groups focus just on meeting group members' particular needs, whereas ChristCare Groups include Biblical Equipping, prayer and worship, and missional service.

There are several kinds of special needs groups. Each fits people in particular circumstances.

- *Recovery groups* help people find healing for acute life crises, such as grief, divorce, abuse, or rape. Recovery groups help people move beyond the crisis. People eventually leave these groups.

- *Support groups* help people deal with long-term challenges, rather than short-term crises. Examples are support groups for single parents, children of aging parents, family members of people with Alzheimer's or other chronic degenerative diseases, or parents of murdered children.

- *Twelve-step groups* are for people trying to overcome addictions or the effects of others' addictions. They help people work on lifelong recovery. Examples are Alcoholics Anonymous, Al-Anon, CODA, and Gamblers Anonymous.

Other Congregational Care

Some challenges are primarily spiritual. These challenges include questions about life, death, and meaning that ultimately have to do with a person's relationship with God. ChristCare Groups certainly address such challenges, but when the challenges become critical, people need to look beyond their groups for additional care.

A pastor or other church staff member may be the best additional care resource if the problem involves any of the following issues:

- questions about doctrine, theology, or the beliefs espoused by your particular congregation or denomination;

- concern about the individual's relationship with God;

- desire for personal spiritual direction;

- questions about, or need for, the sacraments or rites of the church;

Types of Additional Care

Urgent Care	Professional Care	Special Needs Small Groups	Other Congregational Care
Definition: Care that is needed immediately for life-threatening or potentially life-threatening situations and that requires the attention of professionals in particular specialty areas. Necessary for: • threat of suicide • threat of homicide • threat of abuse • evidence of abuse • severe illness or injury **Resources include:** • Psychiatrist, psychologist, or other counselor • Medical doctor • Emergency medical providers • Police • State Division of Family Services: Child Abuse and Neglect • National Child Abuse Hot Line 800/422-4453 • Local hotlines • 911 • Sexual Assault Counselor Centers	**Definition:** Care for serious needs that greatly impair the person's ability to live a happy, productive life. Helpful when situations: • are a continuing, major drain on physical or emotional energy • don't improve, even with support from the group, the congregation, or other informal support systems • keep getting in the way of everyday functioning **Resources include:** Mental Health Professionals • Psychiatrists • Psychologists • Counselors • Social workers • Marriage and family therapists Other Professionals • Medical doctors and other healthcare workers • Vocational counselors • Educational counselors • Financial counselors • Attorneys and other legal experts	**Definition:** Care that involves the participation of other people who are facing the same types of problems and that may or may not involve specially trained professionals. Helpful when a problem fits one or more of the following criteria: • clearly defined • requires a lengthy recovery period • addiction-related • has a support or recovery program available **Resources include:** • The Compassionate Friends • Mothers Against Drunk Driving • Parents of Murdered Children • SIDS Alliance • The Widowed Persons Service • Other local support or recovery groups or people dealing with various difficult issues such as divorce, single parenting or AIDS	**Definition:** Often care of a spiritual nature, when people have questions about God, death, or meaning in their lives; may also involve some emotional care beyond the ability of a ChristCare Group. Helpful when: • people have emotional needs that don't warrant professional care but that are beyond the ChristCare Group's ability • people have urgent questions about the meaning of life • people need the resources of the church for events such as funerals or baptisms **Resources include:** • Pastor • Other congregation leaders • Other church staff members • Stephen Ministers • Food banks • Meal delivery services

- the need for guidance in significant life decisions, such as choosing a vocation, assessing one's own maturity for marriage, or even deciding whether or not to allow doctors to use extraordinary means to maintain a family member on life support;
- funeral planning;
- personal confession and forgiveness;
- church membership.

Stephen Ministry
If your congregation is enrolled in the Stephen Series system of lay caring ministry, you can use this valuable resource as a source for additional care. Trained Stephen Ministers provide one-to-one caring ministry in the following areas:

- Crisis care, including death of a loved one, hospitalization, or loss of employment;
- Follow-up care, including recovery from hospitalization, divorce, or loss of a loved one;
- Chronic care, including care for those in nursing homes, those who are home-bound, and those who are chronically ill;
- Preventive care, including preparing to deal with upcoming childbirth, retirement, or empty nest;
- Supportive care to the family members of people who are dealing with a major life challenge.

Other Congregational Sources of Care
Congregations sometimes have groups that meet particular needs and that might serve to provide additional care for ChristCare Group members. These may include:

- food banks;
- volunteers who provide transportation;
- volunteers who provide respite care for those caring for chronically ill or disabled family members;
- meal service to shut-ins or elderly people;
- discretionary funds for people who need financial help in difficult times.

B. Identifying Sources of Additional Care
There are several methods of identifying sources of additional care for group members.

Consult with Your SEA Group or SEA Group Facilitator
Ask your SEA Group or SEA Group Facilitator for ideas before you do any other research. Perhaps a member of your SEA Group has faced a similar challenge (individually or in his or her ChristCare Group) and can suggest a referral out of personal experience.

You could also ask your SEA Group or SEA Group Facilitator to comment on possible referral sources you have discovered. You may receive information that will either disqualify the source or help you explain it better to the person in need of care.

Ask Those Who Might Know
Check with other knowledgeable individuals available to your ChristCare Ministry through your congregation. For example, ask a pastor about recommendations for a pastoral counselor, a social worker about help with housing or food stamps, an accountant for suggestions about financial counseling, or a medical professional for possible ways to receive low-cost medical care. These individuals may be able to recommend particular specialists. Remember to protect the confidentiality of your group member in any conversation you have about referring this person for additional care.

The ChristCare Series Guide to Community Resources
Another tool you can use to identify sources of additional care is the "ChristCare Series Guide to Community Resources" in Supplement B on pages 121–136. Sometimes this tool will give you the exact information you need, and other times it will give you clues about how to find resources for additional care in your community.

Take some time right now to look over the "ChristCare Series Guide to Community Resources."

Checking the Sources of Additional Care
Be sure to check a resource before you refer someone to it. If your congregation keeps a list of community resources that others have evaluated and approved, you can probably recommend those resources with confidence. You *must not*, however, simply assume that a resource for additional care will provide the services it claims in an acceptable manner.

The Pre-Use Resource Assessment Questionnaire on pages 135–136 of Supplement B shows the information you need to get before you can safely recommend a caring resource. Once you have checked out a resource, pass on that information to your congregation's file of approved community resources.

IV. Recommend Additional Care

After you have consulted with your SEA Group or SEA Group Facilitator, have decided to recommend additional care to a group member, and have checked resources for care, you are ready to talk with the person who needs additional care.

A. Bring Up the Subject

Follow the steps below for mentioning the need for additional care.

Pray

Before you meet with the group member, pray. Ask God to help you speak sensitively and wisely, and to prepare the group member to receive and act on the information you plan to share.

Arrange to Meet Privately with the Person

Choose a place where you and the person needing additional care can speak freely without being overheard or interrupted. Choose a time when neither of you will feel rushed.

Use an I-Statement to Explain What You'd Like to Say

Here are some examples:

- "When I see you struggling so hard to overcome the loss of your spouse, I get concerned about how you're doing. I'd like you to consider talking with someone who can help you work through what has happened."

- "You've mentioned that you've been having a lot of trouble with money since the time when you were unemployed. I've been thinking it might help to work with a financial counselor to see how you can get more control over your finances."

- "During the past few months, I've noticed that you've been hit by several tough challenges. It would be hard for anybody to handle all that. I'd like to talk with you about getting some support that I think could really help."

Be Assertive

By the time you recommend additional care to the group member, you have given the matter much careful thought and prayer, and you have consulted with others to arrive at the best recommendation. It is likely that the group member needs and would benefit from additional care. By assertively recommending care, you are doing the most caring thing.

Being assertive means respecting the person's needs. It also means taking into account both your needs and those of the group. If the person doesn't receive additional care, it may hurt the group by taking away time from others who also need the group's attention. It may also hurt you as group leader if you are expected to take time away from your other responsibilities to meet the person's needs.

Don't aggressively demand that the person seek additional care. Being assertive means recognizing and respecting the other person's right to say yes—or no—to your offer. On the other hand, don't passively avoid sharing your concerns with a person who needs additional care.

Listen to What the Group Member Has to Say about Your Recommendation

The person may agree with what you say and be eager to hear more. Or the person may immediately begin mounting defenses, objecting that "you have it all wrong—I'm doing fine."

If the person agrees with you, that's great. If not, listen to what he or she has to say. The person is more likely to accept your suggestions if he or she believes you have really listened. Also, by listening well you can understand better why the person is unwilling to accept the referral. Then you can deal with those concerns.

Answer Any Questions or Reservations

Address any reservations the group member has expressed about your referral for additional care. You might say, "It seems to me that the idea of receiving financial aid bothers you. But I think that if your neighbor lost a job and needed some help to get back on his feet, you'd feel fine about his receiving aid." Or "I heard you say that it's hard to believe this has happened. Most people feel that way after a loved one dies suddenly. I think it would be encouraging for you to meet other people who have experienced that stage of grief and who could confirm that all these feelings you're having are normal."

B. Recommend One or More Specific Resources

When a group member agrees with your suggestion for additional care, be prepared to share specific care resources. Include the following steps.

Share the Specific Additional Care Resources You've Learned About

Tell the person the names and details of resources you have identified. Say why you believe the resource would work well for him or her. Add any extra information you know, such as, "Several people I know have met with this person and have had good things to say" or "Someone told me that this person really helped, even in just the first meeting" or "I have a friend who was really encouraged by this support group."

Ask For a Commitment to Act

Assertively ask the person to take some specific action on your recommendation. Here are some things you might say:

- "Which of these resources do you think you would like to start with?"
- "Do any of these resources sound better than the others? Would you like me to be there when you call?"
- "When do you think you'd be ready to make a decision about this?"
- "When do you think you'd like to contact this resource?"
- "What questions about this resource could we ask to find out if it's the best one for you?"

In asking for a commitment to act, you might be tempted to call the resource yourself, just to make sure it happens. It's fine to be there when the person makes the call. It's much better, though, for the person to make the call himself or herself because:

- The person is much more likely to follow through in keeping appointments and continuing to use the resource.
- Your relationship with the person will be on a more equal footing: responsible adult to responsible adult.
- The person is accepting responsibility for dealing with his or her own problem.

Even if the person asks you to make the call, do that only as a last resort. Instead, offer to be there in the room when the person makes the call, to help him or her plan what needs to be said during the phone call, or even to go along on the first visit. Assure the person that he or she will benefit most in the end by accepting responsibility from the beginning.

If Necessary, Restate Your Reasons for Recommending Referral

If the person seems hesitant to act on your recommendation, repeat your reasons for suggesting additional care.

Promise to Provide Support and Encouragement

Let the person know that you will continue to care. Promise your support in helpful ways, including phone calls and prayer. Also assure the person that he or she is, and will continue to be, an important part of the ChristCare Group.

Pray with the Person

In your prayer, ask God to assure the person of God's love and presence in his or her life.

C. What to Do When a Group Member Refuses a Referral

There are several reasons a person might refuse a referral for additional care. You need to find out why the person is refusing the referral and then respond to his or her reason. Following are some possible reasons and responses.

The Person Doesn't Understand What It's Like to Receive Additional Care

Some people don't understand and consequently fear professional care, leading them to reject the idea. In such cases, listen to the person and provide an opportunity for him or her to express his or her feelings. Once you have listened, you can address the person's concerns. Here are some examples:

- Explain clearly and thoroughly what would happen if the person were to receive additional care. Clear up any misunderstandings.
- Compare receiving additional care to something the group member understands. For example, compare seeing a counselor for ongoing emotional turmoil to seeing a medical doctor for ongoing stomach pain.
- Tell of your personal experience, if any, in using this resource.
- Share other people's examples of using the resource, being careful to protect confidentiality. Ask permission first if you use names.
- Remind the person that it's natural for people to resist trying something new, but it can be important to overcome that resistance to receive needed care.

- Encourage the person to write down any questions or concerns about the resource, then discuss these concerns during the first visit.

Fear of Consequences in the ChristCare Group

The person who needs additional care might be concerned about what receiving this care will mean to his or her ChristCare Group participation. The person might be thinking, "What if group members think I should be able to handle my own problems?" or "Maybe they won't want me to participate if they find out I'm getting support someplace else" or "What if they find out what's going on?"

If you sense that the person has these kinds of fears, pay attention to them. Listen carefully to what the person has to say. Your attentive listening is the first step toward reassuring the person that his or her position in the ChristCare Group will not be jeopardized by receiving additional care. After taking plenty of time to listen, you might also say:

- "There's no reason for others to find out you are receiving additional care, unless you tell them."

If, for some reason, the group does know about the additional care, you might say:

- "Everyone faces challenges at some point in life. Chances are that other group members have had to face difficult times and may have even received additional care to get through them. Receiving care is not an indication of weakness, but an indication of self-awareness and a willingness to take care of yourself."
- "Any group member who needs additional care is welcome, and wholeheartedly invited, to continue participating in the ChristCare Group. Certainly the group won't be able to do as much as the other caring resource, but we want to continue caring for you as well as we can."
- "By getting additional care when you need it, you are helping other group members learn to do the same if they are ever in similar circumstances."

Fear of Others' Finding Out

If the group member is concerned about confidentiality, remind him or her of these important facts:

- The group member makes the absolute decision whether to speak about this issue during ChristCare Group meetings. No one else will bring it up.
- You will protect confidentiality in SEA Groups.

- Other group members have agreed to keep all information shared in ChristCare Group meetings confidential. You will frequently remind them of this promise.
- Professionals who are involved in providing additional care (for example, physicians, counselors, and social workers) are legally and professionally bound to protect their clients' confidentiality.

Denial

Sometimes group members will refuse a referral because they can't or won't admit they need additional care. Denying problems doesn't make them go away. Keep looking for opportunities to bring up the need for additional care, keep praying, and maintain a good relationship with the person so that once he or she is willing to receive care, you can help him or her find it.

Inability to Pay

If you discover that the person is concerned about the cost of the additional care, you can help in several ways. For instance, you can help the person find helpful services that charge according to a sliding scale. You can also encourage the person to learn about insurance benefits that might help cover the cost. In addition, you can help the person think of other sources for the needed money, such as a loan from a relative or help from a congregational fund.

Belief That the ChristCare Group Should Meet the Need

A group member may ask you, "Why should I get additional care someplace else? Why can't I get it in the ChristCare Group?" In such a case, explain what ChristCare Groups are all about—what they do and don't do. Reaffirm that ChristCare Groups can certainly offer care and support, but that they do not provide the kinds of specialized services that professional caregivers can offer.

Pride

Sometimes a person refuses additional care because he or she believes that people should be able to solve their own problems and that it is a sign of weakness to receive care from others. In such cases it is, again, important to listen while the person tells you what he or she believes. It may also be helpful to share about times when you have received care.

This can show that it is all right to receive care. You might also point out that Jesus himself was not above receiving care from others, such as when he allowed the woman to anoint his head with expensive ointment (Mark 14:3–9).

If the Person Still Refuses

There may be times when, after listening to your explanations, a group member still refuses a referral. This refusal may require you to ask the person to leave the group if the behavior that led to your recommendation disrupts or harms the group. Such occurrences are rare, and almost all group members can continue to participate in the group while receiving additional care.

V. Follow Up After Making a Referral

After making a referral, there are two ways you as ChristCare Group Leader need to follow up:
- with the person you referred;
- with your ChristCare Group.

A. Follow Up with the Person You Referred

After you recommend additional care to a person, follow up in these ways:

- Check in (privately) to find out if the person has followed through on actions he or she decided to take, including thinking about additional care, calling about additional care, or keeping appointments for additional care.

- Continue to pray for the person, asking from time to time if he or she has specific needs for your prayers.

- Stay in touch between group meetings to offer your support.

- Ask (privately) about the quality and effectiveness of care the person is receiving. Sometimes the first resource a person contacts for care doesn't work out well. Let the person know that it's fine to look around a bit to find a more satisfactory resource. Offer to help the person search.

- Continue to uphold confidentiality.

B. Lead Your ChristCare Group in Continuing to Care

Your ChristCare Group may or may not know that you have recommended additional care to the person. It's up to the person to decide whether to let group members know. Even if group members don't know about the additional care, they may well know about the challenges in the person's life

through discussions and sharing during your group meetings.

As you continue leading your group, encourage the group members to care for the person receiving additional care if they know about his or her needs. Feel free to give the person a bit more than his or her share of time to talk about what's going on. At the same time, avoid letting the person monopolize the group's time and caring energy. Focus Box 5 gives you some ideas for accomplishing this.

FOCUS BOX 5

How to Keep a Person Who Needs Additional Care from Monopolizing the ChristCare Group's Time and Caring Energy

Say privately to the person:

- "If you need some extra time to talk about what's going on, why don't we get together or talk on the phone once in a while?"

- "Thanks for keeping us up-to-date on what's going on. I appreciate the way you said what you needed to say fairly quickly so others could share too."

- "Sometimes in our group meetings I might ask you to give us a quick update on what's going on, if you're comfortable doing that. I don't mean to rush you, but I'll use the word *quick* just to help both of us remember that everyone in the group needs time to share."

Say in the ChristCare Group meeting:

- "In order for us to hear from everyone, I'd like to ask all of you to try to keep your sharing/prayer requests to three to five minutes" (depending on the size of the group).

- "I get the feeling that several of you have some important things to share about and ask prayer for. How many need a little extra time? I want to make sure that all of us with urgent needs get adequate care from our group."

The preceding Focus Box gives you some assertive yet sensitive ways to keep a person from monopolizing the group's time and caring energy. If you try these approaches and still find that one group member is continuing to monopolize the time, you might have to be even more assertive. Talk to the person privately and say something like: "I know you're really struggling right now. I can give you extra time outside the meetings to talk about what's going on, or perhaps we can look at the possibility of your receiving some additional care. But we can't take that extra time during the group meetings. As hard as it may be, I need to ask you to limit your sharing time during the meetings so that our group can meet everyone's needs."

Don't think you are the only group member who can provide extra care outside group meetings. While several of the preceding examples featured you as the one who talks with the group member outside group meetings, another group member might be a better choice.

You might ask another group member who has caring gifts to check in regularly with the group member who needs more time to talk. Occasionally talk with that caring group member to see how things are going.

VI. Maintain Confidentiality When Making Referrals for Additional Care

When you make a referral for additional care, you are often dealing with sensitive, private knowledge about another person. Because of that, you need to make sure that you protect confidentiality.

There are some special challenges in maintaining confidentiality when making referrals. For instance, people who need additional care may be reluctant to receive it because they are afraid someone else might find out. Members of your ChristCare Group may know about the person's special need, but may or may not know about the additional care the person is receiving. As always, you'll need to protect confidentiality when you work with your SEA Group and SEA Group Facilitator.

You should not have problems with confidentiality when you understand these special challenges and abide by the rules of confidentiality that you already know.

A. Who Needs to Know?

The first question to ask in preserving confidentiality is: Who needs to know? No one else needs to know *who* is receiving care. You can consult with your SEA Group or your SEA Group Facilitator without revealing the person's name or identifying details. Your ChristCare Group never needs to know that a fellow group member is receiving additional care unless the person chooses to make the fact known. When you identify and check out

additional resources, you can and should do so without revealing the person's name.

B. Follow Good Rules of Confidentiality

When you make a referral for additional care, use your common sense and follow these basic rules of confidentiality:

- Never use the person's name.
- Never reveal unnecessary details about the person. Just say enough to get the help you need to make the referral.
- Trust your SEA Group and your SEA Group Facilitator to maintain confidentiality if they figure out the person's identity.
- When someone is in danger (in cases that involve the threat of suicide, homicide, abuse, or a medical emergency), your first responsibility is getting the person immediate, necessary care. People's lives and safety are more important than confidentiality.

C. In Extremely Sensitive Situations, Get Permission to Find Out about Additional Care

Some referral situations, such as bankruptcy or a diagnosis of AIDS, are extremely sensitive and could cause the person to suffer considerable damage if anyone even suspected what was going on. If that is the case, and if it doesn't involve the threat of suicide, homicide, abuse, or a medical emergency, take these extra steps to preserve confidentiality:

- Ask the person who needs care for permission to find referral resources.

  In such a situation, you will probably already be sure that the person needs additional care, even without the input of your SEA Group. After discussing the need with the person and recommending care, ask permission to check into appropriate resources, assuring the person that you won't use his or her name.

- Consult only with your SEA Group Facilitator or pastor.

  In extremely sensitive situations, inform only your SEA Group Facilitator or pastor about what's going on, still being careful to protect the person's confidentiality. Don't consult with your entire SEA Group.

VII. Getting Ready for the In-Class Session

Now that you've learned more about when and how to refer a group member for additional care, take another look at the situations from the beginning of this Preclass Reading, now shown below in Focus Box 6. This time, each situation is followed by three questions for you to answer. Take some time now to write your answers to those questions for each situation. You'll be referring to these answers during the in-class session, so be thorough.

FOCUS BOX 6

Is Additional Care Needed Here?

Situation 1
Stan and Connie have been members of your ChristCare Group for two years. From the first, this couple shared openly their intense desire to have a child. Your group has supported them through a miscarriage and then through a successful pregnancy. A few months after their baby's birth, however, the baby was diagnosed with cystic fibrosis.

Do you think this situation might warrant a referral for additional care?   ❑ Yes   ❑ No
Why or why not?

If "yes," what steps would you take?

Situation 2
Sandra is a member of your ChristCare Group, which consists of single people in their thirties and forties. Sandra often seems to be sad, even depressed, when she arrives at ChristCare Group meetings. She is usually cheerier by the time the meetings are over.

Do you think this situation might warrant a referral for additional care?   ❑ Yes   ❑ No
Why or why not?

If "yes," what steps would you take?

Situation 3
Julia and Dave are in their fifties and have two college-age children and one teenager. They are concerned about their teen's behavior and are dismayed that he is so different from his older siblings, who were "model" kids. At last week's meeting, Julia shared that her aging father had been hospitalized in another city and now needed to be moved to a nursing home. In addition, Dave learned that his company was downsizing, and his job would be eliminated within the next six months.

Do you think this situation might warrant a referral for additional care?   ❑ Yes   ❑ No
Why or why not?

If "yes," what steps would you take?

Situation 4
Your ChristCare Group meets during lunch on Wednesdays. Charlie, one of the members, has a stressful job that requires long hours away from home. He has said several times in the past that his wife's support and understanding really help him withstand the stress from work. When your group met today, though, Charlie said that his wife announced over the weekend that she has fallen in love with one of her coworkers and wants a divorce.

Do you think this situation might warrant a referral for additional care?   ❑ Yes   ❑ No
Why or why not?

If "yes," what steps would you take?

Situation 5
Mary Jo confided in your ChristCare Group that her 26-year-old brother has AIDS. He has asked her for help in telling their parents.

Do you think this situation might warrant a referral for additional care?   ❑ Yes   ❑ No
Why or why not?

If "yes," what steps would you take?

You'll get some practice in researching community resources before your next class. Your Equipper may assign you a particular resource or let you pick one that interests you. As you discover information about the resource, complete the "Pre-Use Resource Assessment Questionnaire" that your Equipper gave you along with your research assignment. This form is the same as the questionnaire on pages 135–136 of the "ChristCare Series Guide to Community Resources" (Supplement B). Be sure to bring the completed form to your next class.

ENDNOTES

1. Thomas H. Holmes and Richard H. Rahe, "The Social Readjustment Rating Scale," *Journal of Psychosomatic Research* 11 (1967), 213–218.

2. Richard H. Rahe, M.D., "Life Changes Stress Test." This copyrighted test is allowed for use solely by Stephen Ministries by Richard H. Rahe, M.D., President of Health Assessment Programs, Inc., 5209 Boulevard Ext Rd., S.E., Olympia, WA 98501.

Two Helpful Resources from Stephen Ministries

Journeying through Grief
by Kenneth C. Haugk

This is a set of four short books to give to grieving people at four crucial times during the difficult first year after a loved one has died. Each book focuses on what the person is likely to be experiencing at that point in grief and provides care, support, assurance, and hope. These books are an excellent resource for ChristCare Groups that may have a group member—or friend of a member—who is grieving or for groups interested in learning more about the grief process.

To learn more, to read excerpts, or to order a set, log on to www.grief-books.org or call Stephen Ministries at (314) 428-2600.

Don't Sing Songs to a Heavy Heart: How to Relate to Those Who Are Suffering
by Kenneth C. Haugk

Don't Sing Songs to a Heavy Heart blends personal experience, extensive research, and sound psychology, all founded on biblical truths, to provide specific suggestions and practical examples about what to say or do—and what *not* to say or do—as you relate to hurting people. This book will touch your heart, expand your thinking, and guide you in bringing Christ's loving care to hurting people when they need it most. It's a great resource for ChristCare Group Leaders and group members who want to know how to better care for or relate to suffering people.

To learn more, read excerpts, or order a copy, log on to www.stephenministries.org/heavyheart or call Stephen Ministries at (314) 428-2600.

Supplement A: *Signs That Can Indicate the Need for Additional Care*

This supplement includes lists of behaviors, symptoms, and other signs that might indicate a need for additional care. The signs are divided into the following seven categories:

I. **Signs That Can Indicate the Need for Medical or Physical Care**

II. **Signs That Can Indicate the Need for Legal, Criminal Justice, Financial, or Housing Assistance**

III. **Signs That Can Indicate the Need for Educational or Vocational Assistance**

IV. **Signs That Can Indicate the Need for Family, Marital, or Interpersonal Counseling**

V. **Signs That Can Indicate That Emotional or Mental Health Assistance Is Needed**

VI. **Signs That Can Indicate the Need for Assistance with Addictive Behaviors**

VII. **Signs That Can Indicate the Need for Religious or Spiritual Assistance**

As a ChristCare Group Leader, you can use these lists to help you determine if a person needs additional care beyond what the ChristCare Group can provide. Remember that if a sign the person is showing *is* on one of the lists, it's not necessarily a positive indication that additional care is needed; it's a sign that additional care *might* be appropriate. Also, remember that these lists are not exhaustive. A person might show that he or she needs additional care in a way that's not listed here. If that occurs, follow up as you would in any situation that might need additional care.

I. Signs That Can Indicate the Need for Medical or Physical Care

Be alert for the possible need for medical or physical care if the group member:

- is on medication and seems confused or disoriented;
- talks about a sudden change in the senses of sight, hearing, touch, or smell;

- complains of a physical ailment that is one of cancer's warning signals (such as a lump, a swelling, or an unexplained soreness) and has not sought medical help;
- complains of dizziness, disorientation, passing out, fainting, poor balance, or falling as a result of one of these symptoms;
- has physical problems that are chronic or serious enough to warrant a home health care service;
- is ill or incapacitated to the point that 24-hour nursing care is necessary;
- is not interested in eating;
- loses or gains weight suddenly;
- has acute or chronic physical complaints that haven't been brought to the attention of a physician;
- needs but doesn't have adequate medical equipment or supplies for the treatment of a physical ailment;
- appears malnourished or emaciated;
- requires ongoing therapy for chronic physical problems that have resulted from earlier or recent events such as an illness, stroke, accident, or surgery;
- qualifies for food stamps but doesn't use them;
- needs transportation to and from a clinic or hospital for therapy or medical treatment;
- is living in conditions that are unsanitary, unhealthy, or hazardous;
- is experiencing a problem pregnancy.

II. Signs That Can Indicate the Need for Legal, Criminal Justice, Financial, or Housing Assistance

Be alert for the possible need for legal, criminal justice, financial, or housing assistance if the group member:

- has a family member who is in jail or prison or sees this as a realistic possibility;
- has a child who is on probation through juvenile court;
- is in jail or prison himself or herself, or sees this as a realistic possibility;
- is separated or divorced from his or her spouse and is being harassed by that spouse or ex-spouse;

- has decided to divorce his or her spouse but is unsure of the legal procedure;
- has been the victim of rape or another violent crime;
- is being sued;
- is being evicted;
- has experienced a burglary;
- is having difficulty collecting money from an insurance company;
- qualifies for particular benefits but is not receiving them;
- has serious credit problems;
- wants to make a will;
- needs help filing a tax return;
- is an illegal alien or is housing illegal aliens;
- wants to become a naturalized citizen;
- needs to secure a loan and doesn't know how to go about it;
- has a valid complaint about a product or service he or she has purchased but has not been able to get a satisfactory response about it;
- has been threatened with physical violence;
- has bruises, scars, or other characteristics that might indicate abuse;
- has family members, such as children or a spouse, who have bruises, scars, or other characteristics that might indicate abuse;
- has family members who have been threatened with physical violence;
- has threatened you or others with physical violence;
- has experienced discrimination in obtaining housing or other accommodations, products, or services;
- is unable to pay utility bills;
- is being discriminated against by an employer because of race, sex, age, religion, or some other criterion;
- is not receiving rightfully due unemployment compensation.

III. Signs That Can Indicate the Need for Educational or Vocational Assistance

Be alert for the possible need for educational or vocational assistance if the group member:

- needs job counseling, aptitude testing, or vocational placement;

- is disabled and needs vocational evaluation, training, or counseling;
- expresses concern about threats to his or her health or safety in the work environment;
- wants to obtain a GED or other certificate or diploma to become educationally qualified for a job or for personal growth and satisfaction;
- has a grievance against his or her employer or union;
- has a child who requires special educational services;
- believes that his or her child is not receiving good educational services or is being treated unfairly in school;
- is unemployed.

IV. Signs That Can Indicate the Need for Family, Marital, or Interpersonal Counseling

Be alert for the possible need for family, marital, or interpersonal counseling when you notice that the group member:

- is a minor (or the parent of a minor) who expresses the desire to run away from home (or who has run away from home);
- has a child who is hyperkinetic (hyperactive) or exceptionally intelligent, or has other characteristics or behaviors that merit special support or services;
- has a child who is experiencing difficulties that result from divorce;
- has serious marital problems;
- is experiencing serious conflict with in-laws, especially if they are living with the group member and his or her spouse;
- has a child who is not developing along typical physical, mental, or emotional lines;
- expresses a desire to adopt a child but doesn't know how to go about doing so;
- has an unplanned, unwanted pregnancy;
- has serious problems relating to his or her children;
- has recently experienced the birth of a handicapped or disabled child;
- has difficulty admitting a family member's serious problems;
- has difficulty dealing with a family member's serious problems;

- has bruises, scars, or other characteristics that might indicate abuse;
- has family members, such as children or a spouse, who have bruises, scars, or other characteristics that might indicate abuse;
- has serious difficulties relating well to his or her spouse, other family members, coworkers, friends, or others;
- talks about threats made by other family members;
- makes threats to others.

V. Signs That Can Indicate That Emotional or Mental Health Assistance Is Needed

Be alert for the possible need for emotional or mental health assistance if the group member:

- has difficulty responding appropriately in daily interactions, as evidenced by how he or she thinks, responds emotionally, remembers, communicates, interprets reality, and behaves, to the point that it interferes with daily functioning;
- acts as you would expect a young child to act, with inappropriate feelings, lack of self-discipline, lack of impulse control, and excessive daydreaming and fantasizing;
- seems severely depressed;
- seems sad all the time, unable to "bounce back" from a difficult event or circumstance;
- has ongoing sleep disturbances;
- doesn't care about the cleanliness or attractiveness of his or her home or personal appearance;
- gives any sign of suicide;
- is having severe and long-term trouble recovering from the death of a child or other family member or loved one;
- isolates himself or herself from others, including family, friends, coworkers, neighbors, and other usual associates;
- is going through a divorce that is complicated by disagreement in areas such as property settlement or child custody;
- is often or usually late to or absent from school, work, your ChristCare Group, and other normal activities;
- has difficulty making simple decisions about everyday events and occurrences;
- loses track of time or does things at inappropriate times, such as making phone calls in the middle of the night;

- experiences a sudden, severe change in personality or demeanor;
- has hallucinations, including hearing voices that are threatening or intimidating;
- behaves in erratic, bizarre, or dangerous ways;
- has irrational and immobilizing fears;
- experiences memory loss that is not typical for his or her age;
- is cruel to animals;
- expresses anger and hostility inappropriately and in exaggerated ways;
- overreacts to typical, everyday experiences and stresses;
- seems obsessed with homosexual feelings;
- tells you that he or she is a victim of past incest, rape, sexual assault, or molestation;
- tells you that he or she is experiencing sexual dysfunction such as impotence, frigidity, or voyeurism;
- shows inappropriate emotions such as laughing when he or she is obviously sad or angry, or weeping at something that's humorous or enjoyable.

VI. Signs That Can Indicate the Need for Assistance with Addictive Behaviors

Be alert for the possible need for assistance with addictive behaviors (such as alcoholism, chemical dependency, gambling, drug abuse) if the group member:

- is concerned about becoming dependent on prescribed medication;
- is sometimes or often absent from school or work because of substance abuse;
- has alcohol on his or her breath at various times of day;
- seems "drugged out," "spaced out," or out of touch with what is going on around him or her;
- has inappropriate or exaggerated mood elevations;
- has been charged with driving while intoxicated;
- uses excessive amounts of cologne or perfume or mouthwash to cover the odor of alcohol;
- has slurred speech, glazed eyes, or slow physical reactions;
- talks about financial, family, or other problems that you suspect are related to substance abuse;

- shows tendencies toward compulsive gambling;
- makes excessive efforts to disguise/explain evidences of addiction.

VII. Signs That Can Indicate the Need for Religious or Spiritual Assistance

Be alert for the possible need for religious or spiritual assistance if the group member:

- seems seriously disturbed about the prospect of a family member's marrying someone of another faith or religion;
- is struggling with guilt;
- expresses deep inner conflicts or doubts about his or her faith in God;
- is faced with a difficult and complex decision involving moral, ethical, and religious issues;
- wants to change his or her status of membership in the congregation; for instance, he or she wants to become a communicant member;
- moves from inactive status to a more active role in church life, transfers to another church, or is removed from the church roll;
- asks specifically to see an ordained minister or one of the church staff;
- expresses the desire to participate in one of the sacraments or rites of the church requiring the ministry of ordained clergy.

Supplement B: *ChristCare Series Guide to Community Resources*

This ChristCare Series Guide to Community Resources is intended to assist ChristCare Group Leaders and Equippers in providing resources for group members who need additional care. Each item listed is followed by a brief description. The services described are available through resources found in most communities.

The Guide has four sections. **Section I** lists many of the services available through various governmental offices. Services are listed under the type of government that administers the program: federal, state, or city/county. For example, the Social Security program is administered by the federal government, employment service by state governments, and public health services by city or county governments. It is important to note that some programs usually thought of as federal programs are often administered by state or local governments. A good example of this is the Department of Public Assistance, a *county*-run program that administers such services as food stamps and aid to families with dependent children. Therefore, a particular program may be found in an unexpected section.

Section II is an alphabetic listing of "Life Issue Concerns" that ChristCare Group members might experience. An alphabetic list of resources appears under each concern. Cross references to governmental resources offering assistance with a particular life concern are also provided. The resources in this section often appear in the Yellow Pages under the heading of that life concern. Other possible locations are listed when appropriate.

Section III describes methods for locating resources not found in the Guide. It also provides procedures for finding out more information about the listed resources.

Section IV is a "Pre-Use Resource Assessment Questionnaire." This questionnaire is designed to provide a ChristCare Group Leader with information about a particular resource.

We hope you find this guide helpful. Community resources are continually changing, and we welcome any information about additional resources that may exist in most communities. You may send those to:

Stephen Ministries
ChristCare Program Staff
2045 Innerbelt Business Center Drive
St. Louis, MO 63114-5765

I. Government Resources

A. Federal Government

(listed in the blue pages under "United States Government")

1. Department of Housing and Urban Development (HUD)

administers a program of low-cost and/or subsidized housing for people with low incomes; has programs to assist people with low incomes in buying housing; provides help in bringing about healthy environments for urban communities through grants, direct loans, mortgage insurance, technical assistance, or advisory assistance

2. Equal Employment Opportunity Commission (EEOC)

investigates complaints about discrimination in employment because of race, color, religion, sex, age, or national origin; enforces the Equal Pay Act; seeks remedies through conciliation or through federal courts

3. The Federal Information Center

answers questions about federal, state, and local government programs; provides referrals

4. Immigration and Naturalization Service

applies laws and regulations relating to aliens, including entry, reentry, residence, and rights within the United States; administers laws dealing with naturalization

5. National Labor Relations Board

protects individuals' rights to collective bargaining or nonsupport of union activities

6. Social Security Administration

issues Social Security account number cards; takes claims for payment for old-age benefits, disability benefits, survivor benefits, and Medicare health insurance benefits; helps people determine and prove their eligibility for these programs (those eligible include wage earners and self-employed people, as well as their dependents and survivors); people 65 or older, blind, or disabled and eligible may receive payments based on financial need under the federal Supplemental Income program

7. Veterans Administration

administers programs and laws pertaining to veterans of the U.S. Armed Services and their dependents; available programs range from medical care to home-buying assistance

B. State Government

(listed in the blue pages of the phone directory under the name of the state; for instance: "Missouri, State of")

1. Department of Public Assistance (listed under Family Services, Social Services, or Welfare)

usually has offices in each county; administers Aid to Families with Dependent Children (AFDC), General Relief, Aid to the Blind, nursing homes, Medicaid, and other assistance programs; accepts applications for food stamps; benefits and eligibility vary from state to state based on federal guidelines

2. Division of Mental Health

(may be found under "Dept. of Mental Health")

administers programs dealing with mental health, mental retardation, and developmental disabilities; administers state-owned mental health facilities and state-operated residences for the mentally retarded and developmentally disabled; contracts with community agencies to supply support services for those living in their own homes and to provide placement in residential and group homes

3. Employment Services

(affiliated with the U.S. Dept. of Labor)

offers free employment services for potential employees and employers; provides information about the local job market, job counseling, aptitude testing, vocational testing, youth employment services, state unemployment insurance programs, information about employment trends, and in some instances, referral to vocational training; administers the Work Incentive Program (WIN) for Aid to Families with Dependent Children (AFDC) recipients

4. Food Stamps

supplements low-income families' budgets; eligibility is determined by the family's total income and assets relative to its size; application can be made through the Department of Public Assistance

5. Vocational Rehabilitation Service

administers programs for people whose physical, mental, or emotional disabilities interfere with obtaining, continuing, or reaching their employment potential; provides medical examinations, vocational guidance, vocational and on-the-job training, college education, individual counseling, and evaluation of a person's work potential; program covers surgery, hospitalization, prostheses, and other related expenses that the client cannot afford

6. Public Service Commission

provides assistance with problems related to utility (for example, gas and electricity) services

C. City/County Government

(listed in the blue pages of the phone book under the name of city or county)

1. Building Division

(may be found under "Dept. of Public Works" or "Building")

administers laws pertaining to building safety and enforces building codes; acts as a resource for concerns about safe living conditions

2. Jobs Training Partnership Act (JTPA)

provides vocational testing, job opportunities, counseling, classroom instruction, and training for low-income and disadvantaged city residents 16 and older; to locate this program, call the Office of Employment and Training (part of the Department of Human Resources) or its equivalent (department may have a different title in some regions)

3. Public Health Service

a. Public Health Nurses

provide referrals, instruction, and advice, and do home assessments; public health nursing may be available only through agencies or in some areas where public health nurses act independently; to obtain their services, contact the local health department

b. Child Mental Health

provides analysis and treatment for children with emotional problems

c. Clinics

larger metropolitan areas often have medical and dental clinics for low-income families; cost depends on family size and income; service provided varies among cities

d. Hospitals

may provide free or low-cost hospital care for people with low incomes

e. Sanitation Control (may be listed under "Health Division," "General Sanitation," or "Environmental Health Services")

enforces sanitation laws and works to change them in order to correct health hazards and promote a safe, sanitary environment

f. Venereal Disease Clinics

city- or county-operated clinics may provide free confidential consultation and treatment for people who have venereal disease; minors are usually able to obtain treatment without parental knowledge or permission

II. Life Issue Concerns

A. AIDS

1. National AIDS Information Clearinghouse

800/458-5231

offers referrals, information about publications, and other resources (including clinical trials, research studies, and experimental drugs) regarding AIDS and HIV

2. National HIV and AIDS Information Service Hotline

800/342-AIDS

800/AIDS-TTY (hearing impaired)

800/344-SIDA (Spanish)

offers basic information about HIV and AIDS, supplies referrals to medical treatment, testing sites, court groups, and counseling

B. Alcoholism

1. Alcoholics Anonymous (AA)

provides support for people working to overcome alcoholism

2. Al-Anon Family Groups

a fellowship of relatives and friends of alcoholics who share experiences, strength, and hope in order to solve their common problems; Al-Anon believes alcoholism is a family illness and that changed attitudes can aid recovery; Al-Anon has one purpose: to help alcoholics' family members; both AA and Al-Anon practice *the twelve steps*, welcome and comfort families of alcoholics, and give understanding and encouragement to the alcoholic

3. Alateen

provides support for teenagers who have an alcoholic parent or parents; similar to Al-Anon

4. Alcoholism and Drug Abuse, Division of (state)

administers state alcoholism and drug abuse programs, including information distribution, management of monetary grants, and consultation; helps businesses and industries retain and meet the needs of employees with drug or alcohol problems

5. Counselors/Psychotherapists

[See Life Issue Concerns Section II.X.1.]

6. Detoxification Centers

(sometimes affiliated with state hospitals, sometimes privately operated)

found in most states; provide an alcohol- or drug-free environment for people experiencing alcohol or drug abuse problems; offer treatment and counseling

7. Hospitals

May provide programs of information, care, and referral regarding all aspects of alcoholism; state or locally funded hospitals often offer these services

8. National Council on Alcoholism

provides short-term counseling for alcoholics and their families and friends; lists various resources dealing with alcoholism

9. Salvation Army

provides treatment centers and lodging for alcoholics; programs almost always include religious instruction

C. Child Abuse

1. Division of Family Services: Child Abuse and Neglect

investigates child neglect and abuse reports; sometimes a 24-hour service; may be found under a different title under the state government section of the white pages

2. Hospitals

provide emergency medical treatment for child abuse victims

3. National Child Abuse Hotline

800/422-4453

provides crisis counseling, information and referral; available 24 hours a day

4. Childhelp IOF Foresters National Child Abuse Hot Line

800/422-4453

offers information over the phone or by mail about child abuse, family violence, or parenting; can provide referrals for local counseling, social services, and survivor groups

5. National Council on Child Abuse and Family Violence

1155 Connecticut Avenue N.W., Suite 400 Washington, DC 20036

202/429-6695

offers material and information by written request;

800/422-4453

offers advice, information, and referrals about child abuse

6. National Center for Missing and Exploited Children

1825 K Street, N.W., Suite 700, Washington, DC 20006

800/843-5678

acts as a reporting agency that can interface with police departments that investigate sexual abuse of a child outside the family as well as the disappearance of a child; offers information about locating missing children and brochures about child protection

7. National Resource Center on Child Sexual Abuse

Chesapeake Institute, 11141 Georgia Avenue, Suite 310, Wheaton, MD 20902

205/534-6868

offers help primarily to professionals in the field of child abuse; also refers individuals in crisis to local agencies and provides printed information for students

8. Police

have the authority to detain or arrest child abusers pending trial; many states have laws requiring a person who knows of child abuse to report it to the police

9. State Welfare Programs

responsible for enforcement of child protection laws

[See Government Section I.B.1.]

D. Consumer Protection and Information

1. Better Business Bureau

answers inquiries about companies and individuals in business, investigates complaints of deceptive advertising and selling, conducts consumer information programs on basic business procedures, and issues warnings about irregular advertising and business practices; has no legal authority to take action against offenders

2. Consumer Affairs, Regulation, and Licensing

usually a state government organization; develops consumer education programs, handles questions and complaints by consumers; may have the authority to monitor industries and individual programs

3. Legal Aid Society

assists people in securing legal advice and counsel and provides legal services in the areas of housing, employment, consumer and welfare programs, family problems, and marital problems; services are provided only to those unable to afford legal representation

4. Industry Consumer Programs

associations formed by similar businesses; often provide opportunities for complaints against members to be judged by a panel of members; Examples: Car Dealers Associations, Dental Societies; can be found in a directory entitled National Trade and Professional Associations of the U.S. and Canada and Labor Unions; contact your local library

E. Credit Questions and Problems

1. Attorneys

[See Life Issue Concerns Section II.V.2.]

2. Consumer Credit Counseling Services

no-fee organizations formed by lending institutions to assist people who have credit problems; provide families or individuals with credit and money management counseling, and help with developing budgets; work with member institutions to rearrange pay schedules, but members are not obligated to accept suggestions; may provide programs on various aspects of consumer credit to educational groups

F. Crime

1. Aid to Victims of Crime

service available in some communities; provides emergency assistance, legal help, counseling, referral, and educational programs; sometimes works to change the criminal justice system and the social service system

2. Burglary Prevention Divisions

divisions of police departments; examine homes free of charge and suggest burglary prevention measures

3. Federal Crime Insurance Hotline

800/638-8780

provides information on a program that provides crime insurance for those unable to afford private insurance

4. Law Enforcement Agencies

enforce laws and arrest lawbreakers; investigate crime; all crimes should be reported to a law enforcement agency; when in doubt about whom to call, contact the local police department

5. Sexual Assault Counseling Centers

offer counseling, assistance, and legal advice to sexual assault victims; offer assistance in such areas as rape, incest, spouse abuse, and child abuse; may be found under "rape counseling centers" in the white pages or under a variety of titles in the social services section of the Yellow Pages

G. Crisis Pregnancies

1. National Life Center

Birthright North American Directory, 686 N. Broad St., Woodbury, NJ 08096

800/848-LOVE

a pro-life organization offering emotional support for difficult decisions; offers completely confidential, professional, and Christian counseling with a nonjudgmental approach; also offers free pregnancy testing, medical assistance, housing, clothing, and other assistance in extreme circumstances

2. Care Net (Crisis Pregnancy Centers)

109 Carpenter Drive, Sterling, VA 20164

703/478-5661

a nonprofit, Christian organization offering alternatives to abortion; offers free, confidential counseling/peer counseling; also offers free pregnancy testing, legal aid, clothing, furniture, and anything needed to help the mother carry the baby to term

3. Government Programs

[See Government Section I.B.1.]

some states provide services through their public assistance or Child Welfare Departments

4. Hospitals

hospitals may have social service departments that work with unwed mothers; these offer counseling while the mother is still in the hospital and recommend and contact other agencies to assist her after she leaves the hospital

5. Maternity Homes

for single expectant mothers; may provide housing, medical care, and social services; the most common are Florence Crittendon Homes and homes run by the Salvation Army; care is provided both prior to and following the baby's birth; some churches and religious groups also maintain homes for single expectant mothers; many of these homes also help the mother decide whether to keep the baby or place it for adoption

6. Social Services Agencies

provide counseling and other services to single expectant mothers; prefer to see both parents; may provide housing and medical referrals and post-delivery services; if requested, these organizations will usually place children for adoption

H. Death of a Child

1. The Compassionate Friends

P.O. Box 3696, Oak Brook, IL 60522-3696

708/ 990-0010

provides mutual self-help for bereaved parents; local chapters are active in many areas

2. Parents of Murdered Children (POMC)

100 East 8th Street, Room B41, Cincinnati, OH 45202

513/721-5683

provides information, support, and referral to parents and siblings who have lost a family member to violence

3. SIDS Alliance

10500 Little Patuxent Parkway, Suite 420, Columbia, MD 21044

800/221-SIDS

provides information and referral for parents who have lost children as a result of crib death or who have children with crib death-related symptoms;

assistance through local chapters available in some communities

I. Death of a Spouse

1. The Widowed Persons Service

1909 K St., N.W., Washington, DC 20040

available through the American Association for Retired Persons and the National Retired Teachers Association; written materials provided to assist widows and widowers

2. THEOS Foundation

1301 Clark Building, 717 Liberty Ave., Pittsburgh, PA 15222

412/ 471-7779

provides information and support for widows and widowers through a network of self-help groups

J. Divorce/Single Parenting

1. Fresh Start Seminars

63 Chestnut Road, Paoli, PA 19301

610/644-6464

offers congregation-sponsored seminars for people going through separation or divorce; call for brochures, seminar schedules, list of materials (including a workbook on single parenting)

2. Second Chapter

7750 Clayton Road, Suite 102, St. Louis, MO 63117

314/781-9818

offers a 14-week comprehensive program that addresses divorce recovery and rebuilding; now available in just a few cities, but is expanding

K. Drug Abuse

1. Drug Abuse Services

cities or counties may offer drug abuse services; the exact services vary from area to area; these services are usually listed under the county or city listings, either separately or with health department listings; services may be listed under "narcotics"

2. Drug Crisis Intervention Units

normally provide 24-hour, seven-day-a-week crisis service, giving nonmedical support during drug crises; provide drug information, referral services, and educational drug programs; to locate hotline look in the Yellow Pages under "social services" under various names such as Acid Rescue, Drug Abuse, etc.

3. Drug Enforcement Administration

division of the federal Department of Justice that enforces laws relating to the illegal use of narcotics

4. Drug Treatment Centers

a. Government

state and local governments often provide treatment centers for persons suffering from drug abuse; look in the white pages under city, county, or state government

b. Private

many private agencies offer drug abuse treatment; hospitals or physicians should be able to refer to these

5. Hospitals

provide emergency medical treatment for victims of drug abuse; may provide specialized treatment centers or clinics for drug abusers as well

6. Teen Challenge

services include personal counseling, live-in program, group discussion, Bible training, and a 24-hour help line; services are provided within the context of therapeutic communities working primarily with drug-dependent adolescents

7. 1-800-ALCOHOL

provides information and referral services to persons addicted to alcohol and drugs, family members, employers, and social service agencies throughout the United States

L. Education
1. Adult Basic Education

provides free education for people over 16 who are no longer in school; usual programs include high school equivalency training, various vocational classes, and English as a second language; high school graduates may come back for review through Adult Basic Education; a new area Adult Performance Level (APL) Education helps people gain basic living skills

2. Colleges and Universities

provide post-high school education and include a variety of higher education institutions, state schools, city universities, church-related schools, and other private schools; each may provide counseling or guidance programs which may be found in connection with the dean of students' office, student health services, psychology department, or in separate guidance and counseling offices

3. Labor Unions

provide vocational training for people who want to join a union; may provide apprenticeship programs (on-the-job training)

4. Public Schools

provide education, counseling, and vocational guidance for children and adolescents; often conduct night classes for those wishing to complete their high school education or continue their education in areas of interest and concern

5. Vocational Counseling Services

provide counseling, psychological testing, information, training facilities, and occupational information for both able-bodied and handicapped adults already in the job market as well as for youth currently in school who are about to enter the job market; most have a library including vocational and college materials such as information on scholarships and loans

[See Government Section I.C.2. and Life Issue Concerns Section II.N.]

M. Emergency Assistance (Food, Clothing, etc.)
1. American Red Cross

provides emergency food, clothing, and housing assistance for victims of natural disasters; sometimes aid in rebuilding is provided; additional services may be available; for more information, contact your local chapter

2. Food Programs

assist the needy in obtaining food; coordinate emergency food distribution; can sometimes be found in the phone book under such titles as Emergency Assistance, Emergency Food Services, etc.; often it is difficult to find these services listed in the phone book; most community resource directories list these resources under "Food" or "Emergency Food"; to locate these programs, contact United Way referral lines and local churches; some food banks provide referral to emergency food services

3. Government Programs

[See Government Section I.B.1.]

4. Religious Groups

local councils of churches and religious social services agencies often have programs of emergency assistance; individual churches may also have programs

5. Salvation Army

provides emergency assistance; for more information look under Alcoholism in this guide

N. Employment/Unemployment

1. Office of Personnel Management

commission of the federal government; conducts civil examinations; provides information concerning jobs with the United States Government

2. Employment Services

[See Government Section I.B.3.]

3. Employment Agencies for Handicapped People

provide job placement services, training, testing, and sometimes counseling; usually listed in the phone book under "handicapped"; state and federal employment services may provide referral to employment agencies dealing with the handicapped

[See Life Issue Concerns Section II.R.]

4. Private Employment Agencies

secure employment for a fee; either the employee or the employer pays the fee; effectiveness of agencies depends on local labor market and the skills of the individual agency; can be located in the Yellow Pages under "Employment Agencies"

5. Private Temporary Employment Agencies

provide businesses with short-term help and individuals with temporary jobs; jobs can last a few hours to several months and may involve either skilled or unskilled labor; can be located in the Yellow Pages under "Employment Contractors Temporary Help"

6. Unemployment Insurance Program

provides compensation for those who have been fired or have lost their jobs for most reasons (except their own decision to quit); administered by the State Employment Service; listed in the white pages under "State Employment Service"

[See Government Section I.B.3.]

7. Veterans Services Division

division of the Veterans Administration; provides information and aid to veterans and their families concerning claims for benefits and insurance; provides referral information about other government agencies useful to veterans, job advice, and counseling as well as testing for eligible war orphans and disabled veterans

8. Wage and Hour Division

division of the federal government; provides information and enforces laws dealing with minimum wage, child labor, and overtime

O. Energy

1. Housing Development Corporation

evaluates homes' energy efficiency; employs people to do energy-saving work on houses; programs have time and income limits

2. Local Resources Advice

about wise energy use includes: gas and electric companies, building contractors, insulation specialists, heating contractors, solar energy experts, etc.

P. Family Problems (Marital, Parent-Child, Runaways)

1. Attorneys and Courts

provide advice and action on problems such as divorce, child custody, child abuse, or any other family problems that may have legal ramifications

2. Family Social Services

private agencies, often church-related or other nonprofit, that provide marital counseling, family counseling, family life education, and a variety of other services for a fee (usually on a sliding scale); services vary from community to community; listed in the white pages under agency name or in the Yellow Pages under "Social Services"

3. National Runaway Switchboard

800/621-4000

National Runaway Hotline

800/231-6946

both hotlines provide information about runaway services; runaway youths can call these numbers and leave a message to be forwarded to their families without revealing their whereabouts; parents can leave messages; runaway youths can call the hotline and discuss their problems with someone who will listen and offer helpful information

4. Private Counselors/Psychotherapists

clinical psychologists, psychiatric social workers, pastoral counselors, psychiatrists, psychiatric nurses, and other professional counselors provide guidance in premarital counseling and family problems for a fee; listed under "Marriage and Family Counselors" or "Psychologists" in the Yellow Pages

Q. Family Violence

1. National Coalition Against Domestic Violence

Box 15172, Washington, DC 20003-0127

202/638-6388

offers a newsletter or membership information

303/839-1852

offers posters and general information

703/765-0339

offers information on public policies and laws regarding domestic violence

2. Center for the Prevention of Sexual and Domestic Violence

1914 N. 34th Street, Suite 205, Seattle, WA 98103

206/634-1903

provides educational curricula and training for religious organizations

3. National Council on Child Abuse and Family Violence

1155 Connecticut Avenue N.W., Suite 400 Washington, DC 20003

202/429-6695

offers material and information by written request

800/222-2000

offers advice, information, and referrals for elder abuse

R. Handicap Needs

1. Education

public schools must and parochial schools may provide special education and training for the retarded or handicapped; some communities have "homebound" teachers to train children who must remain home; there are also private schools set up just for handicapped persons

2. Employment

a. United States Employment Office

will try to place handicapped people in jobs they are able to handle

[See Government Section, I.B.3.]

b. Goodwill Industries

provides employment, training, and rehabilitation for handicapped people regardless of race, creed, or color; may also provide "sheltered workshop" type of employment

c. Services for the Blind

provides vocational training and operates schools in most states; provides talking books; helps blind people become self-supporting and independent; may operate as a separate office of vocational rehabilitation

3. Vocational Rehabilitation

usually a division of the state government; helps the disabled gain economic independence through useful work; provides diagnostic services to determine a person's capabilities and whenever possible attempts to eliminate or minimize the handicap; also provides counseling, training, and placement; listed in the white pages in the state government section

S. Housing—Discrimination

1. U.S. Department of Housing and Urban Development Discrimination Hotline

800/669-9777

receives discrimination complaints

T. Housing—Emergency

1. American Red Cross

[See Life Issue Concerns Section II.M.1.]

2. Salvation Army

provides temporary housing for families and single persons during disasters; low-cost housing may be provided for a longer period of time; some chapters have housing for the homeless

3. Traveler's Aid Societies

provide referrals to travelers who need emergency housing; may provide counseling services related to adjustment problems due to a move; may also provide protective travel service for the handicapped, runaways, and children traveling alone

U. Housing—Subsidized

[See Government Section I.A.1.]

V. Law or Legal Matters

1. Attorney General, State

receives consumer complaints about fraud or false advertising; authorized to file suit, when it is in the public interest, against those accused of fraud

2. Attorneys

provide legal advice and assistance for a fee; sources for locating a reliable attorney are: friends who have used an attorney, local bar associations, lawyers' reference services (discussed later)

3. Commission on Human Rights

works to bring about just and equal treatment in employment, housing, and public buildings for anyone regardless of race, color, religion, national origin, or sex

4. Lawyers' Reference Services

provides a listing of lawyers in the community and information about each one; assists in locating the appropriate lawyer

5. Law Schools

may offer legal assistance and advice; services are usually provided by law students (supervised by a licensed lawyer)

6. Legal Aid Societies

provide competent legal advice and counsel for those who cannot afford private legal help; may provide educational programs concerning the rights, duties, and responsibilities of citizens under the law, usually emphasizing the rights of the poor

7. Probation and Parole Officers

supervise offenders on probation or parole, or who have recently completed probation or parole

8. Small Claims Court

found in many states; usually simple, inexpensive, quick and informal; normally don't need a lawyer; maximum amounts of claims and awards vary from state to state; look in the phone book under municipal, county, or state government headings for small claims court listings

W. Medical Concerns

1. Hospitals

provide medical care in the form of emergency care and inpatient/outpatient care; hospitals for low-income people are provided by city and county governments

2. Medical Associations (Societies)

provide referral service for physicians and dentists, and also handle complaints about members; listed in the Yellow Pages under "Physicians"

3. Public Health Nurses

[See Government Section I.C.3.a.]

4. Public Health Service (with its various divisions)

[See Government Section I.C.3.]

5. Visiting Nurse Association

VNA nurses provide general care to patients and their families; give bedside care and instruct families as they carry out treatment; instruct in prenatal, maternal, and child care; give information on nutrition, communicable disease prevention, and acute and chronic illnesses; make referrals to other agencies when needed; VNA also provides physical, occupational, and speech therapy as well as the services of social workers, dietitians, and pediatric practitioners

X. Mental Health

1. Community Mental Health Centers

provide comprehensive care in the following five areas: inpatient, outpatient, partial hospitalization, emergency room, consultation/education; designed to meet the total mental health needs of a community; federally funded

2. Mental Health Clinics

communities may operate nonfederally-funded mental health clinics; services are similar to those offered at Community Mental Health Centers; may include a child guidance center

3. Mental Hospitals, Public and Private

provide inpatient treatment for people with emotional problems; adequacy and quality of service and treatment vary greatly, and many hospitals are merely custodial care facilities; private institutions provide more personalized service to a greater or lesser degree, but usually at a greater cost; United States Veterans' Hospitals also operate mental hospital facilities

4. Mental Health Information Referral Services

provide information and referral for the wide spectrum of mental health services and needs

5. Private Psychotherapists

clinical psychologists, psychiatrists, psychiatric social workers, pastoral counselors, and psychi-

atric nurses often provide counseling/psychotherapy for those with emotional struggles

Y. Mental Retardation

1. Community Schools for the Retarded

communities may operate special schools for the intellectually handicapped; these schools teach basic skills according to the abilities of each person while they live at home; schools may be public or private

2. National Association for Retarded Citizens (NARC)

2501 Avenue J, P.O. Box 6109, Arlington, TX 76005

listings of local chapters may be found in the phone book or obtained from the national organization; provides help to parents, individuals, organizations, and communities for jointly solving the problems caused by mental retardation; has a variety of recreational programs; national organization makes available many resources and informational publications

3. Psychologists

give psychological tests to determine the degree of retardation, if any, and also help parents deal with this concern; may provide behavior modification principles to parents and others

4. Public Schools

provide training and education for the retarded child; in some cases, children have special or ungraded classes with teachers who are trained in dealing with retarded children; may attempt to give special care to retarded children who are able to attend regular classes with a minimum of personal attention

5. Residential Facilities

offer intensive individualized care but may be expensive; listed in the white pages under the name of particular institutions, and may be listed under "Homes, Mentally Deficient" or "Schools, Mentally Retarded Children" in the Yellow Pages

6. State Schools

for the mentally retarded; these facilities provide training according to individual needs and abilities

Z. Older Persons

1. Aging Information and Direction Services

provide general information and referral for the elderly, concentrating on information about nursing care and services for the aged

2. Aging Network Services, Inc. (ANS)

is a long-distance care management organization designed to ease the problems confronting adults who have aging parents or other elderly relatives living far away; when you call the central ANS office, you will be interviewed about your specific situation; ANS will then contact your aging relative, and a licensed clinical social worker based in the same area will serve as consultant and care manager

3. Alzheimer's Association

puts caregivers in touch with family support groups, provides information on local chapters, and offers literature describing the causes, symptoms, diagnosis and treatment of Alzheimer's. For one free copy of any of the brochures or for referral to a local chapter, call, toll-free, *800/621-0379*

4. American Association of Retired Persons (AARP)

1909 K St. NW, Washington, DC 20049

provides older Americans with the information they need to live lives of dignity and purpose. In addition, through its literature, AARP is dedicated to answering the questions and concerns of caregivers

5. Children of Aging Parents (CAPS)

serves as a national resource clearinghouse for caregivers, and is currently developing a national network of support groups, workshops, and seminars. Also offers advice and informational leaflets designed to educate the public about the needs of the elderly and their caregivers. For more information, send $1 and a self-addressed, stamped envelope to: CAPS, 2761 Trenton Rd., Levittown, PA 19056

6. Day Centers

provide social and recreational activities for older persons and may provide daily meal services; sponsored by the federal government, local churches, settlement houses, public groups, volunteer groups

7. Family Service America (FSA)

is a nonprofit association consisting of 290 member agencies, the largest network of its kind; one part of its service is helping families solve the complex problems of elder care through counseling, support groups, and specialized services such as meetings with elder-care experts; for the location of the FSA agency nearest you and a copy of the agency's caregiver brochure, send a self-addressed, stamped envelope to: Family Service America, Dept. FC, 11700 West Lake Park Dr., Milwaukee, WI 53224

8. Friends in Service Helping (FISH)

community organization of volunteers who perform various services within the community; most of these organizations provide transportation if needed; may be helpful to older persons; FISH groups also minister to people in a variety of life situations

9. Government Commission on Aging

in many city/county or state governments offering a variety of services; in some areas, these commissions are only advisory

10. Home Delivery Meal Services

provide and deliver meals to older people's homes; there may be a moderate cost for the meals; a typical service is "Meals on Wheels"; such programs may be located under "Social Services" in the Yellow Pages, sometimes with descriptive titles in the white pages under "Meals on Wheels"; many area agencies on aging have federally funded home-delivered meal programs; there is no charge for these meals, but a donation is accepted; contact the local area agency on aging for more information

11. Nursing and Convalescent Homes

provided by government and private agencies for older people, the chronically ill, and those needing care; some provide residential care only; others also may provide a variety of services to older people who do not require residential care; adequacy and cost vary greatly; information can be obtained from local welfare offices or departments of health

12. Organizations for Older People

have a variety of names and purposes; nursing homes, commissions on aging, your pastor, and chaplains of institutions for older people are good sources of information about these organizations; organizations for older people can be a resource in interpreting laws and regulations and bringing about higher levels of patient care in nursing homes

13. Transportation Services

for older people; vary regionally; people who work with the elderly are good sources of information about transportation

AA. Suicide

1. American Association of Suicidology

2459 South Ash, Denver, CO 81222

202/237-2280

acts as a clearinghouse for information on suicide prevention; publishes a directory of crisis centers and survivor organizations; offers other information and materials about suicide

BB. Veterans

[See Federal Government Section I.A.7. and Life Issue Concerns Section II.N.7.]

CC. Victims of Crime

1. National Victim Center

307 W. 7th St., Suite 1001, Ft. Worth, TX 76102

817/877-3355

800/FYI-CALL (for information or referral only)

offers information and referrals for victims of violent crimes; can provide packets of information on different issues regarding crime

2. Mothers Against Drunk Driving (MADD)— National

669 Airport Freeway, Suite 310, Hurst, TX 76053

817/595-0192

offers information and statistics; local chapters offer referrals for legal and medical assistance

3. The Spiritual Dimension in Victim Services

P. O. Box 6736, Denver, CO 80206

303/740-8171

offers seminars and printed information for clergy and religious leaders on assisting victims of crime, including victims of family violence, child abuse, sexual assault, and robbery

DD. Vocational Guidance

[See Life Issue Concerns Sections II.R.3., II.N., and II.L.]

III. Locating Resources Not in This Guide

Some life issue concerns are not listed in this guide. This section suggests other people and organizations for locating further community resources.

A. Other Helping People

It is wise to consult with other people who are in helping, caring ministries. These include the minister, other professional helpers, Stephen Ministers, acquaintances, and friends, especially those who might have used resources in particular areas of concern. Your pastor may be an important source of help; however, pastors cannot be expected to know and be experts about all available community resources.

B. United Way Referral Service

Most United Way agencies have a referral service. It would be listed in the telephone directory's white pages under "United Way." The referral service can provide the names, addresses, and phone numbers of area agencies that deal with certain life issue concerns. This can be a means both of locating and becoming more familiar with a resource.

C. Community Resource Directories

In many communities, particularly larger cities, community resource directories are available. Communities often offer local directories through the United Way, the Council of Churches, or the local government. There is usually a nominal fee for these directories, but they are well worth having as supplements to the "ChristCare Series Guide to Community Resources."

D. Professional Organizations

Many professional organizations have a referral service. A Lawyers' Reference Service is listed in this Guide. Some communities also have medical and dental societies that offer physician and dentist referrals. This can be especially helpful in areas where many physicians or dentists are not accepting new patients.

E. Mental Health Information Referral Services

Many community mental health centers provide information and treatment referrals. They may also provide educational programs and materials. These services often operate independently of community mental health centers.

F. Bridging the Gaps: A Locator of Helping Organizations for the Local Church

Produced by: Health and Welfare Ministries Program Department; General Board of Global Ministries; The United Methodist Church. Order from: The Service Center; 7820 Reading Road; Cincinnati, OH 45237.

A directory of the national headquarters of numerous helping organizations and the services they provide. Resources are listed in four major categories: Aging; Children/Women, Families; Handicapping Conditions; and Health. Its format includes space for the user to fill in the address and telephone number of the nearest local chapter.

G. Love INC

Contact: Dr. Virgil Gulker, President; P.O. Box 1616, Holland, MI 49422; 616/392-8277.

The LOVE, INC. Community Clearinghouse equips communities to use their resources more effectively by organizing church congregations to work cooperatively with public and private helping agencies in meeting human needs. A liaison among needy individuals, agencies, and churches, the LOVE, INC. Clearinghouse reduces unnecessary duplication of agency/church services. It identifies and teaches self-help skills to chronic dependents and generates volunteer and material resources within churches.

H. A Guide to Health and Consumer Toll-Free Hotlines

To order, write: Hotlines Guide, Essential Information, P.O. Box 19405, Washington, DC 20036.

A toll-free hotline directory divided into two categories: Health Issues and Consumer Issues. Organizations are listed alphabetically.

I. Consumer's Resource Handbook

Produced by: United States Office of Consumer Affairs, Consumer Information Center, Pueblo, CO 81009.

An informational and educational tool to help the user communicate more effectively with those who provide products and services, locate sources of help, and resolve complaints in the most effective manner.

J. National Self-Help Clearinghouse

25 West 42nd St., Room 620, New York, NY 10036, 212/840-7606.

Provides access to regional self-help groups dealing with infertility, AIDS, grief, mental illness, addictions, single parenthood, disabilities, and more. Publications include manuals, training materials, booklets, brochures, and a newsletter.

K. CONTACT USA

Pouch A, Harrisburg, PA 17105-1300, 717/232-3501

A Christian-based ministry of more than 70 crisis intervention and helpline centers located across the USA. Its centers offer a wide variety of related services (depending on the needs of their communities) in addition to helplines. There is no fee for their services and calls are confidential. They offer a 50-hour training program. Many of its centers allow outside participants to take this course and can even modify sections to offer as one- or two-day seminars.

ChrisCare Series

Pre-Use Resource Assessment Questionnaire

Name of Resource _____

Address _____

_____

Phone _____

Fax _____

Contact Person _____

A. What services does the resource provide?
(Get as much information as possible.)

B. What hours are the services available?

C. How much do the services cost?

D. Where are the services available?

E. Who is eligible for the services?

F. How does one use the services?

G. What information, if any, is needed on the part of the care receiver?
(For example: rent receipts, proof of income, utility bills, birth certificates, family data, proof of employment, degrees, etc. This is particularly important in dealing with government agencies. Insufficient information can lead to severe delays in receiving services.)

H. What reputation does the resource have for providing consistently good, quality services to its clients?

I. Other helpful information:

When and How to Make Referrals for Additional Care

Outline and Focus Notes

"When you pass through the waters, I will be with you; and when you pass through the rivers, they will not sweep over you. When you walk through the fire, you will not be burned; the flames will not set you ablaze."

Isaiah 43:2

1. Prayer and Worship: Singing and Praising

FOCUS NOTE 1

Psalm 150

Praise the LORD.

Praise God in his sanctuary;
    praise him in his mighty heavens.
Praise him for his acts of power;
    praise him for his surpassing greatness.
Praise him with the sounding of the trumpet,
    praise him with the harp and lyre,
praise him with tambourine and dancing,
    praise him with the strings and flute,
praise him with the clash of cymbals,
    praise him with resounding cymbals.

Let everything that has breath praise the LORD.

Praise the LORD.

---

2. Is Additional Care Needed?

FOCUS NOTE 2

How to Tell When Additional Care May Be Needed

- A person is facing a challenge that is intense, lasts a long time, has severe results or consequences, or comes at the same time as other challenges.

- A person's history or experience hasn't prepared him or her well enough to cope with a particular challenge.

- A person doesn't have an adequate support system to provide help in facing the challenge.

- A person shows one or more of the warning signals listed in "Signs That Can Indicate the Need for Additional Care" (Supplement A from the Preclass Reading, pages 117–120).

- A person indicates by what he or she shares or how he or she behaves in your group meetings that additional care might be needed.

- Your SEA Group or SEA Group Facilitator points out or agrees that additional care might be needed.

FOCUS NOTE 3

Is Additional Care Needed Here?

Situation 1

Stan and Connie have been members of your ChristCare Group for two years. From the first, this couple shared openly their intense desire to have a child. Your group has supported them through a miscarriage and then through a successful pregnancy. A few months after their baby's birth, however, the baby was diagnosed with cystic fibrosis.

Situation 2

Sandra is a member of your ChristCare Group, which consists of single people in their thirties and forties. Sandra often seems to be sad, even depressed, when she arrives at ChristCare Group meetings. She is usually cheerier by the time the meetings are over.

Focus Note 3 is continued on page 139.

Situation 3

Julia and Dave are in their fifties and have two college-age children and one teenager. They are concerned about their teen's behavior and are dismayed that he is so different from his older siblings, who were "model" kids. At last week's meeting, Julia shared that her aging father had been hospitalized in another city and now needed to be moved to a nursing home. In addition, Dave learned that his company was downsizing, and his job would be eliminated within the next six months.

Situation 4

Your ChristCare Group meets during lunch on Wednesdays. Charlie, one of the members, has a stressful job that requires long hours away from home. He has said several times in the past that his wife's support and understanding really help him withstand the stress from work. When your group met today, though, Charlie said that his wife announced over the weekend that she has fallen in love with one of her coworkers and wants a divorce.

Situation 5

Mary Jo confided in your ChristCare Group that her 26-year-old brother has AIDS. He has asked her for help in telling their parents.

---

3. Referral Research

4. An In-Depth Look at Making Referrals for Additional Care

FOCUS NOTE 4

Four Steps in Making a Referral for Additional Care

1. Determine that a person needs additional care.

2. Identify possible sources of additional care.

3. Recommend that the person receive additional care.
   - Pray.
   - Meet privately.
   - Use I-statements.
   - Be assertive.
   - Listen.
   - Answer questions.
   - Recommend a specific resource.
   - Ask for a commitment to act.
   - Promise support and encouragement.
   - Pray with the person.

4. Follow through to make sure the person is receiving the care he or she needs.

FOCUS NOTE 5

How to Handle a Refusal of a Referral for Additional Care

1. Reason for Refusal

The person doesn't understand what it's like to receive additional care
- Explain the care process clearly and thoroughly.
- Compare additional care to a care resource the group member is familiar with, such as medical care.
- Give personal examples of using such a resource.
- Share examples of other people's use of such a resource, while protecting confidentiality.
- Remind the person that it's natural to fear something new.
- Encourage the person to try one visit with the resource.

Focus Note 5 is continued on page 141.

2. *Reason for Refusal*

Fear of consequences in the ChristCare Group

- Assure the person of the group's continued care and confidentiality.
- Explain that it's completely up to the group member whether to mention the additional care in group meetings.

3. *Reason for Refusal*

Fear of others' finding out

- Remind the group member that he or she can choose whether to talk about this issue during ChristCare Group meetings.
- State that you protect confidentiality in SEA Groups.
- Say that other group members have agreed to keep all information shared in ChristCare Group meetings confidential.
- Explain that professional caregivers are required to protect their clients' confidentiality.

4. *Reason for Refusal*

Denial

- Keep praying.
- Keep working on your relationship with the group member.

5. *Reason for Refusal*

Inability to pay

- Help find affordable services.
- Help find alternative funding sources.

6. *Reason for Refusal*

Belief that the ChristCare Group should meet the need

- Explain that ChristCare Groups don't provide specialized additional care services.
- Explain that some needs go beyond the care ChristCare Groups can provide.

7. *Reason for Refusal*

Pride

- Listen to the person.
- Give your own, others', and biblical examples of needs for additional care.

FOCUS NOTE 6

A Situation That Needs Referral for Additional Care

Kelly's spouse died a year and a half ago. At first Kelly seemed able to cope with the loss, but recently Kelly has become more and more depressed about it. He or she has missed work several times in the past month, is losing weight, and doesn't come regularly to ChristCare Group meetings. Some days Kelly doesn't even get out of bed.

FOCUS NOTE 7

Discussion Questions

1. Did the group member get to explain fully his or her objections to the referral? Did he or she get to talk at length about feelings associated with this situation? What else could the ChristCare Group Leader have done to help the group member?

2. Did the ChristCare Group Leader address the group member's objections effectively? What else could have been done?

3. What did your group learn from this role play?

5. Biblical Equipping: Your Spiritual Worship (Romans 12:1–2)

FOCUS NOTE 8

Questions to Focus Sharing of Biblical Equipping Apart

• Share one insight that you've had as a result of your Biblical Equipping Apart this week.

• Describe one change in your life that you've committed to make as a result of your meditation on the Biblical Equipping passage this week.

• Tell about a time when you've met God in a new way through Biblical Equipping Apart this week.

FOCUS NOTE 9

Your Spiritual Worship (Romans 12:1–2 NRSV)

¹I appeal to you therefore, brothers and sisters, by the mercies of God, to present your bodies as a living sacrifice, holy and acceptable to God, which is your spiritual worship. ²Do not be conformed to this world, but be transformed by the renewing of your minds, so that you may discern what is the will of God—what is good and acceptable and perfect.

FOCUS NOTE 10

Explore Questions

1. What did Paul mean when he told the Romans to present their bodies as living sacrifices?

2. What did Paul mean when he wrote that being a living sacrifice is the Christian's spiritual worship?

3. If you knew two Romans back in Paul's day, and one was conformed to that world and the other had been transformed, how do you think their lives would have been different?

4. What did Paul mean when he wrote, "but be transformed by the renewing of your minds"? How was a renewed mind different from a nonrenewed mind?

FOCUS NOTE 11

Connect Questions

1. Can you think of anyone who has been a living sacrifice to God? What was different about her or his life?

2. If you knew two people today, and one was conformed to this world and the other was transformed, how do you think their lives would be different?

3. Paul defines worship as being a living sacrifice. How is that different from what you've always thought worship is? How could you incorporate Paul's definition of worship into your ChristCare Group's worship?

4. What does this passage tell you about how prayer and worship can help you lead a transformational ChristCare Group?

6. Prayer and Worship: Visualization Prayer

7. Assignment: Prepare a Worship Experience

Group-Based Manual for ChristCare Group Leaders
Prayer and Worship in ChristCare Groups

Preclass Reading

Come, let us sing for joy to the LORD; let us shout aloud to the Rock of our salvation. Let us come before him with thanksgiving and extol him with music and song.

Psalm 95:1–2

PRECLASS READING OUTLINE

I. Introduction

Prayer and worship make up one of the four main elements in a ChristCare Group meeting. As a ChristCare Group Leader, you will have primary responsibility for planning and leading your group's prayer and worship. (You may delegate this responsibility to other group members, but you will still need to check its direction and quality.)

This may sound like a big responsibility, especially if you have never done anything like it before. Don't worry. This Preclass Reading and the in-class session will prepare you to facilitate prayer and worship in your ChristCare Group, whether you're a complete beginner or a seasoned veteran. Chapter 4 of *Nuts & Bolts Issues for Small Group Leaders* will also help.

Use the ideas and suggestions in this Preclass Reading—and your group's experiences of prayer and worship in earlier sessions—to prepare a prayer or worship experience for the upcoming session. A number of trainees will be able to present their services during the session.

A. Prayer and Worship in ChristCare Groups

ChristCare Groups' prayer and worship are different from individual prayer and worship because they take place in a small community of Christians. Participants are blessed by one another's faith, needs, and creativity. They also differ from congregational prayer and worship, since they take place in a small, intimate group rather than in a large, less personal one. When the group is small, it is possible for everyone to provide ideas, input, and leadership. Group members can experiment with different styles of prayer and ways of worshiping. As group members meet Christ along new pathways, their relationships with him will deepen and expand.

ChristCare Group prayer and worship can be exciting! Many group members find them to be some of the most meaningful experiences in their lives.

They enjoy thanking and praising God in a community of people they know well and care about deeply.

B. The Scope of This Module

The subject of prayer and worship is a vast one, and there is no way to do it justice in the available space and time. For that reason, this module will only introduce you to some of the varied styles of prayer and worship and suggest how you can incorporate these into your group's time together.

The first part of this Preclass Reading talks about the basics of worship and prayer, and what the Bible has to say about them. If small group prayer and worship are largely new to you, this material will prove useful as you take your first steps with your group. If you already know a great deal about prayer and worship, consider this material a review, a foundation that you can build on with the knowledge and gifts that you possess.

The next part, "First Steps in Prayer and Worship," explains how you can teach your group to pray aloud and offers suggestions for beginning worship activities. This section is most helpful for leaders of ChristCare Groups whose members have never learned to pray aloud and who still feel somewhat uncomfortable with the idea of worshiping together. If your group already feels very comfortable with prayer and worship, this section can still help you teach visitors and new members. Such people may not enter the group knowing what everyone else does, and they will need your help and teaching.

The next section focuses on how to plan and lead your group's worship. It discusses choosing a theme, pulling together the different elements of worship, and staying sensitive to your group's needs. It also offers a look at the many exciting possibilities for prayer and worship together, including ideas from many worship traditions.

II. What Are Prayer and Worship?

It is difficult to separate the subjects of prayer and worship. Both occur when we turn our attention to God and address him, expressing love, thanks, sorrow, awe, or joy. Both are normal activities of Christians alone and in community. Both require the Holy Spirit's help in order to be done properly. Prayer is a way of worshiping; planned worship almost always includes prayer. Many activities, such as meditation or singing, can be used either as worship or prayer.

Although prayer and worship are inextricably intertwined, it is sometimes easier to learn when the two subjects are separated. For this reason, we will look first at what the Bible teaches about prayer, and then consider worship.

A. What Is Prayer?

Put simply, prayer is a conversation with God. When you pray, you can tell God your feelings, fears, needs, and joys. You can speak to God as you speak to a person who loves you, someone you trust completely to care for you. At the same time, you remember that you are speaking to the King of heaven and earth, the one who made you and redeemed you, the one who deserves your worship and has the power to grant your requests.

Prayer is a deliberate way of drawing closer to God. God will draw nearer to you and build his relationship with you. God will bring you closer to him and unite you to him. God himself will guide your prayers, making them acceptable and adding what they lack, as the apostle Paul explains:

> In the same way, the Spirit helps us in our weakness. We do not know what we ought to pray for, but the Spirit himself intercedes for us with groans that words cannot express. And he who searches our hearts knows the mind of the Spirit, because the Spirit intercedes for the saints in accordance with God's will (Romans 8:26–27).

Prayer also involves listening to God. When you are silent before God, God can use that time to speak to you, encourage you, rebuke you, remind you of something important you have forgotten, or guide you about what to do next. Prayer is not a one-sided conversation. It is a dialogue, not a monologue.

What the Bible Says about Prayer

The Bible says a great deal about prayer, both by direct statement and through example. From the examples of Hannah, the tax collector in the parable, and Jesus himself, we see that prayer can be done individually (1 Samuel 1:9–13a; Luke 18:10–13; Luke 6:12). In other cases, it is done as a group. The early church did this (Acts 1:14, 24), as did the people of Israel (2 Chronicles 7:3; Luke 1:10). Jesus promised that God would hear the prayers of two or three Christians gathered in his name (Matthew 18:20).

Prayer in the Bible takes many forms, from adoration (Psalms 95, 100, 104) to confession (Psalm 51;

Daniel 9:3–20) to petition (Matthew 26:39, 42) and even argument (Genesis 18:22–33; Numbers 14:11–25). People prayed simply, using their own words (Luke 18:13) and also liturgically, using beautifully composed prayers (2 Chronicles 6:13–42; Psalm 136). Prayer was sometimes combined with other activities, such as fasting (Acts 9:9–11; 2 Samuel 12:16).

Jesus urged people to persevere in prayer (Luke 18:1–8) and made lavish promises about God's response (Matthew 7:7–11; Luke 18:7–8). He encouraged the disciples to ask in his name (John 16:23–27). Jesus himself prayed for his followers (John 17:14–26), and spent many nights in prayer during his years of ministry (Matthew 14:23; Matthew 26:36; Mark 1:35). We are told that "Christ Jesus, who died—more than that, who was raised to life—is at the right hand of God and is also interceding for us" (Romans 8:34), and also that the "Spirit himself intercedes for us with groans that words cannot express" (Romans 8:26).

The Value of Prayer

First, praying is important because it is a way of showing obedience. Jesus himself told us how to pray (Matthew 6:9–13) and showed us what a life of prayer is like. Paul urges Christians to "pray continually" (1 Thessalonians 5:17).

Prayer is how we bring our needs, hopes, and fears, and those of our fellow group members, before the Lord. Doing this opens the door to God's intervention. It also expresses care for those we pray for, since we are saying in effect, "You and your needs are so important to me that I will even bring them up to God himself."

Second, prayer is a way to know and love God more deeply. As a Christian, you are commanded to "Love the Lord your God with all your heart and with all your soul and with all your mind and with all your strength" (Mark 12:30). One way of loving God is to speak with him, just as you speak with people whom you love.

Third, prayer is valuable for group members as they grow to love and trust one another more. There is something about praying aloud with others that helps cement your relationship with them. Since many people are nervous about praying aloud, when they do so it tells the rest of the group, "I trust you." Such prayer builds intimacy and trust.

Fourth, prayer in ChristCare Groups helps groups remember where their focus needs to be. ChristCare Groups are called "circles of care with Christ at the center." When group members pray

together, they turn to the center of their group, to Christ who is the reason for the group's existence. They remember that their group exists to learn to know Jesus better and to serve him more fully.

Finally, praying together as a ChristCare Group is valuable because it gives individual Christians practice with prayer, helping them to grow in this skill. Group prayer is especially helpful for people who are learning to pray for the first time or who have the conflicting feelings about prayer that Richard Foster expressed:

> We today yearn for prayer and hide from prayer. We are attracted to it and repelled by it. We believe prayer is something we should do, even something we want to do, but it seems like a chasm stands between us and actually praying. We experience the agony of prayerlessness.[1]

The Contents of Prayer

What do group members pray about? People can pray about anything that they wish to bring before God. Most prayers, though, fall into one of the broad categories discussed below: adoration, confession, thanksgiving, lament, and petition.

Adoration

Christian prayers often include adoration. You adore God when you think about who he is—the King of the Universe and the One who made you and everything else that exists. In adoration, you remember that God is a God of power and compassion, a God who created the universe yet remembers every living creature he has made (Matthew 10:29–31). Usually you express your adoration of God through praise, just as the Psalmist did:

> I will sing of the LORD's great love forever;
> > with my mouth I will make your
> > > faithfulness known through all
> > > generations.
> I will declare that your love stands firm
> > forever,
> > that you established your faithfulness in
> > > heaven itself. . . .
>
> The heavens praise your wonders, O LORD,
> > your faithfulness too, in the assembly
> > of the holy ones.
> For who in the skies above can compare
> > with the LORD?
> > Who is like the LORD among the
> > > heavenly beings?

In the council of the holy ones God is
    greatly feared;
  he is more awesome than all who
    surround him.
O Lord God Almighty, who is like you?
  You are mighty, O Lord, and your
    faithfulness surrounds you.

Psalm 89:1–2, 5–8

Such praise is the natural result of knowing God. We cannot help praising him when we have truly come to know him, any more than a person in love can help praising his or her beloved. To adore God is to be in touch with reality, to be in our right minds—for God, above all else that exists, calls forth our love, praise, and admiration.

As noted Christian writer C. S. Lewis points out, to praise and adore God is truly to enjoy him. He writes:

> The Scotch catechism says that man's chief end is "to glorify God and enjoy Him forever." But we shall then [when we are made perfect] know that these are the same thing. Fully to enjoy is to glorify. In commanding us to glorify Him, God is inviting us to enjoy Him.[2]

Confession

Confession is another element of prayer. The New Testament word for confession is *homologeo,* "to say the same thing as." When you confess, you "say the same thing as" God says. You agree with God's truth about your sin and also about the truth of God's forgiveness. There are two types of confession: confession of sins and confession of faith.

- Confessing Sins

  When you confess your sins, you "say the same thing as God" about the wrong things you have said, thought, or done, as well as the right things you have neglected to say or do. Rather than hiding these things or making excuses for them, you bring them out in the open. You don't confess sins to inform God of them. He already knows. Instead, you confess sins to acknowledge that they have hurt your relationship with God. You ask for and receive God's forgiveness, knowing that "If we confess our sins, he is faithful and just and will forgive us our sins and purify us from all unrighteousness" (1 John 1: 9). You don't need to worry that you won't be

forgiven. Jesus' death and resurrection guarantee it.

Most likely, confession of sins will not be a very prominent part of your group's prayer life. It requires an extremely high level of trust, and most Christians handle this need in other ways. This kind of confession might happen, though, when a major conflict has occurred in the group, or when someone has done something to hurt another group member (such as breaking confidentiality). It might also happen when a person feels very guilty about a personal problem and decides to share that with the group. In such a case, a prayer of confession might be very healing. Of course, the group should never require, badger, or intimidate anyone into confession. When group members confess sins, the rest of the group needs to remind them that God forgives our sins because of Jesus.

- Confessing Faith

  When you confess your faith you "say the same as God" about what God is like and about what God does. You express your trust that God will care for you and for others in your group during difficult times because God has promised to do so. In your prayers you remember Jesus' words about the Father's care and you entrust yourself and all that is important to you into God's keeping. Confessing faith means viewing the world and your life through the lens of God's trustworthy promises.

Thanksgiving

Adoration and confession flow naturally into thanksgiving. You thank God for who he is, what he has done, and what he has given you, especially for forgiveness and for making you his child. Most of all, you thank God for his Son Jesus.

Thanksgiving is a good prayer habit to develop. It's easy to forget to take time to thank God for what he has done. Saying "thank you" for both big and little things can fill your heart with joy. Regular thanksgiving also reminds you that God has given you everything you have. This helps you to trust that God will continue to supply all your needs.

Lament

A lament is a prayer that comes out of deep suffering. It expresses pain, sorrow, anxiety, fear, frustration, and even anger. (See the Old Testament book of Lamentations for examples.) Many of the psalms are also laments, notably Psalms 22, 28, 38, and 55.

Such prayers often help those who suffer as they pour out their hearts to God. They can pray in this way knowing that God hears them and has compassion for them. Often, such sufferers receive new strength to bear their burdens.

Sometimes people hesitate to pray in this way. They fear that God will become angry with them or not want to listen to their complaints. Yet Jesus himself prayed in this way on the cross, quoting Psalm 22. Others fear that the rest of the group will question their faith if they pray in this way, although some of God's greatest servants have done so, including Moses, David, Elijah, and Job. As a ChristCare Group Leader, you can encourage group members to try this kind of prayer by modeling it for them.

The prayer of suffering frequently moves into other kinds of prayer, especially supplication and confession. Even the great psalm of suffering, Psalm 22, which begins "My God, my God, why have you forsaken me?," ultimately moves through suffering into praise and thanksgiving. It is likely that your group members will also find God's peace through laments and move through their pain to a renewed sense of God's love and mercy.

Petition

People often think of prayer as petitionary (also called supplication). In petitionary prayer, you come before God to make requests simply and trustingly, as a child asks a parent. You can be sure that God will listen and respond in the way that's best for you. Jesus said:

> "Is there anyone among you who, if your child asks for bread, will give a stone? Or if the child asks for a fish, will give a snake? If you then, who are evil, know how to give good gifts to your children, how much more will your Father in heaven give good things to those who ask him!" (Matthew 7:9–11 NRSV).

ChristCare Group members may sometimes feel embarrassed or self-conscious when asking God for certain requests. They may worry that their requests are not "spiritual" enough, or that their needs are too minor to bother God with. If group members express such concerns, help them see that nothing is too small or mundane to be brought to God in prayer. Jesus said that God knows every strand of hair on our heads (Matthew 10:30). In addition, when Jesus taught his disciples to pray,

he included a supplication for daily bread, a reference to our everyday, practical needs (Matthew 6:11).

Petitionary prayer includes intercessory prayer, which is prayer for others' needs. You and your ChristCare Group will pray for one another, for congregation and community members, and for friends, relatives, and many others. Intercessory prayer can flow out of your community building and care time. You can even pause during check-in time to pray about particular concerns group members share. Bringing one another's needs before God is a powerful way to care.

There are many other kinds of prayer, but these are the ones you will see most often in your ChristCare Group. Keep in mind that confidentiality applies just as strongly to prayer as to anything else said in the group meeting. Many things may be said in prayer that group members would not want repeated outside the group for any reason. Be sure that group members understand that, if they wish to place a certain request on a congregational prayer chain or make it public in some other way, they must always ask the person for permission.

B. What Is Worship?

When Christians think of worship, they most often envision the congregation's weekly worship service. That is an important part of worship, but worship is even more. Worship includes singing, praying, praising, listening, meditating, and hearing or reading about all God has done. Worship can take place at church, in a ChristCare Group, as a family, or even alone. The Scriptures say that every time we respond to God with love and obedience—that is worship.

Worship in the Bible

Worship is a major topic in the Scriptures. It is one of the most important ways people respond to God.

There are many elements of worship in the Old Testament. Worship in Israel consisted of offering various kinds of sacrifices to God, burning incense, and prayers. God instructed Moses about how the Israelites were to worship, including the different kinds of offerings, ceremonies for holidays, how to build the worship area, and even details about what colors the curtains should be (Exodus 26:1). King David made music an important part of worship, using professional singers and instrumentalists. King Solomon built a magnificent temple that was the center of the nation's worship.

In the New Testament, we see the child Jesus worshiping with his parents at the temple, and also attending the synagogue (Luke 2:41–42, 46; Luke 4:16). As an adult, Jesus was often in the temple, and also worshiped with his disciples when they celebrated the Passover together. The new church in the book of Acts worshiped every day, both at the temple and at home:

> Every day they continued to meet together in the temple courts. They broke bread in their homes and ate together with glad and sincere hearts, praising God and enjoying the favor of all the people (Acts 2:46–47).

The book of Revelation pictures heaven as a . place of continual worship, singing and praise. Those who are in God's presence are so filled with joy that they continually break into songs of praise and thanksgiving, throwing themselves down in front of God's throne. The angels also praise God, as we see from Isaiah 6:2–3 (NRSV): "Seraphs were in attendance above [God]; . . . one called to another and said, 'Holy, holy, holy is the LORD of hosts; the whole earth is full of his glory.'"

More Than Just Ceremonies
Of course, worship is far more than just participating in ceremonies held at special locations. Jesus said, "'God is spirit, and his worshipers must worship in spirit and in truth'" (John 4:24). God wants much more from us than the worship we take part in at church services. He wants our entire lives to be worship.

Jesus spoke sternly to people who tried to separate worship from the rest of their lives, believing that as long as they fulfilled their ceremonial obligations, God wouldn't mind what they did in the rest of their lives. He said, "But go and learn what this means: 'I desire mercy, not sacrifice'" (Matthew 9:13). When Jesus said this, he was reiterating a theme from the Old Testament prophets, who reminded people that real worship requires everyday obedience to the will of God:

> Away with the noise of your songs!
>   I will not listen to the music of your
>   harps.
> But let justice roll on like a river,
>   righteousness like a never-failing
>   stream (Amos 5:23–24).

The apostle Paul summed up this biblical idea of worship influencing the Christian's entire life:

> I appeal to you therefore, brothers and sisters, by the mercies of God, to present your bodies as a living sacrifice, holy and acceptable to God, which is your spiritual worship. Do not be conformed to this world, but be transformed by the renewing of your minds, so that you may discern what is the will of God—what is good and acceptable and perfect (Romans 12:1–2 NRSV).

Biblical Worship in ChristCare Groups
Since the Bible makes such a point of connecting worship to the rest of our lives, ChristCare Groups need to find ways to do so also. Special times of worship in ChristCare Groups should be an integral part of group members' overall lives of service and worship. Helping group members make this connection is one challenge that ChristCare Group Leaders face.

Just as the Scriptures show many different ways of worshiping God, so ChristCare Groups may worship in many different ways. The point is always to express the praise and thanks that God deserves from us. Below you'll learn about many different ways of worshiping that you can use in your ChristCare Group.

III. First Steps in Prayer and Worship
This section explains how you can teach group members to pray aloud and offers suggestions for beginning worship activities. As mentioned earlier, this material will be most helpful for groups that have never learned to pray or worship together. But even if your group is very comfortable praying aloud and worshiping as a group, you can still use this material to teach newcomers who may need help.

A. Why Is It So Difficult for Some Groups?
Many groups, especially new ones, have difficulty praying and worshiping together. They may hesitate to pray aloud or to sing together. They may be uncomfortable with any worship activity that requires active participation. Why is this so? There may be several reasons.

First, prayer and worship are very intimate activities. When we pray, we come face to face with God. As far as possible, we take off the "masks" that we wear in public and face God honestly, offering him the truth about ourselves. This is often much easier to do either when alone or in a large crowd, where no one is likely to notice what you are doing. But people may become self-conscious about their words or actions in a small group setting. For this reason, ChristCare Groups need to develop a high level of trust and intimacy in order for group members to pray or worship on more than a superficial level. This is yet another way that community building pays off.

Second, there are some groups of people who are naturally more reserved, for cultural or social reasons. Such groups can certainly learn to pray and worship together, but they will probably need more teaching and encouragement because this kind of expression is new to them. As they do learn to pray and worship together, members often come to find group prayer and worship a very moving, blessed experience.

Finally, there is the obvious problem: many people just don't know how to pray or worship together. They have never been taught. The ChristCare Group is an ideal place for people to learn to pray aloud, even for the first time. It is also a place where group members can try out different ways of prayer and worship than those with which they are familiar.

B. What You Can Do to Make It Easier

As a ChristCare Group Leader, there are a few things you can do to make it easier for your group members to pray and worship together.

Get to Know Your Group Well

The first is to get to know your group well. Find out with what they feel comfortable. Have most of the group members prayed aloud before? Do they enjoy singing, or does that make them feel self-conscious? Reflect on your group's past worship experiences, together and in other settings (such as the congregation). With which kind of worship are they most familiar? What kind of worship do they most enjoy? Thinking about these kinds of questions will give you ideas about where to start.

Take a few minutes at one of your first ChristCare Group meetings to find out what group members think and feel about group prayer. You might draw a scale like the one below on a sheet of paper and make photocopies to hand out. Ask each group member to mark the place on the graph that

fits him or her best. Then, when you collect and look over the sheets later, you will have a much better idea of your group's knowledge, abilities, and feelings about prayer.

Getting to know your group requires time and attention. Never assume that you know where everyone is coming from. You may be surprised at what you find out about group members! Some of them may enjoy worship styles that are very different from those the rest of the group is used to. Others may have difficulties with prayer or worship that have never occurred to you. Take time to discuss prayer and worship with your group, and listen carefully to what they say.

Build Community and Trust

Building community and trust in your ChristCare Group is key to developing a good worship and prayer life. You've learned about building community in the module titled "Building Community in Your ChristCare Group." As you use those insights and techniques with your group, you will be paving the way for your group's prayer and worship.

Take Small Steps

Another thing you can do to make prayer and worship easier for your group is to take small steps. Start with an activity everyone can do. Try to make everyone as comfortable as possible. Later, you can gradually add new elements to prayer and worship, as people gain confidence.

Never throw people "into the deep end." For example, if most of your group members have never prayed aloud, don't plan a half-hour period of spontaneous prayer aloud for your first meeting. In the same way, it's probably not wise to begin with difficult hymns or complicated musical arrangements if your group lacks trained singers or musicians.

C. How to Begin Group Prayer and Worship

How can you begin group prayer and worship? Beginning on the next page are some ideas.

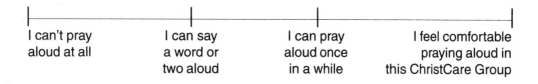

| I can't pray aloud at all | I can say a word or two aloud | I can pray aloud once in a while | I feel comfortable praying aloud in this ChristCare Group |

Start with a Circle Prayer

The circle prayer is probably the most common form of prayer used in small groups, and one of the easiest to learn. Group members stand or sit in a circle. One person (not necessarily the group leader) is responsible for beginning and ending the prayer. Each group member prays in turn, going around the circle to the right (or left). When the last person has prayed, the prayer leader closes for the group.

If you choose this way of praying, explain the format to group members ahead of time. Tell them also that anyone who does not wish to pray aloud should simply say "Thank you, God," and the next person will know it's his or her turn. Don't be surprised if a lot of people choose to pass during your first few meetings. Don't worry—as they come to realize there's nothing to be afraid of, they will eventually try praying aloud also.

Make sure that each group member understands that praying aloud is not a mandatory activity, and that no one will be embarrassed or forced into praying. If you notice any group member putting pressure on others to participate, gently but firmly put a stop to it. For example, if Dean says, "Mary, you always pass. I think you should try it this time," you might say to him, "Let's allow Mary to make that decision herself. There's nothing wrong with praying silently if that's what a person is comfortable with." It also helps to remind your group once in a while about the "passing" rule, just to keep it fresh in group members' minds.

You can add variations to the circle prayer after your group is used to it. For instance, you might say, "Next week when we have circle prayer, I'd like everyone to say one specific thing you're thankful to God for." You can use different prayer topics each week, or simply ask people to pray for whatever is in their hearts. You might also ask for prayer requests before beginning.

Pray often. As with any other activity, the more people pray, the more comfortable they become with it. You'll probably have a special prayer time during each group meeting, but you don't have to limit your praying to that time. For instance, a group member might share a serious concern during community building and care. Your group can stop right then and pray for God's active care in that situation, either by using a circle format or by asking one person to lead the prayer. When you pray together at such times, your group realizes

that prayer is a normal part of life and can be done at any time under any circumstances.

Use Simple Music

Just as with prayer, you will want to start simply in this area of worship. Music is probably the worship element easiest for beginners. Choose one or two familiar songs or hymns to use with your group. You might ask people for their favorites, or use ones that they are very familiar with from congregational worship. Try to avoid songs that are difficult to sing or require complicated arrangements (for example, a song sung as a round or in parts).

Group members may have different tastes in music. For example, you may have some group members who prefer praise choruses while others enjoy traditional hymns. Consider this situation an invitation for the group members to show love to one another by willingly giving up part of their own preferences. You might compromise by having one praise song and one traditional hymn, so that everyone has one thing he or she enjoys.

What about accompaniment? If your group includes people who play musical instruments well, ask them to play for the group. If this is not a possibility, sing without accompaniment or sing along with cassette tapes. There are audiotapes and compact discs available on the market that allow you to play just the music to a hymn or song, allowing your group to sing along. There are even some Christian music videotapes that are done karaoke-style, giving the words on screen so that everyone can sing. Christian bookstores and catalogues are good places to look for these resources.

Model Prayer and Worship

Whenever you pray or worship in your group, remember to be a model. Others will look to your example as they learn to pray and worship. If you participate actively, they will too. If you are enthusiastic and interested, they will probably be too.

Being a model begins with your life outside the group meeting. If you pray regularly yourself, you will be able to lead the group's prayer much more effectively. If you regularly worship God in the congregation and elsewhere and seek to know him better, you will communicate that desire to your group. "You can't give what you haven't got," as the saying goes.

Of course, this doesn't mean your prayer and worship life must be perfect. Like most Christians, you'll probably have "off" days or weeks, or times when prayer and worship seem difficult, boring, or tiring. Don't give up! Instead, try to learn what God wants to teach you. Someday you can pass on what you've learned to others—including ChristCare Group members.

Within the group, your example will show others how they too can take part in worship and prayer. If you pray in very simple language and say only a sentence or two (at least in the first few meetings), then shy group members are encouraged to think, "It's not so hard. I could do that, too." After all, no one is going to criticize them when the group leader him- or herself has set the example of simple prayer! In the same way, if they hear you singing (even off-key), group members are more likely to try singing themselves.

Also help other group members model simple prayer. For instance, you might have a group member who prays such beautiful, elaborate prayers that other group members become intimidated. If you sense such a situation developing, talk with the gifted pray-er privately. Say something like, "Maureen, you seem so comfortable with prayer and always pray so beautifully. God has really gifted you. I was wondering if I could ask you to do something for the sake of some group members who are a bit shyer about praying aloud. Could you make your prayers a little simpler and shorter so they feel encouraged to try praying too? I'm trying to do this myself, and if you could join me, I think we could encourage some group members who aren't so used to prayer."

Be an Encourager

Be an encourager for your group's worship. Find successful aspects of it to affirm, including quality, enthusiasm, and effort. Your encouragement will help build your group's confidence.

As your group becomes comfortable with these first steps in prayer and worship, you will want to start thinking about moving ahead. The section below will describe some next steps you can take, and how to choose the ones that are right for your group.

IV. Moving Ahead in Prayer and Worship

A. Many Different Ways to Pray and Worship

Prayer and worship are what people were made for and can be as individual as each person. Every ChristCare Group worships in ways that reflect its members' needs, backgrounds, experiences, and hopes. The following worship experiences of several ChristCare Groups offer some examples. Notice how each experience is unique.

- Fifteen minutes before the end of the meeting, Alan picks up a copy of his denomination's prayer book from under his chair. "Tonight I thought we'd use the service for evening prayer on page 64," he says. "Since Judy is such a strong singer, she's going to chant the leader's parts, and the rest of us will sing the responses. Tom is going to lead the responsive prayer on page 70. Does anyone have a favorite hymn we could sing?" Lisa turns on the keyboard, and they start together.

- Barbara's group moves naturally into prayer as the group's check-in time ends. Standing in a circle and holding hands, they pray for the needs they have just heard about and give thanks for all the good things God has given them. Barbara starts by praying, "Lord, we thank you for bringing us together tonight. We have much to ask you, and much more for which to thank you." After a moment of silence, Marty speaks up from across the circle: "Lord, thank you that Nola's hospital tests were all right. Please comfort her during her recovery." Peter adds, "Also help her family to adjust to her new needs at home." A few seconds later, Ruth begins to pray about Barbara's job hunting. About ten minutes later, when the silence is long enough that Barbara believes no one else has anything to say, she closes the prayer by saying, "Amen."

The group members sit down and continue worshiping by singing along with a cassette tape of contemporary praise songs. Then they move into Biblical Equipping.

- Another group has planned a special time of worship for this week. Instead of meeting at their usual place, this week they are meeting at Joanne's house. As group members arrive, they sit at a large table, decorated with flowers and lit candles. Wonderful smells come from the kitchen, where Marie and Lucas are preparing dinner. Several group members bring cassette tapes of Christian music, which plays softly during the meal. Then at the end of dinner, the group celebrates the Lord's Supper under the leadership of Pastor John, who is visiting their group this night.

- Ed's group has been experimenting with silence as a time of worship. Group members have agreed that they will not talk once everyone has arrived and the group meeting has begun. A couple of people open their Bibles and read silently; others appear to be praying or thinking. One or two have shut their eyes. After ten minutes, Ed breaks the silence by leading the group in a simple prayer of thanks, asking God to remain with them during the rest of the meeting. Then they begin check-in time.

- Francine has a group of people who love to sing—loudly! Everyone has a favorite song or hymn, usually one he or she memorized while growing up. So they often sing these songs for worship. Since Dan is a gifted guitar player, he accompanies them. These group members usually end their times of worship with a circle prayer.

- First Church has an annual weekend retreat for their ChristCare Groups at a campground 40 minutes away. There, small groups can pray, worship, and build community more intensely. Gina and Harry's group has planned a special worship time for their last morning together. During breakfast, Sam, Tina, and Val have been busy preparing a worship place. They have chosen a small clearing where the trees arch overhead and form a beautiful natural roof. They have set up the chairs in a semicircle and placed a table in front of the chairs. Val placed on the table a wicker basket and a cross made from evergreen branches. Sam made sure there were enough songbooks, pencils, and paper. Then everything was ready.

  After breakfast, the whole group worshiped together in the prepared place. At a special point in their worship, everyone took five minutes to write down a prayer of confession, request, or thanksgiving to God. Then each person came forward to lay his or her folded paper in front of the cross. After the worship, they burned their written prayers.

- Inez's group is interested in Scripture-based prayer. Since the group is currently studying the book of Psalms, tonight they begin their worship by reading Psalm 103, with the men and women alternating verses. After a short time of silence for meditation, one member prays aloud a prayer that he has found based on this psalm. Then group members take turns praying aloud. The group ends worship with a song of praise.

As you can see, there are many different ways to pray and worship, and each ChristCare Group will be unique in the ways it chooses. Some formats, styles, or elements of prayer and worship will be more meaningful to one group than to another. Below you'll learn how to put together a prayer and worship experience that fits your group.

Supplement A contains a "Prayer and Worship Planning Sheet" that will be very helpful to you as you plan. It gives you a place to write your chosen theme as well as room for each of the prayer and worship activities you plan. Using this sheet will help you keep everything organized and make sure nothing gets overlooked. You can get additional copies of the Prayer and Worship Planning Sheet from your Equipper. Take a moment to look over the Prayer and Worship Planning Sheet before you continue with your reading.

B. Choosing a Prayer and Worship Theme

Usually you will start by choosing a theme for your worship experience. (There is a place on the Prayer and Worship Planning Sheet for you to write your chosen theme.) When you choose a theme, consider what is going on in your group:

- the Biblical Equipping topic;
- members' continuing concerns or life situations;
- areas in which your group needs to grow;
- how group members relate to one another; and
- your group's mission.

When you choose a theme that relates to something in the rest of your group's life together, group members see even more clearly how prayer and worship impact every area of life, instead of being separate, rather irrelevant activities.

How does a theme grow out of your group's life together? Let's take Biblical Equipping for an example. If the Bible passage you are working with includes the verse "Give thanks in all circumstances, for this is God's will for you in Christ Jesus" (1 Thessalonians 5:18), you could plan worship around the theme of thanksgiving. You might pray together a psalm of thanksgiving, sing the praise song "Give Thanks," pray sentence prayers of thankfulness, or make a poster or banner that says, "Thank you, Jesus."

Similarly, there may be times when group members' life situations dictate a prayer and worship theme. For instance, when a group member's close friend or relative dies, your worship could focus on remembering God's promises of eternal life and God's presence during difficult times. Your group might pray for the group member and for the family and friends of the person who has died, asking that God comfort and be with them.

Focus Box 1 gives a short list of themes ChristCare Groups might use for prayer and worship. Several bullets are left blank for you to write in your own ideas.

FOCUS BOX 1

Some Themes for Prayer and Worship

- Thanksgiving
- Forgiveness
- Peace
- God's creation
- God's provision for our daily needs
- God as our Father
- God as King
- God's promises
- God's holiness
- Jesus' birth
- Jesus' death
- Jesus' resurrection
- Jesus' second coming
- The work of the Holy Spirit in our lives
- Healing of relationships
- God's gift of our families
- Beginning a new stage of life
- Loss and grief
- Trusting God in hard times
- Living as one body in Christ
- Service
- Evangelism
- Stewardship
- Being Jesus' disciple in our daily lives
- God's will for our missional service
-
-
-
-

C. Using Worship Resources

You will need to think about available prayer and worship resources. These resources fall into three categories: published resources, group members, and people outside the group, such as other ChristCare Group Leaders and Equippers.

Published resources include songbooks, hymnals, prayer books, and collections of litanies and responsive readings. Browse through the ChristCare Group Ministry library if your congregation has one. Look at your denomination's resources: Is there a songbook, hymnal, or prayer book you might use? Check Christian bookstores for other ideas. Stephen Ministries also makes available some worship resources for ChristCare Groups.

Don't forget audiotapes and compact discs. You can purchase some that are wholly instrumental so that your group can sing along. Others have professional singers but are set up in such a way that you can fade out the singing if you wish to and play only the accompaniment. Please see Supplement B for detailed information about using CDs or cassette tapes for worship.

Look at your people resources. For example, you may have group members who enjoy planning worship and would like to help you do so. Identify these people and approach them about serving in this way. As you will read in *Nuts & Bolts Issues for Small Group Leaders*, effective leaders share their leadership with group members. In this way, group members develop leadership skills, and the whole group benefits from their unique ministries. Worship is a perfect opportunity for this.

Consider your group members' gifts and abilities. Do you have a talented guitarist or pianist? Do some group members really enjoy praying aloud? Ask these group members to use their gifts to serve God and the group during worship. Think beyond the obvious. One of your group members might play the harp or saxophone. Another might have an extensive tape library of Christian music. Perhaps one of your group members writes poetry that could be used for worship. Another might be willing to deal with practical tasks such as collecting, transporting, and storing songbooks or setting up tape players or electronic keyboards (with extension cords and adapters). Still another person gifted in prayer might decide to pray every day specifically for God's blessing on your worship times. Each group member can contribute to your worship time in a great variety of ways.

People outside your group also may be able to help. Ask your Equippers and other ChristCare Group Leaders for prayer and worship ideas. They can tell you of ideas that worked well in other groups, as well as direct you to published worship resources such as songbooks and tapes. You might also talk to your congregation's pastor, music director, or youth director.

D. Exploring Alternative Ways of Prayer and Worship

Once you've chosen a theme and looked at available resources, it's time to think about the activities you want to include. You don't need to pray the same way every week or sing the same songs in the same way at every meeting. Add a little variety. Sometimes a little "stretching" helps people come to know God in a different or deeper way. This section offers you many different formats and approaches to prayer and worship.

The different forms of prayer and worship listed below are a smorgasbord. Some you will probably enjoy, and others may make you feel uncomfortable. Use what works for your group. These variations are listed to get you thinking, to help open up new possibilities for you and your group.

Using Different Formats

Spontaneous Prayer
In spontaneous prayer, one person is appointed to begin and one person to end the prayer time. Then, instead of going around a circle, allow people to pray whenever they feel ready to speak, beginning after the first person prays. People can pray more than once if they wish. After a long silence indicates everyone has finished, the person appointed ends with a final prayer.

One Person Prays Aloud
Occasionally have one person pray aloud for the whole group while others pray silently. Usually you will do this after asking for prayer requests.

Sentence Prayer
Ask each group member to say a single-sentence prayer. Group members can pray as often as they like, but just one sentence at a time.

The Lord's Prayer with Festoons
Pray the Lord's Prayer with "festoons," as C. S. Lewis called them.[3] To do this, have one person slowly pray the Lord's Prayer aloud, pausing a minute between each request in the prayer. During the pause, group members pray their own short prayers based on that request. For example, when the leader prays "Give us this day our daily bread," one group member might use that time to thank God for the gift of a newly repaired heating system, while another asks God to provide money for her child's medical treatments.

Simultaneous Prayer
Have the entire group pray aloud simultaneously, without waiting to take turns. The resulting noise will be incomprehensible to anyone but God, but praying this way lets shy group members pray aloud without embarrassment. Figure out ahead of time a signal to indicate the end of prayer time.

Silent Prayer
Ask group members to pray silently for several minutes. You may invite group members to follow silent prayer by praying aloud.

Listening Prayer
Ask group members simply to listen to God during prayer, instead of speaking.

Printed Prayers
Vary your prayers every now and then by using outside sources. Some beautiful songs and poems can be used as prayers or as inspiration for prayers. Here are some specific ways to use printed prayers:

- Scriptural Prayer

  Pray part of the Scriptures aloud as a group. The Psalms are especially good for this. You might also try some of the New Testament prayers, such as Ephesians 1:17–19; Ephesians 3:14–21; or Colossians 1:9–14. You can pray a passage aloud as a whole group or you can divide the group into two parts and have each group take turns praying aloud one verse.

- Reading a Prayer Aloud Together

  Pray the words of a printed prayer, song, or hymn aloud together as a group. You might invite group members to bring copies of items for the group to pray together. Another possibility is to invite extemporary prayers based on the printed prayer after the group has read it aloud.

- Responsive Prayer

  Try responsive prayer. In this kind of praying, the prayer leader says one part of the prayer, and the rest of the group responds with the next part. The prayer continues this way until the end. You can also divide your group into two parts, with the two subgroups reading responsively. Many printed prayers and litanies are structured this way. Psalm 136 is a biblical example of antiphonal prayer.

- Prayer Services

  Use or adapt a prayer service or litany from your denomination's hymnal or prayer book. If your denomination has daily services, such as matins or vespers, you might use those.

Longer Times of Prayer and Worship
Once in a while, devote extra time—half a meeting or more—to prayer and worship. You might try several kinds of prayer during that time. You might also discuss a prayer topic, pray for a while, discuss a different topic, and then pray some more. Or experiment with forms of worship that take more time than your group usually has available.

Have a Different Worship Leader
If the same person usually leads worship at every meeting, have someone else do it one week.

Have Several Worship Leaders
Have several people lead worship, each concentrating on one particular area such as leading prayer, leading singing, or preparing the atmosphere for worship.

Try a New Musical Style
If your group always uses praise choruses, occasionally include a traditional hymn, and vice versa. Or try a musical form that comes from another culture (perhaps by listening to it on tape).

Change Your Worship Schedule
Rearrange the elements of your group's worship time. For example, if you always start with prayer, start with music instead.

Worship Earlier or Later in the Meeting
Change the worship time. If you normally worship at the end of your meetings, do it in the beginning or middle. Some groups intersperse their worship through the whole meeting, taking a few minutes for worship, then moving into Biblical Equipping, and then returning to worship.

Go to Another Place for Worship
Consider moving the group to another location for worship—a different room, a place outdoors, or even the sanctuary if you meet at the church.

Using Multisensory Approaches
God created us with marvelous senses that help us enjoy and discover the world. These same senses can help you and your group members enjoy and discover more about prayer and worship.

Singing a Prayer
Sing your prayers, using a favorite hymn, praise chorus, or liturgical piece set to music. Concentrate on the meaning of the words as you sing them to God.

Music While Praying
Play soft instrumental music in the background while people pray silently.

Praying in Different Postures
Try different physical positions for prayer. The Bible lists many of these, including kneeling, standing, and lying face down before God. Consider holding hands while you pray, if your group is comfortable with this.

Praying and Fasting
If your group is interested, try prayer combined with a short fast (for example, skipping one meal). The Bible records several incidents of fasting and prayer together (Daniel 9:2–3; 2 Samuel 12:16–23; Acts 13:2–3). Of course, it's important to remember that some people should not fast because of medical reasons (such as diabetes or pregnancy).

Using Incense with Prayer
Burn incense while you pray. Incense is a symbol for prayer found in Psalm 141:2, "May my prayer be set before you like incense," and also in Revelation 5:8.

Writing Prayers
Ask group members to write down their prayers, fold up the papers, and place them in a special place, such as at the foot of a cross. Later, these prayer papers can be burned or returned to their owners.

Occasionally you can use a powerful variation of this idea. Each person writes down a particular problem or sin with which he or she needs God's help or forgiveness and folds up the paper. At an appropriate time during group worship, each member comes forward and nails the prayer onto a wooden cross. (Again, preserve confidentiality by burning these unopened papers later.)

Prayer Diaries or Journals

Keep a group prayer journal. Record prayer requests and leave space to describe how and when God answered. Periodically, review the prayer journal with your group and give thanks together for how God has responded.

You can also ask group members to keep individual prayer diaries. A couple of times a year, ask them to bring in their diaries and share from them. They might share things such as how they have changed and grown as pray-ers, how they have seen prayers answered, and how their prayers have changed over time. Be sure group members have the freedom to choose not to share if their prayers are too personal or private.

Drawing Prayers

Have group members draw their prayers. Group members may decide whether to explain their drawings to the rest of the group. If you choose this way of praying, be sure to explain that you don't have to be able to draw well. What's important is finding some way to express your prayer. Even scribbles or doodles will do.

Imagination Prayer

Once in a while, encourage group members to pray by forming mental images. For example, if you are praying for healing in a broken relationship, picture Jesus joining the hands of the two people who need to be reconciled.

Practice Christian Meditation

Ask the group members to sit quietly and contemplate one aspect of God's character, of his work, or of their relationship with him. For example, around Christmas you might ask them to think about the birth of Christ. Group members may close their eyes if they wish. Do this for several minutes.

Use Poetry in Worship

Ask a group member to read a poem aloud, either one that he or she has written or a published poem. Excellent devotional poetry has been written by John Donne, George Herbert, Robert Southwell, Francis Thompson, Edward Taylor, Gerard Manley Hopkins, Sidney Lanier, and T. S. Eliot.

Use Movement While You Sing

Encourage group members to clap their hands, raise their arms, or stamp their feet while you sing together.

Use Unusual Musical Instruments

Use tambourines, drums, or other instruments that anyone can play during your singing.

Celebrate the Lord's Supper Together

This can be a very moving experience for group members. Be sure to stay within your church's customs and guidelines.

Draw an Offering

Ask group members to think about one area of their lives that they would like to offer to God. Then ask them to draw a picture representing it.

Find an Offering

Ask group members to go outside and "find" something to offer to God — a pine cone, flowers, or an unusual stone. You might pile these at the bottom of a cross or on a homemade altar.

Use Responsive Readings

Responsive readings are two-part readings in which one person (or more) reads the first part, and the rest of the group answers with the second. Many denominations print these in their worship books. Or you might choose a favorite passage from the Bible to read aloud in this way, such as Genesis 1, 1 Corinthians 13, or one of the psalms.

Use a Creed

Have your group repeat the Apostles' Creed or the Nicene Creed as a statement affirming to God and to one another the truths they believe.

Use a Litany

Use a printed litany or create your own as a group. You can do this by asking everyone to find his or her favorite Bible verse dealing with a particular theme— for example, God's compassion. Also choose an appropriate refrain such as "Lord, have mercy," "Lord, we thank you," or yet another, very short verse on the topic. After everyone has found a verse, go around the circle asking each person to read his or her verse aloud. After each reader finishes, have the whole group repeat the refrain in unison.

Use a Blessing

At the end of your worship time together, have one person give a blessing, perhaps one based on Scripture (2 Corinthians 13:13, 14; Philippians 4:7; Philemon 25; Revelation 22:21). Or have half of the group say it to the other half, and vice versa. Or sing one together as a group.

Leading with Care and Sensitivity

Whenever you choose a new activity or format, remember to consider your group members' needs and what they feel comfortable with. Don't move too quickly or bring in ideas that will shock group members because they're so far afield from what group members are used to. That defeats the whole purpose of prayer and worship together. If you're not sure whether to use a particular activity, talk to your group about it before you do it.

Remember that the purpose of all these different forms of worship is to honor and please God. It is unnecessary to try to convert the group to a more "correct" form of worship. You are not adding new elements to worship because they are intrinsically better, but rather because they may become a blessing to group members who have not previously encountered them before.

Keep in mind that your ChristCare Group's worship is part of your congregation's overall worship. Stay within congregation guidelines,

especially in areas like the Lord's Supper. Again, if you're in doubt, talk with your pastor or Equipper before trying something new.

E. Pulling It All Together

Let's suppose you've chosen a theme and decided on the formats and activities you want to use for prayer and worship. Now it's time to pull everything together.

On the Prayer and Worship Planning Sheet, there are two vertical columns labeled "When?" and "What?" In these columns, write the activities you intend to use in the order you will do them during the meeting. For example, if you intend to start the meeting with a prayer, put that first. Once you've listed all the activities in order, fill out the columns labeled "Led by whom?" and "Preparations." Focus Box 2 below shows a sample of what your finished sheet might look like, at least in part.

As you look over your Prayer and Worship Planning Sheet, also think about whether your

---

FOCUS BOX 2

Sample Prayer and Worship Planning Sheet

Date: Wednesday, May 5

Theme: "Thanking God"

What to include: Atmosphere, music, prayer, responsive reading or litany, silence, other

When?	What?	Led by whom?	Preparations
Before meeting	atmosphere: soft devotional music playing, small standing cross on table	I will set up	Lee Ann will bring tape, tape recorder and music
Beginning of meeting	Singing: "We Thank the Lord"	John on electronic keyboard	John will bring his keyboard and adapter
After check-in time	Spontaneous prayer	Started and ended by Carl	

[*The planning sheet would continue here.*]

group's prayer and worship needs balance. For example, if your group's prayer and worship always centers around the spoken word, consider using something that appeals to another sense, such as touch. If your group's worship is usually quite complicated, add something very simple. If your group tends to do everything in worship together (such as always singing and speaking in unison), think about ways to split the group up now and then. For example, you might have four people sing one verse, while the other four sing the next. Or perhaps you could ask one group member to pray aloud while the rest pray silently. Your aim is to maintain a rough balance over time—not necessarily within every single group meeting. Again, be guided by your group's needs.

Check your plans to see if they stay within the time constraints of the group meeting. For example, if you have a 90-minute group meeting and you usually pray and worship together for 20 minutes, make sure that whatever you plan will fit comfortably into that time. Never plan so much that you have to hurry through prayer and worship in order to get it all in. That tends to destroy the very prayer and worship you are trying to facilitate.

Finally, look at the column labeled "Preparations" and make any necessary arrangements well in advance of the meeting. For example, if you plan to have one member playing a keyboard, contact him or her and talk about the songs you might sing so he or she can get the sheet music together. Make sure the keyboard will get to your meeting location. Find out if it will require an adapter to fit into the meeting room's electrical outlet.

F. Staying Flexible

Be prepared to change your prayer and worship plans if something unexpected happens. Equipment failure, a musician's or prayer leader's illness, or a sudden crisis in a group member's life may make changing plans necessary. Accept the Holy Spirit's leading, even when it draws you away from your original plans.

For example, imagine that you have planned group worship around the theme of thanksgiving, with a responsive reading from Psalm 136 and lots of upbeat, joyful music. You have planned this for the end of the group meeting. Then one of your group members comes in late and clearly upset. There's a chance that his son in another state may have cancer, but the doctor isn't sure yet and needs to run more tests. You would certainly change your plans for prayer and worship in order to show care for that

member. For example, you might sing hymns that ask for God's help and read a psalm that expresses trust in God during dark times. Or the group might move immediately into prayer and postpone other meeting activities, or cancel them altogether.

G. Using Feedback

Regularly ask ChristCare Group members for their comments about group worship, especially after trying something new. In this way you can make sure that the group's prayer and worship continue to meet group members' needs. Use what you learn as you plan future prayer and worship.

V. Common Questions about Prayer and Worship

This section includes some common questions, with answers, about ChristCare Group prayer and worship.

Q. *Most of my group is very comfortable with prayer, but there are one or two members who have never prayed aloud at all. What should I do?*

A. Don't pressure them to pray aloud or allow other group members to do so. Whether you use a circle prayer, spontaneous prayer, or something else, make sure there is a way for them to "pass" without being embarrassed.

Offer (privately) to teach them how to pray aloud. They may have never learned how. Chapter 16 of *Me, an Evangelist? Every Christian's Guide to Caring Evangelism* has some pointers on how to teach a person to pray aloud.

Set the example of simplicity in your own prayers. For example, if you normally pray in beautiful phrases or lengthy paragraphs, tone it down a bit. Modeling a simple, short, clear prayer style will encourage group members to try it themselves.

Some people who are nervous about praying in large groups are able to do so with a single partner. Consider asking the group to break into twosomes for prayer. You might take one of these group members as your own partner.

Q. *Some of my group members like very traditional forms of worship, and others prefer contemporary worship. What should I do?*

A. Look at such situations as one more opportunity for group members to grow in understanding and care. Explain to group members that you understand their different preferences and that, as a group, you will all care for the others by including everyone's favorite choices at different times.

If six people enjoy singing praise choruses while two members prefer traditional hymns, start with one and end with the other. Or sing one of each kind during your worship time. If some in the group like to raise their hands while singing but others are uncomfortable with that, encourage all to do what makes them feel comfortable without judging one another.

Q. We have problems with music during worship. I can't carry a tune in a basket, the rest of the group isn't much better, and no one can play a musical instrument. Should we just skip music?

A. There are many possible solutions to music problems. For example, an un-musical ChristCare Group Leader might delegate this part of group worship to a more musically talented group member. This would then become the group member's form of ministry. A group without instrumentalists might choose to sing a cappella or to sing along with cassette tapes. Finally, a group that is constantly off-key might discuss whether this is truly a problem. It is right to want to offer God the best possible worship—but your love and thankfulness to God is more important than being on-key.

Q. Our worship is scheduled at the end of our group meeting, and somehow we always run out of time. How can we avoid this?

A. Try scheduling worship earlier in your meeting, perhaps immediately following community building and care. If this is impossible, take a look at what's causing the problem. Are people taking longer than you expected to share about their lives? Are the Biblical Equipping sessions going overtime, and if so, why? Is the meeting itself getting started late? Identifying the particular problem will often suggest solutions. For example, if you find that you're running late because group members get so involved in the Biblical Equipping discussion, you might ask someone to announce worship time. This can be handled with humor (you might give this person a red stop sign to wave). Remember that worship is important because it's group members' time to encounter God in a direct, intimate way. Keep trying until you find a solution.

Q. A couple of our members are very shy and don't feel comfortable joining in the worship. How can I help them get more involved?

A. There are several steps you can take to help shy members participate in group worship. First, talk privately with the person to understand his or her feelings better. Is it simply a case of shyness? Does the person come out of a worship background that is very different from that of the rest of the group? Does the person suffer from hearing loss, tone deafness, or reading difficulties? Has the person never learned to pray aloud?

Your second step will depend on the answers you received in step one. If the person is simply very shy, accept it. His or her silent worship is just as acceptable to God as that of a louder group member. See if you can help alleviate problems caused by hearing loss or vision trouble. If the person has never learned to pray aloud, teach him or her (if he or she is willing) by talking to him or her personally.

VI. Getting Ready for the In-Class Session

During the in-class session, you will learn about prayer and worship in a very experiential way. Be sure to have your ten-minute prayer or worship service ready. Several group members will have the chance to present their prayer and worship experiences during this session.

As you prepare for the in-class session, take a moment to think about this question: Do you know of any songbooks, prayer books, cassette tapes or compact discs, books of poetry, or any other published resources that ChristCare Group Leaders could use as they plan prayer and worship? If so, bring them to the in-class session.

ENDNOTES

1. Richard J. Foster, *Prayer* (New York: Harper Collins Publishers, 1992), page 7.

2. C. S. Lewis, *Reflections on the Psalms* (New York: Harcourt, Brace & World, Inc., 1958), pages 96–97.

3. C. S. Lewis, *Letters to Malcolm: Chiefly on Prayer* (San Diego: Harcourt Brace & Company, 1992).

ChrisӨare Series

Supplement A

Prayer and Worship
Planning Sheet

Date: _____

Theme: _____

What to include: Atmosphere, music, prayer, responsive reading or litany, silence, other

When?	What?	Led by whom?	Preparations

ChrisⒸare Series

Supplement B

Using CDs or Cassette Tapes for Worship

Introduction

Worship is one of the most memorable aspects of small group life. Singing is a big part of worship—but it can be difficult without accompaniment. Many small groups do not have a piano- or guitar-playing member to accompany their singing. Worship CDs or cassette tapes provide these groups an exciting alternative.

Worship CDs and Tapes

Some of the best small group worship resources available come from Brentwood Music. They are called *America's 25 Favorite Praise and Worship Choruses* (Volumes 1 and 2) and *America's 25 Favorite Hymns*. In addition, Brentwood Music has an accompaniment book called *America's 200 Favorite Praise and Worship Choruses and Hymns,* which contains words, piano accompaniments and guitar chords.

These worship CDs and tapes are available in both stereo and split-track format. Split-track format places the accompaniment on one channel and the singing on the other channel. That way you can eliminate the singing (by using the balance knob), and the group can sing with the accompaniment only.

Check your local Christian bookstore to learn about these and other worship CDs and tapes available for purchase.

The Right Equipment

The right equipment can greatly enhance the use of tapes and CDs in worship.

See the chart on the next page for information about features commonly found on such equipment. You may want to consult this chart when purchasing equipment.

Preparing for Worship

It is very important to prepare for worship when using a CD or tape. Here are two important steps:

1. Plan the worship experience using "The Prayer and Worship Planning Sheet" (I.A.4.[24]). Write on the planning sheet the songs you plan to use. If you have a programmable CD player, set it up with the songs you choose.

2. Practice the songs, using the worship book that accompanies the CD or tape you are using, until you are comfortable singing them. Once you're comfortable with the songs, eliminate some or all of the voices and sing only with the musical accompaniment. Practice until you feel confident enough to lead the group in the songs.

Feature	With Feature	Without Feature
Portability	Able to use the stereo anywhere the small group meets, providing flexibility in choosing locations.	Limited to the room where the stereo is set up.
Balance Knob	Able to use split-track CD or tape with the accompaniment on one channel and the voice on the other channel. This allows you to fade out as much of the voice as you want, enhancing the worship experience.	Limited to hearing both the music and voice all the time. Hint: If you plan to use a system without a balance knob, it is better to purchase the CD or tape in stereo, not split-track, format.
CD versus Tape Player	Able to move quickly between tracks (songs) on the CD	Tapes are limited to moving song-by-song in the order recorded.
Programmable CD	Able to pre-program the entire worship time into the CD. For example, you can set up the stereo to play the fifth track, then the first, then the eighth, etc.	Limited to going through the CD by manually advancing tracks.
Multi-CD Changer	Able to use several worship CDs for the same worship service.	Limited to one CD unless you change them manually.
Remote Control	Able to control the CD player from a distance.	Limited to controlling the CD player by sitting right next to it.

Prayer and Worship in ChristCare Groups

Outline and Focus Notes

Come, let us sing for joy to the LORD; let us shout aloud to the Rock of our salvation. Let us come before him with thanksgiving and extol him with music and song.

Psalm 95:1–2

1. Introduction to Prayer and Worship

2. Check-in and Prayer

3. Class Members' Prayer and Worship Experiences

4. Biblical Equipping: Worship at the Temple (2 Chronicles 3:1–5:14, selected verses)

FOCUS NOTE 1

Questions to Focus Sharing of Biblical Equipping Apart

- Share one insight that you've had as a result of your Biblical Equipping Apart this week.

- Describe one change in your life that you've committed to make as a result of your meditation on the Biblical Equipping passage this week.

- Tell about a time when you've met God in a new way through Biblical Equipping Apart this week.

FOCUS NOTE 2

Worship at the Temple (2 Chronicles 3:1–5:14, selected verses)

Then Solomon began to build the temple of the LORD in Jerusalem on Mount Moriah . . .

He overlaid the inside with pure gold. He paneled the main hall with pine and covered it with fine gold and decorated it with palm tree and chain designs. He adorned the temple with precious stones. . . .

In the Most Holy Place he made a pair of sculptured cherubim and overlaid them with gold. . . . The wings of these cherubim extended twenty cubits [30 feet]. They stood on their feet, facing the main hall.

He made the curtain of blue, purple and crimson yarn and fine linen, with cherubim worked into it.

In the front of the temple he made two pillars . . .

He made a bronze altar . . . He made the Sea [a great water tank] of cast metal, circular in shape . . .

The Sea stood on twelve bulls, three facing north, three facing west, three facing south and three facing east. The Sea rested on top of them . . .

The priests then brought the ark of the LORD's covenant to its place in the inner sanctuary of the temple, the Most Holy Place, and put it beneath the wings of the cherubim. . . .

. . . All the Levites who were musicians . . . stood on the east side of the altar, dressed in fine linen and playing cymbals, harps and lyres. They were accompanied by 120 priests sounding trumpets. The trumpeters and

Focus Note 2 is continued on page 167.

singers joined in unison, as with one voice, to give praise and thanks to the Lord. Accompanied by trumpets, cymbals and other instruments, they raised their voices in praise to the Lord and sang:

> "He is good;
> his love endures forever."

Then the temple of the Lord was filled with a cloud, and the priests could not perform their service because of the cloud, for the glory of the Lord filled the temple of God.

FOCUS NOTE 3

Explore Questions

1. What do you think God's purpose was in having the temple builders create such a beautiful, multisensory environment for worship?

2. How do you think such an environment affected their worship?

3. How do you think the people felt when God's glory filled the temple?

FOCUS NOTE 4

Connect Questions

1. Have you ever had a worship experience where you felt God's glory enter the place where you were worshipping?

2. What could ChristCare Groups do to create a beautiful atmosphere for prayer and worship?

3. How might such an environment affect ChristCare worship?

---

5. Missional Service and Worship Leadership

FOCUS NOTE 5

Psalm 100

Shout for joy to the LORD, all the earth.
    Worship the LORD with gladness;
    come before him with joyful songs.
Know that the LORD is God.
    It is he who made us, and we are his;
    we are his people, the sheep of his pasture.

Enter his gates with thanksgiving
    and his courts with praise;
    give thanks to him and praise his name.
For the LORD is good and his love endures forever;
    his faithfulness continues through all generations.

Missional Service
by ChristCare Groups

Preclass Reading

"Instead, whoever wants to become great among you must be your servant, and whoever wants to be first must be your slave—just as the Son of Man did not come to be served, but to serve, and to give his life as a ransom for many."

Matthew 20:26–28

PRECLASS READING OUTLINE

I. What Is Missional Service?

A. Examples of Missional Service

Alan's group met weekly in Sharon and Ed's home. They chose to meet there because Sharon and Ed lived in a large apartment complex where there were many young professionals who were not connected with a church. Maggie also lived in the complex. She regularly put up posters telling the date, time, location, and discussion topic for group meetings. She also invited neighbors to attend group meetings whenever possible. Alan always prepared a simple Biblical Equipping session that dealt with the basics of the Christian faith. Over the past ten months the group had added five members, three of whom had already been baptized and joined the church.

When John and Marcia began their ChristCare Group, their primary aim had been to provide a place where couples could support one another and understand what the Bible had to say to them in their daily lives. As they listened to God's Word, it became clear to them that they also needed to find ways to serve others. For some time Jessica had been helping tutor young children who had difficulty learning. The school district no longer had funds to hire teachers to help these children. Several group members began going with Jessica to help tutor on Tuesday afternoons. When an election created an opportunity to vote for more support for the school district, several other group members carefully studied reports and statistics to make sure the school district used its funds well, then decided to campaign in favor of the tax increase for the schools.

8-PRE.pmd C: 09/01/1997 R: 02/16/2005

After Art heard the missionary from Africa speak about the many different needs at their mission hospital, he enthusiastically shared with his ChristCare Group what he had learned. They decided to support the mission hospital. Group members donated money to help purchase needed equipment and supplies, and they found ways to raise even more money. Ellen corresponded with the missionary in order to learn about specific prayer needs. She reported to the group, and every month or so they spent a large part of their meeting praying for critical needs at the mission. Ellen kept all the correspondence and information they had from the mission. When their group ended after several years, she passed the scrapbook on to another group who took over supporting the mission hospital.

The "Thursday Morning, 6:00 A.M. Group" was made up of six very busy people. Each of them worked at a demanding job and also made time to carry a major volunteer responsibility. Jan was a Sunday school teacher, Pete served as a volunteer for the community telephone "help line," Sondra organized and directed the congregation's annual Vacation Bible School, Vera served on the school board, Bob was a ChristCare Equipper, and Marlene, the ChristCare Group Leader, also served on the congregation's lay governing board. At group meetings they shared about their individual areas of service, prayed for one another, did Biblical Equipping to better understand God's will for their lives, and occasionally even held one another accountable for their areas of Christian service. The group's missional service was to support one another in their individual ministries.

About 20 members of First Church heard God calling them to form a new congregation in the inner city. Together with about 20 people who lived in the area, they started St. Philip's Congregation. As a congregation comprising people of several different races, they saw themselves as a witness to racial harmony and justice in their city. The ChristCare Group that Orrie led decided to support St. Philip's Congregation as its missional service. Members worshiped at First Church on Saturday afternoon so they could be at St. Philip's Congregation on Sunday mornings. They began holding their group meetings at the St. Philip's Congregation's building so people from that neighborhood could attend.

These are examples of how ChristCare Groups can engage in missional service. They represent only a small sample of the broad range of possible missional service opportunities for ChristCare Groups.

While it could be that no two ChristCare Groups will do missional service the same, each ChristCare Group needs to find some way to serve others beyond the group's membership. Helping the group do so will be one of your most important responsibilities as a ChristCare Group Leader.

B. The Definition of Missional Service

Missional service means reaching out with Christ's love to meet the needs of people outside the group.

There are three key aspects to this definition:

- **Reaching out with Christ's love.** Missional service is a way for groups to pass on to others the love they have received from God. The joy that group members find in loving Jesus and knowing of his love for them motivates them to serve. When groups reach out in missional service, they are being the body of Christ, touching others with his love.

- **Meeting needs.** ChristCare Groups can meet a wide variety of needs. God cares for people wholistically—physically, emotionally, spiritually, socially, and intellectually. ChristCare Groups also are called to care in some or all of these dimensions. ChristCare Groups serve Jesus by meeting the needs of those around them (see Matthew 25:31–46).

The Roman Catholic church divides missional service into two helpful categories: corporal (bodily) and spiritual works of mercy. Corporal works of mercy meet basic human needs such as feeding the hungry, sheltering the homeless, clothing the naked, visiting the sick and imprisoned, and burying the dead. Spiritual works of mercy include evangelizing, instructing people in the faith, advising about faith issues, consoling, and comforting.

- **Caring for those outside the group.** Missional service focuses on others' needs, not group members'. That certainly doesn't mean that group members don't provide care for one another. Yet they must also look beyond the group's boundary for service opportunities. Otherwise, the group can become selfish and self-serving—certainly not obedient to Jesus or faithful to his example.

C. Evangelism and Missional Service

Jesus' entire ministry was missional service. He fed the hungry, forgave sins, healed the sick, raised the dead, defended a helpless woman, gave sight to the blind, called people to repentance, and taught people how to live as trusting children of God. Everything Jesus did served to communicate the message he spoke from the very beginning of his ministry—"'The time has come . . . The kingdom of God is near. Repent and believe the good news!'" (Mark 1:15). Jesus' signs and miracles showed that the kingdom of God was right there. His acts of mercy showed how merciful God is. His teachings pointed people toward faith in his loving Father. Jesus came to turn people back toward God, and he did so through both word and deed.

While missional service takes many different forms, the final goal is always the same as Jesus'. Whether Christians serve in their congregations or their community, whether they do acts of mercy or communicate the gospel message, they always do so in order to show that the kingdom of God has come near and to invite people to repent and believe the gospel. Any missional service ChristCare Groups do is a kind of evangelism, and when ChristCare Groups do evangelism, that certainly is missional service.

It is possible for ChristCare Groups to fall into one of two traps in their missional service.

Service without Evangelism

There have been times when Christians were willing to give of themselves to serve others but were not willing ever to bring up Jesus' name. They believed their service to people's physical, emotional, or social needs was enough.

Such service is not enough. It misses the distinctively Christian insight that people also have spiritual needs—for forgiveness, hope, and eternal life. Service is certainly a way to show Christ's love to others and to earn the right to tell others about Jesus. Service that never mentions Jesus is incomplete.

Evangelism without Service

There have also been times when Christians assumed that all others need is to hear the gospel message, even if those to whom they preached lived in terrible conditions. There is a wealth of biblical evidence that this is an unchristian approach. Jesus is the prime example. His ministry was a complete mixture of words and deeds. James

writes, "Suppose a brother or sister is without clothes and daily food. If one of you says to him, 'Go, I wish you well; Keep warm and well fed,' but does nothing about his physical needs, what good is it? In the same way, faith by itself, if it is not accompanied by action, is dead" (James 2:15–17). Old Testament prophets railed against those who thought themselves religious but ignored the poor.

When people are cold, hungry, homeless, or in prison, evangelizing them must include helping meet their physical, emotional, and social needs. They will probably not be able to hear the good news about Jesus if they don't first see Christ's love tangibly lived out for them. If a person is hungry, help him or her find food, then find ways to share the gospel message.

II. Why Do Groups Need to Do Missional Service?

The biggest challenge ChristCare Group Leaders face in the area of missional service is motivating group members to serve. ChristCare Group Leaders must strongly believe in the importance of missional service and be able to communicate their enthusiasm for service to their groups.

A. A Theological Look at Missional Service

Missional service involves the following theological understandings.

Understanding God

God is love. Out of love he created everything that exists. God's greatest desire is to be in relationship with people—he gave his only Son to that end.

God loves all people, not just those of a certain race or status. He especially cares for those who cannot care for themselves, as the psalm in Focus Box 1 shows.

FOCUS BOX 1

Psalm 146

"[The Lord] upholds the cause of the oppressed;
   and gives food to the hungry.
The Lord sets prisoners free,
   the Lord gives sight to the blind,
the Lord lifts up those who are bowed down,
   the Lord loves the righteous.
The Lord watches over the alien
   and sustains the fatherless and the widow."
                                          Psalm 146:7–9

Understanding People

"God created humankind in his image, in the image of God he created them; male and female he created them" (Genesis 1:27 NRSV). All people are God's beloved creation. God cares for people because he loves us. People have rejected God and sinned against him, and they suffer the consequences of that rebellion. Nonetheless God continues to love and care for us.

ChristCare Groups care for people because they are all made in God's image. God doesn't withhold care from people because of their sin, and neither do ChristCare Groups.

Understanding Jesus

Jesus is God's only Son. He was crucified and resurrected so that our sins would be forgiven and so we could enjoy eternity with God as his beloved children.

Jesus told his disciples, "'As the Father has sent me, so I send you'" (John 20:21 NRSV). How did the Father send Jesus? The apostle Paul answers that question beautifully:

> Do nothing from selfish ambition or conceit, but in humility regard others as better than yourselves. Let each of you look not to your own interests, but to the interests of others. Let the same mind be in you that was in Christ Jesus, who, though he was in the form of God, did not regard equality with God as something to be exploited, but emptied himself, taking the form of a slave, being born in human likeness. And being found in human form, he humbled himself and became obedient to the point of death—even death on a cross (Philippians 2:3–8 NRSV).

Jesus is alive and active in us. That shows when we bring his love to people who are broken and lost.

Understanding Salvation

God doesn't care for people because we deserve it. God cares for us because of Jesus, crucified and resurrected. We don't earn salvation; we receive it as a gift. So ChristCare Groups care for others not because they deserve it, but because Jesus gave his life and calls us to follow him.

When God saves people he also transforms them. We can clearly see from James that good works will follow faith: "So faith by itself, if it has no works, is dead. But someone will say, 'You have faith and I have works.' Show me your faith apart from your works, and I by my works will show you my faith" (James 2:17–18 NRSV). As ChristCare Group members grow in faith, they will naturally reach out in service to others.

Understanding the Church

The church is the place where God gathers Christian people together so they can praise and glorify God, hear his word, receive his gracious gifts, grow in faith, and care for one another. The church is the launching pad for Christian service in the world.

Paul defined the church as "the body of Christ" (1 Corinthians 12:27). The church is a tool Jesus uses to act in the world. Jesus wants to reach out to the poor and needy; he wants to communicate the good news of salvation by grace through faith. He uses the church to do so.

ChristCare Groups are parts of the church. They don't replace the larger congregation, they participate in it—receiving the benefits God gives there and helping carry out the congregation's mission. In ChristCare Groups the Holy Spirit builds members' faith as they hear God's Word. Then the Spirit uses ChristCare Groups as small parts of the body of Christ, reaching out to do God's will through ChristCare Groups and their members.

B. Groups Exist to Minister beyond Themselves—and Suffer When They Don't

ChristCare Groups are not exclusive clubs. Members are called to minister: to God, to one another, to those outside the group, and to God's creation. Spend a few minutes thinking about the statement by Gareth Icenogle in Focus Box 2.

FOCUS BOX 2

The Journey Christ Desires for Small Groups

Christ desires to take each group on a journey, to travel together into the places and among the people where individuals alone would not dare venture. Small groups are exodus bands who are moving from the control of life's negative systems to be servants of freedom with the present Christ. Group leaders need to understand the fullness of a healthy small group model: from discipleship into mission, from safety into risk, from old ways into new ways. This is the model of Christ among the disciples. The group's journey inward to Christ and one another must become a journey outward into the world.[1]

There are often negative effects in a group that does not follow Jesus into missional service. A group that does not want to participate in missional service:

- is probably unhealthy or not experiencing spiritual growth;
- can become ingrown and insensitive to the wider world;
- can become self-protective and self-satisfied;
- avoids and withdraws from the congregation and the outside world;
- can develop an us-against-them mentality instead of rich involvement in life;
- does not advance group members' lives of discipleship.

As a ChristCare Group Leader you need to understand the reasons for missional service so well that you can explain them to others in your group. You also need to believe in missional service so strongly that you can pass on your enthusiasm and commitment to your group members. It may be easier just to focus on group members' needs and forget the rest of the world—but you know that such a choice would be unfaithful and harm your group. In your SEA Group you and other ChristCare Group Leaders will give and receive support and encouragement to lead your groups into missional service. You will also hold one another accountable for this aspect of your ministry when necessary.

III. What Is Involved in Missional Service?

FOCUS BOX 3

The Four Components of Missional Service

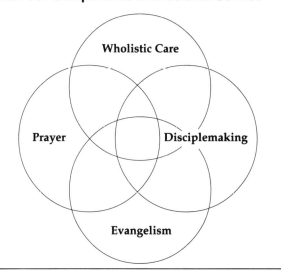

A. Four Components of Missional Service

Missional service involves four components, illustrated in Focus Box 3.

A group's missional service will usually include all four components, although some groups will give more emphasis to one or more of the components.

Prayer

Prayer will probably be part of a group's missional service. Group members will ask for God's guidance as they choose and carry out their missional service. Group members will also pray for those they serve. They not only want others to benefit from what they can do, they also want to ask God's blessings on those they serve.

Some groups may focus most of their missional service on praying for others outside the group. Such groups may spend half or more of their group meetings in prayer. Group members learn of others' needs and bring them to the group (without revealing confidential information). Groups may pray for missionaries' needs, for countries that need to hear the gospel, for community needs, for their nation's leaders, or for their congregation or denomination. Group members may also communicate prayer needs between meetings and commit themselves to daily intercession.

Wholistic Care

Missional service is defined as care for others, and Christian care is always for whole people. You can't care for one need without meeting the rest. There are two sides to this kind of missional service: social service and social action. The chart in Focus Box 4 shows the differences between them.

FOCUS BOX 4

Social Service	Social Action
Relieving human need	Removing the causes of human need
Philanthropic activity	Political and economic activity
Seeking to minister to individuals and families	Seeking to transform societal structures
Works of mercy	The quest for justice

Fully meeting people's needs may require both service and action. Think about the parable of the good Samaritan on the Jerusalem-Jericho road (Luke 10:30–35). The good Samaritan was deeply involved in missional service when he helped the wounded Jew at the side of the road. But what if the Jew's beating had not been an isolated incident? If the bandits had continued to wound and kill people on the road to Jericho, it would have been important to remove the cause of such human need. In this case it might have involved petitioning the authorities to do something about the bandits so that people would no longer be wounded and killed on the route.

There are a variety of ways groups can get involved in both service and action. Group members might work together at a food pantry, visit and pray with nursing home residents, or rehabilitate houses for homeless people. They might tackle one-time projects, such as cleaning up a park or a stream or providing summer recreational opportunities for underprivileged children. There are endless opportunities for this kind of service.

Groups can also become involved in social action to help remove causes of need. They may become involved in a neighborhood watch program or petition local, state, or national authorities about community problems. Groups may work politically to combat oppression or threats to life such as crime, abuse, or environmental issues.

Disciplemaking

Disciplemaking is at the heart of missional service. Every ChristCare Group will help members grow as Jesus' disciples. This equips group members to reach out with Christ's love and serve others.

Some groups will focus most or all of their energy on disciplemaking. The group may covenant for a period of time when their focus is completely on one another. This can be missional service if the group makes its covenant with the understanding that their inward focus is temporary, and that the end result will be that group members will be better able to serve others in Jesus' name.

ChristCare Group Leaders need to understand the danger here. Some groups may start off focusing on their own growth as disciples, fully intending to limit that emphasis to a specific period of time. After a while, however, they become so involved in themselves that they forget about the need to reach out to others. A group that chooses to focus on its own discipleship growth for a period of time needs to spell out clearly how long it will do so and to have a clear idea of the missional service to be done after that time is up. Every time the group recovenants, members need to ask themselves honestly if they are still doing what God wants them to be doing.

Evangelism

ChristCare Groups always need to help equip and support members for daily life evangelism. Sending members out as Christ's ambassadors into the workaday world is a powerful ministry of ChristCare Groups. You will learn more about this when you study session 22, Evangelism in and through ChristCare Groups.

Some groups will make evangelism their primary missional service focus. Group members will intentionally reach out to non-Christians and invite them to group meetings. Then the group meeting will be tailored to the visitors' needs. Some people who would never come to a regular church service may agree to visit a ChristCare Group. Then group members can demonstrate Christ's love through their care, talk about their lives of faith, share the truth about Jesus from the Scriptures, talk to God in prayer, and otherwise show what it means to be a Christian. The Holy Spirit will use such a witness to bring people to faith in Jesus.

B. Ways Groups Do Missional Service

Groups can do missional service in a wide variety of ways. You read about several of those ways in the examples at the beginning of this module. The method is not that important. What is important is that group members are reaching out to serve others in Jesus' name.

Most often ChristCare Groups do missional service as a group. They may do short-term, one-time projects or become involved in regular service that could last for years. They may work with other groups, with the entire congregation, with other Christian or community service organizations, or alone.

Frequently a group's missional service will include bringing new members into the group. The challenges of growing, bringing closure, and birthing new groups will be all the missional service some groups do. Members of such groups will give up some closeness and depth in order to reach out to others and involve them in the group.

IV. Leading Your ChristCare Group into Missional Service

Some ChristCare Groups will be ready to do missional service from the very beginning. Indeed, some groups will form primarily to do evangelism or some other missional service. Other ChristCare Groups will need to take some time to catch the vision and grow in faith until they are ready for service. Even for those groups, however, it is only a matter of time before missional service becomes a central part of their life together.

ChristCare Group Leaders need to lead their groups to a decision about missional service. There are six steps to take in leading your ChristCare Group into missional service:

1. Prepare

2. Investigate

3 Select

4. Plan

5. Carry out

6. Review

A. Step 1: Prepare

When you help your ChristCare Group prepare for missional service, you help them believe in the necessity and value of serving Jesus by serving others. You also make sure they are ready to go out and serve.

Jesus did not throw unprepared people into advanced ministry situations. Mark's Gospel tells us that Jesus "appointed twelve—designating them apostles—that they might be with him and that he might send them out to preach and to have authority to drive out demons" (Mark 3:14–15). Note the order of events:

- Jesus formed his small group (the 12 apostles).

- He helped them understand their calling by naming them apostles. The word *apostle* means a person who is sent out on a mission.

- Jesus spent time with them. We know that he taught them, showed them how to minister, challenged them to believe in him, and cared for them.

- It was only after those steps that Jesus sent them out to proclaim the gospel message. The Gospels show Jesus sending out the apostles several times, and then meeting with them again to learn about their experiences and to continue teaching them.

- Finally the apostles grew in faith and obedience to the point where they were able to perform signs the way Jesus had, including casting out demons.

ChristCare Group Leaders have many tools to help prepare their groups for missional service.

The group covenant in the *Beginnings* course asks group members to decide how they will serve. Whenever groups recovenant, they evaluate their service and ask themselves if they could be serving Jesus even more effectively. The covenant helps make missional service a part of the very definition of each ChristCare Group.

Prayer is a powerful tool for preparing ChristCare Groups for missional service. ChristCare Group Leaders commit to praying regularly for their groups, including asking the Holy Spirit to lead the group into deeper service. As group members pray together, they can ask God to show them his will for their service and to give them the faith they need to follow Jesus in lives of servanthood.

Biblical Equipping will help group members to hear God's call to service and to grow in faith. ChristCare Group Leaders might even lead their groups to focus Biblical Equipping on parts of the Bible that teach about the need to serve, such as John 12–13, the book of James, or prophets like Amos or Micah. You can count on God's Word to help group members understand that "'whoever wants to become great among you must be your servant, and whoever wants to be first must be your slave—just as the Son of Man did not come to be served, but to serve, and to give his life as a ransom for many'" (Matthew 20:26–28).

ChristCare Group Leaders need to help group members see and support the congregation's vision for ministry. Groups need to talk about the congregation's vision or mission statement and ask themselves what they are doing to help carry out the congregation's mission. ChristCare Group Leaders must cast the vision in group meetings or talk about occasions when the pastor or other congregation leaders have done so. Group leaders need to help group members catch the excitement and commitment of a vision and help them see the effect their service will have.

Some groups need to focus on caring for one another before they can move into missional service. For example, a group may have a member who is working through a challenge such as the death of a family member. The group will certainly need and want to turn its focus inward and care for the hurting member. That experience of grieving may help the group care for others in similar crises in the future.

As ChristCare Group members share about their lives, group leaders need to encourage them to talk about what it means to live as Jesus' disciples. As they answer that question, the Spirit will lead them deeper into service. Talking about discipleship will help group members understand the choices they must make to follow Jesus.

B. Step 2: Investigate

Once the ChristCare Group is prepared to start a missional service project, members will need to investigate possibilities. Sometimes the entire group will do this together. For instance, groups may find that a member is already doing missional service and decide to join him or her. Or group members may know about missional service opportunities and report on them to the entire group.

Other times the ChristCare Group Leader will take the lead.

You can find a list of possible missional service activities in Supplement A. Use the list to find ideas that might work for your group. Then contact those organizations to learn how your group might be able to participate in the services the organizations provide. Focus Box 5 provides several questions you might ask.

FOCUS BOX 5

Questions for Investigating Missional Service Possibilities

- Does the missional service project fit your group's commitment level? A group whose members have never done missional service might be better suited to a short-term project rather than one requiring months or years of commitment.

- Does the missional service fit your group's gifts? Some groups may have members with lots of non-Christian friends, which may make that group a good one for evangelism. Another group may be made up of men who have skill and experience in construction—perfect for building or renovating housing for homeless persons.

- Does the missional service project fit with the congregation's overall mission? ChristCare Groups are part of the larger congregation and need to find ways to support it. If the congregation's vision is to reach the unchurched,

ChristCare Groups need to consider evangelistic mission. If the congregation's mission is equipping and supporting members for daily-life ministry, ChristCare Groups can be "mission outposts" that provide ministry direction and support.

- Does the missional service project's time frame fit your group's time frame? For example, don't plan to begin a project during a time when many group members will be on vacation.

Supplement B contains a copy of the "Missional Service Opportunity Information Sheet." Take a moment to look it over. You can get a copy of the form from your Equippers. Use it to gather the information you need about organizations that might provide missional service opportunities.

Your Equippers can gather these forms into a binder that ChristCare Group Leaders can consult to find ideas for their groups' missional service.

C. Step 3: Select

Once you've gathered three or four possibilities, present them to the group and let members pick a project. Don't try to choose one and then impose it on the group! Members are much more likely to support a project if they've helped select it.

D. Step 4: Plan

Missional service projects require planning. Planning means finding answers to questions like:

- When will the group do the missional service?
- Where?
- Are any tools or supplies needed?
- How can all group members be involved?
- What does the group need to know and by when?
- How will you communicate to group members?
- What does the group hope to accomplish, over what period of time, and how will you know if you have succeeded?

You may want to ask Equippers for a copy of the "Action Plan Form" from the *ChristCare Series Equipper's Manual* (I.A.4.[1]). It can be a useful tool for putting your plan together.

You also can consider delegating some or all of the planning. It is still your responsibility, though, to make sure the right questions have been asked and answered.

E. Step 5: Carry Out

This is the moment you have been waiting for. Depending on the type of missional service that the group has chosen, many months may have passed since you did your initial preparation and investigation. Group members are no doubt eager to get involved in your selected project.

Some missional service events (for example, a short-term mission trip) may require your ChristCare Group to suspend its normal meeting time. If that is the case, plan to incorporate some times of prayer and worship and Biblical Equipping into your daily schedule. If your ChristCare Group has selected a missional service project in your community, you will need to decide whether the project will replace or be in addition to your ChristCare Group meeting for that week. If group members decide not to meet at their regular time, be prepared to allow additional time at subsequent meetings to review your missional service activity.

F. Step 6: Review

Regularly evaluate your group's missional service (perhaps each time the group recovenants). Make sure you are obeying God, meeting others' needs, and serving in ways that fit and are a blessing for group members. Focus Box 6 contains a list of questions to ask as groups review their missional service.

FOCUS BOX 6

Questions for Evaluating Missional Service

- Does our missional service serve Jesus? If not, how do we need to change?

- Is God calling us to a different kind of missional service? If so, what?

- Is our missional service meeting others' needs? If not, how do we need to change?

- How might we do our missional service even more faithfully and effectively?

- Is our missional service gratifying for group members? If not, how do we need to change?

- Does our missional service challenge us to grow as disciples? If not, how do we need to change?

Based on the answers to those questions, group members can either continue with the missional service they have been doing, change the way they are serving, or investigate new service opportunities.

V. A New Paradigm for Mission

It used to be that mission was something missionaries did in far-off lands. Now, every Christian lives in a mission field. Depending on where you live, anywhere from 20 to 90 percent of the people in your community are unchurched. It is no longer necessary to go overseas to be a missionary.

That means that it is no longer sufficient for Christians to send missionaries to foreign lands and support them with money and prayers. That is certainly still important, but it is not enough. Now, every Christian needs to be a missionary—at work, at school, in the neighborhood, in the community. We are all called to tell the same message Jesus proclaimed, "'The time has come . . . The kingdom of God is near. Repent and believe the good news!'" (Mark 1:15).

ChristCare Groups are the bases from which daily life missionaries go out. In ChristCare Groups members help one another grow as disciples. They work together to discover mission opportunities—both for the entire group and for individual members. Group members support one another as they try to live as obedient disciples. Sometimes they gently hold one another accountable to Jesus' command to serve as he did. When the mission field gets tough, group members care for one another; they "encourage one another and build each other up" (1 Thessalonians 5:11).

As ChristCare Group members reach out, caring and sharing in the name of Jesus, they touch their world with Christ's healing, saving presence. You will learn more about this in session 22, Evangelism in and through ChristCare Groups.

VI. Preparing for the In-Class Session

In preparation for the in-class session, find a way to serve God by serving someone outside this training group before the class meets again. Be prepared to share what you did as missional service.

ENDNOTE

1. Gareth Weldon Icenogle, *Biblical Foundations for Small Group Ministry: An Integrational Approach* (Downers Grove: Intervarsity Press, 1994), page 159.

Supplement A: *ChristCare Series Guide to Missional Service Opportunities*

The ChristCare Series Guide to Missional Service Opportunities is intended to help ChristCare Group Leaders and ChristCare Equippers identify missional service opportunities. It is organized according to the following kinds of missional service:

- Your Congregation's Ministry
- Home Missions (in your own country)
- World Missions (in other countries)
- Social Needs
- Educational Outreach
- Political Activity
- Influencing Community Values

Examples are listed under each of these kinds of missional service. Each example includes a brief description of ways the need can be met. There is some overlap between examples.

This guide is not meant to be exhaustive, but to stimulate your own creativity as your ChristCare Group seeks to reach out. As you consider each possibility, keep in mind three questions:

1. How can our group plug into what our local church is already doing in this area?
2. How can our group plug into what our denomination is already doing in this area?
3. How can our group plug into a Christian ministry already working in this area?

It is usually best to complement the work that your local church or denomination is already doing or to work with a community organization. If none of these offer service opportunities, then try to find national ministries specializing in those areas.

Read through this supplement in one sitting. Allow it to excite you about the possibilities for your ChristCare Group's missional service!

I. Your Congregation's Ministry

A. Prayer

- Pray for the congregation, for the pastor(s), and for other leaders and staff.
- Pray for particular mission concerns of the overall congregation.

B. Serve the Congregation's Needs

- Help prepare for church holidays. Design a special worship booklet for Advent or help decorate the church.
- Have a workday and paint a church room or work on the landscaping.
- Keep the pews stocked with sharpened pencils and an even distribution of hymnbooks.

C. Participate in Congregational Mission Activities

- Raise funds to support a child's attendance to regional or national youth events or to go on a short-term mission project.
- Canvass a neighborhood to invite children to Vacation Bible School.
- Participate in a congregational mission trip.

II. Home Missions

A. Prayer

- Pray for mission work in the United States. This includes ministry to the poor, to particular religious groups, international student outreach, campus ministry, ministries to the disabled, church planting, etc.
- Contact your denomination's headquarters for information about mission activity. You may also want to consult *Operation World: The Day-by-Day Guide to Praying for the World* by Patrick Johnstone (Grand Rapids: Zondervan, 1992). The section on the United States can give you information about nationwide needs.

B. Adopt a Missionary

- Pray for a missionary and the area he or she is seeking to reach.
- Care for missionaries in the field by writing or sending care packages.
- Help a missionary working nearby with special projects he or she may have.
- Raise funds for the missionary's specific needs, such as a computer, office furniture, or Bibles for distribution.
- Keep the congregation informed about the missionary's work. Make a display using maps, information about the work, photographs and

letters. Briefly report to the congregation about the missionary's work and needs. If practical, have the missionary personally speak to the congregation.

- Help a visiting missionary with mailings, phone calls, a place to stay, a ride from the airport, or child care.

- Keep a binder of the group's relationship with the missionary. Include photographs, letters, and correspondence. Pass on the binder to another ChristCare Group when yours closes.

C. Adopt a Home Mission Agency

- Study a mission agency and find out what it does.

- Pray for the agency's work.

- Inform the congregation about the agency's work.

- Do some practical projects with or for the agency, such as a fundraiser.

- Support a ChristCare Group member involved in the work of a home mission agency. For example, host an international student or work among the poor.

- Keep a notebook of the group's relationship to the agency. Include photographs, letters, and correspondence. Pass the notebook to another ChristCare Group when yours closes.

D. Go on a Short-Term Mission

- Go on a short-term mission, individually or as a group. (Call your denomination headquarters and ask if there are any opportunities in your area.)

- Write or call mission agencies for short-term service opportunities. *Operation World: The Day-by-Day Guide to Praying for the World* lists most major mission agencies' addresses and phone numbers.

- InterChristo (800/426-1342) has a host of short-term volunteer opportunities.

III. World Missions

A. Pray for the World's Needs

- Pray for a different country each week, or devote one meeting a quarter to pray for a specific part of the world.

- *Operation World: The Day-by-Day Guide to Praying for the World* lists the specific prayer needs of

every country in the world. The following publications also do so:

- o AD 2000 Global Monitor (Newsletter). Global Evangelization Movement, P.O. Box 129, Rockville, VA 23146.

- o Church Around the World. Tyndale House Publishers, P.O. Box 80, Wheaton, IL 60189.

- o DAWN Report. DAWN Ministries, 7899 Lexington Drive, Suite 200B, Colorado Springs, CO 80920.

- o Evangelical Missions Quarterly. Evangelical Missions Information Service, P.O. Box 794, Wheaton, IL 60189.

- o FrontierScan. U.S. Center for World Mission, 1605 Elizabeth St., Pasadena, CA 91104.

- o Global Prayer Digest. U.S. Center for World Mission, 1605 Elizabeth St., Pasadena, CA 91104.

- o International Journal of Frontier Missions. International Student Leaders Coalition for Frontier Missions, P.O. Box 27266, El Paso, TX 79926.

- o Mission Frontiers. U.S. Center for World Mission, 1605 Elizabeth St., Pasadena, CA 91104.

- o News Network International News Service. News Network International, P.O. Box 28001, Santa Ana, CA 92799.

- o Pulse. Evangelical Missions Information Service, P.O. Box 794, Wheaton, IL 60189.

- o World Christian News. YWAM International Research and Information, P.O. Box 26479, Colorado Springs, CO 80936-6479.

- Subscribe to some of these publications and make them available to other ChristCare Group Leaders.

B. Adopt a Missionary

- Pray for a missionary and the country he or she is seeking to reach.

- Write, call, or send care packages to missionaries in the field.

- Raise funds for the missionary's specific needs, such as a computer, office furniture, or Bibles to distribute.

- Keep the congregation informed about the missionary and his or her country. Make a display using maps, information about the country, photographs and letters. Briefly report to the congregation about the missionary's work and needs.

- Help a visiting missionary with mailings, phone calls, a place to stay, a ride from the airport, or babysitting.

- Keep a binder of the group's relationship to the missionary family. Include photographs, letters, and correspondence. Pass the binder to another ChristCare Group when yours closes.

C. Adopt a Mission Agency

- Study an agency to find out what it does. There are many specialized agencies. Bible translation organizations (American Bible Society, United Bible Society and Wycliffe Bible Translators) can provide some interesting material.

- Pray for the agency's work.

- Inform the congregation about the agency's work.

- Adopt a specific mission project that the agency sponsors and pray for it, help fund it, or participate in it.

- Do some practical projects with or for the agency, such as hosting a fundraiser.

- Keep a notebook that chronicles the group's relationship with the agency. Include photographs, letters, and correspondence. Pass the notebook to another ChristCare Group when yours closes.

D. Go on a Short-Term Mission

- Groups or individuals can go on short-term missions. Call your denomination headquarters and ask if there are any opportunities of this kind.

- You can also write or call agencies for information. *Operation World: The Day-by-Day Guide to Praying for the World* lists most major mission agencies' addresses and phone numbers. If you're interested in a specific country, you can easily find out which mission agencies are working there.

- InterChristo (800/426-1342) has a host of short-term volunteer opportunities.

IV. Social Needs

A. Hunger

- Collect food for a church or community food bank. Volunteer once a month to restock the shelves or distribute food. Community food banks

are often listed in the phone book under Emergency Assistance or Emergency Food Services. Most community resource directories list these resources under "Food" or "Emergency Food." Contact your local United Way office and churches to find these programs.

- Set up a food collection station in the church foyer. Promote the food drive through the newsletter, bulletin and announcements. Deliver the food to the pantry after the drive is over.

- Volunteer one evening or weekend day a month to work in a soup kitchen.

- Provide sandwiches once a month to a homeless shelter. Involve group members' families in making and delivering the sandwiches.

- Raise pledges and participate in a walk-a-thon for hunger.

- Work for world hunger. Mercy Corps International is a nonprofit, voluntary agency that exists to assist the world's suffering, impoverished, and oppressed through emergency relief, self-help projects, and development education (3030 S.W. First Avenue, Portland, OR 97201, 503/242-1032, FAX 503/796-6844). World Vision (800/423-4200, 919 W. Huntington Drive, Monrovia, CA 91016) also helps the poor. Groups can sponsor a child in a foreign country through a number of organizations, including Christian Children's Fund (2821 Emerywood Parkway, P.O. Box 26507, Richmond, VA, 23261-6507, 800/776-6767). The group will receive a photo and information about the child's family, community, country, and progress and will be able to communicate with the child.

B. Housing

- Help a retiree, widow or widower, or single parent with home maintenance work.

- Work with Habitat for Humanity (800/334-3308 or 912/924-6935, 121 Habitat Street, Americus, GA 31709-3498). Founded in 1976 by Millard and Linda Fuller, Habitat for Humanity International (HFHI) is a nonprofit, ecumenical Christian housing ministry. Habitat uses volunteer labor (including the homeowner's) and donated materials to build or rehabilitate simple, modest homes. There are active affiliates in all 50 states, and some projects are coordinated by international affiliates.

- Many communities have short-term opportunities to help build or refurbish homes to be used by poor persons.

- Volunteer to help at a homeless shelter. You might work with children, conduct Bible studies, or clean bathrooms.

C. Incarceration

- Get connected to a prison ministry through Prison Fellowship (800/398-HOPE; 800/497-0122). Give Prison Fellowship your phone number and ZIP code and they will have a representative call you with needs in your area. The Angel Tree project is one of their large outreach ministries. It provides holiday gifts for prisoners' children.

- Adopt a prisoner through support and prayer. Group members could take turns writing, allowing the prisoner to be connected to an entire family of people, not just one. This would also give the entire ChristCare Group the opportunity to understand what life is like behind bars.

- Support a group member who wants to receive additional training from Prison Fellowship so that he or she can visit prisoners or their families.

- Adopt a parolee and provide mentoring and support as the person readjusts to life outside prison. Invite the person to join the group.

D. Disaster Relief

- Help victims of floods, earthquakes, tornadoes, fires, or hurricanes. Contact your community's chapter of the American Red Cross to find out what needs to be done. Also call the Salvation Army.

E. HIV/AIDS

- People with HIV/AIDS need much care and assistance. ChristCare Groups could work with an AIDS organization to do everything from helping with bulk mailings to planning fundraisers. The National AIDS Information Clearinghouse (800/458-5231) can provide names of AIDS organizations in your area.

- Support a group member who wants to be a buddy or support group facilitator with an AIDS organization.

F. Nursing Homes

- Work with a nursing home's activities director or chaplain to provide residents with entertainment, such as skits or singing.

- Assist in a nursing home ministry in many practical ways. Members could provide the singing

or teaching or simply wheel residents to the services.

- "Adopt" nursing home residents without nearby family and be family for them. Spend time with them, celebrate holidays and birthdays with them, and generally be there for them.

G. Disabilities

- Groups can help make their congregations accessible for the disabled. This may involve reserving parking places near the church's entrance for people with disabilities. It may involve building a wheelchair ramp or lift or installing an elevator so that disabled people have full access to facilities. Group members can agree to help disabled congregation members move around the congregation, such as from Sunday school to the service. Obviously, many of these projects would require the consent and cooperation of congregation leaders.

- Sponsor a Disability Awareness Sunday. Develop a segment of the church library or resource center with books about disabilities.

- Groups could learn sign language and reach out to the hearing impaired. Group members could translate the worship service or hymns into sign language. They could also reach out to the hearing impaired in their communities.

- Work with Joni and Friends (800/523-5777) as they work with the disabled. You can get an information packet about Wheels for the World and how you can help the disabled in the United States and overseas.

- Volunteer to work in or visit residents of a group home (mental retardation, blindness, hearing impaired, etc.).

- Raise funds for necessary medical equipment that is not covered by insurance.

V. Educational Outreach

- Present topical lectures, films, displays, literature, or fairs to the congregation and community.

- Educate the congregation about psychological health issues such as grief and addiction and the proper responses to them.

- Educate the congregation and community about physical health issues. Work at a health fair in an inner-city neighborhood. Provide pregnant women with information about nutrition and prenatal care.

- Help staff an after-school tutoring program for children who have difficulty learning.
- Volunteer one day a month to help out at a job re-education program.

VI. Political Activity

- Write to national, state, or local legislators about issues of concern.
- Advocate for the rights of oppressed people through action or indirect action like writing letters to appropriate people.
- Campaign for a legislator who supports an important cause.
- Help staff the polls on election day.

VII. Influencing Community Values

- Underwrite and publicize a Christian radio broadcast.
- Inform the congregation or community about Christian stewardship of the earth. Set up exhibits or give lectures about environmental issues.
- Identify a moral need in the community, such as crime, gambling, abortion, poverty, or inadequate support for schools. Find ways to provide a Christian perspective. Means might include speakers, literature, activities to draw attention to the problem, community Bible studies to present the biblical point of view, and attempts to draw media attention to the issue.

Two Helpful Resources from Stephen Ministries

Spiritual Growth through Spiritual Gifts: A ChristCare Group Experience
by Kenneth C. Haugk, William J. McKay, Sandra A. Ashby

ChristCare Groups are a great place to discover and exercise spiritual gifts. *Spiritual Growth through Spiritual Gifts* is an eight-session ChristCare Group curriculum (similar in format and style to *Beginnings*) that helps group members discover and develop their own spiritual gifts and then decide how to use their gifts to serve God and the church.

Missional service can transform lives—of those serving as well as those being served. *Spiritual Growth through Spiritual Gifts* will help your ChristCare Group find that place where members' gifts and passions meet the needs of others, and life-transforming missional service results.

To learn more, log on to www.ChristCare.org/Gifts or call Stephen Ministries at (314) 428-2600.

www.ChristCare.org/Mission

This special section of the Stephen Ministries Web site provides ChristCare Group Leaders with missional service stories and ideas from other ChristCare Groups. Group leaders can also share their own missional service ideas and experiences to encourage and inspire ChristCare Groups from hundreds of other congregations to engage in transforming service.

Missional Service Opportunity Information Sheet

ChristCare Series

Name of Organization _____

Address _____

City/State/ZIP_____

Phone ( )_____   Fax ( )_____

Name of Contact Person_____

Describe the missional service activity.

How many people are needed/can be involved? _____

What are the dates, if any, within which the project must be done? _____

Is this a one-time project or an ongoing project? _____

What special skills are needed?

What costs, if any, are there? _____

What lead time is required to arrange to participate? _____

Other important information:

Group-Based Manual for ChristCare Group Leaders

Missional Service by ChristCare Groups

Outline and Focus Notes

"Instead, whoever wants to become great among you must be your servant, and whoever wants to be first must be your slave—just as the Son of Man did not come to be served, but to serve, and to give his life as a ransom for many."

Matthew 20:26–28

1. Class Member-Led Prayer and Worship

2. Biblical Equipping: Least-of-These Care (Matthew 25:31–40)

FOCUS NOTE 1

Questions to Focus Sharing of Biblical Equipping Apart

• Share one insight that you've had as a result of your Biblical Equipping Apart this week.

• Describe one change in your life that you've committed to make as a result of your meditation on the Biblical Equipping passage this week.

• Tell about a time when you've met God in a new way through Biblical Equipping Apart this week.

8-OFN.pmd C: 02/25/2004 R: 12/10/2004

Least-of-These Care (Matthew 25:31–40)

[31] "When the Son of Man comes in his glory, and all the angels with him, he will sit on his throne in heavenly glory. [32] All the nations will be gathered before him, and he will separate the people one from another as a shepherd separates the sheep from the goats. [33] He will put the sheep on his right and the goats on his left.

[34] "Then the King will say to those on his right, 'Come, you who are blessed by my Father; take your inheritance, the kingdom prepared for you since the creation of the world. [35] For I was hungry and you gave me something to eat, I was thirsty and you gave me something to drink, I was a stranger and you invited me in, [36] I needed clothes and you clothed me, I was sick and you looked after me, I was in prison and you came to visit me.'

[37] "Then the righteous will answer him, 'Lord, when did we see you hungry and feed you, or thirsty and give you something to drink? [38] When did we see you a stranger and invite you in, or needing clothes and clothe you? [39] When did we see you sick or in prison and go to visit you?'

[40] "The King will reply, 'I tell you the truth, whatever you did for one of the least of these brothers of mine, you did for me.'"

Explore Questions

1. How is the caring that Jesus commends the "sheep" for similar to the care that he provided during his earthly ministry?

2. Why do you think the righteous ones cared for those in need when they didn't know that they actually were caring for Jesus?

3. What does Jesus mean when he says, "Whatever you did for one of the least of these [sisters and] brothers of mine, you did for me"?

Connect Questions

1. What do you think Jesus would say to you and your ChristCare Group about the importance of doing missional service?

2. What are some specific kinds of missional service through which your ChristCare Group could meet and care for Jesus himself?

3. How will you help the members of your ChristCare Group understand the necessity and value of missional service?

3. Share Your Missional Service Experiences

Questions about Your Missional Service

1. What did you do?
2. What made you decide to do this activity?
3. What did you enjoy most about the experience?
4. What did you find to be hardest about doing missional service?

4. Missional Service Opportunities

Definition of Missional Service

Missional service means reaching out with Christ's love to meet the needs of people outside the group.

5. What Will Our Class Do for Missional Service?

6. Prayer as Missional Service

7. Assignments and Reminders

How to Use the Bible as an Equipping Tool

Preclass Reading

All scripture is inspired by God and is useful for teaching, for reproof, for correction, and for training in righteousness, so that everyone who belongs to God may be proficient, equipped for every good work.

2 Timothy 3:16–17 NRSV

PRECLASS READING OUTLINE

I. Introduction

Before you can lead your ChristCare Group in Biblical Equipping, you'll need to prepare the materials you will use. Sections I through IV of this Preclass Reading explain how to make those preparations, including how to:

9-PRE.pmd C: 08/23/1994 R: 02/16/2005

- choose subject matter for a Biblical Equipping series;
- choose curriculum materials;
- use reference resources;
- prepare introductory information for the first Biblical Equipping session of a new series.

Sections V and VI of this Preclass Reading give in-depth information on how to prepare for and lead Biblical Equipping sessions with your ChristCare Group.

Sections VII, VIII, and IX provide information on several other Biblical Equipping issues that are also important to ChristCare Group Leaders.

II. How to Use Published Resources in Biblical Equipping

You've learned that Biblical Equipping is a distinct way of encountering the Bible. There are no published small group curricula that will lead you step by step through the Biblical Equipping cycle. Even so, Biblical Equipping does not eliminate the need for published background materials and curricula for small group Bible study. Instead, Biblical Equipping will enable you to use these materials in ways you've never used them before—and with effective results. You will tailor those resources to your group members' specific needs and circumstances. You need to know how you will use materials in order to choose effective ones.

A. Three Main Uses for Bible Study Curricula

You will use published Bible study curricula in three important ways.

To Provide Background Information

When you begin a new Biblical Equipping series, you'll prepare information for the group members about the topic you're going to study, including the cultural and historical context of a book or passage, the author of the book, and unfamiliar words and concepts. These facts will help group members get the most out of the Biblical Equipping series.

Try to anticipate before each Biblical Equipping session the questions that group members might have. As a general rule, if you have a question about something in the passage, group members probably will too. You'll use published materials to research the answers to these questions in case they come up during your ChristCare Group meeting.

To Provide a Structure for the Series

Every Biblical Equipping series needs a structure. Structures indicate the theme for each Biblical Equipping session and tell what portions of Scripture you'll encounter at each group meeting. Creating a structure can take a great deal of time and energy if you do it yourself. In addition, some people find it difficult to do. It's easier to use materials already published on your topic that provide a structure. Then you can simply organize your series around it.

To Give Group Members Reading Assignments

Some small group curricula have booklets with readings for group members. These readings may introduce the topic for the next group meeting or explain the Bible passage that the group will work with. If the curriculum you choose has group member readings, get a copy for each group member.

B. Parts of Published Curricula You Will and Won't Use

Parts to Use

- Background information about the book of the Bible or the topic of the Biblical Equipping series.
- Information to help you answer questions about particular words or verses.
- The outline of the study—which passages you encounter each session.
- Reading assignments for group members.

Supplement B contains an excerpt from *Mastering the Basics—Philippians*.[1] Take a few minutes to look at pages 205–207, 210–211, and 214–215 of Supplement B for an example of material that will work with Biblical Equipping.

Parts Not to Use

- Discussion questions the curriculum suggests (you'll use the Biblical Equipping discussion questions instead).
- Directions for what to do during the Biblical Equipping portion of the group meeting (you'll follow Steps 1–5 of the Biblical Equipping cycle).

Note that, unless you make reading assignments, you will be the only one who needs a copy of the published materials.

Take a few minutes to look at pages 208–209 and 212–213 of Supplement B for an example of material that will not work with Biblical Equipping.

C. What Other Resources Might You Use?

Focus Box 1 lists different kinds of Bible reference materials that you may find useful as you lead Biblical Equipping. Supplement A describes in detail these resources and their uses. If you do not already know how to use any of the references listed below, take a look at Supplement A on pages 201–202.

FOCUS BOX 1

Reference Resources for Biblical Equipping Leaders

- Commentaries
- Concordances
- Study Bibles
- Chain Reference Bibles
- *Nave's Topical Bible*
- Bible Dictionaries

D. Creating Your Own Biblical Equipping Series

Once in a while, a ChristCare Group Leader may decide to create his or her own Biblical Equipping series from scratch. Instead of relying on a published curriculum, he or she would use the Bible and reference resources like dictionaries and concordances to come up with a structure and to research the passages. This is a good approach but it requires a great deal of time and energy.

III. How to Choose a Biblical Equipping Series

You will usually lead your ChristCare Group in a *series* of sessions on a particular book of the Bible or biblical topic. A series helps you build continuity from week to week and also helps group members focus on growth in particular areas of their lives or on one book of the Bible. As the ChristCare Group Leader, you will have responsibility for helping your group choose subjects for Biblical Equipping series.

A. Consider Your Particular Group

The first step in preparing for Biblical Equipping in your ChristCare Group is choosing the subject. Consider the following every time you choose a series:

What Is Your Group's Mission or Purpose?

Always remember the missional reason your ChristCare Group exists.

Is your group's purpose evangelism? If it is, you may choose a subject that prepares group members to be everyday evangelists. Or, if group members often invite visitors who aren't Christians to the group meetings, you might choose a subject that covers the basics of Christian faith or topics on contemporary issues that would interest newcomers.

Perhaps your group's main purpose is helping members deepen their relationships with God and become better disciples of Jesus. If so, consider topics that dig deeply into God's Word and challenge group members to grow.

What Is the Level of Christian Experience of Your Group Members?

Each member of a ChristCare Group will probably be at a different level of experience. When you look at your group as a whole, however, you can usually find a level that you wouldn't want to go too far under or over when choosing a series topic.

For instance, if your group is mostly made up of new Christians, you would choose topics that would help them learn to pray, study the Scriptures, and learn what happened in Jesus' life. Instead of studying Revelation, you might choose one of the Gospels, the story of the young church in Acts, or one of Paul's letters (such as Galatians) that spell out the basics of the Christian faith.

On the other hand, a group made up of experienced Christians needs to be challenged to keep growing spiritually. You may still study one of the Gospels, but you'll look for a deeper level of understanding. You may also move on to more challenging parts of the Scriptures to learn more about who God is and how to live for God.

What Are the Group Members' Needs or Interests?

Have group members asked for help or shown evidence that they need guidance in particular areas? If so, consider a topic that focuses on that area.

B. Ask Group Members for Their Opinions

Even if you believe you already know what group members would say, always ask them what they would like to focus on in a Biblical Equipping series. Sometimes their responses will surprise you. Even if they don't, people prefer to have input in decisions that affect them.

You can gather group members' input through informal discussion or through a more formal time of brainstorming. You might give group members a couple of weeks' notice so they have time to think of topics or books that interest them.

The answers to the question "What would you like to focus on?" usually fall into one of two categories:

Topical Series
Spending some time gathering your group's input will usually result in rich ideas for topical series, such as studies on prayer, faith, biblical people, or what the Bible says about contemporary issues. People have varied interests and experiences, and they often come up with intriguing ideas. In addition, you can suggest topics to group members and find out how much enthusiasm they generate.

Book-of-the-Bible Series
Book-of-the-Bible series give your group the chance to work through an entire book from beginning to end. You get to see the author's ideas develop, and you come to understand passages in their larger context. Tackling an entire book of the Bible also gives you the chance to learn from less well-known Bible passages and keeps you from skipping over the parts that are harder or more challenging to understand.

Groups usually appreciate variety. If your group often chooses topical series, consider using a book-of-the-Bible series once in a while as a change of pace. Likewise, you can punctuate book-of-the-Bible series with a topical series.

C. Find Out What Materials Are Available
After you have considered the needs and interests of the group and have asked group members what they'd like to focus on, find out what materials are available. Your selection of a topic may depend in part on what curriculum or study resources you can find. If your group is intensely interested in a topic for which you cannot find published resources, you can still choose that topic, but you need to realize that it will take much more of your time and energy to prepare for each Biblical Equipping session.

There are several ways to go about finding published resources.

Ask Your ChristCare Equippers
Your ChristCare Equippers have information on curricula that may be readily available to you through your congregation's ChristCare Ministry. During this in-class session, you may see some examples of these curricula.

In addition, your ChristCare Equippers may have set up a ChristCare Group Ministry library in your congregation. If so, you can probably find good resources available there. Check with your Equippers about this.

Check with Local Christian Bookstores
Most Christian bookstores carry small group curricula and other resources.

D. Take a Couple of Suggestions to Your ChristCare Group
Choose two or three strong possibilities for your next Biblical Equipping series topic. Suggest these possibilities to your ChristCare Group members, and ask for their feedback. Arrive together at a good decision on the Biblical Equipping topic.

IV. Getting Ready to Begin a Biblical Equipping Series
After you've chosen a Biblical Equipping subject and curriculum, you will need to prepare written and verbal information to present to your ChristCare Group during the first session. The information you prepare will depend in part on the kind of series you have chosen.

You will gather this information for the first session from the published materials you learned about in section I of this Preclass Reading (for example, prepared curricula and reference resources for background information).

A. Preparing for a Book-of-the-Bible Series
If you choose a book-of-the-Bible series, you'll want to give your group members the following information during the first Biblical Equipping session:

- a schedule showing what portion of the book you will work with at each session;
- any additional reading assignments;
- what is known about the author, including when and where the author wrote the book and to whom;
- what is known about the original readers, including who they were, where they lived, and

what problems, questions, or challenges the readers faced;

- an outline of the book;
- the main ideas of the book.

Make a one- or two-page, easily understood handout. Supplement C on pages 216 and 217 gives you an example of a two-page handout that could be distributed at the beginning of a Biblical Equipping series on the book of Philippians.

B. Preparing for a Topical Series

If you choose a topical series, the handout you distribute at your first Biblical Equipping session will include the following kinds of information:

- the number and dates of the sessions;
- the theme for each session;
- the Scripture passage for each session;
- any additional reading assignments required for the sessions.

Supplement D on page 218 contains an example of what a topical introductory handout would look like. If the study on Gideon were the first session of a topical series called "First Steps in Faith," the introductory handout might look like the one in Supplement D. Be aware that "First Steps in Faith" is a fictitious example. Such a topical Biblical Equipping series does not actually exist. It simply provides an example of an introductory handout for a topical Biblical Equipping series.

C. How You Will Use the Introductory Handout

After you have prepared the introductory handout, you will be ready to use it to introduce the new Biblical Equipping series to your ChristCare Group.

At the beginning of the first Biblical Equipping session in a new series, you will review the handout for five to ten minutes. After you answer any questions, you will proceed right into your first Biblical Equipping session.

V. Getting Ready to Lead Each Biblical Equipping Session

You will need to prepare to lead each Biblical Equipping session. Focus Box 2 gives you a brief overview of what that preparation involves.

FOCUS BOX 2

Preparing to Lead a Biblical Equipping Session

1. Pray.
2. Read the Scripture and its surrounding context.
3. Look up difficult words and concepts.
4. Choose three questions each for Explore and Connect.
5. Think about your own personal response to Step 5: Prepare.
6. Keep up with your own Biblical Equipping Apart.

Much of your preparation centers on understanding what the passage originally meant—to the writer and to those who first read it. It's important, first of all, to understand what God was saying to the original readers before talking about what the passage means to us today. That way group members focus on God's truth instead of trying to impose their own ideas on the passage.

This is also why groups discuss Explore questions before they discuss Connect questions. The Explore questions get at the original meaning—to the writer, the readers, and God. Then Connect questions help group members apply the original meaning to their own lives.

The following paragraphs describe each preparation step in more detail.

Pray

In all matters that concern your ChristCare Group, begin with prayer. Ask for the Holy Spirit's help as you prepare for the next Biblical Equipping session.

Read the Scripture and Its Surrounding Context

Read the Scripture passage for that session several times. Sharpen your awareness by reading it aloud at least once. Read the chapter that contains the passage, as well as the chapter before and after it. If you are reading several verses in different locations in the Bible, read at least the paragraph in which each verse appears.

Write down your preliminary ideas about what this text meant to the author and original hearers.

Look Up Difficult Words and Concepts

Mark any words, phrases, or sentences that are hard for you to understand. Consider your group members. Mark portions of the Scripture you think they'll have trouble understanding.

If you have questions about the passage or anticipate that your group members will have questions, do your best to find the answers.

Use your published materials (prepared curricula or Bible reference resources) to look up definitions of unfamiliar words. Look up words that might have several meanings or special cultural or historical significance, such as *covenant* or *synagogue*.

If you wish, use a Bible commentary or a study Bible to find out other information that may not be readily evident just from reading the passage.

Choose Three Explore Questions and Three Connect Questions

Right now, take a look at Supplement E on pages 219–222 to see a list of Explore and Connect questions you can choose from.

Remember that you ask Explore questions in order to help the group get at what God was saying when the text was written. What did it mean to the writer and those who first read it? Once the group has talked about the original meaning, then you can use Connect questions to help group members apply God's truth to their lives.

You will notice, however, some overlap between the two kinds of questions. Sometimes your group will discuss the original meaning and then jump right into applying it without asking a Connect question. Other times Connect questions will require group members to think more about the original meaning. That's okay, because Explore and Connect are closely related.

As you think about the Explore and Connect questions, consider how you can tailor them to the specific Scripture passages your group will encounter, or to the particular needs in your ChristCare Group. You may reword the questions to make them fit for your passage or group. As you gain experience, you may even make up your own discussion questions.

Take a few minutes now to practice choosing Explore and Connect questions. Focus Box 3 contains a Scripture passage about Gideon. Read the passage and then follow the directions written after the passage.

Gideon Destroys Idols

The Israelites did what was evil in the sight of the LORD, and the LORD gave them into the hand of Midian seven years. The hand of Midian prevailed over Israel; and because of Midian the Israelites provided for themselves hiding places in the mountains, caves and strongholds. For whenever the Israelites put in seed, the Midianites and the Amalekites and the people of the east would come up against them. They would encamp against them and destroy the produce of the land, as far as the neighborhood of Gaza, and leave no sustenance in Israel, and no sheep or ox or donkey. Thus Israel was greatly impoverished because of Midian; and the Israelites cried out to the LORD for help.

Now the angel of the LORD came and sat under the oak at Ophrah, which belonged to Joash the Abiezrite, as his son Gideon was beating out wheat in the wine press, to hide it from the Midianites. The angel of the LORD appeared to him and said to him, "The LORD is with you, you mighty warrior." Gideon answered him, "But sir, if the LORD is with us, why then has all this happened to us? And where are all his wonderful deeds that our ancestors recounted to us, saying, 'Did not the LORD bring us up from Egypt?' But now the LORD has cast us off, and given us into the hand of Midian." Then the LORD turned to him and said, "Go in this might of yours and deliver Israel from the hand of Midian; I hereby commission you." He responded, "But sir, how can I deliver Israel? My clan is the weakest in Manasseh, and I am the least in my family." The LORD said to him, "But I will be with you, and you shall strike down the Midianites, every one of them."

That night the LORD said to him, "Take your father's bull, the second bull seven years old, and pull down the altar of Baal that belongs to your father, and cut down the sacred pole that is beside it; and build an altar to the LORD your God on the top of the stronghold here, in proper order; then take the second bull, and offer it as a burnt offering with the wood of the sacred pole that you shall cut down." So Gideon took ten of his servants, and did as the LORD had told him; but because he was too afraid of his family and the townspeople to do it by day, he did it by night.

When the townspeople rose early in the morning, the altar of Baal was broken down, and the sacred pole beside it was cut down, and the second bull was offered on the altar that had been built. So they said to one another, "Who has done this?" After searching and inquiring, they were told, "Gideon son of Joash did it." Then the townspeople said to Joash, "Bring out your son, so that he may die, for he has pulled down the altar of Baal and cut down the sacred pole beside it." But Joash said to all who were arrayed against him, "Will you contend for Baal? Or will you defend his cause? Whoever contends for him shall be put to death by morning. If he is a god, let him contend for himself, because his altar has been pulled down." Therefore on that day Gideon was called Jerubbaal, that is to say, "Let Baal contend against him," because he pulled down his altar (Judges 6:1–4, 6, 11–16, 25–32 NRSV).

When you look at the Explore and Connect questions in Supplement E, you'll realize that many of the questions listed there would be appropriate choices for the discussion. In Focus Boxes 4 and 5, you'll see several questions, all of which are appropriate to the Gideon passage. After you read the questions in the following Focus Boxes, choose two more questions from both the Explore and Connect lists that you think would also be likely candidates and write them in the spaces provided.

FOCUS BOX 4

Choosing Explore Questions

Possible Explore Questions

- What is important to God in this passage?
- What was life like for Gideon and his community? Why do you think life was like that for them?
- How does God care for Gideon in this passage?

Additional Appropriate Explore Questions

- How does Gideon change in this passage? Why?
- What surprised you in this passage?
- What feelings did Gideon experience in this passage?

Two Additional Explore Questions of Your Choice

-

-

FOCUS BOX 5

Choosing Connect Questions

Possible Connect Questions

- What does God ask of Gideon in this passage? What is God asking of you now?
- How does God change Gideon in this passage? How is God changing you?
- Are you ever afraid to obey God or try something God is calling you to do?

Additional Appropriate Explore Questions

- What does this passage tell us about how God deals with us when we are afraid?
- Can you recall a time when you chose to obey God? What happened?
- Is God calling you to obey in a special way now?

Two Additional Connect Questions of Your Choice

-

-

Think about Step 5: Prepare

At the end of Biblical Equipping together, you will give group members some time to think about how they will carry what they have learned into their daily lives as part of their Biblical Equipping Apart. You will introduce Step 5: Prepare and invite them to think about specific ways they might obey God, or about a passage they might meditate on between group meetings. Then you will give them four or five minutes of silence to write down their ideas. (Have a *Biblical Equipping Weekly Guide* for each group member; bring extra pencils in case members forget.)

As you get ready to lead Step 5: Prepare, think about what you yourself would carry from the passage into your daily life. How is God calling you to obey? What verses might you meditate on? By having your response ready, you can help any group members who have trouble coming up with their own ideas.

Keep Up with Your Own Biblical Equipping Apart

In addition to your role as ChristCare Group Leader, you are also a group member. So, like the other members, you'll need to take time between group meetings to follow Step 6: Obey, Step 7: Meditate, and Step 8: Reflect.

As the leader of your ChristCare Group, you will model faithfulness to Biblical Equipping Apart for the rest of the group. They may not follow your example to the fullest, but they are unlikely to be more committed to Biblical Equipping Apart than you are.

VI. Leading the Biblical Equipping Session

After you have chosen your topic, prepared to introduce your Biblical Equipping series, and prepared for your first session, you'll be ready to jump in and lead a real Biblical Equipping session. With all the preparation you've done, you're going to do a great job!

A. How to Manage the Time

As a ChristCare Group Leader, you are responsible for keeping the meeting and the Biblical Equipping session moving, as well as starting and ending on time. This can be a challenge, especially during your first few sessions.

Don't Worry Too Much about Time

The first few times you lead a Biblical Equipping session, you'll be especially conscious of the time allotted for each step. Don't be overly concerned about time, though. If you find that Biblical Equipping has taken more or less time than you anticipated, just shorten or extend another part of your group meeting. The more sessions you lead, the more you'll begin to get a feel for how much time you need for each step of Biblical Equipping

Together. Just be sure always to end your ChristCare Group meeting on time.

Think about When to Schedule Sharing

ChristCare Group meetings have two possible times of sharing: one during community building and care, and another at the beginning of Biblical Equipping.

Note that these two times of sharing are not the same. The community building and care sharing focuses on what's going on in group members' lives—their hopes and fears, worries and joys. In contrast, the Biblical Equipping sharing (Step 1: Share) focuses on group members' experiences of Biblical Equipping Apart.

There are different ways you can handle sharing:

- Schedule two sharing times.

  Schedule general community building and care sharing at the beginning of the meeting, then proceed with worship or prayer or both. Group members will share specifically about their experiences with Biblical Equipping Apart at the beginning of the Biblical Equipping session.

- Schedule one extended sharing time.

  Let the community building sharing flow right into Biblical Equipping sharing. In this way, you can move the discussion logically from "What is going on in your life?" to "What is going on for you in Biblical Equipping Apart?" You can then move into the rest of your Biblical Equipping and end your group meeting with worship and prayer.

B. What to Do during Steps 1 through 5

Step 1: Share

This step should take about ten to 15 minutes—maybe more, maybe less. The length of time depends largely on the size of your group. Avoid the temptation to spend so much time on this step that you don't have adequate time to encounter the Scriptures. Also avoid the opposite temptation to rush through this step so that group members feel pushed or don't have time to share.

As you begin your Biblical Equipping session with this step, invite group members to share their experience with Biblical Equipping Apart. Remember to model this type of sharing and to affirm group members for what they share. Be sensitive to shy or quiet group members who may need some time to get used to this kind of sharing.

Use a Question to Get Started
It helps to have a question in mind that you can use to begin the sharing. In a newly organized ChristCare Group, you'll want to answer the question yourself first so you can model the length and kind of sharing you hope for at this time. Focus Box 6 gives you examples of questions you might use.

FOCUS BOX 6

Questions to Get Sharing Started in Step 1: Share

1. What has God taught you in Biblical Equipping Apart since our last meeting?

2. What Bible promises are you having success or trouble in trusting?

3. How has the Biblical Equipping we've done together and apart been affecting your life?

4. How has it been going with your obedience, meditation, and reflection between group meetings?

Step 2: Hear
In this second step of the Biblical Equipping cycle, prepare group members to hear God's Word, listen to God's Word, and think about what they've heard.

Invite Group Members to Silence
After group members have finished sharing, you will invite them to participate in a time of silence in preparation to hear God's Word. You can decide how long the silence will last, but usually it will be one or two minutes. Focus Box 7 gives you an idea of what you might say at the beginning of Step 2.

FOCUS BOX 7

Inviting Group Members to a Time of Silence

"Now that we've shared about our encounters with God's Word, let's prepare to hear the verses we will focus on today. Let's take a couple of minutes to be silent and focus our minds and hearts on our loving Lord so we will be ready to hear what God has to say to us. I'll end the silence by saying 'Amen.'"

Arrange for God's Word to Be Read Aloud
After silence, ask someone to read aloud the Scripture verses on which you're going to focus. You might ask one person (or several) to do this. Or you might read the verses yourself. Sometimes, the entire group might read the verses aloud. You might choose a different way of reading aloud every week, or you might find one way that seems to work best in your group and stick with it.

Avoid putting on the spot someone who doesn't like to read aloud. If you suspect someone has trouble reading aloud or is uncomfortable with it, ask ahead of time (when the person can say no without embarrassment). If someone hesitates when you ask, don't push it. Your objective is for everyone to get the most out of reading or hearing God's Word, not for everyone to read aloud.

Invite the Group to Silence Again
After the reading, invite the group to be silent and think about what they've heard. Focus Box 8 gives you an idea of what you might say.

FOCUS BOX 8

Invitation to Silence Again

"Now that we've heard God's Word, let's be silent again for a couple of minutes. Let God's Word speak to you. I'll end the silence by saying 'Thank you, God.'"

End the silence when you believe the time is right, usually after one or two minutes.

Step 3: Explore
Some weeks group members may focus more on Explore, while other weeks they may have more to say about Connect. Some weeks the Bible passage will lend itself better to Explore than to Connect or vice versa. That's fine. You may want to spend about 20 minutes total time for both the Explore and Connect steps.

As you and your group members explore God's Word, your role is that of facilitator. You will encourage group members to share their ideas. When necessary, you will give additional information, answer questions, or correct misinformation, but avoid lecturing or coming across as a teacher.

Share Important Information
Sometimes you will need to explain certain confusing points about the verses you have read.

Earlier in this Preclass Reading, you read a passage from Judges about Gideon. Focus Box 9 contains a script of what you might say to your ChristCare Group to clarify that passage.

FOCUS BOX 9

Explaining Difficult Parts of a Scripture Selection

The ChristCare Group Leader says:

"Before we begin talking about this passage, I'd like to share just a couple of things with you that might make these verses a little more clear. As you probably figured out, Midian was a neighboring country that periodically invaded or raided Israel. The Midianites would carry off anything they wanted, then destroy the rest. That's why Gideon hid out in the winepress when he was threshing wheat—so no one would see him and steal his wheat and maybe even kill him.

"I also wanted to mention that in the Old Testament, the expression 'the angel of the Lord' sometimes means what we would call an angel—a supernatural messenger. But other times it means God himself. In verses 14 and 16, it looks as if this angel of the Lord might have actually been the Lord.

"Just one more thing—you read about how Gideon's father had an altar to Baal and a sacred pole for Asherah. Baal and Asherah were a Canaanite god and goddess, both of them connected with fertility worship. Farmers sacrificed to them in the hope of getting good crops and many children. Even though God forbade the Israelites to worship any other god, many Israelites still followed these gods and built altars and sacred poles for them."

Note how brief and clear the ChristCare Group Leader's comments are. He or she didn't turn the explanation into a long lecture but kept it simple, giving the group members just the amount of information they needed to know.

Ask the First Explore Question
After giving any necessary information, you will begin a discussion in your ChristCare Group by asking the first Explore question. In addition to discussing answers to Explore questions, you and the group members will discuss any other questions group members bring up. As you facilitate the discussion, remember:

- When someone asks a question no one can answer, ask someone in the group to research the answer or offer to research it yourself.
- Use your facilitation skills to include as many group members as possible in the discussion.
- Help the group focus on the clearest meaning of the biblical text instead of drifting off into fantastic, questionable interpretations.

Ask More Explore Questions
If there's time, ask one or both of the additional Explore questions you have chosen. Sometimes you won't have time to do this, but other times you'll need one or two more questions to stimulate discussion or to clear up confusion.

Step 4: Connect
In Step 4 you lead group members to focus on what meaning God's Word has for them in their lives. Encourage group members to talk freely and openly about encountering God. As you facilitate the discussion, start off with one of the questions you have chosen, but let group members follow up with questions of their own if they wish. Make sure group members' questions are heard and discussed.

Ask More Connect Questions
As your group discusses the first Connect question and any others they might have, look for opportunities to ask one or two more Connect questions. Sometimes you won't have time to get to these extra questions, and other times you'll need them to help carry on a meaningful discussion.

Step 5: Prepare
The final step of Biblical Equipping Together is to get ready for Biblical Equipping Apart. Group members might do this by deciding on a way they will try to obey God, or by identifying a passage to meditate on, or both. Your job as leader is to introduce the Prepare time and remind group members what to think about. Then give them four or five minutes to write down what they

come up with. (Have a *Biblical Equipping Weekly Guide* for each group member. Bring extra pencils in case members forget theirs.)

At the end of four or five minutes, ask group members to give you their attention again, and continue with the rest of your meeting.

Focus Box 10 shows how you might introduce Step 5: Prepare to your group.

FOCUS BOX 10

Introducing Step 5: Prepare

"As we bring our time of Biblical Equipping Together to a close, let's take about five minutes to prepare for Biblical Equipping Apart.

"Our Biblical Equipping Apart will involve us in trying to obey God's truth as we've learned it. Has this Biblical Equipping session shown you any specific way God wants you to obey through our encounter with the Scriptures? If so, write it down. It would be easy for us to talk about obedience here at our group meeting but then forget about it once we return to our daily lives. Writing it down is a way to prepare to obey.

"During Biblical Equipping Apart we will also meditate. Is there a particular portion of the passage we worked with today that really stood out for you, that grabbed your interest, challenged you, or clearly spoke God's grace to you? If so, make a note to yourself that you will meditate on it during Biblical Equipping Apart. You may even want to write it down or start to memorize it.

"You may not finish preparing for Biblical Equipping Apart during the short time we have left, but at least make a start. I'll let you know when the time is up."

Ending the Biblical Equipping Session
After you have led the group members in Step 5: Prepare, close the Biblical Equipping session and move on to the next part of your meeting.

C. Encouraging Group Members to Do Biblical Equipping Apart

Your ChristCare Group members will do fine when they begin Biblical Equipping Together because you'll be there to lead them through it. But between group meetings, they'll be on their own.

Group members can run into several common challenges when they begin to do Biblical Equipping Apart. They may simply forget at first. If they remember, they may have trouble finding time for it. Or they may not understand exactly what to do. Some members may not immediately realize the importance of Biblical Equipping Apart.

There are several ways you as ChristCare Group Leader can encourage group members in Biblical Equipping.

- Explain each step carefully and clarify your explanations if you believe some group members still don't understand the steps.

- Briefly remind the group members from time to time of the Biblical Equipping steps.

- Expect group members to have completed Biblical Equipping Apart by asking them how it went during Step 1: Share.

- Model Biblical Equipping Apart by relating your own experiences with it during Step 1: Share.

- Affirm group members for sharing their experiences in Biblical Equipping Apart.

VII. Biblical Equipping for Leaders between ChristCare Group Meetings

After each ChristCare Group meeting, spend some time thinking about how the Biblical Equipping session went. Take a few minutes to do each of the following activities.

A. Evaluate the Biblical Equipping Session

1. Pray that God will give you insight into how the meeting went and what you could do to make the next Biblical Equipping session better.

2. Evaluate your own impressions of how the meeting went. Also consider group members' remarks and comments.

3. Ask yourself how you could make Biblical Equipping more effective at the next ChristCare Group meeting.

You might write down your thoughts on each of the items above in a notebook reserved especially for this purpose. Then you can look back over your notes from time to time for insights.

B. Keep Up with Your Own Biblical Equipping Apart

You—like the other members of your ChristCare Group—will spend some time between ChristCare Group meetings in Steps 6, 7, and 8 of the Biblical Equipping cycle. By going through the same activities your group members are experiencing, you will understand them better and grow with them. But most important, you will be continuing the disciplines of Biblical Equipping and regularly encountering God in the Scriptures.

C. Begin Planning for the Next ChristCare Group Meeting

Between each ChristCare Group meeting, you will need to spend time preparing for the next meeting, including the Biblical Equipping session. Do this early—don't wait until the day before the meeting.

VIII. Introducing Your ChristCare Group to Biblical Equipping

Your ChristCare Group members will need to learn about Biblical Equipping so they can participate in it. They don't need to learn as much as you because they are participants, not group leaders. They don't have to understand all the ins and outs at first. They just need to know enough to understand where you're headed.

A. Introducing Biblical Equipping to Group Members

The best way to introduce ChristCare Group members to Biblical Equipping is to take them through the *Beginnings* course. Biblical Equipping is carefully interwoven into all the sessions of the *Beginnings* course. Session 7 is devoted to Biblical Equipping. If your group is not able to go through the *Beginnings* course, you may still want to use session 7 to introduce them to Biblical Equipping.

B. Introducing Guests and New Members to Biblical Equipping

If your group has regular guests or new members, you will want to introduce them to Biblical Equipping.

Introduce guests and new members to Biblical Equipping by giving them a copy of the *Beginnings Group Member Guide*. Invite them to read session 7, and then follow up at the next group meeting to see if they have any questions about Biblical Equipping.

IX. Sharing Leadership in Biblical Equipping

As a ChristCare Group Leader, you have the responsibility for making sure Biblical Equipping works well in your ChristCare Group. But that doesn't mean you have to do all the work or all the leading involved in Biblical Equipping. After all, Biblical Equipping involves everyone in your ChristCare Group, and some group members may be involved as leaders, not just as participants.

A. Partially Delegating Leadership

In some ChristCare Groups, leaders delegate some of the responsibilities of leading Biblical Equipping. For instance, a ChristCare Group Leader might share leadership by asking other group members to:

- research possible curriculum choices;
- prepare the introductory handout for a new Biblical Equipping series;
- research background information on a passage;
- find out the answers to group members' difficult questions;
- prepare a Biblical Equipping session to lead in case you are unexpectedly absent from a group meeting.

Consider the interests, abilities, and gifts of your group members when you ask them to assume a leadership role in Biblical Equipping. For instance, a quiet group member may appreciate being asked to do research, but might not enjoy leading a Biblical Equipping session in your absence.

B. Completely Delegating Leadership

In some cases, ChristCare Group Leaders completely delegate their Biblical Equipping leadership role to a group member. The group member becomes a "Biblical Equipping leader" and performs all the tasks associated with Biblical Equipping.

It's important to note that *delegate* means "to *assign* responsibility," not "to *give up* responsibility." Even if your group has a Biblical Equipping leader, you—as ChristCare Group Leader—are still responsible for the overall quality and effectiveness of Biblical Equipping in your group.

If you consider delegating the role of Biblical Equipping leadership, you must be able to fulfill the following two requirements.

- **Identify a person in your group who can do a good job as Biblical Equipping leader.** Assess group members carefully in terms of their skills, abilities, experience, and gifts. Make sure the person you have in mind really wants to take on this responsibility.

If you have an Apprentice Leader in your group, he or she may be a good choice. Or you may have a group member who really enjoys leading Bible study sessions and is eager to do so in your group. Perhaps you have a group member who believes he or she would be good at leading Biblical Equipping sessions and wants to give it a try.

- **Provide resources and support for the Biblical Equipping leader.** As a ChristCare Group Leader, you have received extensive training in leading Biblical Equipping. You'll need to share some of what you know if you delegate Biblical Equipping leadership. Prepare and support your Biblical Equipping leader by:

  o asking him or her to read the book *Biblical Equipping* and then discussing it after he or she has read it;

  o lending him or her your copy of this Preclass Reading and then discussing it after he or she has read it;

  o making sure he or she has experience watching you lead several Biblical Equipping sessions so he or she has a model to follow;

  o sharing your list of Explore and Connect questions;

  o working closely with him or her to prepare for the first few sessions;

  o talking about a couple of Biblical Equipping sessions right after the group meetings in which they occur, to answer questions or point out ways the leadership was good or could improve;

  o setting regular check-in times to discuss how Biblical Equipping is going.

X. Getting Ready for the In-Class Session

During the next in-class session, you'll begin preparing to lead a Biblical Equipping session, which you will present during session 10. Choose a portion of the Bible, anything from a single verse to an entire chapter, for which you'd like to prepare a Biblical Equipping session. Read the entire chapter to see the passage in context. Think about the passage and pray for a clear understanding of what God is saying through it.

You've been participating in Biblical Equipping all during training. You already have a strong background, a good basis upon which to build your own leadership of Biblical Equipping.

ENDNOTE

1. Lyman Coleman and Richard Peace, *Mastering the Basics: Personal Excellence through Bible Study. Philippians* (Littleton: Serendipity, 1986).

Reference Resources for Biblical Equipping Leaders

ChrisꝶCare Series

These resources can be helpful in preparing to lead Biblical Equipping sessions and series.

Commentaries

Commentaries are books that discuss Bible passages verse by verse. They clarify each passage's meaning as much as possible. They do this by identifying names, places, and stories that you might not recognize; describing ancient customs; and explaining any religious or social issues at the time the book was written that might affect the way you understand the passage. You can find commentaries written about a single book of the Bible or ones that deal with the whole Bible.

How do you choose a commentary? Some commentaries are much easier to understand than others. Your denomination may recommend a particular commentary series. You may even be able to borrow a commentary from your small group ministry library or from your pastor.

Concordances

Concordances are reference books that allow you to find any verse in the Bible from just a word. For example, if you remember the verse "In the beginning God created the heavens and the earth" but you don't know where it is in the Bible, you can find out by looking up the word *beginning* in your concordance. Under the word *beginning*, you will find a list of Bible verses that include that word. Usually you will also find a short phrase from each verse, so that you don't have to look up 50 verses in order to tell which one is the one you want. For example, under *beginning* you might find an entry like this:

beginning

In the beginning, God created   Genesis 1:1

the beginning of birth pains   Matthew 24:8

By reading the short phrases, you can tell that the verse you want is Genesis 1:1—not Matthew 24:8.

(You could also have found this verse by looking up *created*, *heavens*, or *earth*. It's wise, however, to pick the most unusual word in the passage, since picking a word like *God*, *Lord*, or *the* might mean you have to look through a 15-page-long list.)

Keep in mind that versions of the Bible differ in the exact words that they use to translate each verse into English. This means that, if you are looking up a verse that you once memorized in the King James Version, you had better use a concordance prepared for the King James Version. For example, if you are trying to find the verse "My soul doth magnify the Lord, and my spirit hath rejoiced in God my Savior," and you want to use the key word *magnify*, you'd need a King James concordance. If you use a New International Version (NIV) concordance, you won't find the word *magnify* at all, since the NIV translates that verse "My soul glorifies the Lord." In an NIV concordance, you'd have to look up the word *glorifies* instead.

Study Bibles occasionally include a short concordance section at the end of the Bible, listing only the most important verses and words. There are also computer concordances that will locate your verse in a matter of seconds.

While most people use concordances to find verses whose locations they can't remember, there's another good use for them. You can use a concordance to find all the places where the Bible uses a word like *peace*, *love*, or *righteousness*. Then you can create your own Bible study by looking up these verses and seeing what the whole Bible has to teach on that subject.

Study Bibles

Study Bibles are ordinary Bibles that contain additional special helps such as dictionaries, maps, concordances, book introductions and outlines, or footnotes that carry commentary on each verse. Some also carry features like a list of Jesus' miracles or a reading plan for people who want to read the whole Bible in a year.

Every study Bible is slightly different, so you will need to look through several in order to find the one that is most helpful to you. Your pastor or Equipper may be able to make a recommendation.

When you choose a study Bible, make sure it uses the translation you prefer. Some study Bibles come in more than one version.

Chain Reference Bibles

A chain reference Bible is a special kind of study Bible that allows you to follow one topic or idea throughout the Bible. For example, suppose you are reading what Jesus says about the Holy Spirit in John 14:16–17. At the bottom of the page, or perhaps in a column next to the text, you'll find a note that tells you to look up John 14:26, Genesis 1:2, Matthew 28:19, or Acts 2:1–4. If you look up those verses, you will discover more of what the Bible says about the Holy Spirit. Each of those verses usually has another list of verses to look up if you wish. This is why it is called a chain reference Bible. If you have the time and patience to follow the chain, you can learn a lot.

Keep in mind that chain reference Bibles, like other study Bibles, come in different translations.

Nave's Topical Bible

Nave's Topical Bible comes in King James[1] or New International Version.[2] It is a cross between a concordance and a Bible dictionary. Here's how it works.

Look up the biblical topic you'd like to explore (they are listed alphabetically). For example, if you want to learn about the names of "God," then you look up the topic God. Since this is a very large topic, you'll find many subsections listed, including "God—Name of." Under that section you'll find verses listed from all over the Bible that deal with that topic. You'll also find definitions and explanations for the names, and important verses on each subject printed out in full. This saves considerable time, since you don't have to flip through the Bible looking up every one of a hundred or so verses.

Nave's can be used like a concordance to find verses whose locations you have forgotten. But its most important use is providing an overview of a whole biblical subject, such as marriage or baptism. You can create topical Bible studies quite easily with the help of *Nave's*. In fact, *Nave's* is often better than a concordance for this use. You will find verses in it that deal with your subject even though the actual key word (for example, *peace*) never appears in the verse.

Bible Dictionaries

Bible dictionaries are a useful resource when you want to discover the meaning behind an unknown person, place, or item. For example, if you are reading the story of Jesus' birth and his family's escape to Egypt, you will understand it much better if you know a little bit about King Herod, the magi, Bethlehem, Ramah, and Rachel (mentioned in Jeremiah's prophecy). A Bible dictionary can give you the basic information you need to understand your passage without being confused when you run into a strange word like *synagogue*. Many Bible dictionaries are available. Choose one that suits your needs and is easy for you to use.

ENDNOTES

1. Orville J. Nave, *Nave's Topical Bible* (New York: International Bible Agency, 1897).

2. John R. Kohlenberger and David J. Jirak, eds., *NIV Nave's Topical Bible* (Grand Rapids: Zondervan, 1992).

Supplement B: Excerpt from *Mastering the Basics—Philippians*

PROJECT ENGINEER: Lyman Coleman, Serendipity House

WRITER FOR NOTES/COMMENTARY: Richard Peace, Gordon Conwell Seminary.

CONTRIBUTORS: Denny Rydberg, University Presbyterian Church, Seattle □ Gordon Fee, Gordon Conwell Seminary, Boston □ Virginia Zachert, Medical College of Georgia, Augusta □ Margaret Coleman, Serendipity House, Denver □ Peter Menconi, Professional Consultants, Denver □ John Mallison, Board of Education, Uniting Church in Australia, Sydney □ John U'Ren, Scripture Union, Melbourne □ Ken Anderson, Synod of South Australia, Uniting Church of Australia, Adelaide □ Anton Baumohl, Scripture Union, Bristol, England □ Lance Pierson, Freelance writer, London □ Emlyn Williams, Scripture Union, Cambridge, England.

PUBLISHER: Serendipity House is a resource community specializing in the equipping of pastors and church leaders for small group ministry in the local church in the English speaking world. A list of training events and resources can be obtained by writing one of the addresses below.

SERENDIPITY U.S.A.
Serendipity House
Box 1012
Littleton, Colorado 80160

Telephone: 800-525-9563

SERENDIPITY AUSTRALIA
Serendipity Christian Resources
P.O. Box 130
West Ryde, NSW 2114

Telephone: SYDNEY 858-1778

SERENDIPITY GREAT BRITAIN
c/o Serendipity U.K.
48 Peterborough Road
London SW6 3EB

Telephone: LONDON 01-731-6544

PHILIPPIANS

LYMAN COLEMAN and RICHARD PEACE

MASTERING THE BASICS
PERSONAL EXCELLENCE THROUGH BIBLE STUDY

7 WEEKS (OR MORE) THROUGH PHILIPPIANS

This schedule gives two plans: ☐ 7-week economy tour and ☐ 13-week grand tour. Use the first column for 7-week tour, the second column for 13-week tour, one week per unit.

7-week plan	13-week plan	PHILIPPIANS	SUBJECT	PAGE
1	1	1:1-2	Salutation	12
	2	1:3-11	Thanksgiving and Prayer	16
2	3	1:12-18a	Paul's Chains Advance the Gospel	20
	4	1:18b-26	Life or Death?	24
3	5	1:27 — 2:4	Living Worthy of the Gospel	28
	6	2:5-11	The Humility of Christ	32
4	7	2:12-18	Shining as Stars	36
	8	2:19-30	Timothy and Epaphroditus	40
5	9	3:1-11	No Confidence in the Flesh	44
	10	3:12 — 4:1	Pressing on Toward the Goal	48
6	11	4:2-9	Exhortations	52
7	12	4:10-20	Thanks for Their Gifts	56
	13	4:21-23	Final Greetings	60

INTRODUCTION TO THE BOOK OF PHILIPPIANS

Philippians is the letter of joy. Joy permeates its pages from start to finish. But this is not joy forged out of privilege and abundance. It is not the joy of people who have no problems to face. This is joy in the midst of hard situations. Paul is writing from prison. He faces the very real possibility of execution. The Philippian church is confronted with internal dissension and with false teachers who would seduce it away from the gospel. Furthermore, both Paul and the Philippians live with the sense that the world might end any day. The second coming of Jesus was a living reality for them.

How can you be joyful in that kind of world? How can you urge joy when your fellowship is pressed from within and without? How can you be joyful when the world is about to end? The average twentieth-century American Christian does not know how to answer these questions. To him or her joy is what comes with prosperity and success. Joy is what happens when your church is growing and when its influence is spreading in the community. Joy is the anticipation of grandchildren who will build on the accomplishments of the family and do even better for themselves than you have done. Joy is the lack of pressure and hardship.

Since most of us are authentically puzzled by the emphasis in this epistle, it is therefore most important to listen carefully to what Paul has to say. It is not that we do not want joy. We do. We go to incredible lengths to find satisfaction (which is how we often define joy). It is just that we do not want joy in the midst of hardship. We want the hardship to go away. Yet, the hardship would not go away for either Paul or the Philippians. This was the reality in which they lived and out of which this letter, brimming with joy, was written.

The City of Philippi
Philippi was located in the Roman province of Macedonia (modern Greece), eight miles from the Mediterranean Sea in a fertile area known for its fresh water springs and gold mines.

Philippi was founded around 360 B.C. by Philip II, the King of Macedonia, so that he could mine its gold in order to finance his army. The city was named after him. Philip was the father of Alexander the Great. After the Romans defeated the Persians in 168 B.C., Philippi became part of the Roman Empire. It rose to some importance then because of its strategic location on the *Via Egnatia,* the great road that linked Rome with the Byzantium Empire in the East. But its real prominence came later as the result of two battles. In 42 B.C., in the plains of Philippi, the Caesarean forces of Antony and Octavian defeated the Republican forces led by Brutus and Cassius, the assassins of Julius Caesar. A number of the soldiers from the victorious army were then settled there. A few years later, in 31 B.C., the two former allies fought each other. Octavian emerged victorious over the forces of Antony and the Egyptian Queen Cleopatra. Octavian later became the Emperor Caesar Augustus. After this second battle, yet more veterans were settled in Philippi, and it became a Roman colony. This meant that to live in Philippi was like living in Rome itself. One had all the rights and privileges accorded those in the capital. Its citizens were considered Roman citizens. Its governmental structure was modeled on that of Rome. The citizens were exempt from land tax and poll tax. At the time of Paul the citizens of Philippi, who were mostly Romans (though there were some Greeks and a few Jews), were very proud of their city and its special tie to Rome.

The Founding of the Church
The church at Philippi was founded during Paul's second missionary journey. This had not been an easy journey for Paul. It had begun badly. Barnabas, his companion on the first missionary journey, wanted to take along Mark. But Paul would not hear of it, since Mark had deserted them on the previous trip. So Paul and Barnabas split up (Acts 15:36-41). Paul set out this time with Silas. But after a while, they found themselves struggling to know where God wanted them to go. Acts 16:6-7 states:

> Paul and his companions traveled throughout the region of Phrygia and Galatia, having been kept by the Holy Spirit from preaching the word in the province of Asia. When they came to the border of Mysia, they tried to enter Bithynia, but the Spirit of Jesus would not allow them to. So they passed by Mysia and went down to Troas.

It is in this context that Paul had his famous "night vision" in which a "man from Macedonia" beckoned him to "Come over and help us" (Acts 16:9). Paul did just that. He sailed almost immediately from Asia and after two days arrived at the Macedonian seaport of Neapolis. He was accompanied by Silas, Timothy, and now Luke (at this point in Acts the report switches to the first person plural "we," indicating that Luke had joined the party).

Paul and his party did not remain at Neapolis but pressed on to the city of Philippi to begin work. Paul's custom was to preach first in the local synagogue. But it seems that the Jewish population in Philippi was so small that there was no synagogue. Instead, a group of women met on the Sabbath by the banks of the river Gangites in order to recite prayers. Paul joined them and there he met Lydia, a successful merchant whose business was trading in the purple cloth for which her home town of Thyatira was famous. She listened to Paul's message and was converted along with her whole household. They were the first European Christians. Lydia was not Jewish, but was a "god-fearer," that is, a Gentile who participated in Jewish worship without becoming a proselyte. Her house became the center of missionary activity in Philippi.

Paul soon ran into trouble in Philippi, however. It seems that he cast out a demon from a fortune-telling slave girl (though not without some hesitation on his part). She promptly lost her ability to predict the future. This outraged her owners who saw that they stood to lose a great deal of money now that the girl was out from under the bondage of the demon. So they had Paul and Silas thrown in jail. That night, while the two of them were singing hymns and praying, an earthquake shook open the jail. The jailer saw the open door, and fearing that all his prisoners had fled, he was about to commit suicide. But Paul stopped him and reported that all the prisoners were still there. With great emotion, the Philippian jailer inquired of Paul and Silas how he might be saved. Thus he and his household became Christians.

The next day when the magistrates discovered that Paul and Silas were Roman citizens, they released them with some alarm. They did, however, "request" that they leave the city (you couldn't just throw a Roman citizen out of a Roman city). Thus Paul and Silas left Philippi, leaving behind them the first European church.

This church was always special to Paul and he to it. Years later there was still a warm feeling of mutual care and concern between Paul and the Philippians, so much so that in his Epistle Paul calls them his "joy and crown" (4:1).

It is quite possible that even though Paul and Silas had to leave Philippi, the church was not left without guidance. Luke may have stayed behind. The first "we" passage in Acts ends in Philippi (Acts 16:17) and the second "we" passage begins some years later in Philippi (Acts 20:5).

Origin of the Letter

When and where did Paul write Philippians? This is a question to which no certain answer can be given. However, one thing is clear. Paul was in prison when he wrote. Which prison he was in is not quite so clear. It is known that Paul was in at least four prisons. Chances are that he was also in other prisons on occasions not recorded in the New Testament. The four known imprisonments occurred in Philippia itself (Acts 16:19-40); in Jerusalem following the riot when it was rumored that Paul had brought Gentiles into the forbidden precincts of the temple (Acts 21:27—23:30); in Caesarea when he was awaiting a verdict on the charges leveled against him in Jerusalem (Acts 23:31—26:32); and in Rome where he was sent finally to be tried on the charges originating back in Jerusalem (Acts 28:30-31). Scholars also suggest that he was probably in jail in Ephesus on at least one occasion and possibly in Corinth as well.

Paul didn't write from the Philippian jail obviously. And while some case can be made that he wrote from each of the other prisons, the probable origin of the letter is Rome (though this only a "best guess"). In this case, the date of the letter would be some time after A.D. 60.

The Occasion

Paul is in prison when Epaphroditus, an old friend from Philippi, arrives bearing a gift from the church. Unfortunately, Epaphroditus falls gravely ill. His home church hears about it and is deeply concerned. In due course he does recover and Paul is anxious that he return home and so relieve the fears of his friends and family. Epaphroditus' return to Philippi affords Paul the opportunity to send along a letter thanking them for their gift and for all that they mean to him. This also enables Paul to inform them that he hopes to send Timothy to see them soon and that he himself will come when

he is released from prison. He also warns them about the danger they face from certain troublemakers who seek to undermine both their doctrine and their morals, and to warn them about the internal danger they face due to their lack of unity.

This is the most personal of all Paul's epistles. He is writing to old friends and colleagues who have long supported his ministry. He doesn't have to assert his authority as an apostle (as he does in other letters). He is free to express his strong feelings toward them. There is an informality to this letter not found in others of Paul's epistles.

One Letter or Two?

There is a problem with the Epistle to the Philippians. It opens in a traditional way. Paul talks about his imprisonment and about how the gospel is advancing. He makes an appeal for harmony among the members of the Philippian church. He tells them that he will be sending both Epaphroditus and Timothy to see them. And then in 3:1 he says "Finally, my brothers . . ." as if he is about to close the letter. But then he abruptly launches into a warning about dangerous men who will harm the church (3:2-21). This is followed by more exhortations (4:1-9) and by thanks for their gifts (4:10-20) after which he actually concludes his letter. So the question is raised, is this a single unified letter or the composite of two (or more) letters?

Most commentators regard Philippians as a single letter, but it is instructive to note the two sections that could be separate letters. First, there is the warning about troublemakers that begins in 3:2 and goes to at least 4:1 and possibly to 4:9. Then, second, there is Paul's note of thanks in 4:10-20. Still, these parts do not have to stand alone. The way in which they can be understood to be part of the whole letter will be made clear in the notes on each section.

Outline

At first glance this appears to be an informal, *ad hoc* letter dashed off by Paul to his friends in Philippi and filled with news about himself and his plans. As Hawthorne writes:

Philippians bears all the characteristics of a very personal letter, where the reasons for writing are various and numerous. It is like a chat, the subject matter changing without notice as in an informal conversation between friends. For this reason an outline of the letter is not easy to make. The letter follows no logical progression. Swift changes of topic and even of tone come as no surprise. Philippians is the antithesis of Romans.

And yet, under this guise of informality there lurks a very serious concern on Paul's part. There is a problem in the Philippian church. Two of the leaders are at odds with one another. Their disunity threatens the unity of the whole church. The church needs to be reunited. But Paul knows that to tackle this issue head on would hinder, not help, the very unity he craves. Thus he deals with it indirectly.

So, in his letter, first he conveys news of his situation to them. He is in prison, but this is a matter of no importance to Paul since the gospel is being preached. He knows that they too share this same passion to see the gospel advance. But they have a problem. There are false teachers in Philippi who are opposing them. And in order to resist successfully these enemies of the gospel they must be unified as a church. At this point in his letter Paul launches into an eloquent discussion of the nature of unity and how to achieve it. Then he illustrates his point with three case studies that show what unity in relationships is all about. It is only in the last case study that he finally gets to the core problem: the feud between Euodia and Syntyche. By this point in his argument it is

overwhelmingly clear that they must resolve their differences. In other words, Paul says what needs to be said to the Philippians without alienating anyone. Here is an outline of this letter, based on this understanding:

I. Introduction (1:1-11)
   A. Salutation (1:1-2)
   B. Thanksgiving and Prayer (1:3-11)
II. The Advance of the Gospel (1:12-26) (News about Paul and his situation)
III. The Need for Unity (1:27—2:18) (Instructions for the Philippians in their situation)
   A. A Call to Unity (1:27-30)
   B. The Way to Achieve Unity: The Path of Humility (2:1-4)
   C. An Example of Humility: The Incarnation of Christ (2:5-11)
   D. An Exhortation to Unity (2:12-18)
IV. Examples from Three Relationships (2:19—4:9)
   A. A Positive Example: The Relationship of Paul to Timothy and Epaphroditus (2:19-30)
   B. The Opposite Problem: Warning Against False Teachers (3:1—4:1)
   C. A Negative Example: The Relationship between Euodia and Syntyche (4:2-9)
V. Conclusion (4:10-23)
   A. Thanks for Their Gift (4:10-20)
   B. Final Greetings (4:21-23)

Further Study

1. Read Philippians quickly in one sitting. Then try to sum up in one paragraph what Paul is saying in this letter.
2. Paul uses the noun "joy" and the verb "rejoice" some fourteen times—even though he is writing from prison! See if you can locate the fourteen times these words occur in the NIV translation. (In fact, you will find fifteen uses of these words! But the word translated "joy" in 1:26 is actually from

a different Greek word, one that is sometimes translated "boast.")
3. Read about Paul's first visit to Philippi in Acts 16. How did Paul happen to visit Philippi? What success did he have there? What problems?
4. Read about Paul's return visit to Philippi in Acts 20:1-6. See also 1 Corinthians 16:5; 2 Corinthians 7:5; and 8:1-5. What further light do these texts shed on Paul's relationship to the Philippians?
5. In Acts 16:9, Paul has a "vision" during the night of a man from Macedonia who begs him to come and help them. What do you recall about the role of dreams and visions in the early Christian church? (See also Matthew 1:18—2:23.) What impact have dreams and visions had on your own Christian experience? On that of your church? What is the role of dreams and visions today?
6. Think about how you would write a *formal* letter (for example, to a company where you were seeking a job) as against how you would construct an *informal* letter (for example, to your best friend). Compare and contrast the differences between the two types of letters and then examine Philippians on the basis of these characteristics. What kind of letter is it and why did you come to this conclusion?
7. Paul is concerned about foes from without (false teachers) and foes from within (rival parties). Is your church facing either problem? If so, describe it and how you are dealing with it.

UNIT 1—Salutation/Philippians 1:1-2

TEXT

1 Paul and Timothy, servants of Christ Jesus.
To all the saints in Christ Jesus at Philippi,
together with the overseers[a] and deacons:
²Grace and peace to you from God our
Father and the Lord Jesus Christ.

᷇ᵃ1 Traditionally *bishops*

STUDY

READ

Two readings of the passage are suggested—each with a response to be checked or filled in on the worksheet.

First Reading/First Impressions: To get familiar with the Scripture passage as though you are reading the passage for the first time and to record your "first impressions" on the worksheet.

Practice: Read through the entire letter (in a modern translation) and check two boxes below that best describe the *tone* or *mood* of this letter.

☐ Stiff and formal—a business letter
☐ Warm and friendly—to old friends
☐ Cold and frosty—from a lawyer
☐ Light and chatty—from a college roommate
☐ Polite and diplomatic—from a politician

☐ Serious and sombre—a general to his army
☐ Heavy and theological—from a professor
☐ Fatherly and pastoral—a pastor to his flock
☐ _____

Second Reading/Theme or Headline: To get the overall idea, thought or "gist" of the book, as though you are seeing the action from the press box—high above the stadium.

Practice: Read the entire book a second time and check the box that best describes the "big idea" in this book.

☐ Paint or get off the ladder
☐ Tough times never last but tough people do
☐ Every day with Jesus is sweeter than the day before
☐ You only go around once, so reach for the gusto

☐ Who said you can't have it all?
☐ Look for the silver lining
☐ Winning isn't everything. It is the only thing.
☐ Live one day at a time.
☐ Let the good times roll.
☐ _____

SEARCH

1. What are the circumstances surrounding Paul's first visit to Philippi? (Acts 16:6-12)

2. What happened on Paul's first visit to Philippi that caused the church there to feel a special debt of gratitude to Paul? (Acts 16:13-40)

3. Who was one of the early converts to Christ in Philippi? (Acts 16:27-34)

4. What caused Paul to make a second visit to Philippi? (Acts 20:1-6)

5. How did the church in Philippi show their concern for Paul and what did Paul promise them? (Phil. 2:25 and 4:19)

6. How does Paul refer to himself and Timothy? (Phil. 1:1)

7. To what three groups in Philippi does Paul address this letter? (v. 1)

APPLY

As you begin this course, what are some goals you would like to work on? Check one or two from the list below and add anything that you would like to add.

☐ To get to know God in a more personal way.

☐ To understand what I believe as a Christian and where I stand on issues.

☐ To develop my skills in Bible study and personal devotions.

☐ To belong to a small group that will support me in my growth.

☐ To think through my values and priorities in light of God's will

☐ To wrestle with the next step in my spiritual journey with others who care.

What are you willing to commit to in the way of disciplines during the time you are in this course?

☐ To complete the Bible study home assignment before the group meets.

☐ To attend the group meetings except in cases of emergency.

☐ To share in leading the group—taking my turn in rotation.

☐ To keep confidential anything that is shared in the group.

☐ To reach out to others who are not in a group and invite them in.

☐ To attend the teaching session with the Pastor/Teacher.

GROUP AGENDA

Divide into groups of 4 before starting on these questions. Follow the time recommendations.

To Begin/10 Minutes (Choose 1 or 2)

☐ Who is a good letter writer in your family? How good are you at writing letters? ☐ What TV commercial immediately comes to mind when you think of the word "joy"? ☐ From your knowledge of history, what famous battle took place in Philippi? How did this affect world history? ☐ What did you jot down under READ on your worksheet after the first reading? Second reading?

TO GO DEEPER/15 Minutes (Choose 2 or 3)

☐ Go around your group and answer the questions under SEARCH on your worksheet—one person answering question 1, the next person answering question 2, etc. ☐ What is significant about Paul's decision to cross over from Troas to Macedonia and go to Philippi? (Acts 16:9-12) What would this be comparable to today? ☐ What is the difference between Paul's concept of "joy" and today's concept of "happiness"? ☐ CASE HISTORY: Mary has been laid up in a nursing home for several years. There is little hope of her getting out for a visit to her family and friends this Christmas, so she decides to send them a letter. If you were Mary, what would you want to say in the Christmas letter? If some of your family and friends had given up their Christian faith, how would you explain your faith?

TO CLOSE/5 to 20 Minutes (Choose 1 or 2)

☐ Discuss what you jotted down under APPLY on your worksheet. How can you help each other reach the goals you set? ☐ Who was the Apostle Paul in your life—who introduced you to Christ or wrote encouraging letters to you? ☐ Why did you decide to join this study? What do you need out of this group?

NOTES ON PHILIPPIANS 1:1-2

Summary . . . Paul begins this letter in typical fashion. He includes the three elements normally found in a Greek letter: the name of the sender or senders, the name or names of the recipients, and a word of greeting. This is the pattern followed by all New Testament letters. "X to Y, greetings." In this case, Paul and Timothy are the ones sending this letter. It is addressed to "all the saints in Christ Jesus at Philippi, together with the overseers and deacons." And the greeting is: "grace and peace." However, this salutation does differ in one respect from those in other letters written by Paul. In this letter, Paul does not identify himself as an "apostle." In all his other letters, except for Philemon, when he states his name it is "Paul, called to be an apostle" (1 Corinthians 1:1) or something equivalent. The reason for the omission of his apostolic title is clear. In both Philippians and Philemon, Paul is writing more a personal letter than an official communique. He is writing to friends. Furthermore, in other letters he is often dealing with controversial issues in situations where not everyone recognizes his authority. By including his title he makes it clear that he is not just sharing his private feelings about the matter but communicating God's Word to them in his role as an apostle.

v. 1 Paul and Timothy . . . This is not really a joint letter written by the two men. It is Paul's letter as becomes clear in 1:3 when he states "*I* give thanks," not "*we* give thanks." Then in 2:19, he refers to Timothy by name: "I hope . . . to send Timothy to you. . . ." Paul includes Timothy's name in the salutation perhaps because he was with him when the letter was written and because he was well known in Philippi. Timothy may even have been the one who actually wrote out the letter while Paul dictated it. (Paul

generally dictated his letters—see Romans 16:22.) In any case, this is Paul's letter and it is a very personal document.

Timothy . . . Timothy had long been a companion of Paul. He was converted as a young man, perhaps during the visit by Paul and Barnabas to his hometown of Lystra (Acts 14:8-20). Several years later when Paul returned to Lystra, he heard good reports about Timothy and so he asked him to join his band as a co-worker (Acts 16:1-3). Timothy was with Paul when he visited Philippi for the first time and so was well known there.

servants . . . The Greek word used here (*doulos*) means literally "slaves." In this context *doulos* has two possible meanings. In the Greek version of the Old Testament this was a word that denoted those individuals who had been chosen by God for a special task (like Moses—see Nehemiah 10:29, and David—see Psalm 89:20). But *doulos* also referred to the countless slaves in the first-century Roman world. In the Old Testament sense, *doulos* is a positive word and signifies those who have been specially chosen by God. In the Greek sense, *doulos* was an ugly word, connoting absolute subservience. It is not clear in which sense Paul means it here, but it is likely that his readers heard it in the second way: "Paul and Timothy, *slaves* of Christ Jesus." Certainly Paul lived a life of total (and willing) submission to the Lord. And in Philippians this is one point he will stress—that the Christians need to serve one another. (See also Romans 6:16-23 and 1 Corinthians 7:22-23.)

The unique thing about the use of this word here, however, is that it is plural and

applies to both Paul and Timothy. In other letters Paul calls himself "a servant of Christ Jesus" (Romans 1:1) but he never gives this title to anyone else. This seems to be part of his apostolic designation. When others are mentioned—including Timothy—they are called "brothers." For example, in Colossians 1:1 he writes: "Paul, an apostle of Christ Jesus by the will of God, and Timothy our brother . . ." (See also 1 and 2 Corinthians 1:1; Galatians 1:2; and Philemon 1.) As Hawthorne writes:

> Why then did the apostle dare to share, for this one time only, his otherwise carefully and jealously guarded uniqueness? The best explanation seems to be that Paul, by such condescension, was most effectively able to teach the Philippians a lesson they needed to learn—"that relationships in the bosom of the church between collaborators were not those of authority, superiority or inferiority but of humble equality" (Collange; cf. Phil. 2:5-11).

to all . . . This letter is addressed not just to a select few in the church at Philippi, but to everyone. Paul does not often stress this point in his letters. In fact, the only other letter which he addresses to *all* in the church is Romans (see Romans 1:7). But here in this letter, it is important for Paul to emphasize the fact that he is grateful to everyone and concerned about the welfare of the whole church, lest any feel that he is taking sides in the internal dissension they are experiencing. The problem in Philippi is the lack of unity—and here Paul teaches in a subtle way that they are all one. He continues this stress by using the inclusive phrase *all of you* throughout his letter. This phrase is found in 1:4, 7 (twice), 8, 25; 2:17, and 26.

saints . . . The Greek word used here is *hagios* and means "saints" when it is a noun and "holy" when it is an adjective. This designation is not meant to imply that the individuals to whom Paul was writing were especially pious or that they lived lives of exceptional character. It is a word used to denote those who are Christians, who because of their union with Christ have been set apart to serve God. In fact, this is the word that is customarily used in the New Testament instead of the word "Christians." It occurs some 60 times in the New Testament while the word "Christian" occurs only three times (Acts 11:26; 26:28, and 1 Peter 4:16). At the root of the word is the idea of being "separate" or "set apart." "Saints" are those who have been set apart to be God's people. This word was used in the Old Testament to describe God who alone was "holy," (i.e., different from all others. See Leviticus 19:2). Because of their special relationship with God, priests came to be called "holy," since they were set apart to do special work for God (Leviticus 21:6). Eventually the whole nation of Israel was considered "holy" by virtue of the covenant between them and God (Exodus 19:5-6). God set apart this nation to be his people. In the New Testament this word was applied to the church, which was seen as the new Israel.

in Christ Jesus . . . The people to whom Paul is writing became "saints" not by any virtue of their own but because of their union with Christ. The phrase "in Christ Jesus" is one of Paul's favorites. He uses it literally hundreds of times, and by it he describes the essence of the Christian experience.

together with . . . Having addressed the fellowship ("all the saints"), Paul now addresses the leadership. As indicated by this phrase, the relationship between the two is horizontal, not vertical. The members are not *under* the leaders but *in company with* them.

overseers and deacons . . . The function of these individuals is not completely clear, except that they are leaders of some sort, quite possibly appointed by Paul. The Philippian church was now large enough to require regularized leadership. The Greek word translated "overseers" is *episkopoi*. It is often translated "bishops," as in the KJV, RSV, and NEB. In its secular use, *episkopoi* was a title given to individuals who held a variety of jobs ranging from tutors to temple officials. It carries with it the idea of supervision. The Greek word for "deacons" is *diakonoi* and refers to those who served others in some way, such as by being a messenger or a temple attendant. It is possible to translate this phrase "overseers and deacons" as "overseers who serve," in which case it would refer to one group of individuals, not two. Thus it would reinforce what Paul is trying to teach the Philippians about service. In whatever way it is translated, the reference is plural. There is not just one bishop/overseer but several.

v. 2 **grace and peace** . . . At this point in a secular Greek letter, the writer would normally say "rejoice." But here Paul wishes them "grace" which is a word that comes from the same Greek root as the secular greeting "rejoice." In a Hebrew letter the writer would say "peace" *(shalom)*. Paul links the two wishes together to form a distinctively Christian greeting.

grace . . . Grace is central to the Christian life. It is at the heart of the Christian gospel. It speaks of God's saving work in Christ Jesus whereby men and women can experience forgiveness and new life—not because of what they have done by way of good works—but because of what Jesus has done for them on the cross. To wish grace for others is to wish for them that they will be able to live on the basis of the freely given love and power of Jesus Christ in their lives—and not try to make it on their own in their own power.

peace . . . peace also lies at the heart of the gospel. It too is a gift of God. It defines the results of Christ's saving activities. It is what people experience as a result of having accepted the gift of grace. To wish peace for persons is to wish for their wholeness and well-being. It is to wish for their salvation on the deepest level of their personalities. It is to wish that they will live their lives on the basis of the secure knowledge that they are, indeed, reconciled to God.

from God our Father and the Lord Jesus Christ . . . The co-source of such "grace and peace" is, of course, God the Father and Jesus the Son.

UNIT 2—Thanksgiving and Prayer/Philippians 1:3-11

TEXT

Thanksgiving and Prayer

³I thank my God every time I remember you. ⁴In all my prayers for all of you, I always pray with joy ⁵because of your partnership in the gospel from the first day until now, ⁶being confident of this, that he who began a good work in you will carry it on to completion until the day of Christ Jesus.

⁷It is right for me to feel this way about all of you, since I have you in my heart; for whether I am in chains or defending and confirming the gospel, all of you share in God's grace with me. ⁸God can testify how I long for all of you with the affection of Christ Jesus.

⁹And this is my prayer: that your love may abound more and more in knowledge and depth of insight, ¹⁰so that you may be able to discern what is best and may be pure and blameless until the day of Christ, ¹¹filled with the fruit of righteousness that comes through Jesus Christ—to the glory and praise of God.

STUDY

READ

First Reading/First Impressions
What's going on here? (Check two) ☐ Preaching ☐ Teaching ☐ Warning ☐ Comforting ☐ Pleading

☐ Defending ☐ Other _____

Second Reading/Big Idea
What's the main point or topic? (Fill in the box)

SEARCH

1. How does Paul feel about the church in Philippi? (vv. 3-6)

2. How did the relationship Paul had with this church affect his prayers for them? (vv. 3-6)

3. Why did Paul feel as he did toward these people? (v. 5)

4. What is his sure hope for these Christians? (v. 6)

5. How does Paul explain and defend his feelings? (vv. 7-8)

6. What is Paul's prayer for these Christians? (v. 9)

7. What are the results that will follow if this happens? (v. 10)

$$\begin{pmatrix} \\ \\ \end{pmatrix}$$

8. What is the ultimate dream for the Philippians? (v. 11)

$$\begin{pmatrix} \\ \end{pmatrix}$$

APPLY

Paraphrase. From now on in the APPLY phase, you will be asked to try a different form of application in each unit. In this unit we want you to try Paraphrase—the most basic of all forms of Bible study application.

Go back and read verse 6—phrase by phrase. Close your eyes and try to restate the thought here *in your own everyday words*—like you were explaining the thought to your next-door neighbor.

Then, in the space below, write you own original expanded translation, using your own slang and street language. For example:

"I am sure of this, God is doing his thing in you and will continue to do his thing.... You may not see anything happening ... but God is not going to let you go until ..." etc.

Be creative. Be original. And use a little "literary license" if you wish, but get the main idea across in verse 6.

GROUP AGENDA

Divide into groups of 4 before starting on these questions. Watch the time and ask the group to "move on" after the recommended time.

TO BEGIN/10 Minutes (Choose 1 or 2)

☐ Are you better at expressing your feelings in a letter or face to face? ☐ When you really care about someone, are you more likely to send them a funny card or a touching one? ☐ Who do you look up to for their ability to "rejoice" in times of confinement? ☐ When you were growing up, who was the person that believed in you and assured you that "everything would turn out all right"? ☐ What did you jot down under READ on your worksheet?

TO GO DEEPER/15 Minutes (Choose 2 or 3)

☐ Go around and share what you jotted down under SEARCH on your worksheet—one person answering question 1, the next person question 2, etc. ☐ Rumor has it that Paul was a cold, unfeeling sort of person. How does this passage fit that stereotype? ☐ From the prayer that Paul explains in verses 9-11, what is he concerned about in this young church? What does he want them to do? ☐ CASE HISTORY: You tried to raise your children in the Christian faith, but one by one they have slipped away from their faith in God. Recently you discovered you have cancer and not very long to live. What do you say to your children?

TO CLOSE/5 to 20 Minutes (Choose 1 or 2)

☐ How did you paraphrase verse 6 under APPLY on the worksheet? ☐ How are you at believing that God is at work in the lives of your children—particularly when you see no evidence of it? ☐ How would you describe your spiritual life this past week in terms of weather: sunny and warm? stormy? cold and foggy? etc.

NOTES ON PHILIPPIANS 1:3-11

Summary . . . In a typical Greek letter following the salutation a prayer was offered on behalf of the recipients. Paul follows this custom here, as he does in most of his letters. Specifically, he thanks God for the long partnership he has had with the Philippians. He expresses his gratitude (vv. 3-6) and his affection for them (vv. 7-8). Then he describes his prayer for them (vv. 9-11). In the course of this thanksgiving and prayer, Paul touches upon many of the themes that he will deal with in the letter: joy, thankfulness, love and affection, partnership/fellowship in the gospel, the day of Christ, his imprisonment, the completion of one's faith, and so on.

vv. 3-6 . . . Paul begins by expressing how thankful he is for the Philippians.

v. 4 with joy . . . "Joy" is the theme that pervades Philippians. It is appropriate that the first reference to joy is in connection with prayer. Paul says that it is easy for him to pray for the Philippians. They are dear friends. But even more than that, they have long been partners with him in the work of the gospel. Thus, when he prays for them, it is with "inward rejoicing."

This is the first of some fourteen times in Philippians that Paul will use the noun "joy" (*chara*—5 times) or the related verb "rejoice" (*chairein*—9 times). In addition, he mentions "shared joy" twice (*sun-chairein*) and uses the related concept "boasting" three times (*kauchema* twice and *kauchasthai* once). Of all the New Testament writers, Paul is the one who refers most to "joy" in all its aspects. For Paul, the gospel was about "joy" as well as about "grace." (It is interesting to note that the Greek word for "grace" — *charis*, comes from the same root, *char-*, as that for "joy" — *chara*. The connection

between these two words is that "grace" which is "unmerited favor" brings "joy" to the recipient.)

For the most part in the New Testament, *chara* and *chairein* are used to express an attitude of inward joy or delight. "Joy" was a characteristic of the teaching of Jesus (Luke 15:5, 32; Matthew 13:44-46). There is "joy" in believing the gospel (Acts 8:4-8, 39; 13:48). Paul "rejoiced" over his converts and friends in the church (1 Thessalonians 3:9; Colossians 2:5; Romans 16:19). But "joy" is also connected with suffering (Matthew 5:12; Acts 5:41; Colossians 1:11-12, 24; 1 Peter 4:13; Hebrews 12:2). Still, it is the hope of glory that brings this "inward joy" to the Christian. "Christianity is a message of joy from beginning to end" (Morrice).

v. 5 partnership . . . The Greek word rendered here as "partnership" is the familiar word *koinonia*, translated elsewhere as "fellowship." It means, literally, "having something in common." In the New Testament it carries with it the idea of men and women bound together in a community of love, sharing, and active burden-bearing. In this context it communicates the idea that ministry is not something which only select individuals like Paul do. The whole fellowship shares together as partners in ministry, each contributing what they can.

in the gospel . . . The Philippians were partners with Paul in spreading the gospel. Specifically, they supported him financially in his ministry (2:25; 4:10-20); they worked with him to spread the gospel (4:3); they prayed for him (1:19); and they contributed generously to the

fund he raised in aid of the poor Christians in Jerusalem (2 Corinthians 8:1-5).

v. 6 confident . . . To be confident is to be sure of something, to be convinced that it is so. This is yet another of the underlying themes in Philippians—confidence. Paul is *confident* that he will go on living in order to encourage them in the faith (1:25—the word translated "convinced" is the same Greek word as used here). He is *confident* that he will be released from prison and that he will visit them (2:24). Others have been made *confident* by his example of preaching the gospel while in chains and so are bolder in their own proclamation (1:14—the word translated "encouraged" is the same Greek word as used here). Paul makes it very clear what lies at the root of this confidence. It is not human accomplishment or ritual of any sort (3:3-4). This is conviction that springs out of faith in who God is and what he is doing. Paul is confident *"in the Lord"* (2:24—see also 2:13). Confidence, like joy, permeates this epistle.

good work . . . There is a difference of opinion as to the nature of this "good work." Some would see this as the work of salvation begun in the lives of the Philippians which will be consummated when the Lord returns. Others see this as a reference to the work of advancing the gospel which will be carried on by the Philippians right up until the Second Coming. In this second sense, the idea is that they would not cease in their support of Paul's ministry.

vv. 7-8 . . . From *thanksgiving*, Paul now turns to an expression of his *affection* for the Philippians.

v. 7 feel ... This is another favorite word of Paul. He uses it ten times in Philippians (1:7; 2:2 [twice]; 2:5; 3:15 [twice]; 3:19; 4:2, 10 [twice]). It is translated various ways in these verses because it is not an easy word to render into English. It carries not only the idea of an attitude or an emotion (as in English) but also the concept of how one thinks about someone (or something) and what one plans to do because of these thoughts and feelings (which is not part of the English concept of "feeling"). "This word signifies a combination of intellectual and affective activity which touches head and heart, and leads to a positive course of action" (Martin).

defending and confirming the gospel ... These are legal terms. The reference is to Paul's defense before the Roman court in which he hopes to be able not only to vindicate himself and the gospel from false charges, but to proclaim the gospel in life-changing power to those in the courtroom. (See Acts 26 for an example of how Paul did this when he stood in court before Agrippa and Festus.)

grace ... In this context, "grace" does not refer to God's saving act (as in 1:2—see note), but to God's granting of spiritual gifts. In this case, the reference would be to Paul's gifting to be an apostle. The Philippians shared in Paul's gift through their continued support of his ministry.

v. 8 God can testify ... In moments of deep feeling, Paul will sometimes invoke God to bear witness to the authenticity of these feelings. (See also Romans 1:9; 2 Corinthians 11:11, 31; 1 Thessalonians 2:5.)

I long ... This is a strong word which expresses the depth of Paul's feelings for them, his desire to be with them, and his wish to minister to them.

all of you ... Once again Paul emphasizes that his care is for every person in the church, not just for one group or for certain individuals. He loves the warring women (4:2-3) as much as Epaphroditus who brought the church's gift to him. In first-century culture a solemn oath such as he has just taken ("God can testify") would be considered "proof" of the genuineness of his feelings (see Hebrews 6:16).

with the affection of Christ Jesus ... This phrase in Greek is literally, "in the viscera of Christ Jesus."

In Greek the viscera were the nobler organs of the body—the heart, liver and lungs (not the intestines)—and were regarded as the seat and origin of the deeply felt emotions such as anger and love. So Paul is saying, in effect: 'If it is true that you hold me in your heart (v. 7), and this is the measure of your affection for me, I wish to assure you that I long for you. I hold you in the heart of Christ Jesus! This is the measure and meaning of my affection for you.' Surely this astonishing metaphor powerfully drove home to the Philippians the depth and reality of Paul's love for them! (Hawthorne).

vv. 9-11 ... Paul began this unit with thanksgiving (vv. 3-6), moved to affection (vv. 7-8) and now he ends with intercession (vv. 9-11).

v. 9 this is my prayer ... Paul's love for the Philippians leads him to pray on their behalf. What he prays is that they will

overflow with love. He prays that this love will increase (i.e., that it will go on developing) and that it will be regulated by knowledge and discernment.

knowledge and depth of insight ... This growing love is to be focused by intellectual and moral insight. Both qualities are gifts from God. Both are nurtured by listening to wise teachers and learning from experience.

v. 10 to discern what is best ... The Philippians are being confronted with competing ideologies. They are being given different information from what they had been taught as to what is true and how to live. (The problem with the false teachers will be made clear as the epistle unfolds.) They need "knowledge" and "insight" in order to choose and follow that which is of God and so results in "purity" and "blamelessness." The word translated "discern" is used to describe the process of testing coins so as to distinguish between those that are real and those that are counterfeit.

vv. 10-11 pure/blameless/fruit of righteousness ... These three terms describe the kind of people this sort of focused love produces. These are people who are morally pure (i.e., their lives are transparent, free from stain); who give no offense or bring no harm to others; and who are authentically good people.

through Jesus Christ ... the source of such goodness is the Lord.

Introductory Handout for Philippians[1]

ChristCare Series

SESSION	DATE	PASSAGE	THEME
1	9/9	1:1–11	Salutation (1:1–2) Thanksgiving and Prayer (1:3–11)
2	9/23	1:12–26	Paul's Chains Advance the Gospel (1:12–18a) Life or Death? (1:18b–26)
3	9/30	1:27–2:11	Living Worthy of the Gospel (1:27–2:4) The Humility of Christ (2:5–11)
4	10/14	2:12–2:30	Shining as Stars (2:12–18) Timothy and Epaphroditus (2:19–30)
5	10/28	3:1–4:1	No Confidence in the Flesh (3:1–11) Pressing On toward the Goal (3:12–4:1)
6	11/11	4:2–9	Exhortations (4:2–9)
7	12/2	4:10–23	Thanks for Their Gifts (4:10–20) Final Greetings (4:21–23)

Christmas Break

General Background Information on Philippians

Author

Paul wrote the book of Philippians from prison. The best guess about the location of his imprisonment is Rome. This would place the writing of Philippians a little after A.D. 60.

Addressee

Paul wrote this letter to the church in Philippi. Philippi was the leading city of Macedonia, which enjoyed special prominence during the time of Paul. The city was a Roman colony enjoying all the rights and privileges of Rome itself. The citizens were even exempt from land tax and poll tax. The citizens of Philippi felt much pride in their city and position in the Roman Empire.

Paul founded the church during his second missionary journey (Acts 16:12–40). Lydia, a merchant of purple cloth, was his first contact. She and her whole household became followers of Jesus.

Paul also cast out a demon from a fortune-telling slave girl. Without the demon she was unable to predict the future and her owners lost a major source of income. Paul and Silas were imprisoned. That night an earthquake released them from prison while they sang hymns and prayed. This escape resulted in the conversion of the jailer and his household.

The following day the magistrates discovered that Paul and Silas were Roman citizens and asked them to leave the city.

Occasion

The church in Philippi had sent Epaphroditus with a monetary gift for Paul. Epaphroditus became very sick while delivering the money. This caused much concern in the church at Philippi. After Epaphroditus recovered, Paul sent him back to Philippi to ease the minds of his friends and family. Paul writes Philippians to pave the way for Epaphroditus' return and to thank the church at Philippi for their gift. He also tells them of his desire to send Timothy. Paul also takes the opportunity to warn them about certain troublemakers who seek to undermine both their doctrine and morals, and to warn them about disunity in their ranks. This is one of Paul's most personal letters because he's writing to old friends and colleagues. He views the Philippians as his "crown and joy" (4:1).[2]

Outline of the Book of Philippians
I. Introduction (1:1–11)
II. The Advance of the Gospel (1:12–26)
III. The Need for Unity (1:27–2:18)
IV. Examples from Three Relationships (2:19–4:9)
V. Conclusion (4:10–23)[3]

ENDNOTES

1. Adapted from *Mastering the Basics: Study Guide for the Book of Philippians* by Lyman Coleman and Richard Peace (Littleton: Serendipity, 1986), inside front cover.

2. Adapted from *Mastering the Basics: Study Guide for the Book of Philippians* by Lyman Coleman and Richard Peace (Littleton: Serendipity, 1986), pages 9–11.

3. Adapted from *Mastering the Basics: Study Guide for the Book of Philippians* by Lyman Coleman and Richard Peace (Littleton: Serendipity, 1986), page 11.

ChrisᏟare Series

First Steps in Faith
A Topical Biblical Equipping Series

Introductory Handout

Session	Date	Theme	Scripture
1	7/11	Gideon: Learning to Try	Judges 6:1–4, 6, 11–16, 25–32
2	7/18	Abraham: Learning to Leave	Genesis 12:1–9 Hebrews 11:8–10
3	7/25	Samuel: Learning to Listen	1 Samuel 3:1–10
4	8/1	Naaman: Learning to Obey	2 Kings 5:1–19
5	8/8	Jonah: Learning to Love	Jonah 3 and 4
6	8/15	Mary: Learning to Trust	Luke 1:26–38
7	8/22	Paul: Learning to Repent	Acts 9:1–20
8	8/29	Lydia: Learning to Serve	Acts 16:11–15, 40
9	9/5	The Canaanite Woman: Learning to Persevere	Matthew 15:21–28

"First Steps in Faith" is a fictitious example.
Such a topical Biblical Equipping series
does not actually exist.

Supplement E

Biblical Equipping Questions for ChristCare Group Leaders

ChrisƟare Series

Ideas for using these questions:

- Change the wording to fit your needs.
- Freely substitute *Jesus* or *the Holy Spirit* for *God*, or vice versa, except where that obviously won't work.
- Use these questions as a starting point for your own creativity. When you come up with new questions, add them to the list. Then you will have them for future use or adaptation.
- There are many questions in these lists, so you can find questions that fit your group and the passage you are encountering. You may come back to some questions again and again. You may never use others.
- Note that there is some overlap between Explore and Connect questions. You will find this same kind of overlap between Explore and Connect in your group's discussions. That's fine, as long as you avoid emphasizing one type of question to the exclusion of the other.
- Questions that fit in more than one category are listed more than once.

Explore Questions

It's important to know the purpose of Explore questions—to try to understand:

- what the text meant to the person who wrote it and to those who first read it;
- what God is communicating through this passage.

When you understand the purpose of Explore questions, you can either choose questions from this list or make up your own—whatever best gets at the original meaning.

A. What Is God Like?

1. What basic truths about God do you find in this passage?
2. What does this passage teach you about Jesus? About his personality? About what is important to him?

3. What does this passage show you about what God was like then? What does it tell you about what God is like now?
4. What does God think in this passage? What do God's thoughts tell you about who God is?
5. What does God feel in this passage? What do God's feelings tell you about who God is?
6. What does God do in this passage? What do God's actions tell you about who God is?
7. What does God say in this passage? What do God's words tell you about who God is?
8. What name or names is God called in this passage? What do those names mean? What do they tell you about who God is?
9. Brainstorm as many one-word descriptions as you can of God as you see him in this passage.
10. What does this passage tell you about the character of God?
11. How does the picture of God in this passage contradict our current cultural stereotypes about God?
12. What does God do when he gets angry?
13. How does this passage demonstrate God's mercy?
14. How does this passage demonstrate God's patience?
15. How does this passage demonstrate God's love?
16. What about God in this passage surprises you?
17. How does this passage change the way you think about God?
18. How did God seem to change in this passage? What brought about this change?

B. What Does God Want?

1. What values does God hold to in this passage?
2. What is important to God in this passage?

3. What does this passage teach about what it means to live as a disciple of Jesus?

C. How Does God Relate to People?

1. What spiritual gifts does God give people in this passage? What does that tell you about what God is like?

2. Does Jesus relate to different people in different ways in this passage? How so? How are the people different? How do their differences influence the way Jesus treats them?

3. Does God relate to people differently at the end of this passage than at the beginning? To what do you attribute the differences?

4. How does God help people be the people God wants them to be in this passage?

5. How does Jesus relate to people in this passage? What does he give them? What does he demand of them?

6. What is the situation for the people in this passage? Why do you think they are in that situation?

D. How Does God Love Us?

1. What evidence of God's love do you see in this passage?

2. How does God love in this passage? What does it cost God to love in this way?

3. What do people do that makes God angry in this passage? How does God treat people when God gets angry?

4. How did God care for people in this passage?

5. How did God meet people's needs in this passage?

6. Did the people in this passage deserve God's love? Why or why not? Is it possible for us to deserve God's love?

Connect Questions

It's important to know the purpose of Connect questions—to try to understand how the original meaning of the passage applies in group members' lives today. When you understand the purpose of Connect questions, you can either choose questions from this list or make up your own—whatever best applies the original meaning.

When a question refers to the person or people in this passage, it can mean the people in the story

or incident described or, in the case of a passage from an epistle, for example, the people to whom the epistle was written.

A. God's Care

1. How does this passage help you see God's love more clearly in your own life?

2. If God were like this all the time, how do you think your life would be different?

3. How did God sustain this biblical character, or the people to whom this passage is written, through their time of difficulty? How has God sustained you through times of difficulty? How do you *wish* God would sustain you through times of difficulty? How might God use you to help sustain others through times of difficulty?

4. How does God care for people wholistically (physically, emotionally, socially, intellectually, and spiritually) in this passage? What does that teach you about how God cares for us?

5. What does God give to people in this passage? What has God given to you recently?

6. How did the people in this passage trust God to meet their needs? How can you trust in similar ways?

B. God's Will

1. How is God challenging the person in the passage, or those to whom the passage was written? How is God challenging you in similar ways?

2. What do you see in this passage that shows how God wants Christians to relate to each other? To the world? How is God calling you to relate with others differently?

3. What does God give to people in this passage? What has God given to you recently?

4. How is God calling you to change now? What help is God giving you to help you change?

C. God at Work in Our Lives

1. How is the Spirit leading you to apply these truths to your own life?

2. What lesson is there for you in this passage?

3. What spiritual gifts does the Spirit give people in this passage? Why does the Spirit give those gifts? What does God expect people to do with their spiritual gifts?

4. How did God respond to people's feelings in this passage? How does God respond to you when you have feelings like those?

5. How did God respond to people's thoughts in this passage? How does God respond to you when you have thoughts like those?

6. How did God respond to people's words in this passage? How does God respond to you when you say things like that?

7. How did God respond to people's actions in this passage? How does God respond to you when you act that way?

8. How was the character in this passage transformed? How is God transforming you right now?

9. How does this passage help you understand and receive the Spirit's power and wisdom so that you can be and do what God wants?

10. How does this passage teach you to communicate with God? How does it teach you to pray?

11. What does our study of this passage teach you about how to study the Bible on your own?

12. How did the people in this passage trust God to meet their every need? In what specific area of your life is God calling you to give up trying to run things yourself and trust completely in God's love and power?

13. What was it that made it possible for the person in this passage to live in ways that pleased God? How can you live in ways that please God?

14. What does this passage show you about ways you need to grow in order to serve God more effectively? How can this small group help you grow in those ways?

15. What spiritual gifts did you learn about or see people using in this passage? What does that suggest to you about your own spiritual gifts?

16. How did people use, or misuse, their spiritual gifts in this passage? What does the passage suggest to you about how to use your spiritual gifts?

D. Our Response to God's Love

1. What is the question God is asking of the person in the passage? Is God asking the same question of you? If so, what is your answer?

2. How did the people in this passage change their ideas about God? How does this passage cause you to change your ideas about God?

3. How does this passage give you hope for the future?

4. What does God want of people in this passage? What does God want of you now?

5. Who is God calling you to be through this passage?

6. What is God calling you to do through this passage?

7. How did people in this passage obey God? What does this passage teach you about how you can obey God?

8. What changes does this passage challenge you to make in your life? How can the group help and support you in making those changes?

9. How did the people in this passage, or those to whom this passage was written, live as witnesses to Jesus? What does this passage show you about how you can live as a witness too?

10. How did the people in this passage communicate the truth about God to others? What is one situation in your life in which you have an opportunity to communicate God's truth to others? What does this passage tell you about how to do that?

11. What does God want from people in this passage? How do (or don't) they give God what he wants? What does God want from you? How can you give God what he wants?

12. How do people in this passage respond to God's love? How might you respond to God's love?

13. How do people in this passage worship God? Does this passage give you any ideas about how you might worship God?

14. How did the people in this passage serve God? How does their example help you choose kinds of service you might engage in? What does their service teach you about how you might serve God?

15. What does this passage teach you about what it means to live as a disciple of Jesus? How do you need to grow and change in order to live as a more effective disciple of Jesus? How can this small group help you grow and change in those ways?

16. How does this passage help you become more loving?

17. How does this passage help you become more peaceful?

18. How does this passage help you become more patient?

19. How does this passage help you become kinder?

20. How does this passage help you become more generous?

21. How does this passage help you become more faithful?

22. How does this passage help you exercise more self-control?

23. How does this passage help you become more like Jesus?

24. How does this passage help you know better how to pray?

25. How does this passage help you better understand and do God's will in a particular circumstance in your life right now?

26. How does this passage challenge unquestioned traditions?

27. What does this passage show you about how we can be more faithful followers of Jesus?

How to Use the Bible as an Equipping Tool—Part 1

Group-Based Manual for ChristCare Group Leaders

Outline and Focus Notes

All scripture is inspired by God and is useful for teaching, for reproof, for correction, and for training in righteousness, so that everyone who belongs to God may be proficient, equipped for every good work.

2 Timothy 3:16–17 NRSV

1. Class Member-Led Prayer and Worship

2. Biblical Equipping: The Crop That God's Word Grows in Our Lives (Matthew 13:1-9, 18-23)

FOCUS NOTE 1

The Crop That God's Word Grows in Our Lives (Matthew 13:1–9, 18–23)

13:1 That same day Jesus went out of the house and sat by the lake. 2 Such large crowds gathered around him that he got into a boat and sat in it, while all the people stood on the shore. 3 Then he told them many things in parables, saying: "A farmer went out to sow his seed. 4 As he was scattering the seed, some fell along the path, and the birds came and ate it up. 5 Some fell on rocky places, where it did not have much soil. It sprang up quickly, because the soil was shallow. 6 But when the sun came up, the plants were scorched, and they withered because they had no root. 7 Other seed fell among thorns, which grew up and choked the plants. 8 Still other seed fell on good soil, where it produced a crop—a hundred, sixty or thirty times what was sown. 9 He who has ears, let him hear." . . .

18 "Listen then to what the parable of the sower means: 19 When anyone hears the message about the kingdom and does not understand it, the evil one comes and snatches away what was sown in his heart. This is the seed sown along the path. 20 The one who received the seed that fell on rocky places is the man who hears the word and at once receives it with joy. 21 But since he has no root, he lasts only a short time. When trouble or

Focus Note 1 is continued on page 224.

9-OFN.pmd C: 03/02/2004 R: 11/17/2004

persecution comes because of the word, he quickly falls away. [22] The one who received the seed that fell among the thorns is the man who hears the word, but the worries of this life and the deceitfulness of wealth choke it, making it unfruitful. [23] But the one who received the seed that fell on good soil is the man who hears the word and understands it. He produces a crop, yielding a hundred, sixty or thirty times what was sown."

FOCUS NOTE 2

Explore Questions

1. What did Jesus mean when he said that the person who hears and understands God's Word "produces a crop, yielding a hundred, sixty or thirty times what was sown"? What do you think that "crop" looks like in a person's life?

2. What did Jesus mean when he talked about "hearing and understanding" God's Word?

3. What can get in the way of a person's hearing and understanding God's Word?

FOCUS NOTE 3

Connect Questions

1. What "crop" has God's Word grown in your life? In other words, how is your life different than it would have been if God had never planted his Word in your heart?

2. What can get in the way of our hearing and understanding Jesus' message today?

3. How can we help one another to hear and understand God's Word and to grow God's crop in our lives?

4. How will you help the members of your ChristCare Group to hear and understand God's Word and grow God's crop?

---

3. Biblical Equipping Apart

FOCUS NOTE 4
Biblical Equipping: An Overview

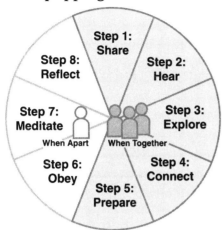

What Is Biblical Equipping?

Biblical Equipping is a disciplined way of encountering the Bible—by yourself and with your ChristCare Group—for the purpose of hearing and understanding God's Word more clearly, knowing and loving God and others more deeply, and living for and serving God more joyfully and obediently.

Steps 1 to 5 are done together in ChristCare Groups, and steps 6 to 8 are done individually by group members during the time in between group meetings.

Biblical Equipping Together

 These steps are done together in ChristCare Groups.

Step 1: Share
Talk with your ChristCare Group about your experience in living as Jesus' disciple and how God's Word has affected your life since the last group meeting.

Step 2: Hear
Begin with silence to open your heart to God's Word. Then listen together as the Bible passage is read. End with silence to receive the message the Holy Spirit would give you.

Step 3: Explore
Together explore the passage in depth. Your group leader will ask focused questions to help you discover what the passage meant to those who wrote and originally heard it.

Step 4: Connect
Apply the Bible's truth to your own life. How do those truths change the way you understand God and others? How do Jesus' teaching and example connect with your own life? How does the Holy Spirit address your needs and challenges in this passage?

Step 5: Prepare
Make a conscious plan to apply the Word to your daily life. Choose a portion of the Bible passage you have just explored to concentrate on during the time between group meetings. What specific steps can you take to live by God's Word, relying on God for the strength to take those steps?

Biblical Equipping Apart

These steps are done individually by group members between group meetings.

Step 6: Obey
Respond to God's Word by living according to what you heard and learned. Conform your thoughts to God's Word. Let it shape your behavior and the way you think about and relate to others and situations you encounter.

Step 7: Meditate
Set aside time daily to meditate. Use the portion of the Bible passage you selected (Step 5), pray about it, and ponder it in your heart. Connect it to what you are thinking, feeling, and experiencing. What is God revealing to you?

Step 8: Reflect
Think about how God is working in your life and how you are doing at living according to God's Word. Decide what experiences you will share with others in your ChristCare Group at your next meeting.

FOCUS NOTE 5

Helping Group Members Find Verses for Meditation

ChristCare Group Leaders can:

• suggest the passage the group worked on in Biblical Equipping;

• suggest another passage that illustrates a concept worked on in Biblical Equipping; or

• invite group members to come up with their own verses or passages from their personal Bible reading.

FOCUS NOTE 6

Meditation

"Fear not, for I have redeemed you;

I have summoned you by name; you are mine.

When you pass through the waters,

I will be with you;

and when you pass through the rivers,

they will not sweep over you.

When you walk through the fire,

you will not be burned;

the flames will not set you ablaze" (Isaiah 43:1b–2).

1. Pray for the Holy Spirit's wisdom and guidance as you meditate.

2. Relax and appreciate this time of calm and quiet. Clear your mind of other concerns. Ask God to fill your mind and speak to you through the passage.

3. Read the passage. Imagine what it would be like to be trapped in a flood or fire, knowing God was protecting you.

4. Think about what these verses say about God, about you, about your ChristCare Group, or about your congregation.

5. Repeat the verses. Say them to yourself several times. Memorize them if you can.

6. Connect these verses with what is going on with you this minute, this day, this month. Ask yourself what God is saying to you or asking you through these verses. How does God want you to respond?

7. Pray, giving thanks for what God has shown you. Ask for God's help in meeting the challenges you've been shown. Pray for other people or situations God brings to mind.

---

4. Using Published Materials

A. How to Use Published Curriculum Materials

B. A Sample of Published Curriculum Materials

C. Other Samples of Published Curriculum Materials

5. How to Prepare a Biblical Equipping Session

FOCUS NOTE 7

Preparing to Lead a Biblical Equipping Session

1. Pray.
2. Read the Scripture and its surrounding context.
3. Look up difficult words and concepts.
4. Choose a way to introduce and focus Step 1: Share.
5. Choose three questions each for Explore and Connect.
6. Decide on which verse you will recommend for Step 5: Prepare, or decide how to help group members choose a verse.

Questions to Get Sharing Started in Step 1: Share

1. What has God taught you in Biblical Equipping Apart since our last meeting?

2. What Bible promises are you having success or trouble in trusting?

3. How has the Biblical Equipping we've done together and apart been affecting your life?

4. How has it been going with your obedience, meditation, and reflection between group meetings?

6. Preparing Your Own Biblical Equipping Session

7. Missional Service Check-in

How to Use the Bible as an Equipping Tool—Part 2

Outline

Your word is a lamp to my feet and a light for my path.

Psalm 119:105

1. How Did Your Preparations Go?

2. Group Members Lead Biblical Equipping

3. Class Member-Led Prayer and Worship

Group-Based Manual for ChristCare Group Leaders
Being a Process-Oriented Leader

Preclass Reading

*Now faith is being sure of what we hope for
and certain of what we do not see.*

Hebrews 11:1

PRECLASS READING OUTLINE

I. Why Is a Process Orientation Important?

II. What Is Process-Oriented Leadership?

   A. Process versus Results

   B. A Biblical Perspective on Process versus Results

   C. God's Results

III. Helping ChristCare Group Members Be Process Oriented

IV. The Results of a Process Orientation

V. Getting Ready for the In-Class Session

I. Why Is a Process Orientation Important?

Consider this scenario:

Jim is a ChristCare Group Leader for six people of varying ages and interests. Jim really enjoyed the first four meetings with his group, but during the next meeting the atmosphere in the group began to change. Mike, an attorney, started to express disappointment that the "group isn't going anywhere." He said things like, "It's frustrating that we haven't really done anything yet." He asked, "When do you think we'll start making some progress . . . you know, really start doing something?" Several group members nodded in agreement. Jim realized that his group had moved to the Ask stage.

By the seventh meeting, several group members openly challenged Jim's leadership. Mike suggested a different meeting format. Jeff and Linda also thought changes were needed, though they disagreed with Mike's solution, and complained that Jim hadn't taken a more active role in solving the group's problems.

Jim doesn't like taking blame he doesn't really deserve, and he doesn't like watching the group members go through seemingly unproductive turmoil. Jim wonders how much longer this will go on.

Jim has two choices at this point:

1. He could take control in order to get quick *results*.

   Jim could choose to pick up his ChristCare Group's reins, get people back into shape, and force the group members to behave in the way he thinks best.

2. He could allow the *process* of maturing to take place.

Jim could choose to keep listening, caring, and affirming while he allows the group to grow through the Test stage at its own pace.

Taking Control and Getting Results

Here's what could happen if Jim chooses the first option:

- The group's outward behavior will shape up, but their inner feelings will not change.
- If Jim forces the group to be polite instead of letting them express conflict, it may stunt the group's growth. They will communicate in a guarded, polite way, but never learn to share deeply with one another.
- The group probably will never come together as a team. They may take on some projects, but they probably won't work together smoothly.
- Group members probably will not develop as leaders.
- Jim will have to keep doing everything for the group by himself.
- The Test stage will be postponed. The group either will go through it later, or they will eventually disband because they have not been allowed to mature.

Allowing the Maturing Process to Take Place

Here's what could happen if Jim chooses the second option:

- The group's behavior may continue to be chaotic and unproductive for a while.
- The group may continue to attack Jim's leadership.
- Group members eventually may recognize their unproductive behavior.
- Some of Jim's messages and modeling will start to get through to the group members.
- Group members will begin to acknowledge their brokenness and turn to one another for acceptance and support.
- Eventually the group members will begin to trust one another and build community.
- Finally the group will move into the Undertake stage of group development and continue the maturing process.

Jim's options can be summed up by the terms *results-oriented* (the first one) and *process-oriented* (the second). As you can tell, process-oriented leadership is better for his group in the long run.

As a ChristCare Group Leader, you'll face many situations in which you could be either a process- or results-oriented leader. In this module you'll gain a better understanding of both relating styles. You'll also see how a process-oriented relating style is the better choice for a ChristCare Group Leader.

II. What Is Process-Oriented Leadership?

A. Process versus Results

What is a process orientation? Simply put, you are process oriented when you focus on the relationship process itself instead of concentrating on the results you want to get. You focus on caring, listening, and accepting people as they are *right now.*

The opposite of process-oriented leadership is results-oriented leadership. Results-oriented leaders focus on achieving a result they want rather than on understanding what the other person is going through. The results are so important to them that they might even use bullying, guilt, or manipulation to get their way.

Notice the differences between a process-oriented leader and a results-oriented leader in the chart on the next page.

It takes patience to be a process-oriented leader. Results-oriented leaders may seem to achieve results quickly, but often those results backfire. Imagine how results could backfire in these situations if a results-oriented ChristCare Group Leader would:

- push a new group member into accepting Christ (results-oriented) rather than focus on his needs and—over time—allow him to see how Christ can meet him (process-oriented);
- tell a grieving group member to pick up the pieces and get on with her life (results-oriented) rather than share her suffering and allow her to work through her grief (process-oriented);
- tell a person struggling with doubts about his faith to "pray and read the Bible and everything will be fine" (results-oriented) rather than patiently listen while he tells about the same doubts over and over again until he works through them to a stronger faith (process-oriented).

Process-Oriented Leaders	Results-Oriented Leaders
1. Build relationships with others	1. Push to achieve their own goals for others or for the group
2. Control their own behavior as ChristCare Group Leaders	2. Try to control group members' behavior
3. Support others in finding their own solutions	3. Try to fix others' problems for them
4. Support group members in developing their leadership skills	4. Keep all leadership tasks to themselves to make sure they are done right
5. Help group members discover their spiritual gifts	5. Discourage individual growth because they fear it will disturb the group's equilibrium
6. Build trust and community within the group	6. Push for accomplishing goals they set for the group
7. Enable group members to grow in a variety of ways as Jesus' disciples	7. Impose on group members their own ideas of what it means to grow in Christ
8. Enable group members to express their brokenness and truly care for one another	8. Expect group members to keep up an appearance of "having it all together" and not needing care
9. Welcome visitors to the group and allow them to be who they are	9. Let visitors know they must conform to a certain pattern of behavior or they won't fit in
10. Give the group the responsibility to set and achieve its own goals	10. Take responsibility for setting goals for the group
11. Encourage group members to express their feelings even when that may lead to conflict in the group	11. Delay or prevent true maturing by forcing the group to stay polite and thus remain in the early stages of development
12. Promote open, honest communication	12. Restrict communication to the "right" topics and opinions
13. Help group members learn to resolve conflict and work together productively	13. Expect group members to rely on the ChristCare Group Leader to sort out differences and direct the work

Our Caring Action	Bible Verse
Sharing others' difficulties instead of trying to fix them	*Carry each other's burdens, and in this way you will fulfill the law of Christ.* Galatians 6:2
Listening to others	*Everyone should be quick to listen, slow to speak and slow to become angry.* James 1:19
Accepting others unconditionally	*Accept one another, then, just as Christ accepted you, in order to bring praise to God.* Romans 15:7
Encouraging others to find their own answers to their challenges	*Therefore encourage one another and build each other up.* 1 Thessalonians 5:11
Acting with humility instead of managing others' lives for them	*Do nothing out of selfish ambition or vain conceit, but in humility consider others better than yourselves.* Philippians 2:3
Respecting others	*Be devoted to one another in brotherly love. Honor one another above yourselves.* Romans 12:10
Showing kindness and forgiveness	*Be kind and compassionate to one another, forgiving each other, just as in Christ God forgave you.* Ephesians 4:32
Being gentle instead of trying to force solutions on others	*But we were gentle among you, like a mother caring for her little children.* 1 Thessalonians 2:7
Being patient while others work through their own pain	*Love is patient.* 1 Corinthians 13:4
Being considerate of others' needs to share their pain	*Remind them . . . to be gentle, and to show every courtesy to everyone.* Titus 3:1–2 NRSV
Showing sympathy toward those in difficult circumstances	*Finally, all of you, have unity of spirit, sympathy, love for one another . . .* 1 Peter 3:8 NRSV
Showing empathy—that is, understanding and sharing others' feelings	*Rejoice with those who rejoice, mourn with those who mourn.* Romans 12:15
Being compassionate	*Finally, all of you, have unity of spirit . . . a tender heart . . .* 1 Peter 3:8 NRSV
Praying for and with others	*Therefore confess your sins to each other and pray for each other so that you may be healed. The prayer of a righteous man is powerful and effective.* James 5:16
Admonishing, but only after building a strong relationship and demonstrating Christian care in other ways	*Let the word of Christ dwell in you richly as you teach and admonish one another with all wisdom . . .* Colossians 3:16

B. A Biblical Perspective on Process versus Results

The concept of process orientation is firmly grounded in Scripture, as you can see from the chart above.

C. God's Results

At this point, you may be wondering, "But what about results? Aren't they important?" Certainly they are! As a ChristCare Group Leader you do want to see people come to believe in Jesus, to work through their grief, or to heal wounded relationships. But you need to remember that *results are up to God*—not to you.

Leaving results up to God requires a great deal of faith and trust from you as a ChristCare Group Leader. Sometimes you will intensely want a particular result in your group. For example, you may deeply care for a group member and really want him or her to trust in Jesus. Or there may be a group member who keeps talking about the same depressing problems over and over again, and you wish he or she could move beyond the need to do so. It's perfectly normal for you to want good results like these; just make sure you don't bypass God and push for the results yourself. Instead, stick patiently with a process orientation and wait for God to bring about results in God's good time.

A good motto for ChristCare Group Leaders to remember is, "Christians are responsible for the care; God is responsible for the cure." The phrases and Bible verses listed in the chart on page 235 describe God's role in bringing results.

As a ChristCare Group Leader, your process-oriented leadership will help your group members grow as individuals and as a community. As you focus on the process, God will bless your ChristCare Group with results.

III. Helping ChristCare Group Members Be Process Oriented

As a process-oriented ChristCare Group Leader, you can help members relate to one another with a process orientation. When both the leader and the members understand and use a process orientation, everyone benefits.

Group members may experience many difficulties that cannot be fixed with a quick suggestion or by a demand that they shape up. Your group may have members who are grieving, looking for a new job, adjusting to a newborn, getting used to being married, or moving into retirement. All of these circumstances require process-oriented care that happens over weeks or months. Quick-fix solutions don't exist. If your ChristCare Group wants to care for those in such crises, its members will need to walk with the hurting people through their process of adjusting. Part of your job as ChristCare Group Leader is to help group members stay process oriented in their care for one another.

Sometimes you will notice small group members responding to each other in a results-oriented way. Here are some examples:

- Group members urge a grieving member to "get over it" and "get on with life."
- One group member believes the group should progress more quickly and pushes the group to do so.
- Whenever a group member talks about a problem, several other group members jump in with advice.
- When a group conflict erupts, one side accuses the other of being faithless and not acting according to God's will.
- One group member regularly coaxes and prods a quiet person to speak up.
- Group members pressure one member to pray aloud even though he or she feels uncomfortable doing this.

When situations like these arise in your ChristCare Group, exert your leadership and move the group toward a process orientation. Here's a list of things you might do.

1. Recognize what's going on.

   This may take some practice. Most people are used to a results orientation and may start relating that way without even realizing it. This can also happen to ChristCare Group Leaders! Get in the habit of asking yourself, "Are we relating in a process-oriented way, or are we pushing for results?"

2. Model a process-oriented approach.

   As a ChristCare Group Leader, be very careful to focus on process rather than results. Group members often notice this, follow your lead, and respond in a process-oriented way themselves.

3. Remind members what a process-oriented approach is.

   Process-oriented relating isn't a secret. Talk about it openly. Teach a lesson on it or lead a discussion about it. One of the simplest ways to explain a process-oriented approach is to use or review session 4 from the *Beginnings* course, "Process-Oriented Caring." Or, if you want to create your own lesson, you can use some of the information and activities from this ChristCare Group Leader training module.

4. Put "process orientation" into your group's vocabulary.

   Work this term into what you say once in a while. Say something like, "Hmm. Now that's a good, process-oriented idea," or "I wonder if we're getting a little results oriented here?" This keeps the two concepts fresh in group members' minds.

Results	Bible Verse
Convincing people of their sin and their need for a Savior	*"When he comes, he will convict the world of guilt in regard to sin and righteousness and judgment."* John 16:8
Giving people faith	*Yet to all who received him, to those who believed in his name, he gave the right to become children of God.* John 1:12 *For it is by grace you have been saved, through faith—and this not from yourselves, it is the gift of God—not by works, so that no one can boast.* Ephesians 2:8–9
Defeating death and providing eternal life	*"My sheep listen to my voice; I know them, and they follow me. I give them eternal life, and they shall never perish; no one can snatch them out of my hand."* John 10:27–28 *Jesus said to her, "I am the resurrection and the life. Those who believe in me, even though they die, will live, and everyone who lives and believes in me will never die. Do you believe this?"* John 11: 25–26 NRSV
Forgiving sin and freeing people from guilt	*Cleanse me with hyssop, and I will be clean; wash me, and I will be whiter than snow.* Psalm 51:7 *Then I acknowledged my sin to you and did not cover up my iniquity. I said, "I will confess my transgressions to the LORD"—and you forgave the guilt of my sin.* Psalm 32:5 *If we confess our sins, he is faithful and just and will forgive us our sins and purify us from all unrighteousness.* 1 John 1:9
Bringing people to conversion and repentance	*Jesus answered, "I am the way and the truth and the life. No one comes to the Father except through me."* John 14:6 *. . . correcting opponents with gentleness. God may perhaps grant that they will repent and come to know the truth . . .* 2 Timothy 2:25 NRSV
Giving people real peace	*Those of steadfast mind you keep in peace—in peace because they trust in you.* Isaiah 26:3 NRSV *Peace I leave with you; my peace I give you. I do not give to you as the world gives. Do not let your hearts be troubled and do not be afraid.* John 14:27 *Do not be anxious about anything, but in everything, by prayer and petition, with thanksgiving, present your requests to God. And the peace of God, which transcends all understanding, will guard your hearts and your minds in Christ Jesus.* Philippians 4:6–7
Giving people lasting hope	*Praise be to the God and Father of our Lord Jesus Christ! In his great mercy he has given us new birth into a living hope through the resurrection of Jesus Christ from the dead.* 1 Peter 1:3

5. Use affirmation and self-disclosure to remind group members about process orientation.

When a group member approaches a situation in a process-oriented way, say, "Marge, I appreciate how you responded to Phyllis. You didn't push her to follow your advice." Or say, "I'm glad you're supporting Dave right now without expecting him to feel better right away." When you catch yourself slipping into a results orientation, say, "Sometimes it's so hard for me to see someone hurting and so easy for me to give advice. John, I'd like you to know that I want to be here for you while you're going through this tough time."

6. Set up a structure for a process-oriented approach.

When your group is facing a problem, has to make a decision, or needs to respond to a group member's pain, guide them into a process-oriented approach. Steer the group away from results-oriented activities such as fixing and giving advice. Steer them toward process-oriented activities such as listening, accepting, and understanding. Say something like, "Let's let Terry know we're going to hang in there with her through this difficult time." Or say, "Some of us have different opinions about this. Let's take some time to hear one another out."

7. Invite the group to step back and analyze.

When you catch a results-oriented approach, ask the group to take a minute to evaluate how they've been relating to one another. Suggest that they brainstorm some ways they could move away from a results-orientation focus and toward a process orientation.

IV. The Results of a Process Orientation

Surprisingly, results start happening when you stop pushing for them! People can actually work against their own goal when they focus on the result, not the process. A lonely person who latches on to people he or she wants to make friends with may actually push people away instead of drawing them closer, while a person who patiently lets relationships grow naturally will more easily make new friends. Similarly, a church member who pushes a friend to accept Christ may harden the person to Christ, while a church member who consistently cares for a friend may eventually draw that person to Jesus.

You can help your ChristCare Group focus on process as they learn to work together and care for one another. As group members learn the process of caring, God will bless your group with results, including:

- An increase in trust, growth, and community

  As group members begin to feel really cared for, they develop deeper relationships with one another. Process-oriented caring helps people feel accepted as they are and gives them the courage to trust others, make changes in themselves, and grow in Christ.

- A new perspective on suffering

  As you and your ChristCare Group members learn to care in a process-oriented way, you gain a new perspective on suffering. You begin to see suffering less as an unexpected catastrophe and more as a painful but expected part of our lives in an imperfect world. You will become better able to live with suffering and to help others live with it too.

- Deepening relationships with God

  As Jesus becomes real in and through the process-oriented care of group members, others meet him and come to know and trust him more completely. Then they begin to share Christ's love with others.

- Increasing hope

  Process-oriented caring gives group members hope as they face big and little crises in their daily lives. It helps so much to know that someone will take the time to understand you and share your burdens.

Can you think of any additional results of leading a ChristCare Group in a process-oriented way?

V. Getting Ready for the In-Class Session

After completing this Preclass Reading, you've learned:

- what process-oriented leadership is;
- the importance of process orientation in a ChristCare Group;
- the results that come naturally when you use a process orientation.

During the in-class training session that's coming up, members will have a chance to practice being a process-oriented ChristCare Group Leader.

In preparation for the in-class training session, recall times when you have experienced a results orientation.

Being a Process-Oriented Leader

Outline and Focus Notes

*Now faith is being sure of what we hope for
and certain of what we do not see.*

Hebrews 11:1

1. Process versus Results Role Play

FOCUS NOTE 1

Roles

• ChristCare Group Leader

• Group member who is always late

• Other ChristCare Group members

FOCUS NOTE 2

Discussion Questions

1. How did it feel to play the role of the group member who's always late?

2. How did it feel to be in the role of the ChristCare Group Leader under pressure to solve the problem of late starts?

3. How did the ChristCare Group members feel as they watched the interaction between the ChristCare Group Leader and the habitually late member?

4. What do you think would be the result of such interaction for the group member who's always late? For the rest of the group?

11-OFN.pmd C: 03/03/2004 R: 12/03/2004

A Process-Oriented Approach

- The ChristCare Group Leader states the problem.

- The ChristCare Group Leader invites group members (including the one who's always late) to offer comments about the problem.

- The ChristCare Group Leader and group members willingly listen to and care for the group member who is always late, allow that group member to express his or her feelings and thoughts, and ask that group member how they can help.

- The ChristCare Group Leader invites group members to offer possible solutions.

2. Process or Results?

Too Shy to Pray

Madeline has been a member of a ChristCare Group for four months. She is a very shy person and doesn't want to pray aloud when the rest of the group does, even just a few words. But Madeline enjoys the group and believes she is growing in her relationship with Jesus because of it.

Amanda, another group member, has noticed that Madeline never prays aloud. Amanda believes that Madeline needs to pray aloud in order to grow in her relationship with Jesus. So Amanda takes Madeline aside and says, "I didn't start growing as a Christian until I overcame my shyness and started praying aloud with others. I think you need to pray aloud too, and I'd like to help. Here are some things you can do. You can write out a prayer and memorize it. Then you can have more confidence when you pray. Or we could try praying aloud, just the two of us. Which one do you choose?"

FOCUS NOTE 5

An Absent Group Member

Martha has missed the last two group meetings and Karen, the ChristCare Group Leader, calls her at home to find out what's going on. Martha talks about some difficulties at work that are interfering with her attendance. Karen listens and lets Martha know that the group members miss her, are praying for her, and will be glad to see her when she can return.

FOCUS NOTE 6

Dealing with an Emergency

Jane and Tom were in the same ChristCare Group. They had dated for several months, but had just stopped seeing each other two weeks earlier. As the ChristCare Group meeting started, Tom arrived with a woman no one had seen before. Jane looked angry. Mary, the ChristCare Group Leader, said, "Tom, could you please introduce your guest?"

Tom smiled and replied, "I'd like to introduce Sue. We met about a week ago through a mutual friend, and we've been seeing each other quite a bit in the last few days."

"That's just great," shouted Jane. "Dump me and grab the first woman you find. How do you think that makes me feel?" Jane stood and approached Tom with her fists clenched.

"Jane," Mary intervened, "I understand that you may be feeling hurt, but . . ."

"Stay out of this," Jane retorted, standing over Tom.

"Jane," Mary said calmly, "this is a matter you need to take up with Tom in private."

Jane took a deep breath. She apologized to Sue and to the rest of the group and then took her seat. Her face was flushed. After a few seconds, Jane stood up and said, "I'm sorry. I have to leave," and she left the room.

Mary nodded at Jane's friend Alexis, who got up and followed Jane.

Mary continued, "Sue, you really are welcome to our group. We appreciate having you here."

A New Group Project

Jack's congregation has decided to build a house for a homeless family. Jack asks his ChristCare Group if they would like to be involved. The group members say they would like to consider some type of involvement. Jack leads a discussion to explore the ways the group could be involved.

3. Biblical Equipping: A Process-Oriented Approach to Growing as Disciples (Matthew 6:19–34)

A Process-Oriented Approach to Growing as Disciples (Matthew 6:19–34)

[19] "Do not store up for yourselves treasures on earth, where moth and rust destroy, and where thieves break in and steal. [20] But store up for yourselves treasures in heaven, where moth and rust do not destroy, and where thieves do not break in and steal. [21] For where your treasure is, there your heart will be also.

[22] "The eye is the lamp of the body. If your eyes are good, your whole body will be full of light. [23] But if your eyes are bad, your whole body will be full of darkness. If then the light within you is darkness, how great is that darkness!

[24] "No one can serve two masters. Either he will hate the one and love the other, or he will be devoted to the one and despise the other. You cannot serve both God and Money.

[25] "Therefore I tell you, do not worry about your life, what you will eat or drink; or about your body, what you will wear. Is not life more important than food, and the body more important than clothes? [26] Look at the birds of the air; they do not sow or reap or store away in barns, and yet your heavenly Father feeds them. Are you not much more valuable than they? [27] Who of you by worrying can add a single hour to his life?

Focus Note 8 is continued on page 241.

²⁸ "And why do you worry about clothes? See how the lilies of the field grow. They do not labor or spin. ²⁹ Yet I tell you that not even Solomon in all his splendor was dressed like one of these. ³⁰ If that is how God clothes the grass of the field, which is here today and tomorrow is thrown into the fire, will he not much more clothe you, O you of little faith? ³¹ So do not worry, saying, 'What shall we eat?' or 'What shall we drink?' or 'What shall we wear?' ³² For the pagans run after all these things, and your heavenly Father knows that you need them. ³³ But seek first his kingdom and his righteousness, and all these things will be given to you as well. ³⁴ Therefore do not worry about tomorrow, for tomorrow will worry about itself. Each day has enough trouble of its own."

FOCUS NOTE 9

Explore Questions

1. What does Jesus say people are to do in this passage, and what does he say people are not to do?

2. What seems to be the main difference between the behavior of the "pagans" Jesus describes and the behavior he instructs his disciples to have?

3. Sum up the process that Jesus instructs people to follow and the results that Jesus says will come.

FOCUS NOTE 10

Connect Questions

1. What specific and practical actions would someone today do in order to seek first God's kingdom and his righteousness?

2. What helps you live as Jesus instructed, and what keeps you from living that way?

3. When it comes to growing as disciples, there are some things that we can do and some things only God can do. What can we do? What can only God do?

4. How could you help members of your ChristCare Group take a process-oriented approach to living as Jesus' disciples?

Questions to Focus Sharing of Biblical Equipping Apart

- Share one insight that you've had as a result of your Biblical Equipping Apart this week.

- Describe one change in your life that you've committed to make as a result of your meditation on the Biblical Equipping passage this week.

- Tell about a time when you've met God in a new way through Biblical Equipping Apart this week.

4. Missional Service Check-in

5. Class Member-Led Prayer and Worship

ChristCare Group Facilitation Skills

Preclass Reading

Therefore, if anyone is in Christ, he (or she) is a new creation; the old has gone, the new has come!

2 Corinthians 5:17

PRECLASS READING OUTLINE

I. What Is Facilitation?

Imagine the following scenario:

Kyle was leading his ChristCare Group in a Biblical Equipping discussion. His group challenged him to pay close attention and help their discussion in several ways.

- Kyle set the tone for the group members' sharing by briefly telling them about something that happened to him in the past week that forced him to rely on God in ways he hadn't expected.

- Arlene always had a lot to say. At that meeting she would have talked non-stop if Kyle hadn't interrupted, thanked her for her contribution, and asked Ed what he was thinking.

- Kyle noticed that Julie was unusually quiet that evening. He made a point of drawing her into the conversation and invited her to share her thoughts.

- There was a tense moment when Al and Ty began debating a doctrinal issue. Their argument would have escalated and taken over the rest of the meeting if Kyle hadn't refocused the conversation.

- The ideas Ed shared directly illustrated the main point of the Biblical Equipping session. Kyle summarized what Ed had said and asked others what they thought.

- The Biblical Equipping session gave the group ideas about how they could do missional service. Kyle led them in a process of deciding on exactly how they would do missional service in the next few months.

A common dictionary definition of *facilitate* reads "to make easy or easier." For a ChristCare Group Leader to facilitate means to assist, encourage, foster, and support group members in order to

12-PRE.pmd C: 12/02/1993 R: 12/08/2004

make it easier for them to participate successfully in the group, care for one another, and grow as Jesus' followers. In the example, Kyle used several small group facilitation skills to help the group function smoothly. As you read on you'll see that group leaders use facilitation skills to help group members communicate, participate, and build trust, and to help the group make difficult decisions.

II. Facilitating Effective Group Communication

An effective ChristCare Group Leader keeps a pulse on communication in the group. One way leaders do this is by periodically asking themselves questions such as: "Is everyone getting a chance to speak?" "Are the speakers' true messages being heard?" "Is the communication fostering the personal growth of both the speakers and the listeners?" "Are there any topics the group is avoiding?"

Here are some techniques for facilitating effective communication in your ChristCare Group.

A. Active Listening

Active listening means listening beyond the facts for feelings, attitudes, assumptions, and beliefs. You listen in a way that lets speakers know they are being heard, understood, and encouraged to say more.

When you use this skill, you:

- clarify—ask for more information;

- reflect—say back the content, feelings, attitudes, or opinions that you heard;

- encourage—assure the speaker you'd like to hear more;

- summarize—sum up what was said;

- explore implications—what does the speaker think this means?

What you might say when you use this skill:

- "Tell me more about that."

- "It sounds as if that really upsets you."

- "Then what happened?"

- "What do you think about that?"

- "Let me make sure I understand everything . . ."

- "How do you think this will affect . . ."

B. I-Messages

I-Messages are a way to take ownership for your feelings and actions. When you model this skill

you teach group members to take responsibility. I-Messages provide appropriate ways of expressing anger, frustration, or other strong feelings to another person or to the group while lessening the risk that the listener will feel defensive.

When you use this skill, you include the following steps:

1. Describe the situation or behavior nonjudgmentally ("When you . . .")

2. Say how you feel about the effect of the situation on you ("I feel . . .")

3. State why you feel as you do ("because . . .")

4. Say what you want done ("I would like . . .")

What you might say when you use this skill:

- "When you criticize others in our church, I feel uncomfortable hearing about it because it isn't really a problem our group can do anything about. I would like you to try to work out the problems with those who are involved."

- "When you seem so angry but won't share why, I feel frustrated because I'm concerned I might be the reason for your anger. I would like you to tell me why you're angry."

C. Asking for Clarification

Asking for clarification includes: asking group members to give reasons for what they have said, encouraging group members to think through what they're saying, and encouraging the expression of wide-ranging and well-thought-out opinions.

When you use this skill, you:

- use open-ended questions, those that can't be answered with only "yes" or "no";

- ask a group member to clarify a comment he or she has made;

- ask other group members to express their thoughts on a comment someone else has made.

What you might say when you use this skill:

- "How do you . . ."

- "What do you think about . . ."

- "Could you tell us more about . . ."

- "I've never thought of it quite like that. What brought you to that conclusion?"

- "That's an interesting idea. I'll bet it's something we all have opinions about. What are some ideas the rest of you have?"

III. Encouraging Group Participation

An effective ChristCare Group Leader makes sure each group member has a chance to participate. The leader not only encourages quieter group members to get more involved, but also keeps more active members from taking over. The following techniques will help you manage participation in your ChristCare Group.

A. Including

Including means drawing more reluctant or quieter participants into discussions and sharing.

When you use this skill, you:

- provide nonthreatening sharing situations in which group members can share with a minimum of risk;

- request, but don't force involvement;

- acknowledge quieter individuals' comments to build their confidence, but don't overdo it and embarrass them.

What you might say when you use this skill:

- "Let's hear from each of you about a time when you got a new piece of clothing that was very special to you—like Joseph's many-colored coat was to him."

- "Last week we talked about dealing with difficult people. How did that discussion affect your dealings with people this week? If you can't come up with anything, just say so when we get to you."

- "Thanks for sharing that."

- "That helps me understand where you're coming from."

B. Affirming

When you affirm, you respond positively to group members as they participate in group activities.

When you use this skill, you:

- openly thank a group member for a comment, and say why you're expressing your thanks;

- make a positive observation about what a group member says;

- agree with what someone says;

- are on the lookout to affirm each person in the group, including quieter individuals.

What you might say when you use this skill:

- "Thanks for sharing that with us, Tom. I appreciate your trusting us enough to say that."

- "I can tell you've really thought carefully about that."

- "What an interesting way to look at it!"

- "I really agree with what you said."

- "That's right! I've noticed that before too."

- "Pat, I've noticed that you really know your way around the Old Testament. Would you look up one of these verses? Thanks."

- "George, thanks for letting me know that you couldn't come last week. I'm glad to see you tonight. Are you feeling better?"

C. Extending

Extending is a way to get the most out of group members' comments during a discussion. When you extend a group member's comment, you invite others in the group to share their thoughts on the same topic.

When you use this skill, you draw attention to a group member's comment in an affirming way in order to:

- get a discussion going;

- draw others into discussion;

- enliven a discussion.

What you might say when you use this skill:

- "That's a creative approach to this situation. What do you say about that, Tom?"

- "Thanks for that interesting insight, Nancy. Does that bring a new idea to mind for anyone else?"

- "That's an interesting piece of information on this subject. Has anyone else read or heard of something they'd like to share?"

D. Refocusing

Refocusing means getting a discussion back on track, ending a discussion, or keeping a discussion appropriate.

When you use this skill, you:

- point out that the group has gotten sidetracked;

- give an alternative to continuing the discussion now;

- end or postpone the discussion or bring it back within appropriate limits.

What you might say when you use this skill:

- "I think we've gotten off the track a bit. Let's get back to our discussion of . . ."

- "I can tell this is really important to several of us. Let's take some time to think, pray, and study about it this week. Next week we'll put it first on our agenda."

- "You know, this issue is *[confidential, extremely sensitive, something that needs to be dealt with by those directly involved]*. Let's table our discussion of it for now. Those of you who still have concerns, let's talk privately after the meeting."

E. Redirecting

Redirecting is encouraging the flow of communication in all directions, not just between you and one other individual at a time.

When you use this skill, you:

- ask another group member what he or she thinks, instead of answering a question yourself;
- wait for others in the group to respond to comments or questions directed at you, even if that means a period of silence;
- invite group members to interact with one another, not just with one other person.

What you might say when you use this skill:

- "Mike, what do you think about what Pat said?"
- "Somebody else share a time when you felt that way too."
- "I'd love to know what Jean is thinking after you said that, Marie!"

It is also possible to redirect nonverbally. In order to do this, catch the eye of the one who is speaking, then look at another person. Often the speaker's eyes will follow yours. You can try this several times while a person is speaking.

F. Limit Setting

When you gently let the group know that it's time to stop something, that's limit setting.

When you use this skill, you:

- assertively manage the behavior of individuals in the group when necessary—for example, with those who monopolize discussion;
- matter-of-factly direct the actions of the entire group when necessary.

What you might say when you use this skill:

- "Jan, let's hear some other people's ideas on that."
- "Mark, I want to make sure everyone has time to share."
- "Let's get back to the subject."
- "We've spent all the time we can on that."
- "Let's get started."

G. Intervening

Intervening is stronger than limit setting, and you save this skill for when it is needed. Intervening means doing what you must to stop potentially destructive behaviors, such as ganging up on one group member, breaking confidentiality, bullying, or being insensitive to others' feelings. Use as little force as necessary to end a destructive behavior, but make sure it stops.

When you use this skill, you:

- call attention to something that has hurt someone's feelings;
- point out a dynamic in the group that is not in the group's best interest or in the best interest of a group member;
- help group members resolve a conflict.

What you might say when you use this skill:

- "Some things have been said here that might have hurt the feelings of a few people in this group."
- "It seems to me that whenever someone talks about a problem, the rest of the group wants to 'fix it' right away."
- "Jack and Bill, it seems to me that our discussion has turned into a disagreement. Let's take some time to try to work it out."

IV. Building Trust and Group Cohesion

A ChristCare Group's cohesiveness increases in proportion to the trust its members feel in one another. A group leader can use the following skills to offer ongoing opportunities to group members to build and maintain trust.

A. Self-Disclosure

This skill involves sharing your own thoughts, feelings, and experiences.

When you use this skill, you:

- share from your life experiences to let group members know that you—like they—are not perfect, but are still in the process of being refined by God;
- model self-disclosure as a way of teaching group members about this important tool for building relationships;
- sense that a group member has something especially personal or difficult to share, and model self-disclosure at a deep level. This will often help group members respond by sharing at that level too.

What you might say when you use this skill:

- "Now here is something I've always had to struggle with . . ."
- "'I really wish this weren't so hard for me . . ."
- "I sure blew it once when I . . ."
- "When something like that happens, I feel so *[inadequate, unprepared, frightened, unsure].* Do you ever feel that way?"
- "This is really difficult for me to talk about because . . ."
- "I don't usually share this with very many people, but I'd like to tell you about it . . ."

B. Sharing Questions

Sharing questions give group members opportunities to tell about their past and present circumstances, their joys and sorrows, their hopes and fears, their struggles and successes.

When you use this skill, you:

- ask group members to share something meaningful about themselves;
- encourage the listeners to affirm the speakers;
- take a group into deeper levels of relationship building with questions that require trust to answer.

What you might say when you use this skill:

- "What are three words that would describe you?"
- "If someone could add another word to those three that Larry shared about himself, what would it be?"
- "When you've had to deal with a significant loss, what was the one thing that helped most?"
- "If you could put your finger on the one thing you *[fear, hope for, look forward to, regret]* most, what would it be?"
- "Have you ever . . ."
- "How would it make you feel . . ."
- "What would you do . . ."

C. Inviting Positive Reflection

This skill involves building trust by inviting group members to say something positive about the group or about other group members.

When you use this skill, you:

- give group members a chance to reflect on the group as it relates to them personally;
- ask group members to reflect on their feelings about other group members.

What you might say when you use this skill:

- "What is one thing you've learned in our group tonight?"
- "What is something you like or value about *[each individual here, the individual next to you, your sharing partner]?"*
- "What is something positive you've learned about the person sitting next to you?"
- "What spiritual gifts do you see represented in this group?"

V. Group Decision Making

From a group's first meeting to its final stages of maturity, group members need to know how to make decisions. Decisions can range from the very simple (deciding on a starting time) to the challenging decisions (figuring out how to support a group member in crisis). Here are three steps that are useful in many different decision-making situations.

A. Step One: Brainstorming

Brainstorming is a creative way to come up with more than one "right answer." Here are the rules for this technique: Anything goes! All ideas are welcome. It's okay to piggy-back on someone else's idea. The wilder the ideas are, the better. No negative comments, criticisms, or evaluations are allowed—just ideas.

When you use this skill, you:

- explain the rules;
- write the ideas on a chalkboard or easel;
- solicit ideas "free-flow" (as fast as they come from whoever has them) or "round-robin" (going around the group, letting group members know it's okay to "pass" at any time).

What you might say when you use this skill:

- "How can we handle the child care?" Possible answers include:
  - leave the kids at home with sitters;
  - meet at a home with a playroom and hire a sitter;
  - use the church nursery;
  - trade child care with another group.

B. Step Two: Sorting Down

After brainstorming you help the group "sort down." This involves deciding which of the brainstormed ideas merit serious consideration. You give each group member input as you move toward a decision, and enable each group member to see the process clearly as it unfolds.

When you use this skill, you:

- give each group member a certain number of votes (maybe three votes if you have ten items to vote on);
- take a show-of-hands vote on each item, noting the number of votes by item;
- sort the list down to items that received the most votes;
- repeat the process if you still need to reduce the total number of ideas.

What you might say when you use this skill:

"These two ideas received six or more votes, out of 12 possible:

- meet at a home with a playroom and hire a sitter;
- trade child care with another group."

To reach a final decision, the group leader may use "gaining consensus" (see next technique).

C. Step Three: Gaining Consensus

Consensus involves enabling a group to reach a decision that all can accept.

When you use this skill, you:

- tell what the options are, after brainstorming, or when you have sorted down to a couple of options;
- if you sense disagreement, ask each group member to share his or her thoughts, ideas, or feelings, or simply invite comments from the group;
- if you reach an impasse, try these strategies:
  - o wait a week or two to decide (often time and prayer will result in agreement or even in a new solution);
  - o try one of the ideas for a while, then evaluate it;
  - o come up with a compromise;
- avoid pressuring individuals into a solution they're not comfortable with.

What you might say when you use this skill regarding the preceding example ("How can we handle child care?"):

- "I have a feeling some of you think that children, even if they're in a playroom, might be disruptive. Let's talk about it."

- "It looks as if we're divided right down the middle here. What if we tried the playroom idea for the next two weeks? That would give us some time to find out if trading child care with another group is even feasible."
- "This is an important issue to us. Let's pray about it this week. Maybe God will give us a solution we haven't thought of yet."

VI. Techniques to Avoid in Leading ChristCare Groups

The following techniques really get in the way of ChristCare Group Leaders' effective communication and group growth. Guard against them yourself, and also be on the alert for them in other group members. Most of us have used these techniques before, and it's easy to slip into using them again, especially in tense situations or when we aren't feeling confident.

- Ordering, directing, commanding
- Warning, admonishing, threatening
- Exhorting, preaching, moralizing
- Giving solutions
- Judging, criticizing, blaming
- Name-calling, ridiculing, shaming
- Interpreting, diagnosing, psychoanalyzing

Can you think of any other techniques that could be added to this category?

VII. Test Your Knowledge of Facilitation Skills

In order to participate successfully in the in-class session, you will need to know what the facilitation skills are and be able to use them. Use the quiz on the next page to test your recollection of the facilitation skills. If you need to, go back over the Preclass Reading and review the skills in order to become very familiar with them.

This is a matching quiz. In the left column are descriptions of facilitation skills; in the right column you'll find a list of all the facilitation skills mentioned in this Preclass Reading. Write the number of the correct facilitation skill in front of each skill description. The answers to the quiz appear at the bottom of the page.

Facilitation Skills Quiz

_____ A. Ask open-ended questions, request more information, invite others' questions or comments.

_____ B. Share your own thoughts, feelings, and experiences.

_____ C. Let the group know that it's time to stop something.

_____ D. Invite others in the group to share their thoughts on the same topic.

_____ E. Decide which of the brainstormed ideas merit serious consideration.

_____ F. Get a discussion back on track, end a discussion, or keep a discussion appropriate.

_____ G. Help the group reach a decision that all can accept.

_____ H. Involve others in the conversation when a group member is trying to talk only to you.

_____ I. Invite group members to say something positive about the group or about other group members.

_____ J. By intensive listening, encourage the other person to say more in order to clarify, reflect, encourage, summarize, and explore implications.

_____ K. Respond positively to group members.

_____ L. "When you_____," "I feel_____," "Because_____," "I would like_____."

_____ M. Do what you must to stop potentially destructive behaviors.

_____ N. Ask questions that invite group members to tell about their personal histories, experiences, and feelings.

_____ O. Come up with ideas.

_____ P. Draw reluctant or quieter participants into discussions.

1. Active Listening

2. I-Messages

3. Asking for Clarification

4. Including

5. Affirming

6. Extending

7. Refocusing

8. Redirecting

9. Limit Setting

10. Intervening

11. Self-Disclosure

12. Sharing Questions

13. Inviting Positive Reflection

14. a. Decision Making: Brainstorming

14. b. Decision Making: Sorting Down

14. c. Decision Making: Gaining Consensus

Answers: A.3, B.11, C.9, D.6, E.14b, F.7, G.14c, H.8, I.13, J.1, K.5, L.2, M.10, N.12, O.14a, P.4

VIII. Getting Ready for the In-Class Training Session

Here are two things you can do to help apply what you've learned in this Preclass Reading and to prepare for the in-class training session:

- Quickly review small group facilitation skills a couple of times before the in-class training session so these skills are fresh in your mind. This will help you to get the most out of the training session.

- As you relate with coworkers, friends, and family members, try out some of the skills you've learned about in this Preclass Reading. These skills are useful in all kinds of relationships and settings, so practice them whenever you have a chance.

Group-Based Manual for ChristCare Group Leaders
ChristCare Group Facilitation Skills

Outline and Focus Notes

*Therefore, if anyone is in Christ, he (or she) is a new creation;
the old has gone, the new has come!*

2 Corinthians 5:17

1. Discuss Facilitation Skills

2. Practice Facilitation Skills

FOCUS NOTE 1

Directions for the "Practice Facilitation Skills" Exercise

1. **Read the appropriate instructions for the upcoming role play (1 minute).**
   - Group leaders, read group leader instructions.
   - Group members, read group member instructions.
   - Observers, read both sets of instructions.

2. **Prepare for the role play (1 minute).**
   - Group leaders, review the facilitation skills you will use.
   - Group members, think about how you will play your roles.
   - Observers, find your Facilitation Skills Observation Sheet and prepare to use it.

3. **Conduct the role play (4 minutes).**
   - Group leaders, lead the role play; group members, participate according to instructions.
   - Observers, note and evaluate facilitation skills that the group leader exercises on the Facilitation Skills Observation Sheet.

4. **Discuss the role play using the following questions (5 minutes).**
   - How did it feel for the group leader to exercise facilitation skills?
   - What facilitation skills did the group leader exercise?
   - How well did the facilitation skills work?
   - What other facilitation skills might the group leader have exercised?

5. **Repeat this process for the three remaining role plays (11 minutes each).**

12-OFN.pmd C: 03/03/2004 R: 12/03/2004

Role Play 1: Group Leader Information

Situation:

Two new members have come to your group for the first time. You want to help all group members get to know one another and help them learn to trust one another.

Facilitation Skills to Exercise:

- Self-Disclosure
- Sharing Questions
- Inviting Positive Reflection
- Others, as needed

Discussion Topic:

"Tell about your family—when you were a child and now."

Facilitation Skills Observation Sheet: Role Play 1

List of Skills	Observations		
Active Listening Clarify, reflect, encourage, summarize, point out implications.	☐ Very Effective **Key Word(s):**	☐ Somewhat Effective	☐ Not Effective
I-Messages "When you . . . , I feel . . . ," "Because . . . , I would like . . ."	☐ Very Effective **Key Word(s):**	☐ Somewhat Effective	☐ Not Effective
Asking for Clarification Ask open-ended questions, request more information, invite others' questions or comments.	☐ Very Effective **Key Word(s):**	☐ Somewhat Effective	☐ Not Effective
Including Draw reluctant or quieter participants into discussions.	☐ Very Effective **Key Word(s):**	☐ Somewhat Effective	☐ Not Effective
Affirming Respond positively to group members.	☐ Very Effective **Key Word(s):**	☐ Somewhat Effective	☐ Not Effective
Extending Invite others in the group to share their thoughts on the same topic.	☐ Very Effective **Key Word(s):**	☐ Somewhat Effective	☐ Not Effective
Refocusing Get a discussion back on track, end a discussion, or keep a discussion appropriate.	☐ Very Effective **Key Word(s):**	☐ Somewhat Effective	☐ Not Effective
Redirecting Involve others in the conversation when a group member is trying to talk only to you.	☐ Very Effective **Key Word(s):**	☐ Somewhat Effective	☐ Not Effective
Limit Setting Let the group know that it's time to stop something.	☐ Very Effective **Key Word(s):**	☐ Somewhat Effective	☐ Not Effective
Intervening Do what you must to stop potentially destructive behaviors.	☐ Very Effective **Key Word(s):**	☐ Somewhat Effective	☐ Not Effective
Self-Disclosure Share your own thoughts, feelings, and experiences.	☐ Very Effective **Key Word(s):**	☐ Somewhat Effective	☐ Not Effective
Sharing Questions Invite group members to tell about their personal histories, experiences, and feelings.	☐ Very Effective **Key Word(s):**	☐ Somewhat Effective	☐ Not Effective
Inviting Positive Reflection Invite group members to say something positive about the group or about other group members.	☐ Very Effective **Key Word(s):**	☐ Somewhat Effective	☐ Not Effective
Group Decision Making a. Brainstorming: Come up with ideas.	☐ Very Effective **Key Word(s):**	☐ Somewhat Effective	☐ Not Effective
b. Sorting Down: Decide which of the brainstormed ideas merit serious consideration.	☐ Very Effective **Key Word(s):**	☐ Somewhat Effective	☐ Not Effective
c. Gaining Consensus: Help the group reach a decision that all can accept.	☐ Very Effective **Key Word(s):**	☐ Somewhat Effective	☐ Not Effective

FOCUS NOTE 3

Role Play 1: Group Member Roles

Group Member 1:

This is your first group meeting. You don't understand what the group leader wants you to talk about until he or she asks the question a couple of different ways. Then you participate in the discussion.

Group Member 2:

Be the model group member. Share your answer to the question, making sure to leave time for others.

Group Member 3:

This is your first group meeting. Talk too much. Try to monopolize the discussion.

FOCUS NOTE 4

Role Play 2: Group Leader Information

Situation:

The group is engaged in a Biblical Equipping discussion of the passage, "The LORD is my shepherd, I shall not want" (Psalm 23:1).

Facilitation Skills to Exercise:

- I-Messages
- Active Listening
- Asking for Clarification
- Others, as needed

Discussion Topic:

Discuss questions such as

- What did a shepherd do at the time the psalm was written?
- Why did sheep need a shepherd?
- Why do we need God to be our shepherd?
- How is God like a shepherd to us?

Facilitation Skills Observation Sheet: Role Play 2

List of Skills	Observations		

Active Listening
Clarify, reflect, encourage, summarize, point out implications.

☐ Very Effective   ☐ Somewhat Effective   ☐ Not Effective
Key Word(s):

I-Messages
"When you . . . , I feel . . . ," "Because . . . , I would like . . ."

☐ Very Effective   ☐ Somewhat Effective   ☐ Not Effective
Key Word(s):

Asking for Clarification
Ask open-ended questions, request more information, invite others' questions or comments.

☐ Very Effective   ☐ Somewhat Effective   ☐ Not Effective
Key Word(s):

Including
Draw reluctant or quieter participants into discussions.

☐ Very Effective   ☐ Somewhat Effective   ☐ Not Effective
Key Word(s):

Affirming
Respond positively to group members.

☐ Very Effective   ☐ Somewhat Effective   ☐ Not Effective
Key Word(s):

Extending
Invite others in the group to share their thoughts on the same topic.

☐ Very Effective   ☐ Somewhat Effective   ☐ Not Effective
Key Word(s):

Refocusing
Get a discussion back on track, end a discussion, or keep a discussion appropriate.

☐ Very Effective   ☐ Somewhat Effective   ☐ Not Effective
Key Word(s):

Redirecting
Involve others in the conversation when a group member is trying to talk only to you.

☐ Very Effective   ☐ Somewhat Effective   ☐ Not Effective
Key Word(s):

Limit Setting
Let the group know that it's time to stop something.

☐ Very Effective   ☐ Somewhat Effective   ☐ Not Effective
Key Word(s):

Intervening
Do what you must to stop potentially destructive behaviors.

☐ Very Effective   ☐ Somewhat Effective   ☐ Not Effective
Key Word(s):

Self-Disclosure
Share your own thoughts, feelings, and experiences.

☐ Very Effective   ☐ Somewhat Effective   ☐ Not Effective
Key Word(s):

Sharing Questions
Invite group members to tell about their personal histories, experiences, and feelings.

☐ Very Effective   ☐ Somewhat Effective   ☐ Not Effective
Key Word(s):

Inviting Positive Reflection
Invite group members to say something positive about the group or about other group members.

☐ Very Effective   ☐ Somewhat Effective   ☐ Not Effective
Key Word(s):

Group Decision Making
a. Brainstorming: Come up with ideas.

☐ Very Effective   ☐ Somewhat Effective   ☐ Not Effective
Key Word(s):

b. Sorting Down: Decide which of the brainstormed ideas merit serious consideration.

☐ Very Effective   ☐ Somewhat Effective   ☐ Not Effective
Key Word(s):

c. Gaining Consensus: Help the group reach a decision that all can accept.

☐ Very Effective   ☐ Somewhat Effective   ☐ Not Effective
Key Word(s):

FOCUS NOTE 5

Role Play 2: Group Member Roles

Your group is exploring the passage, "The LORD is my shepherd, I shall not want" (Psalm 23:1).

Group Member 1:

Be reluctant to say much, but open up as the group leader exercises active listening skills with you.

Group Member 2:

Sit and sulk. When called on, say something like, "This is a stupid discussion. I am not a sheep. You are wasting our time."

Group Member 3:

When you share, be so vague and unclear that the group leader has to ask follow-up questions to clarify what you are saying.

FOCUS NOTE 6

Role Play 3: Group Leader Information

Situation:

Group members are checking in during a time of community building and care.

Facilitation Skills to Exercise:

• Including
• Limit Setting
• Intervening
• Refocusing
• Redirecting
• Others, as needed

Discussion Topic:

Invite group members to share about what has happened in their lives in the past week.

Facilitation Skills Observation Sheet: Role Play 3

List of Skills	Observations		
Active Listening Clarify, reflect, encourage, summarize, point out implications.	☐ Very Effective **Key Word(s):**	☐ Somewhat Effective	☐ Not Effective
I-Messages "When you ... , I feel ... ," "Because ... , I would like ... ."	☐ Very Effective **Key Word(s):**	☐ Somewhat Effective	☐ Not Effective
Asking for Clarification Ask open-ended questions, request more information, invite others' questions or comments.	☐ Very Effective **Key Word(s):**	☐ Somewhat Effective	☐ Not Effective
Including Draw reluctant or quieter participants into discussions.	☐ Very Effective **Key Word(s):**	☐ Somewhat Effective	☐ Not Effective
Affirming Respond positively to group members.	☐ Very Effective **Key Word(s):**	☐ Somewhat Effective	☐ Not Effective
Extending Invite others in the group to share their thoughts on the same topic.	☐ Very Effective **Key Word(s):**	☐ Somewhat Effective	☐ Not Effective
Refocusing Get a discussion back on track, end a discussion, or keep a discussion appropriate.	☐ Very Effective **Key Word(s):**	☐ Somewhat Effective	☐ Not Effective
Redirecting Involve others in the conversation when a group member is trying to talk only to you.	☐ Very Effective **Key Word(s):**	☐ Somewhat Effective	☐ Not Effective
Limit Setting Let the group know that it's time to stop something.	☐ Very Effective **Key Word(s):**	☐ Somewhat Effective	☐ Not Effective
Intervening Do what you must to stop potentially destructive behaviors.	☐ Very Effective **Key Word(s):**	☐ Somewhat Effective	☐ Not Effective
Self-Disclosure Share your own thoughts, feelings, and experiences.	☐ Very Effective **Key Word(s):**	☐ Somewhat Effective	☐ Not Effective
Sharing Questions Invite group members to tell about their personal histories, experiences, and feelings.	☐ Very Effective **Key Word(s):**	☐ Somewhat Effective	☐ Not Effective
Inviting Positive Reflection Invite group members to say something positive about the group or about other group members.	☐ Very Effective **Key Word(s):**	☐ Somewhat Effective	☐ Not Effective
Group Decision Making a. Brainstorming: Come up with ideas.	☐ Very Effective **Key Word(s):**	☐ Somewhat Effective	☐ Not Effective
b. Sorting Down: Decide which of the brainstormed ideas merit serious consideration.	☐ Very Effective **Key Word(s):**	☐ Somewhat Effective	☐ Not Effective
c. Gaining Consensus: Help the group reach a decision that all can accept.	☐ Very Effective **Key Word(s):**	☐ Somewhat Effective	☐ Not Effective

Role Play 3: Group Member Roles

Group Member 1:

Be very shy and quiet. Don't say anything unless the group leader asks you to.

Group Member 2:

Announce that you are going to change the subject and share confidential information about another group member who is not at the meeting. (You might say something like, "All this stuff is sort of interesting, but I can tell you something about Yolanda that is really hot stuff. Nobody knows about this. Yolanda isn't here tonight, but she probably won't mind if I tell you.") Even when the group leader asks you not to share that information, brush him or her off and go ahead and tell confidential information such as the fact that Yolanda is back together with the boyfriend she swore she would never date again. Stop when the group leader exercises the facilitation skill of intervening.

Group Member 3:

Try to engage the group leader in a one-to-one conversation, excluding all the other group members.

Role Play 4: Group Leader Information

Situation:

The group is trying to decide several nuts and bolts issues.

Facilitation Skills to Exercise:

Exercise whatever facilitation skills are called for by group members' behavior.

Discussion Topic:

Get the group to decide on the following questions.

• Who will bring refreshments to the next meeting?

• Should the group meet from 7:00–8:30 P.M. or from 7:30–9:00 P.M.?

• Should everyone use the same Bible translation at group meetings?

Facilitation Skills Observation Sheet: Role Play 4

List of Skills	Observations		
Active Listening Clarify, reflect, encourage, summarize, point out implications.	☐ Very Effective **Key Word(s):**	☐ Somewhat Effective	☐ Not Effective
I-Messages "When you . . . , I feel . . . ," "Because . . . , I would like . . ."	☐ Very Effective **Key Word(s):**	☐ Somewhat Effective	☐ Not Effective
Asking for Clarification Ask open-ended questions, request more information, invite others' questions or comments.	☐ Very Effective **Key Word(s):**	☐ Somewhat Effective	☐ Not Effective
Including Draw reluctant or quieter participants into discussions.	☐ Very Effective **Key Word(s):**	☐ Somewhat Effective	☐ Not Effective
Affirming Respond positively to group members.	☐ Very Effective **Key Word(s):**	☐ Somewhat Effective	☐ Not Effective
Extending Invite others in the group to share their thoughts on the same topic.	☐ Very Effective **Key Word(s):**	☐ Somewhat Effective	☐ Not Effective
Refocusing Get a discussion back on track, end a discussion, or keep a discussion appropriate.	☐ Very Effective **Key Word(s):**	☐ Somewhat Effective	☐ Not Effective
Redirecting Involve others in the conversation when a group member is trying to talk only to you.	☐ Very Effective **Key Word(s):**	☐ Somewhat Effective	☐ Not Effective
Limit Setting Let the group know that it's time to stop something.	☐ Very Effective **Key Word(s):**	☐ Somewhat Effective	☐ Not Effective
Intervening Do what you must to stop potentially destructive behaviors.	☐ Very Effective **Key Word(s):**	☐ Somewhat Effective	☐ Not Effective
Self-Disclosure Share your own thoughts, feelings, and experiences.	☐ Very Effective **Key Word(s):**	☐ Somewhat Effective	☐ Not Effective
Sharing Questions Invite group members to tell about their personal histories, experiences, and feelings.	☐ Very Effective **Key Word(s):**	☐ Somewhat Effective	☐ Not Effective
Inviting Positive Reflection Invite group members to say something positive about the group or about other group members.	☐ Very Effective **Key Word(s):**	☐ Somewhat Effective	☐ Not Effective
Group Decision Making a. Brainstorming: Come up with ideas.	☐ Very Effective **Key Word(s):**	☐ Somewhat Effective	☐ Not Effective
b. Sorting Down: Decide which of the brainstormed ideas merit serious consideration.	☐ Very Effective **Key Word(s):**	☐ Somewhat Effective	☐ Not Effective
c. Gaining Consensus: Help the group reach a decision that all can accept.	☐ Very Effective **Key Word(s):**	☐ Somewhat Effective	☐ Not Effective

Role Play 4: Group Member Roles

The group is deciding some nuts and bolts issues.

Group Member 1:

Whatever the group leader asks you to talk about, talk about something different.

Group Member 2:

Engage in a conversation with group member 3 while group member 1 and the group leader are talking.

Group Member 3:

Whenever the group leader asks you a question or says anything to you, say you don't understand and ask him or her to restate the question or comment.

---

3. Biblical Equipping: Taking Risks and Being Transformed (Luke 19:1–10)

FOCUS NOTE 10

Taking Risks and Being Transformed (Luke 19:1–10)

¹Jesus entered Jericho and was passing through. ²A man was there by the name of Zacchaeus; he was a chief tax collector and was wealthy. ³He wanted to see who Jesus was, but being a short man he could not, because of the crowd. ⁴So he ran ahead and climbed a sycamore-fig tree to see him, since Jesus was coming that way.

⁵When Jesus reached the spot, he looked up and said to him, "Zacchaeus, come down immediately. I must stay at your house today." ⁶So he came down at once and welcomed him gladly.

⁷All the people saw this and began to mutter, "He has gone to be the guest of a 'sinner.'"

⁸But Zacchaeus stood up and said to the Lord, "Look, Lord! Here and now I give half of my possessions to the poor, and if I have cheated anybody out of anything, I will pay back four times the amount."

⁹Jesus said to him, "Today salvation has come to this house, because this man, too, is a son of Abraham. ¹⁰For the Son of Man came to seek and to save what was lost."

FOCUS NOTE 11

Explore Questions

1. What small group facilitation skills did Jesus exercise with Zacchaeus? Which ones did he exercise with the crowd?

2. What happened to Zacchaeus as a result of Jesus' relating to him?

3. What evidence shows the depth of Zacchaeus' transformation?

4. How did Zacchaeus take risks and make himself vulnerable? How do you think this contributed to his transformation?

5. How did Jesus make it safe for Zacchaeus to respond to God?

FOCUS NOTE 12

Connect Questions

1. How have you taken risks and made yourself vulnerable in your quest to know and follow Jesus?

2. What risks might members of your ChristCare Group need to take as they are transformed in order to know and follow Jesus more completely?

3. What could keep people in a ChristCare Group from taking the risks necessary to be transformed as Zacchaeus was?

4. How will you make your group a safe place for members to take risks and be transformed as Zacchaeus was?

---

4. Missional Service Check-in

5. Class Member-Led Prayer and Worship

The Nuts and Bolts of Leading a ChristCare Group

Outline and Focus Notes

For God is not a God of disorder but of peace. . . .
Everything should be done in a fitting and orderly way.

1 Corinthians 14:33a, 40

1. Nuts and Bolts in Our Congregation

2. Working with People, Personalities, and Problems

FOCUS NOTE 1

Problem-Solving Steps

1. Meet privately
2. Identify the problem
3. Listen
4. Think about changes the group can make
5. Explain the changes you'd like the person to make
6. Listen again
7. Give the person time to change
8. Affirm the changes the person makes
9. If the behavior doesn't change, try to find a different solution
10. If change still doesn't take place, make a final decision
11. Follow up and follow through

13-OFN.pmd C: 03/03/2004 R: 12/10/2004

FOCUS NOTE 2

Situation 1

The ChristCare Group Leader calls the group member, who has been ten minutes late to the last few meetings. The group leader learns that the group member has been late because of a problem that recently developed in his or her life. (The group member chooses his or her own problem—such as being required to work longer hours or driving a car that doesn't always start easily—and does not share this problem until the role play begins.)

Situation 2

The ChristCare Group Leader calls the group member and discovers he or she missed the last group meeting because he or she has a problem with the group and doesn't know what to do about it. (The group member decides what the problem is—such as feeling left out because the group has grown larger, feeling embarrassed at having revealed too much personal information, or feeling angry at another group member—and does not share this problem until the role play begins.)

FOCUS NOTE 3

Discussion Questions

1. ChristCare Group Leader, how did you feel about the phone call? What was difficult about it? What surprised you about it? What would you do differently next time?

2. Group member, how did you feel about the phone call? What did the group leader do well in helping you solve your problem? What else could the group leader have done to help you solve your problem?

3. Observer, what did you notice about the phone conversation? What good things took place? What could have been improved?

3. Biblical Equipping: Being a Transformational Leader (2 Timothy 3:10–4:8)

FOCUS NOTE 4

Questions to Focus Sharing of Biblical Equipping Apart

- Share one insight that you've had as a result of your Biblical Equipping Apart this week.

- Describe one change in your life that you've committed to make as a result of your meditation on the Biblical Equipping passage this week.

- Tell about a time when you've met God in a new way through Biblical Equipping Apart this week.

FOCUS NOTE 5

Being a Transformational Leader (2 Timothy 3:10–4:8)

[10] You, however, know all about my teaching, my way of life, my purpose, faith, patience, love, endurance, [11] persecutions, sufferings—what kinds of things happened to me in Antioch, Iconium and Lystra, the persecutions I endured. Yet the Lord rescued me from all of them. [12] In fact, everyone who wants to live a godly life in Christ Jesus will be persecuted, [13] while evil men and impostors will go from bad to worse, deceiving and being deceived. [14] But as for you, continue in what you have learned and have become convinced of, because you know those from whom you learned it, [15] and how from infancy you have known the holy Scriptures, which are able to make you wise for salvation through faith in Christ Jesus. [16] All Scripture is God-breathed and is useful for teaching, rebuking, correcting and training in righteousness, [17] so that the man of God may be thoroughly equipped for every good work.

[4:1] In the presence of God and of Christ Jesus, who will judge the living and the dead, and in view of his appearing and his kingdom, I give you this charge: [2] Preach the Word; be prepared in season and out of season; correct, rebuke and encourage—with great patience and careful instruction. [3] For the time will come when men will not put up with sound doctrine. Instead, to suit their own desires, they will gather around them a

Focus Note 5 is continued on page 265.

---

great number of teachers to say what their itching ears want to hear. [4]They will turn their ears away from the truth and turn aside to myths. [5]But you, keep your head in all situations, endure hardship, do the work of an evangelist, discharge all the duties of your ministry.

[6]For I am already being poured out like a drink offering, and the time has come for my departure. [7]I have fought the good fight, I have finished the race, I have kept the faith. [8]Now there is in store for me the crown of righteousness, which the Lord, the righteous Judge, will award to me on that day—and not only to me, but also to all who have longed for his appearing.

FOCUS NOTE 6

Explore Questions

1. How would you describe the example that Paul gives as a leader?

2. How would you summarize the leadership instructions that Paul wrote to Timothy? What is the importance of the Bible in Paul's instructions to Timothy?

3. What kinds of challenges did Paul warn Timothy to expect?

4. What kind of treatment can transformational leaders expect from people? From God?

FOCUS NOTE 7

Connect Questions

1. Who has provided an excellent example of a transformational leader for you? What did she or he do to help lead others into greater faith and discipleship?

2. How has God transformed you? What have you learned from your experience about how God might transform others?

Focus Note 7 is continued on page 266.

3. Discuss how you could follow the instructions Paul gives in chapter 4, verses 2 and 5 as you lead your ChristCare Group.

4. What hardships might you experience as a leader? How can we support and encourage one another when we experience the hardships that inevitably come to transformational leaders?

4. Facilitating Transformation and Missional Service in Your Group

FOCUS NOTE 8

Three Groups with Specific Emphases

Group 1

Group Emphasis: In-Depth Disciplemaking

The group members are:

- Art, 47, divorced, who has three high school- and college-aged children and works as an airline mechanic

- Charles, 35, who has two elementary school-aged children and works as an economics professor at a local junior college

- Diana, 28 and married to Charles, who works as a homemaker and mother, teaches Sunday school, and volunteers in various activities at her children's school

- Ellie, 64 and widowed, who retired last year from practicing medicine

- Fred, 56, the ChristCare Group Leader, married with four grown children, who took early retirement from a computer manufacturer and recently committed himself to doing at least 30 hours a week of volunteer church work

Focus Note 8 is continued on page 267.

Group 2

Group Emphasis: Supporting Group Members Individually Involved in Service

The group members are:

- Arlene, 59 and married with one grown child, who serves as the president of the congregation's women's group and as a member of the church council

- Dan, 30 and married, who is one of the congregation's pastors

- Ed, 22 and unmarried, who works as the director of a shelter for homeless men

- Gerald, 42 and married to Helen, who has one child in kindergarten and another in second grade and who works as Minister of Music, choir director, and organist for the congregation

- Helen, 38, the ChristCare Group Leader, who works as a manager at a large corporation

Group 3

Group Emphasis: Evangelism, with Plans to Triple in Size and Subdivide within a Year

The group members are:

- Adam, 25 and married to Bea, who has two preschool-aged children and works as a computer technician

- Bea, 25, who provides day care for six children in her home; she and Adam exercise their gifts of hospitality by hosting group meetings in their home

- Cathy, 29, mother of a two-year-old and attending law school, who shares leadership of the ChristCare Group with her husband, David

- David, 28, who shares leadership of the ChristCare Group with Cathy and who works out of his home as a freelance writer; David and Cathy live in the same subdivision as Adam and Bea

Questions to Consider in Striving for a Transformational, Missional Focus

By answering some of the following questions, your group members can make decisions that will guide the group into missional service.

1. What is the mission (or purpose) of this group?

2. Should this group be open or closed? Why?

3. Assuming we have chosen to have a 90-minute group meeting, how much meeting time would our group spend on each of the following activities, and why?

Activity	Number of Minutes
Community building and care	
Biblical Equipping	
Prayer and worship	
Missional service	

4. How often should our group meet, and for how long?

5. What, if anything, will our group do about child care?

6. What other "nuts and bolts" decisions might we need to make in order for our group to be transformational and mission-centered?

5. Missional Service Check-in

6. Class Member-Led Prayer and Worship

Group-Based Manual for ChristCare Group Leaders

How to Build Membership in Your ChristCare Group

Preclass Reading

Unless the LORD builds the house, its builders labor in vain.

Psalm 127:1

PRECLASS READING OUTLINE

I. The Benefits and Challenges of Growth

Consider the following two ChristCare Groups.

George enjoys the small group of six members he leads. He can't wait for Wednesday night meetings to catch up on what is happening in their lives, to pray, and to discuss the Scriptures with them. His group members are all comfortable with one another. There is a warm, caring, safe atmosphere in George's group that keeps members coming back.

George is not terribly interested in seeing his ChristCare Group grow. In fact, the thought of dealing with visitors makes him uncomfortable. It also makes group members uneasy. The last time anyone invited a visitor to attend was more than six months ago, and it was a disaster. People felt awkward and the discussions dragged. The visitor never came back.

Maria leads another group at the same congregation. She likes to compare her ChristCare Group to a childhood experience. She says, "My group reminds me of the dining room table in my family's farmhouse. People were always stopping by and joining us for dinner. How often I heard my mother say, 'There is always room for one

14-PRE.pmd C: 08/31/1994 R: 12/03/2004

more at our table.'" Indeed, visitors to Maria's group always find that there is room for them, not just in a physical sense, but also in the hearts of those present. There is a welcoming spirit in this group that always makes room for "one more." This attitude attracts and holds visitors to Maria's group. Not surprisingly, this group has experienced steady growth and expects to give birth to a new group in the near future.

As you reflect on George's and Maria's ChristCare Groups, and as you consider your own ChristCare Group leadership, write your answers to the following questions:

1. In what ways are George's group and Maria's group different from each other?

2. How do those differences affect growth in these two groups?

II. Open and Closed ChristCare Groups

Whether a group grows depends partly on what kind of group it is. There are two kinds of groups: those that intend to build membership and are open to receiving new members, and those that limit their membership, either intentionally or unintentionally.

A. Open ChristCare Groups

This session focuses on open groups and what they can do to grow in membership. Almost all ChristCare Groups are "open." Open groups intentionally invite guests, eagerly welcome them, and warmly receive them as new members. Open groups expect to build membership and give birth to new groups. A ChristCare Group cannot grow unless it is an open group.

B. Closed ChristCare Groups

There are some ChristCare Groups that choose not to be open to guests. They have made an intentional decision not to grow. Usually, such a group is closed for a missional reason. For example, a group may choose to close its membership so it can focus on intensive discipleship—a focus that guests would disrupt. Groups might be intentionally closed for a limited period or for the group's life. Lack of membership growth is normal in such groups.

Unfortunately, some ChristCare Groups unintentionally become closed. Leaders and members of such groups may tell you that their groups are open, but in reality that is not the case. They rarely invite visitors and tend to "freeze out" any visitors who do come. These groups do not have a missional reason to be closed. They simply allow themselves to dwindle into a comfortable clique or an exclusive club. Like George's group, their members establish close relationships with one another, but avoid the discomfort of dealing with people who are not part of that close-knit group. This kind of closed group is probably unhealthy. Such groups usually become self-centered and selfish. They often don't follow Jesus' missional example or his commands to be witnesses and serve others. ChristCare Groups exist to serve Jesus and build disciples, and these purposes are not likely to be fulfilled when the group exists just for its members' pleasure. As a ChristCare Group Leader, make sure your group never becomes like this.

C. Factors That Influence Group Growth

As you have seen, the fact that a group calls itself "open" does not guarantee that the group will grow. Many factors affect building membership in an open group, including:

- the kind of missional service the group chooses to do;
- the ChristCare Group Leader's attitude and leadership;
- the quality of interaction among group members;
- the way the group engages in Biblical Equipping, community building and care, missional service, and prayer and worship;
- the way group members invite and welcome guests; and
- the way the group assimilates new members.

III. The ChristCare Group Leader: A Key to Building Membership

In order to grow, a ChristCare Group needs its leader's enthusiastic participation and encouragement. The ChristCare Group Leader's attitude and actions are major factors in whether the group chooses to grow. If a group leader doesn't wholeheartedly support group-building efforts, the group is unlikely to grow, no matter what group members do.

A ChristCare Group Leader's effectiveness in building membership results from many qualities: personal discipleship, vision for ChristCare Group Ministry, a positive attitude, a willingness to work as a team member, and a strong motivation to see more people experience the benefits ChristCare Groups provide.

IV. Building Membership in Your ChristCare Group Is a Team Effort

Building your group's membership may seem like an overwhelming task. Take heart: you don't have to do it alone! You and your pastors, Equippers Team, fellow group leaders, and group members will work together to bring new members into your group.

A. Work with Your Equippers and Pastoral Staff

Equippers Team members and pastoral staff help build group membership. They help your congregation become familiar with and excited about ChristCare Group participation. They can do this in many ways: through bulletin announcements, sermons, brochures, corporate prayers, pastoral letters to the congregation, flyers, posters, newsletter articles, special displays, or informational events. All of these activities help your group gain new members. If people know what ChristCare Groups are and how they work, they are much more likely to accept an invitation to visit one. In fact, if the publicity campaign is successful, you'll notice congregation members actively seeking groups to join!

Work with the Group-Building Coordinator

As a ChristCare Group Leader, you'll work closely with the Equipper who serves as the Group-Building Coordinator. The Group-Building Coordinator is responsible for establishing ChristCare Groups and helping them build membership. He or she recruits congregation members and helps them find a ChristCare Group to join. The Group-Building Coordinator will also help you when your group gets large enough that you need to form two new groups.

There are many ways you might work with the Group-Building Coordinator. For example, he or she may ask you to give a brief talk or personal testimony during a worship service or at a special meeting about ChristCare Group Ministry, to participate in a skit during a worship service or other congregational event, or to write a testimonial or description of your group's mission to include in the newsletter or bulletin.

Of course, the Group-Building Coordinator's main job is finding potential ChristCare Group

members and guiding them into an appropriate ChristCare Group. Take a moment now to look over Supplement A, the "Group-Building Flow Chart." It illustrates what happens when someone expresses interest in visiting a ChristCare Group. The chart refers you to a document titled "Prospective ChristCare Group Member Information Form" (Supplement B). This is the form your Group-Building Coordinator will give you when he or she wants to recommend a new member for your group.

Look over the "Prospective ChristCare Group Member Information Form." Take a moment to imagine how the information on this form might help you tailor a personal invitation. For example, if the potential member has small children, you might mention your group's child care arrangements. Or, if you know that the person does not drive, you could be prepared to offer him or her a ride with another group member (assuming, of course, that the group member is willing and able to do this).

To keep the Group-Building Coordinator informed about your group's membership, you will use the "ChristCare Group Leader Administrative Report" (Supplement C). You will learn to use this form in session 15, How to Participate Effectively in a SEA Group.

Work with the Foundation-Building Coordinator

You also will work with the Equipper who serves as the Foundation-Building Coordinator. This person plans and oversees activities that build the congregation's strong foundation of understanding, appreciation, and support for the whole ChristCare Group Ministry. He or she helps the pastoral staff and Equippers communicate to the congregation the ChristCare Group Ministry vision.

As a ChristCare Group Leader, you form an important link between your group and the Foundation Building Coordinator. Building the congregation's foundation for ChristCare Group Ministry involves telling the ChristCare Group Ministry story in a variety of ways. As a ChristCare Group Leader, you see up close how ChristCare Group Ministry affects group members' lives, which gives you many stories to tell. If the people involved give you permission to use their stories, you can share some of them with the Foundation-Building Coordinator. Such stories work well in pastoral letters, sermons, newsletters, and bulletin inserts. You might even know group members who would be willing to talk during a worship service. Their stories can be very encouraging, especially to people who are unsure about participating in a ChristCare Group.

B. Work with Your SEA Group

In a sense, everything you and your fellow ChristCare Group Leaders do in your SEA Group helps to build ChristCare Group membership. As you work to ensure that all group members have the best, most distinctively Christian experience possible, you are building a strong congregational foundation for ChristCare Group Ministry. When ChristCare Group Ministry is strong and healthy, people are more likely to want to participate.

In addition, SEA Group meetings allow group leaders to learn from one another's experiences, insights, and ideas about building group membership.

C. Work with Your Group Members

Foundation-building and group-building activities are tremendously valuable, but a personal invitation is still the best way to encourage a visit to a ChristCare Group. The most effective personal invitations come from ChristCare Group members.

The Potential for Personal Invitations

People are most likely to accept an invitation to a ChristCare Group from someone they know and trust. Every ChristCare Group member has trusting relationships with family, friends, neighbors, and coworkers. All of these relationships mean that group members have a tremendous opportunity to help your group grow by personally inviting others to participate.

Your Attitude and Motivation Are Key Factors

Earlier in this reading, you saw how important it is for the ChristCare Group Leader to be enthusiastic about building membership. Your attitude affects your group members'. If you are excited about building your group's membership, your group members are likely to share your excitement. If you make inviting others a top priority, your group members will do the same.

How to Motivate Group Members to Help Build Membership

You can motivate group members and give them an exciting vision for growth by following these practical guidelines.

Pray
Relying on the Holy Spirit is the most important thing you can do as you seek to build your ChristCare Group's membership. Pray for help as you work at motivating members to invite others to the group. You also can pray about this subject during your group's prayer and worship times. Ask the Holy Spirit to prepare the hearts of those you will invite. Ask God to show you whom to invite, and to give each of you the understanding and encouragement to invite people effectively and caringly. You might also ask group members to pray for specific people they want to invite to the ChristCare Group.

Remind Them of the Benefits They Experience
Another way to motivate group members to invite others is to remind them of the benefits they have experienced in the ChristCare Group. When group members remember the blessings they have received, they often want their friends to enjoy those blessings. Here are a few benefits of ChristCare Group membership:

- enjoying a place of acceptance, warmth, and belonging;
- giving and receiving care and support;
- coming to know Jesus better;
- growing and maturing in faith;
- finding new ways to serve God.

Emphasize Growth in the Covenant
The covenant your group establishes at its beginning should express a commitment to growth. One of the promises you can make to one another is to "stay evangelistic and missional by welcoming guests and new members at any meeting." As newcomers join your group and you review the group covenant with them, you can make certain they understand from the beginning that adding new members is an important goal for your group.

Affirm Group Members Who Invite Others
Yet another way to motivate group members to invite others is by encouraging them when they try it. For example, during group check-in time you might ask people to talk about their difficulties and successes in inviting others to the group. Affirm their attempts to invite others and encourage the rest of the group to do the same. This can be a good opportunity to teach ways to invite others effectively and appropriately.

Use Visual Reminders

Visual reminders can encourage your group members to invite others. Here are a few ideas:

- Before each meeting, post a sign at the entrance. The sign could read "Welcome to our ChristCare Group" or "Welcome, Guests!" This will not only convey a warm welcome to the guests, it will also remind group members to think about inviting and welcoming guests. If you have a group member who enjoys doing crafts, this sign might be done in needlework or in some other artistic way.

- Leave an empty chair at each meeting to remind members that there is always room for one more person.

- Create a construction paper tree and put each group member's name and each guest's name on a leaf. Display it at every meeting.

- Purchase creative and colorful party invitations or cards. Write each guest's name on the invitation or card and tack it on a special display below the words: "Welcome to the celebration!"

- Take a picture of each new member and add it to a collage.

- Create a ChristCare Group banner, and have temporary squares that can be pinned on to represent each guest. Put the guests' names on the squares. When the guests become permanent members, they can decorate and permanently attach their squares to the group banner. (For instructions on making a banner, see Supplement E in session 21, How to Bring Closure to ChristCare Groups.)

Look for Chances to Give Short Reminders

You will have many chances to remind group members about building membership through just a sentence or two. For example, when you welcome a guest, you might say something like: "Kim, thank you for visiting with us today. As a group, we really enjoy having guests."

Use the Beginnings *Course*

Appendix B of the *Group Member Guide* of the *Beginnings* course teaches group members how to invite and welcome new group members in a clear and encouraging way.

Affirm Group Members' Other Membership-Building Activities

If one of your group members helps publicize ChristCare Group Ministry by writing an article for the church newsletter or by sharing a personal testimony during worship, be sure to affirm him or her in front of the group. His or her example may lead other group members to try this kind of membership-building activity.

V. The Process of Building ChristCare Group Membership

Building ChristCare Group membership involves three steps. They are summarized in Focus Box 1.

FOCUS BOX 1

The Process of Building ChristCare Group Membership

Inviting

How group leaders and members bring new people to a ChristCare Group

Welcoming

The caring reception groups give to their guests before, during, and after a ChristCare Group meeting

Assimilating

How a guest becomes a permanent group member

Let's take a closer look at each of these activities. The following information is not only for your own use. Sharing it with your ChristCare Group members will help them understand the process better.

VI. How to Invite

A. Be Process Oriented

When you invite others to visit the ChristCare Group, always be process oriented. This is important both for the sake of the people you are inviting and for the sake of your group members, who will be watching your example.

It is easy to become results oriented when you invite others to visit your group. This can happen when you or a group member becomes so excited about the benefits of the group that you put undue pressure on others to attend and enjoy those benefits also. Or it can happen when you realize that the group is not growing as fast or as easily as you expected. If you become overly concerned about this, you may begin to issue inappropriate, insensitive invitations. You also may pressure group members to invite in results-oriented ways.

Focus Box 2 contains an example of a results-oriented invitation:

FOCUS BOX 2

A Results-Oriented Invitation

James: Hi, Rich, how are you?

Rich: Well, things have been better.

James: What's wrong?

Rich: I just feel completely overwhelmed by work right now. My wife is feeling neglected and I never seem to have time for my children.

James: Have you thought about my invitation to come to our ChristCare Group? We're discussing the topic of balancing priorities. I think it would help you.

Rich: Well, thanks for the invitation, but as I said, I'm overwhelmed right now. I don't think I could add another . . .

James: Well, I'm sure the group would help you. Why don't you give it a try? You could also bring your wife and have time together. There's babysitting for the children as well.

Rich: But . . .

James: Trust me. I really think you'll find it helpful in balancing your priorities.

Although James cared about Rich, it's clear from this example that James expected immediate results. He wanted Rich to join his ChristCare Group—regardless of what Rich wanted. James did not take enough time to listen to Rich and really hear what he was saying. He didn't take seriously what Rich said about needing more time for his family. If James had really listened, he would have realized that this was not a good time to invite Rich to another activity, no matter how beneficial.

Focus Box 3 shows how this conversation might have gone if James had related in a process-oriented way:

FOCUS BOX 3

A Process-Oriented Invitation

James: Hi, Rich, how are you?

Rich: Well, things have been better.

James: What's wrong?

Rich: I just feel completely overwhelmed by work right now. My wife is feeling neglected and I never seem to have time for my children.

James: Sounds terrible. What's taking up all your time?

Rich: Well, it's the Simons Project. Lately I've been here sixty hours a week trying to meet the deadlines.

James: Is there anything I can do?

Rich: Not really; I just have to finish this project. Things will ease up in a month or so.

James: Well, if I can be of any help, please let me know.

Rich: Thanks so much. I've been thinking about that ChristCare Group you mentioned last week, the group that's studying how to balance priorities. When I get through this project, I might come to a few meetings with you. I'm sure it would help me.

James: We'd love to have you when the time is right for you.

A process-oriented approach to extending invitations means taking time to build a caring relationship. Spending time with a person, listening, and getting to know his or her needs and interests leads to a trusting relationship in which the person knows, respects, and feels comfortable with you. In the context of such a caring relationship, you can invite someone to visit your ChristCare Group when he or she lets you know it would benefit him or her.

B. Questions to Consider Before Inviting

Is the Group Right for the Person?

Before you invite someone to visit a ChristCare Group, you should ask yourself "Is this group right for this person?" Some people fit better into certain ChristCare Groups than they do into other groups. For example, a sixty-year-old widower may not feel comfortable in a ChristCare Group made up of singles in their twenties and thirties. Consider the person's life circumstances, personal needs, and interests when you decide which ChristCare Group might be best for him or her. Of course, if it's clear that the person would do better in a ChristCare Group other than your own, you would certainly recommend a visit there.

Is the Person Right for the Group?
Will the ChristCare Group benefit from having this person visit? Most of the time, the answer will be yes. There are some special cases, however, when care for the individual or care for the group may mean it is better not to invite the person to visit. Focus Box 4 lists situations in which it is usually better not to invite someone to visit a ChristCare Group.

FOCUS BOX 4

When Not to Invite

- When the person is unable or unwilling to maintain confidentiality.

- When the person is so hostile or emotionally unstable that he or she is likely to disrupt the group.

- When the person has needs for care so great that he or she should be referred to a pastor, a mental health professional, a parish nurse, or a lay person trained to do one-to-one caring ministry (such as a Stephen Minister).

- When the person has serious relationship problems with someone already in the group.

- When the person has behavior patterns that could overwhelm the group (such as someone who talks incessantly and never listens to others).

- When the person is so heavily committed to other activities that regular participation in a ChristCare Group would be impossible.

Additional Questions
In Focus Box 5 you will find a list of additional questions that can help you decide whether the person you're listening to could benefit from visiting a ChristCare Group.

FOCUS BOX 5

Additional Questions to Consider Before Extending an Invitation

- Is this person searching for "community" or "a place to belong"?

- Is this person hungry for spiritual growth?

- Is this person lonely or lacking social support and friendship?

- Is this person experiencing a life transition, such as a move to a new city, a change of career, or retirement?

- Does this person desire to pray and worship with a smaller group of Christians?

- Would this person like to work with a handful of dedicated Christians who are committed to doing meaningful ministry?

- Has this person expressed a desire for personal growth?

- Has this person expressed a desire to become more disciplined in his or her spiritual life?

- Has this person had a positive experience with a previous small group?

If the answer to one or more of these questions is yes, then the person might enjoy being part of a ChristCare Group. In addition, now that you've stopped to think through the person's needs, you will know better how you can give a process-oriented invitation that focuses on those needs.

C. Characteristics of an Effective Invitation
There are three ways to make an invitation most effective: invite clearly, enthusiastically, and assertively.

Invite Clearly
Whenever you invite someone to visit, tell him or her what a ChristCare Group is and what goes on at a typical meeting. Trying something new is a little frightening for most people, so tell the person that he or she will not be pressured to do anything he or she finds uncomfortable, such as read or pray aloud.

If the person accepts your invitation, give additional information. Be sure the person knows the meeting date, time, location, and directions for getting there. It's a good idea to provide him or her with the host's name and telephone number.

Also make sure the person understands any arrangements you are making about transportation or child care. If the person needs to bring anything, such as a Bible, be sure to mention that. You might also want to describe the way that your ChristCare Group members usually dress, so that the person isn't embarrassed by showing up formally dressed at an informal meeting, or vice versa.

Invite Enthusiastically

Enthusiasm is contagious! If people can see from the expression on your face, your body language, and your tone of voice that you believe being in a ChristCare Group is a valuable experience, then the people you invite are more likely to want to try it.

Invite Assertively

An assertive invitation is one that respects the other person's intelligence, his or her ability to make good choices, and his or her right to say no. Following is an example of one way (and two ways not) to offer invitations.

FOCUS BOX 6

Assertive and Nonassertive Invitations

Example of an Assertive Invitation

"Laura, we've talked quite a bit about whether a ChristCare Group would be right for you. I'm wondering if you would like to visit the ChristCare Group I'm attending."

Example of a Passive Invitation

"Laura, I don't suppose you'd ever consider visiting my ChristCare Group, would you?"

Example of an Aggressive Invitation

"Laura, if you knew what was good for you and if you valued my opinion, you'd visit my ChristCare Group."

You'll learn much more about assertiveness in sessions 18 and 19, Assertiveness Skills for ChristCare Group Leaders.

D. How to Respond to a Declined Invitation

If people refuse your invitation to visit your ChristCare Group, don't get upset or defensive. Instead, maintain a caring attitude. There are several ways you can respond assertively to their decision:

- Try to understand their reasons for refusing your invitation. This will involve some listening. Repeat those reasons to make sure you understand them correctly.

- Make sure people understand that it's all right for them to say no to you. Let them know that you still care for and accept them.

- Also assure people that they are welcome to visit a ChristCare Group in the future if they change their minds.

VII. How to Welcome

When a guest accepts an invitation and visits your ChristCare Group, you need to make sure he or she feels welcome. Otherwise the invitation will have been worthless. Welcoming involves practicing the art of hospitality. Pages 130–133 of *Nuts & Bolts Issues for Small Group Leaders* describe specific ways you can help group members make guests feel welcome. Review those pages now.

VIII. How to Assimilate

A. What Does Assimilation Mean?

Assimilation is the process through which a guest becomes a permanent group member. Focus Box 7 describes how you can know when a person is fully assimilated.

FOCUS BOX 7

Characteristics of an Assimilated ChristCare Group Member

A fully assimilated ChristCare Group member:

- regularly attends group meetings;
- actively participates in group activities;
- accepts the group covenant;
- expresses satisfaction with his or her participation in the group;
- has friends in the group and socializes with them apart from the group (Note: people who make new friends during the first few months in the group are much more likely to continue as active members);
- takes on a task or role in the group appropriate to his or her talents and available time.

B. Steps to Facilitate Assimilation

There are four steps you can take to facilitate the assimilation of new members into your group.

Follow Up Carefully

When a guest has visited the group several times, follow up in these ways:

- Call the person, thank him or her for coming, and find out if he or she has any questions you can answer.

- Send a card thanking the person for visiting your group. Be sure to enclose your phone number, along with a note encouraging the guest to call you if he or she has any questions. Remember that a thank-you note can also be effective when it comes from a group member instead of the group leader. Consider asking one or more volunteers from the group to handle this responsibility.

Review the Group Covenant

Pages 81–82 of *Nuts & Bolts Issues for Small Group Leaders* suggest ways to explain the group covenant both to guests and new members. Signing a copy of the covenant helps cement a new member's commitment to the group.

Explain Biblical Equipping

You also can help assimilate new members by explaining Biblical Equipping. You may wish to give the new group members a copy of *Beginnings Group Member Guide* and encourage them to read through session 7 on Biblical Equipping. You can then answer any questions they might have. This will help them participate during Biblical Equipping sessions and encourage them to make the Biblical Equipping cycle part of their lives.

Involvement

Involvement is one of the most effective ways groups assimilate new members. Remember that your new group members have gifts, talents, time, energy, and a desire to use these gifts in meaningful ministry. Help them find ways they can get involved with service in the group. Being able to contribute something to the group can be very satisfying and rewarding for new members, and also builds a sense of belonging. See pages 107–110 of *Nuts & Bolts Issues for Small Group Leaders* for a discussion of how you can share many responsibilities with group members.

IX. Go and Build

At the very beginning of this module, you read the words from Psalm 127:1, "Unless the LORD builds the house, its builders labor in vain." As you have seen, there are many things you and the members of your group can do to build membership in the ChristCare Group. Ultimately, however, it is God who builds membership in your group. As your group gains new members, remember to give thanks and glory to God.

X. Getting Ready for the In-Class Session

Look back at the two questions you answered at the beginning of this Preclass Reading. Would you change either of your answers? Also, are there any questions you wish to bring to the in-class session? If so, note those questions here:

ChrisCare Series

Group-Building Flow Chart

 START

Person communicates an interest in visiting a ChristCare Group

- person submits a ChristCare Interest Card
- person speaks to the Group-Building Coordinator
- person speaks to pastor, church staff, or friend, who relays interest to the GBC

GBC = Group-Building
       Coordinator
CGL = ChristCare
       Group Leader

GBC determines whether ChristCare Group is appropriate for interested person

- GBC reviews ChristCare Interest Card (if submitted)
- GBC, with an understanding spirit, calls the interested person to gain further information
- GBC completes a Prospective ChristCare Group Member Information Form
- GBC prayerfully considers person's interest

* The ChristCare Group Leader may be the leader of an existing group or the person chosen to lead a group under development. He or she may be a veteran, newly commissioned, or about to be released from an existing group where an apprentice will take over.

YES

- GBC reviews the characteristics of current ChristCare Groups using GBC's ChristCare Group Profile and prayerfully considers which group would be most appropriate

–OR–

GBC notes a growing desire to begin a group for people with a similar interest or situation

- GBC relays Prospective ChristCare Group Member Information Form to an appropriate ChristCare Group Leader* (retains copy)

NO

GBC contacts interested person to explain why it can't work for the person to be in a ChristCare Group at that time. If it's because all the groups are full, the GBC explains that and tells when new groups will be formed. If the reason is because the potential group member has needs that are greater than a group can meet, the GBC suggests referral to an appropriate caring ministry resource

 PROCEED TO TOP OF NEXT PAGE

ChristCare Group Leader contacts interested person

CGL, with a welcoming spirit, calls the interested person and issues a personal invitation to visit his/her existing group or to attend an initial meeting of a developing group.

Interested person visits ChristCare Group and decides whether or not to join it

YES

CGL relays membership status to GBC via the ChristCare Group Leader Administrative Report

NO

- CGL meets with person to discuss interest in visiting another ChristCare Group
- Person decides whether or not to visit another group

YES

CGL notifies GBC via phone of person's continuing interest

NO

- CGL responds with an understanding spirit and keeps the door open
- CGL relays information to GBC via ChristCare Group Leader Administrative Report

GBC selects another ChristCare Group

- GBC, with an understanding spirit, calls the interested person to gain further information
- GBC prayerfully considers which group would be most appropriate
- GBC relays Prospective ChristCare Group Member Information Form to an appropriate CGL (retains copy)

CGL contacts interested person

(Follow procedure beginning at top of page)

Prospective ChristCare Group Member Information Form

ChrisCare Series

Name: _____

Address: _____

City/State/ZIP: _____

Phone: _____
      (Home)   (Work)

Referral

What was the source?
❏ Name (of person who made referral)_____

  ❏ ChristCare Group member   ❏ Church staff

  ❏ ChristCare Group Leader   ❏ Lay leader

  ❏ Equipper   ❏ Member

  ❏ Pastor   ❏ Other

❏ Response form. Which one? _____

Characteristics of Prospective Member

❏ Male   ❏ Female

❏ 18–24   ❏ 25–34   ❏ 35–44   ❏ 45–54   ❏ 55–64   ❏ 65–74   ❏ 75+

❏ Never married   ❏ Newly married   ❏ Newly remarried   ❏ Married

          ❏ Widowed   ❏ Separated/divorced

❏ Congregation member   ❏ Spouse of member   ❏ Friend of member

❏ Other connection to congregation:

❏ New in community

❏ Children
    Number: _____   Age range: _____ – _____

Special Interests in Relation to ChristCare Group

❏ Prayer   ❏ Bible study   ❏ Spiritual growth   ❏ Relationships

❏ Evangelism   ❏ Social ministry   ❏ Service: _____

❏ Other: _____

Parameters for Group Selection

Would others (friends or relatives) visit the group with this person? If so, how many?

❏ 1   ❏ 2   ❏ 3   ❏ More: _____

Transportation to/from group meeting needed?   ❏ Yes   ❏ No

❏ Only for night meetings   ❏ Only during inclement weather

Child care needed?   ❏ Yes   ❏ No

Days/times person is available (check **all** days and times that apply)

	SUN	MON	TUES	WED	THUR	FRI	SAT
Morning							
Afternoon							
Evening							

Notes _____

_____

Geographical location of group—requirements or limitations _____

_____

Accessibility of group meeting place—requirements or limitations _____

_____

ChristCare Group Leader Administrative Report

ChrisCare Series

Name: _____ **Date:** _____

Write out answers to any of the questions that apply to your group or to you as a ChristCare Group Leader. Write "NA" next to questions that do not apply. All questions pertain to issues and information since your last administrative report.

Meeting Dates and Attendance

Dates of ChristCare Group meetings held since last report				
Total attendance (including leader) at each meeting				
Number of first-time visitors at each meeting				

Membership Update (include meeting dates after names)

Name of apprentice leader: _____

Names of visitors:

_____   _____

_____   _____

Names of potential group members:

_____   _____

_____   _____

Names of new group members:

_____   _____

_____   _____

Names of those who are thinking about leaving the group:

_____   _____

_____   _____

Names of those who have left the group:

(For each name, choose reason for leaving from the following list and check number after name.)

1. Part of a new group that has just been born
2. Relocated to another ChristCare Group
3. No longer active in a ChristCare Group (explain)
4. Left our congregation
5. Other (briefly explain)

Name: _____ 1_____ 2_____ 3_____ 4_____ 5_____

    Briefly explain_____

    _____

Name: _____ 1_____ 2_____ 3_____ 4_____ 5_____

    Briefly explain_____

    _____

Name: _____ 1_____ 2_____ 3_____ 4_____ 5_____

    Briefly explain_____

    _____

Information for the Equippers Team

Y N	Do any members of the group need referral for additional care?
Y N	Is there an area in which you need continuing education? **Topic(s):**
Y N	Do you need help finding Biblical Equipping resources? **Bible Book(s):** **Topic(s):**
Y N	Do you or a member of your group have a story that could promote ChristCare Groups? **Who?** **What?**
Y N	Do you need help finding more members for your group?
Y N	Do you need to talk to your SEA Group Facilitator about anything?

How to Build Membership in Your ChristCare Group

Outline and Focus Notes

Unless the LORD builds the house, its builders labor in vain.

Psalm 127:1

1. Modeling Welcoming

2. Biblical Equipping: Follow Me—Inviting as Jesus Did (John 1:35–51)

FOCUS NOTE 1

Follow Me—Inviting as Jesus Did (John 1:35–51)

[35] The next day John was there again with two of his disciples. [36] When he saw Jesus passing by, he said, "Look, the Lamb of God!"

[37] When the two disciples heard him say this, they followed Jesus. [38] Turning around, Jesus saw them following and asked, "What do you want?"

They said, "Rabbi" (which means Teacher), "where are you staying?"

[39] "Come," he replied, "and you will see."

So they went and saw where he was staying, and spent that day with him. It was about the tenth hour.

[40] Andrew, Simon Peter's brother, was one of the two who heard what John had said and who had followed Jesus. [41] The first thing Andrew did was to find his brother Simon and tell him, "We have found the Messiah" (that is, the Christ). [42] And he brought him to Jesus.

Jesus looked at him and said, "You are Simon son of John. You will be called Cephas" (which, when translated, is Peter).

Focus Note 1 is continued on page 286.

285

14-OFN.pmd C: 03/03/2004 R: 12/03/2004

[43] The next day Jesus decided to leave for Galilee. Finding Philip, he said to him, "Follow me."

[44] Philip, like Andrew and Peter, was from the town of Bethsaida. [45] Philip found Nathanael and told him, "We have found the one Moses wrote about in the Law, and about whom the prophets also wrote—Jesus of Nazareth, the son of Joseph."

[46] "Nazareth! Can anything good come from there?" Nathanael asked.

"Come and see," said Philip.

[47] When Jesus saw Nathanael approaching, he said of him, "Here is a true Israelite, in whom there is nothing false."

[48] "How do you know me?" Nathanael asked.

Jesus answered, "I saw you while you were still under the fig tree before Philip called you."

[49] Then Nathanael declared, "Rabbi, you are the Son of God; you are the King of Israel."

[50] Jesus said, "You believe because I told you I saw you under the fig tree. You shall see greater things than that." [51] He then added, "I tell you the truth, you shall see heaven open, and the angels of God ascending and descending on the Son of Man."

FOCUS NOTE 2

Explore Questions

1. What are the ways in which different people find out about Jesus in this passage?

2. Does Jesus do all the inviting in this passage? Who else does? Whom do they invite—not the people's names but their relationship? Why do you think they invite these people to meet Jesus?

3. Find the people Jesus invites in this passage and describe what relationship Jesus has with them before he invites them.

4. How do people in this passage respond to Jesus' invitations?

FOCUS NOTE 3

Connect Questions

1. Who invited you to come and meet Jesus? How did he or she or they invite you? What was helpful about that invitation? What, if anything, was unhelpful?

2. Whom have you invited to join your ChristCare Group or to meet Jesus? How did you invite him or her? What was helpful about your invitation? What, if anything, was unhelpful?

3. What do you know about Jesus that you would like to share with others and that you would like to invite someone else to come and experience?

4. How could you help members of your ChristCare Group become inviters who introduce others to your group and to Jesus?

FOCUS NOTE 4

Questions to Focus Sharing of Biblical Equipping Apart

- Share one insight that you've had as a result of your Biblical Equipping Apart this week.

- Describe one change in your life that you've committed to make as a result of your meditation on the Biblical Equipping passage this week.

- Tell about a time when you've met God in a new way through Biblical Equipping Apart this week.

---

3. Role-Play Inviting

FOCUS NOTE 5

Scenarios for Role-Playing Invitations

Scenario 1

Inviter: Your friend went through a divorce about a year ago. He or she seems to be relieved that the marriage is over, but also very lonely. You believe your group would welcome your friend and provide needed friendship.

Invited: You went through a painful divorce about a year ago. Some of your church friends rejected you during the divorce, and you worry that the ChristCare Group also might reject you.

Scenario 2

Inviter: You've become friends with your next-door neighbor since he or she moved in four months ago. You'd like to invite your neighbor to your ChristCare Group because you believe the group could help your neighbor come to know Jesus.

Invited: You like your new neighbor, but you are not at all a religious person. You didn't grow up going to church, and you've never had any interest in God.

Scenario 3

Inviter: You've had several lunchtime discussions with a coworker who's interested in Jesus and in what you believe. You can't always answer your coworker's questions about Christianity, but you think he or she could experience what it means to be a Christian in your ChristCare Group.

Invited: You had a bad experience with a religious cult many years ago, and you're suspicious of religious fanatics. You're interested in Christianity, and you've felt comfortable talking to your coworker because he or she has never pushed you to believe or join the church.

Scenario 4

Inviter: A fellow church choir member tells you that he or she only comes to church because his or her family does and that he or she really doesn't get anything out of it—it's boring. You believe this person would be a lot more enthusiastic about all the discussion and missional service activities that take place in your ChristCare Group.

Invited: You've gone to church all your life out of obligation to your family, but you've never really gotten it. You wish you understood what it is that people get out of going to church.

Focus Note 5 is continued on page 289.

Scenario 5

Inviter: Five years ago your close friend stopped attending your church because he or she was deeply hurt by the pastor during a particularly vulnerable time. You've tried to talk with him or her about it, but he or she says, "I don't have anything against God, but I'm not going back to church." You wonder if your friend would be willing to visit your ChristCare Group.

Invited: Five years ago you filed for divorce because of physical and emotional abuse. Your pastor didn't support your decision and told you that you were sinning. You are still deeply hurt. You miss worshipping God, but you are too angry to go back to church.

FOCUS NOTE 6

Discussion Questions

1. What did the inviter do well?

2. How might the inviter have been even more effective?

---

4. Building Groups in Our Congregation

5. Class Member-Led Prayer and Worship

6. Assignments for the Next Class

Group-Based Manual for ChristCare Group Leaders
How to Participate Effectively in a SEA Group

Therefore encourage one another and build each other up, just as in fact you are doing.

1 Thessalonians 5:11

PRECLASS READING OUTLINE

I. What Is a SEA Group?

First Church has had ChristCare Group Ministry in its congregation for about a year. Twelve ChristCare Group Leaders have completed their training and are now leading small groups. Right now it's 5:30 P.M. on a Tuesday evening. Here's what's going on in the minds of four of the 12 ChristCare Group Leaders:

Dean is driving home from work. The rush-hour traffic is terrible. But Dean realizes that it's upsetting him more than usual. As his car crawls along he starts thinking about why he's upset. "It's Allen! That's why I'm so angry. He did it again last night. Every time my ChristCare Group meets, he tries to take it over. It makes me mad!"

Maria is struggling up to her front door, her arms full of work papers, groceries, a diaper bag, and a two-year-old. She says to herself, "Oh, I've got to remember to put those folding chairs in the trunk. That way we'll at least have enough seats next week. What if even more people show up? Sixteen in a group—that's way too many!"

Lee is picking up something to fix for dinner. As he wanders through the grocery store aisles, he starts thinking about why he's felt "down" for a few days. "It's my ChristCare Group. People have stopped coming. I don't know why—maybe I'm just not doing a good job as a leader. Why did I ever say I would be a ChristCare Group Leader?"

Sally is folding laundry and keeping an eye on dinner as it cooks. Her thoughts turn again to something that's been at the back of her mind for several days. "Irene seems so depressed at every meeting. Everyone cares for her so much, but it seems like all we do recently is talk about her problems. Irene's needs are important, but so are the other members of the group. I feel stuck. I don't know what to do."

John is also thinking about ChristCare Groups on this Tuesday. He is a ChristCare Equipper at First Church, and the Facilitator for the SEA Group that Dean, Lee, Maria, and Sally attend. As John watches his daughter's hockey game, he's thinking about the ChristCare Group Leaders in his SEA Group. "I really need to find out what's going on in Lee's group. I can tell something's bothering him. And Maria's group has gotten way too big. We really need to help move it along toward birthing new groups."

Later that evening, each of these four ChristCare Group Leaders, together with their SEA Group Facilitator, brings his or her concerns to one another and to God. They attend a twice-monthly SEA Group meeting. At this meeting, they receive and give support and encouragement. They hold one another accountable for their valuable ministry. They leave the meeting feeling affirmed, revitalized, and capable of leading their ChristCare Groups even more effectively.

Without a SEA Group, Dean might blow up at Allen, Maria might struggle along with a group that's too large, Lee might decide to quit being a ChristCare Group Leader, and Sally's group might crumble under the pressure of trying to provide care it can't provide well enough. Without a SEA Group, John might continue wondering how the groups are going, never knowing for sure if they are operating effectively and according to First Church's mission.

The name, SEA, spells out the purpose of a SEA Group:

Support
Four to six ChristCare Group Leaders, meeting with a SEA Group Facilitator, listen to one another, offer different perspectives on difficult situations, suggest options to explore, and help identify next steps to take.

Encouragement
The members of a SEA Group affirm one another, empathize with one another, care and pray for each other. They celebrate the high points and provide a safe place during the low points of a ChristCare Group's life.

Accountability
In the SEA Group, ChristCare Group Leaders help one another stay connected to the congregation's mission and accountable for their ministry.

Working with small groups can be a challenge even for professionally trained group leaders. ChristCare Group Leaders in congregations also face many challenges, and they deserve the best support and guidance they can get. SEA Groups provide what ChristCare Group Leaders need in order to lead the highest quality, most distinctively Christian groups possible.

II. How SEA Groups Work
Here's a basic overview of SEA Groups.

Administrative Leadership
SEA Group leadership involves two Equipper roles: the SEA Group Coordinator and the SEA Group Facilitators.

The SEA Group Coordinator oversees all the SEA Groups. He or she assigns ChristCare Group Leaders to SEA Groups and appoints SEA Group Facilitators to lead them. He or she also meets regularly with SEA Group Facilitators to monitor SEA Groups' effectiveness.

SEA Group Facilitators, trained ChristCare Equippers, are the leaders of the individual SEA Groups. Their responsibilities are to:

- plan, guide, and review their SEA Group meeting;
- assure that confidentiality is maintained in their SEA Group;
- facilitate interaction among SEA Group members;
- facilitate community building in their SEA Group;
- conduct assessments of their SEA Group;
- maintain the distinctively Christian nature of their SEA Group;

- facilitate the closure and group growth processes;
- serve as liaison between their SEA Group and other members of the Equippers Team, such as the SEA Group Coordinator and the Continuing Education Coordinator.

In many ways, the SEA Group Facilitator is like a ChristCare Group Leader for the SEA Group.

Meeting Frequency
SEA Group meetings begin as soon as ChristCare Group Leaders finish their training and are commissioned. ChristCare Group Leaders attend SEA Group meetings twice a month.

Meeting Place and Time
SEA Group members decide together when and where to meet. For example, meetings might occur at church or in a home, in the evening, on a Saturday morning, or at some other time convenient for all the SEA Group members. SEA Group meetings last ninety minutes.

Attendance
Attendance at a SEA Group isn't optional. ChristCare Group Leaders who can't attend because of an emergency, or because they're ill or going out of town, must let the SEA Group Facilitator know ahead of time. ChristCare Group Leaders value consistent attendance because they care about their groups, themselves, other leaders, and their call to this ministry. SEA Groups are the most effective way to make sure their ChristCare Groups are top-quality and faith-building for everyone involved.

Group Size
One SEA Group contains four to six ChristCare Group Leaders, led by one SEA Group Facilitator.

What Is a SEA Group?

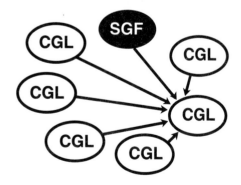

Peers provide Support, Encouragement, Accountability.

As new ChristCare Group Leaders are commissioned, SEA Groups add new members. When the SEA Group grows beyond its maximum size of six ChristCare Group Leaders, the group divides into two new SEA Groups, each with a mixture of new and experienced leaders. (This process of growing and creating new SEA Groups gives ChristCare Group Leaders valuable experience in handling this same growing and dividing process in their own ChristCare Groups.)

Confidentiality in SEA Groups
You've read about how to maintain confidentiality in SEA Groups in session 5, Confidentiality in ChristCare Groups. You may want to go back and review the section of the Preclass Reading for that session that deals specifically with SEA Groups.

III. Preparing for a SEA Group Session
You will need to prepare for each SEA Group session in advance. This section will help you to understand the various forms used in SEA Groups. Make sure you take the time to look at the sample forms at the back of this Preclass Reading when they are referred to.

A. Pray
As with most things you prepare for, prayer is the place to start. It's important to pray for your SEA Group Facilitator, for the group members, about your role in the SEA Group, and for the time your group is going to spend together.

B. Prepare Your Administrative Report
Take a minute now to look over the sample "ChristCare Group Leader Administrative Report" on pages 300–302. This report was filled out by the Maria you met in the vignette in section I, "What Is a SEA Group?"

Here are some important points about this form:
- You will pick up this blank form at each SEA Group session, complete it before the next session, turn it in, and pick up another blank form to fill out for the next meeting.
- Most of the time this form will take only a few minutes to fill out.
- This form will help you focus on basic events and critical issues that occur in your ChristCare Group's life. Answering the questions is a good way to review the values and the principles

(quality care, group growth, evangelism, and leadership) that undergird this ministry.

- The SEA Group Facilitator will read your report and pass on any pertinent information to other appropriate Equippers Team members. For instance, if you report that you need to know more about referring a group member to another caring resource, the Continuing Education Coordinator might schedule a training session on that topic.

The diagram below shows how the information you put into this report is passed on to the Equippers Team so they can manage the ChristCare Group Ministry and maintain its high quality.

C. Prepare Your Check-in Report

The check-in report will give you a chance to share about what's going on in your ChristCare Group. You, the SEA Group Facilitator, and the other group members will use your report to "keep tabs" on the general health of your group and your feelings about your leadership, and to help you determine if you need immediate assistance.

You use the form called "ChristCare Group Leader Check-in Report" to write out the report you plan to give at your SEA Group session. Take a minute now to look over the sample "ChristCare Group Leader Check-in Report" on pages 303–304. This report was filled out by the Sally you met in the vignette in section I, "What Is a SEA Group?" You'll recall that Sally was worried about Irene, who took up much of the group's time with her problems.

Here are some important points about this form:

- You will pick up this blank form at each SEA Group session, complete it before the next session, turn it in, and pick up another blank form to fill out for the next meeting.

- Most of the time this form will take only a few minutes to fill out.

- This form will help you prepare to give a brief oral report to your SEA Group about your ChristCare Group. It helps you give the SEA Group members the information they need to know and say it concisely.

- Question 2 on this report, the "Current Need or Challenge," needs careful consideration. Your answer to this question will give the other SEA Group members a "window" into how your ChristCare Group is doing. They may be facing similar circumstances now, or they may in the future. Your ideas about the causes and solutions can help them. And, in turn, their responses to you can help you in your leadership.

Following are some guidelines that tell how to make your check-in report as helpful as possible— for you, for your ChristCare Group, and for your SEA Group.

- Be brief.

Take just a few minutes to report on the basic status of your ChristCare Group. Describe the major need or primary challenge, and your response to it, in a couple of sentences each.

- Be honest.

Tell the truth about the status of your ChristCare Group and the need or challenge facing it (item 2 on the report) so the SEA Group can respond to what's really going on.

- Be confidential.

Remember to keep this report confidential: Never mention names and do not share irrelevant or identifying details about a person or a situation.

- Be prepared.

Write out your report ahead of time.

- Be current.

Your check-in report should change from session to session because your ChristCare Group will be changing. Report about the different stages and challenges as they occur.

- Let the report guide, not restrict, you.

You may find that your major need or challenge isn't related to the activity ratings. For instance, you might rate your group high in all areas, yet still be concerned about where it's going from here. That's okay.

D. Prepare Your In-Depth Report

Those SEA Group members who will be giving an in-depth report at the SEA Group meeting (usually two members each meeting) will need to fill out an in-depth report form prior to the meeting. This report gives your SEA Group members the information they need to discuss your ChristCare Group and provide you with the in-depth support, encouragement, and accountability you need.

There are two forms that help you prepare your in-depth report. Which one you use depends on what you want to emphasize. The forms are described in Focus Box 1.

FOCUS BOX 1

In-Depth Report: How Is It Going for You as a ChristCare Group Leader?

If you as a ChristCare Group Leader are wrestling with a particular challenge (for example, how to handle a group member who monopolizes discussions or how to help your group make decisions), this is the form to use.

In-Depth Report: How Is It Going for Your ChristCare Group?

If your ChristCare Group is wrestling with a need or challenge (for example, the group can't seem to get out of the Test stage of group development, or the group has experienced a breach of confidentiality), this is the form to use.

To decide which of the two in-depth report forms to use, ask yourself this question:

In light of my major need or primary challenge, which report would better help the SEA Group understand the situation?

The answer to this question will determine which report to choose. In addition, either your SEA Group Facilitator or your SEA Group may suggest that you use one form or the other.

Take a minute now to look over the two sample ChristCare Group Leader in-depth report forms on pages 305–309. The sample "In-Depth Report: How Is It Going for You as a ChristCare Group Leader?" was filled out by the Lee you met in section I, "What Is a SEA Group?" Lee doubted his leadership ability because people had stopped

coming to his group. The "In-Depth Report: How Is It Going for Your ChristCare Group?" was filled out by the Dean you met in section I, "What Is a SEA Group?" Dean felt threatened by Allen, who wanted to take over his group.

Here are some important points about these forms:

- You will pick up a blank form at the SEA Group session before you give your report. You will complete the report, bring it to the session, present your report orally, then turn it in to the SEA Group Facilitator. If you aren't sure which report form you'll use, pick up a copy of each. It's also fine to take several of each so you'll have them handy when you need them.

- Either of these forms will require about 15–30 minutes to complete.

- The information you present to the SEA Group from these forms will help them understand fully the need or challenge you are facing. Your report will be the starting point for your SEA Group's in-depth discussion of your ChristCare Group.

As you fill out your in-depth report, make your answers as clear and to-the-point as possible. Try to limit yourself to four or five sentences for each essay-type question. That way, your oral report will be brief and to the point.

Remember that the SEA Group members will be listening for information that will help them fully understand your major need or challenge. If you are specific and clear, they will be better able to help you analyze the problem and come up with an action plan that will work.

IV. The Beginning of the SEA Group Session

What happens in a SEA Group session, and what do you do to participate? This section of your Preclass Reading, and the two following sections, will give you a detailed look at each part of a SEA Group session.

The beginning of the SEA Group session has two parts:

- convening; and
- check-in reports.

A. Convening (Five Minutes)

At the very beginning of the SEA Group session the Facilitator welcomes each member, makes necessary announcements, and either prays or

---

asks a group member to pray. In his or her training, your SEA Group Facilitator has learned two important things about convening a SEA Group: start on time, and keep opening comments to a minimum so the group can get right to work.

B. Check-in Reports (15 to 20 Minutes)

As you've read, check-in reports give you a chance to share briefly about what's happening in your ChristCare Group. Sometimes you may feel like spending lots of time with check-in reports—both your own report and others'. But realize that the in-depth discussion time is where the most important work of the SEA Group gets done. You need to keep the check-in reports short so there is enough time left for the in-depth discussion.

Be Brief and Supportive When You Respond to a Check-in Report

Your SEA Group Facilitator will invite one or two responses from the group after each member gives his or her check-in report. One or two SEA Group members can respond with short, supportive statements. These statements will boost the confidence of the check-in reporter. Affirming positive trends in the ChristCare Group's life will contribute to the overall atmosphere of care and trust that is essential in a SEA Group. Save lengthy statements or probing questions for the in-depth discussions that will take place later.

V. The Middle of the SEA Group Session

The middle portion of a SEA Group meeting is the core of what SEA Groups do. During this time, group members dig deeply into issues that seriously affect their ChristCare Groups. The middle of the SEA Group session has five parts:

- in-depth report;
- analysis (including Focus Questions);
- possibilities;
- action plan; and
- summary.

A. In-Depth Report (Five to Ten Minutes)

In-depth reports focus the SEA Group members' attention and skills on important issues facing ChristCare Group Leaders.

Who Reports?

At most sessions, two SEA Group members will give in-depth reports. The SEA Group Facilitator designates the next-session reporters at the end of each session. If your SEA Group has six members, and two members give an in-depth report at each session, you will give a report every third session.

Needs for Immediate Assistance Take Priority

Sometimes it becomes clear during the check-in reports that a group member needs immediate assistance. The member might make this clear during the course of the report, or the SEA Group members might decide immediate assistance is needed after hearing the report.

If you ever discover, between SEA Group meetings, that you will need immediate assistance at your next SEA Group session, call your SEA Group Facilitator before the meeting. He or she can then formally include you in the schedule ahead of time, and you can write out your in-depth report prior to the session. Even if you have not had time to prepare a report because you learned about a need for immediate assistance just before the SEA Group session, you can still receive immediate assistance from the SEA Group.

Here are some examples of major needs that could require the SEA Group's immediate assistance.

- "I think a member of my ChristCare Group may need professional care."
- "The problems of one member of my group dominate every meeting. I don't know what to do about it."
- "Five people have joined our group, and that brings us to 12 members. I think we need to form two new groups, and I need help with that."
- "I'm feeling lousy about my performance as a ChristCare Group Leader right now. I'm thinking it's time to step down."

B. Analysis (Ten to 15 Minutes)

After a SEA Group member gives an in-depth report, the group analyzes the information he or she has presented. Here are some things to remember when you help analyze a group member's ChristCare Group.

Pray

After you have learned more about the in-depth reporter's situation, prayer may be the most natural response. Such prayer acknowledges that all ministry is under the Spirit's control and done with the Spirit's power. It also helps group members to keep on trusting God instead of trying to solve problems on their own. Your SEA Group Facilitator may lead a prayer, or you might suggest prayer and pray out loud.

Don't think you must pray every time a SEA Group member shares an in-depth report, but always ask yourself whether prayer would be an appropriate response.

Start with Affirmation
Find ways to affirm what the in-depth reporter is doing right. Recognize his or her effort and hard work. Point out how the in-depth reporter's ChristCare Group has changed and grown.

Such affirmation will help the in-depth reporter see more clearly his or her gifts and achievements. It will help him or her trust the SEA Group and become better able to accept and respond to the SEA Group's suggestions and questions.

Keep in Mind the Purposes of Analysis
Your purpose in analyzing is to understand the in-depth reporter's situation better, especially the major need or challenge that he or she identified. You want to gather enough information that you can respond with ideas for meeting the need or challenge.

You also want to make sure the in-depth reporter is carrying out his or her responsibilities.

Use Focus Questions
Focus Questions are important tools for SEA Group members. They probe the most important aspects of leading a ChristCare Group and help the SEA Group spend enough time discussing each issue to get beneath the surface. Focus Questions also help the entire SEA Group work together to analyze the in-depth reporter's situation—without Focus Questions each SEA Group member might be asking about a different topic and the SEA Group would get nowhere.

Take time to look over and become familiar with the "Focus Questions for SEA Groups" included in your manual on pages 310–319. Notice the instructions for using Focus Questions below each set of questions.

Focus Box 2 highlights how to and how *not* to use these Focus Questions.

FOCUS BOX 2

How and How Not to Use Focus Questions
Focus Questions *should* be used to:
- provide the in-depth reporter with care, support, and encouragement;
- help SEA Group members to concentrate on one issue at a time;
- hold the in-depth reporter accountable for his or her ChristCare Group leadership;
- clarify the issues, thoughts, concerns, and feelings expressed by the in-depth reporter;
- explore other factors that may be affecting the situation or issue described by the in-depth reporter;
- size up the challenges facing the in-depth reporter and his or her ChristCare Group;
- evaluate strategies or actions that have worked and strategies that have not worked;
- identify options, alternatives, or possibilities for the in-depth reporter;
- come up with new strategies or action plans;
- invite the reporter to express needs, concerns, ideas, and beliefs;
- stimulate and guide group members' questions so the discussion is productive.

Focus Questions *should not* be used to:
- interrogate the in-depth reporter;
- stifle creativity by limiting discussion;
- push people toward results.

Choose and Use Focus Questions Wisely
Focus Box 3 describes how SEA Groups choose which Focus Questions they will discuss.

FOCUS BOX 3

How to Choose Focus Questions
1. At the end of his or her report, the in-depth reporter suggests a set of Focus Questions to use.
2. The other SEA Group members may also suggest additional Focus Question sets.
3. The SEA Group Facilitator guides the group in deciding on a set of Focus Questions and in choosing one question in that set as a starting point.

---

4. Some groups may want to stop at this point and give everyone time to read the questions in that set, then choose the starting question.

5. As the discussion progresses, group members:
   - may ask additional questions from the set.
   - may add their own questions on that topic.
   - may move to additional Focus Question sets, with the consent of the rest of the SEA Group.

Know and Meet the Challenges of Using Focus Questions

Focus Questions are an essential and effective tool for SEA Groups. But they do present some challenges. For instance, the sheer number of Focus Questions can be overwhelming. Here are some suggestions for making the most of Focus Questions while minimizing any possible disadvantages they might present:

- Become very familiar with each set of Focus Questions and how to use them. Then, as you listen to an in-depth report, you'll be better able to sense which set or sets of Focus Questions will be most appropriate.

- Use the Focus Questions and encourage others to use them. The more you use Focus Questions, the more comfortable you'll become with them. Soon they'll be second nature and your SEA Group will benefit from the high-quality sessions that result.

C. Possibilities (Five Minutes)

After the in-depth report and analysis, SEA Group members will clearly understand what the in-depth reporter's needs and concerns are. Now it's time to come up with some possible responses.

Brainstorm

Your SEA Group Facilitator may ask you at this time to use the skills of brainstorming, sorting down, and gaining consensus that you learned in session 12, ChristCare Group Facilitation Skills. The idea is to come up with plenty of responses to the need that's been presented.

Be Process Oriented

It's very tempting at this point to become results oriented. But instead of trying to solve problems and fix what's wrong, stay process oriented. The in-depth reporter doesn't need you to solve his or her needs and challenges. He or she needs you to listen, to care for him or her, to ask questions, to

understand, to offer ideas, and to allow him or her to decide what to do. That is the process that will lead to the best results in a SEA Group.

There will be times when a ChristCare Group Leader presents a need that can only be responded to with listening, caring, and sharing the burden. For instance, if a group member dies, the ChristCare Group Leader will grieve, and there's nothing you can do to solve that problem. You are called upon to "mourn with those who mourn" (Romans 12:15). In such a situation, to become results oriented and try to solve the other person's problem would be uncaring.

D. Action Plan (Five Minutes)

An in-depth reporter should leave the SEA Group with a clear plan for what to do next. The SEA Group helps develop that plan.

Evaluate the Possibilities

Your SEA Group might come up with ten great ideas, but the in-depth reporter may be able to implement only one or two. You and the other SEA Group members will help him or her select the ideas or activities that will best meet the needs or challenges.

Develop an Action Plan

The SEA Group will help the in-depth reporter decide what to do, when to do it, and how to do it, based on the work they've done to this point. Future check-in reports will tell how the action plan is working out.

Focus Box 4 shows what an action plan might look like.

FOCUS BOX 4

Sample Action Plan

Action
Give possible apprentice responsibility for leading the Biblical Equipping at one ChristCare Group meeting to see if she handles the responsibility well.

Steps
- Decide which meeting you want her to lead.
- Prepare the materials she will need for her own preparations and teaching.
- Ask her to lead a Biblical Equipping session.
- Tell her exactly how you want her to prepare, how long the Biblical Equipping should last, and when you want her to lead Biblical Equipping.

- Set up a day when you will call and check on her preparations.
- Answer any questions she has.
- Tell her you will provide any help she needs.

E. Summary (Two to Three Minutes)

When your SEA Group reaches the end of an in-depth round, the SEA Group Facilitator will summarize the issues you've covered, the ideas you've come up with, and the action plan you've helped create.

F. If Time Allows, Repeat Steps A through E

If there's time, your SEA Group will go through another in-depth round. If not, you'll move on to the end of the SEA Group session.

VI. The End of the SEA Group Session

There are two parts to the end of the SEA Group session:

- assessment; and
- wrap-up.

A. Assessment (Five Minutes)

Each time the SEA Group meets, members will assess how well it is functioning. Usually your group will conduct a regular assessment. Occasionally you'll do a periodic assessment.

Both types of assessments give SEA Group members an opportunity to ask and answer some important questions about the SEA Group, how it functions, and their commitment to it. When you assess your SEA Group, you will ask questions such as:

- How effectively is the SEA Group meeting my needs and those of other members?
- In what way am I contributing to the SEA Group process?
- How am I helping the SEA Group to function effectively?
- What do we want our SEA Group to accomplish?
- Are we all participating actively and contributing fully?
- How can we improve our effectiveness as a supportive and encouraging community?
- How are we fulfilling our commitment and responsibilities to one another?

Regular Assessment

Take a minute now to look at "Questions for Regular SEA Group Assessment" on pages 320–321. Here are some important points to note about this form:

- SEA Group Facilitators distribute this form at the end of each session (except in sessions in which periodic assessments are conducted). You'll take about five minutes to complete your copy, then return it to the SEA Group Facilitator.
- This form provides SEA Group Facilitators with immediate and regular feedback on each SEA Group session. By using this form, you can help improve the SEA Group's quality.

Periodic Assessment

Take a minute now to look at "Questions for Periodic SEA Group Assessment" on pages 322–326. Here are some important points to note about this form:

- This form is a tool that helps SEA Group members think deeply about their SEA Group experience in preparation for an extended discussion in the next SEA Group session. The discussion will focus on your personal participation in, and perspective on, the SEA Group. Complete this form carefully and thoughtfully.
- Your SEA Group Facilitator will distribute this form three or four times a year, at the session prior to the one when your SEA Group will discuss it. You will complete the form at home, then share your assessments with the group at the next session. You will not turn it in. A periodic assessment form takes about 20 minutes to complete.

Assessment—A Joint Effort

The nature of these two forms and the way in which you use them make it clear that the SEA Group's success depends on a united effort, not just on the SEA Group Facilitator or a few group members.

B. Wrap-Up (Three to Five Minutes)

Your SEA Group Facilitator will do several things to close each SEA Group Session.

Distributing Forms

The SEA Group Facilitator will pass out any forms SEA Group members need, including any of the following:

- "ChristCare Group Leader Administrative Report"
- "ChristCare Group Leader Check-in Report"
- "In-Depth Report: How Is It Going for Your ChristCare Group?"
- "In-Depth Report: How Is It Going for You as a ChristCare Group Leader?"
- "Questions for Periodic SEA Group Assessment"

Preparing for the Next Session

The SEA Group Facilitator will choose members to lead the opening and closing prayer at the next SEA Group session. He or she also will announce who will present in-depth reports at the next session and (perhaps) which report forms they will use.

Close with Prayer

Finally, the SEA Group Facilitator will ask for a closing prayer by a SEA Group member, thanking the Spirit of God for community, guidance, and mutual care.

VII. Getting Ready for the In-Class Training Session

In the in-class training session that's coming up, you'll have a chance to practice being a SEA Group member. In preparation for the in-class, please prepare two reports—a check-in report and an in-depth report. You should have received blank copies of these reports from your trainer. This is the same preparation you'll do for SEA Group sessions.

Be sure to prepare these reports. If you don't, you will not be prepared for the in-class session.

Check-in Report

If you are currently a small group leader of some kind, report on that group in your check-in report. If you are not currently a group leader, here are some other groups you may want to use as a basis for your report:

- The group you were in as you worked through the *Beginnings* course.
- A small group in which you are now a member.

- A small group to which you once belonged.
- Another small group situation you have experienced.
- As a last resort you may use one of the situations from the beginning of your Preclass Reading.
- See the sample check-in report on pages 303–304 for an example of how to prepare your own.

In-Depth Report

Prepare an in-depth report about the same small group that you used in your check-in report. Allow the Preclass Reading and the sample in-depth reports to guide you.

The first thing you'll need to do is figure out which in-depth report best fits the primary challenge mentioned in your check-in report. Remember the key question to ask in selecting the correct form:

> In light of my major need or primary challenge, which report would better help the SEA Group understand the situation?

See the sample in-depth reports on pages 305–309 for examples of how to prepare your own.

Here are several other things you can do to help apply what you've learned in this Preclass Reading and to prepare yourself for the in-class training session:

- Review all the documents that follow this Preclass Reading.
- Review the ten sets of Focus Questions on pages 310–319.
- Review "When to Use" information below each set of Focus Questions.
- Make a list of questions you've thought of while reading through this information. Be prepared to ask them in class.
- Pat yourself on the back for finishing this Preclass Reading! You'll be glad for the background when it's time to participate in the exercises in the in-class session. But you'll be even more glad when you participate in your first SEA Group.

ChristCare Group Leader Administrative Report

ChrisӨare Series

Name: Maria Lopez   **Date:** 3/4/03

Write out answers to any of the questions that apply to your group or to you as a ChristCare Group Leader. Write "NA" next to questions that do not apply. All questions pertain to issues and information since your last administrative report.

Meeting Dates and Attendance

Dates of ChristCare Group meetings held since last report	2/14	2/28		
Total attendance (including leader) at each meeting	13	16		
Number of first-time visitors at each meeting	5	3		

Membership Update (include meeting dates after names)

Name of apprentice leader: ___None___

Names of visitors:

John and Peggy Stevens (2/14)   Linda and Jeff Makin (2/14)

Joan Brownstone (2/14, 2/28)   Joel Fredrickson (2/14)

Jeff Dare (2/14, 2/28)   Yvonne Cordell (2/28)

Names of potential group members:

John and Peggy Stevens   Yvonne Cordell

Jeff Dare

Names of new group members:

Bill Johnson   Scott Meirose

George Brown

Names of those who are thinking about leaving the group:

_____None_____   _____

_____   _____

Names of those who have left the group:

(For each name, choose reason for leaving from the following list and check number after name.)

1. Part of a new group that has just been born
2. Relocated to another ChristCare Group
3. No longer active in a ChristCare Group (explain)
4. Left our congregation
5. Other (briefly explain)

Name: _____ 1_____ 2_____ 3_____ 4_____ 5_____

    Briefly explain_____

    _____

Name: _____ 1_____ 2_____ 3_____ 4_____ 5_____

    Briefly explain_____

    _____

Name: _____ 1_____ 2_____ 3_____ 4_____ 5_____

    Briefly explain_____

    _____

Information for the Equippers Team

Y (N)	Do any members of the group need referral for additional care?
Y (N)	Is there an area in which you need continuing education? **Topic(s):**
Y (N)	Do you need help finding Biblical Equipping resources? **Bible Book(s):** **Topic(s):**
(Y) N	Do you or a member of your group have a story that could promote ChristCare Groups? **Who?** Me **What?** I could talk about how we've grown.
Y (N)	Do you need help finding more members for your group?
Y (N)	Do you need to talk to your SEA Group Facilitator about anything?

ChristCare Group Leader Check-in Report

ChrisCare Series

Name: Sally Hammer   **Date:** 3/4/03

1. Activity Ratings

Based on your own observations and feedback from ChristCare Group members, on a scale of 1 to 5 rate each of the four major activities of ChristCare Group life. Be prepared to share briefly your reasons for each rating.

1 = very low

- reluctant or no participation by group members
- activity does not carry out the group's purpose or mission
- activity does not meet group members' needs

5 = very high

- group members participate enthusiastically
- activity clearly carries out the group's purpose or mission
- activity definitely meets group members' needs

Activity	1	2	3	4	5
Community Building and Care					(5)
Biblical Equipping			(3)		
Prayer and Worship		(2)			
Missional Service	(1)				

2. Current Need or Challenge

Briefly describe the major need or primary challenge that you or your group faces at this time.

One of my group members is seriously depressed. She comes to group meetings weighed down with her problems. Group meetings are often filled with care for her. Unfortunately other people are feeling cheated of time to share their needs. We are also shortchanging other group activities.

Briefly describe how you or your group has handled this need or challenge thus far.

```
This group member dominates our time. It is hard for us
to be there for her because of her great needs.
```

3. Is This an Emergency?

Do you need the immediate assistance of the SEA Group to deal with this need or challenge?

☒ yes ❑ no

```
This is a serious challenge — I need help.
```

ChrisΦare Series

Supplement C

In-Depth Report: How Is It Going for You as a ChristCare Group Leader?

1. Identify and report on the most significant ChristCare Group meeting since the last time you gave an in-depth report to the SEA Group.

   a. How did you feel about yourself?

   ```
   I felt like a failure. We dropped attendance from 8 people to 3
   people. I think my leadership ability is lacking.
   ```

   b. What were your feelings toward the group?

   ```
   I'm hurt that people seem to care so little about the group. It
   seems like their priorities are in reverse. Anything takes pre-
   cedence over the group. I must be a really dull leader.
   ```

   c. What do you wish you would have said or done differently?

   ```
   I wish I'd spent more time focusing on the covenanting process.
   I felt bad being assertive about the covenant. People are so
   busy, I just rushed through it.
   ```

2. How have you grown as a ChristCare Group Leader?

   ```
   I don't feel like I've grown that much.
   ```

3. How have your feelings about being a ChristCare Group Leader, or your feelings about your ChristCare Group, changed since your last in-depth report to the SEA Group?

   ```
   I'm pretty discouraged right now. With the lack of attendance
   in my ChristCare Group things are not very exciting anymore.
   ```

4. How does your relationship with God affect your ministry as a ChristCare Group Leader? How does your ministry as a ChristCare Group Leader affect your relationship with God? How has this relationship changed over time?

   ```
   I'm frustrated with God for allowing me to get into this ministry.
   I'm not sure God cares about my group.
   ```

5. On a scale of 1 to 5, identify who is taking most of the leadership responsibility in your group in the following areas.

   1 = I take all the responsibility.

   2 = I take the majority of the responsibility.

   3 = The responsibility is split in half between me and group members.

   4 = Group members take the majority of the responsibility.

   5 = Group members take all the responsibility.

	1	2	3	4	5
Setting and carrying out goals		②			
Making sure that the group lives up to its covenant		②			
Prayer and worship			③		
Biblical Equipping		②			
Providing care for group members			③		
Reaching out with Christ's love beyond the group (missional service)		②			

   How are you feeling about sharing responsibility with other group members?

   ```
   Other group members don't seem to want to take responsibility.
   ```

6. Describe how you currently manage your group's missional service activities. How are you feeling about how you are managing these activities?

```
We're not ready for this yet.
```

7. Describe your current relationship with your apprentice and your thoughts and feelings about the future of that relationship.

```
No apprentice.
```

8. Give an example of how you transmit the congregation's vision for ministry to the members of your group.

```
I guess I don't know what the vision is.
```

9. What additional information would help the SEA Group better understand the major need or primary challenge you identified in your check-in report?

```
The group is made up of single people. Is this the reason?
```

10. What Focus Question Set and Focus Question might the SEA Group use to address the major need or primary challenge you identified in your check-in report?

```
Set B, Question 2
Set C, Question 7
Set G, Question 3
```

In-Depth Report: How Is It Going for Your ChristCare Group?

ChristCare Series

1. On a scale of 1 to 5, how would you characterize the overall emotional climate or tone of the group?

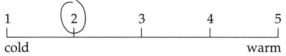

Share an example that illustrates your rating.

```
There is some tension in the group. There's a group member that
keeps trying to take over the group. He's well
respected by many of the group members and I'm the new
kid on the block.
```

2. On a scale of 1 to 5, how would you characterize the level of trust within the group?

Share an example that illustrates your rating.

```
People seem to be holding back because of the tension
between this group member who wants to dominate the group
and me.
```

3. Is the group maintaining confidentiality?   ☒ yes   ☐ no

4. Report on your group's current prayer and worship.

```
We spend about 15 minutes singing together.
```

5. What are your group members doing to promote one another's growth as Jesus' disciples?

```
There is a fair amount of participation in worship and Biblical
Equipping. The only drawback is this group member who constantly
wants to air his opinions or say things like, "A better way to
ask that would be . . . "
```

6. Report on your group's response to current needs or opportunities for caregiving among group members.

   ```
   As previously mentioned, the trust level is a little low.
   ```

7. What are the members of your group doing to reach out to others with God's love?

   ```
   We're waiting to bond as a group before participating in
   missional service.
   ```

8. Briefly tell a story that illustrates how your small group carries out your congregation's mission and ministry.

   ```
   N.A.
   ```

9. Describe your group's numerical growth and indicate its prospects for giving birth.

   ```
   We've remained around seven for a month.
   ```

10. What challenges could soon appear or are just coming into view? How might they be addressed now?

    ```
    This group member is a major challenge. I'm the only one trained
    to be in charge. I need help figuring out how to deal with him.
    ```

11. What additional information would help the SEA Group better understand the major need or primary challenge you identified in your check-in report?

    ```
    This group member who wants to take over used to lead some of the
    group members in a discipleship group. I think some of those mem-
    bers want him to lead this group.
    ```

12. What Focus Question Set and Focus Question might the SEA Group use to address the major need or primary challenge you identified in your check-in report?

    ```
    Set A: Question 8
    Set G: Question 5d
    ```

Focus Questions for SEA Groups

ChristCare Series

Set A: Focus on the Interaction between ChristCare Group Members

1. How would you describe group members' relationships? Are there specific subgroups?

2. How openly do group members express difficult feelings? How does the group respond when someone expresses difficult feelings?

3. Do you think the level of trust among group members has grown enough, given how long they've been together? If not, what might be done to build trust among group members?

4. How would you rate your group in the following areas? Give examples.

   a. Respect

   b. Genuineness

   c. Warmth

   d. Affirmation

   e. Acceptance

   f. Listening

5. What do group members expect of one another?

   a. Are their expectations realistic?

   b. How do they feel about unmet expectations?

6. How well do group members handle the tension between process and results?

   a. To what extent do group members offer solutions, give advice, or attempt to heal, convert, or rescue others? Give an example.

   b. Do any group members pressure others to act differently in order to gain acceptance? Give an example.

7. Do group members look to one another or just to the group leader for care and guidance?

8. To what extent do group members encourage or sustain another group member's unhelpful or inappropriate behavior?

9. What impact have group members' life crises had on relationships among group members?

10. Does one group member seem to monopolize the group's time and caring energy?

    a. How are you helping the group respond to this situation?

    b. Does this person need to be referred to another caregiver?

11. How effectively do group members handle decision making and problem solving? Give examples.

When to Use Set A: Focus on the Interaction between ChristCare Group Members

This set emphasizes:

- the group's interaction, its strengths and weaknesses;
- group members' feelings, decision making, and problem-solving abilities;
- the group's level of trust.

A SEA Group might use this set to:

- Focus on how group members get along.
- Analyze why relationships within the group seem to be going sour.

- Zero in on why a group does not seem to value the relationships within the group.
- Help ChristCare Group Leaders see that group members' relationships affect the group's ministry and quality of life.
- Figure out why group members often experience tension or conflict.
- Support a ChristCare Group Leader who feels overwhelmed by the way group members relate to one another.

Set B: Focus on the ChristCare Group's Distinctively Christian Nature

1. How do group members convey Jesus' love to one another?

2. How do you see God at work among group members?

3. What questions arise about God or God's relationship with people? How do group members respond when such questions are raised?

4. Are there faith issues that cause difficulty? If so, what are they? How do group members respond when such issues are raised?

5. How appropriately and effectively do group members use Scripture with one another?

6. Do group members share their personal faith experiences? If not, why not? If so, do they do so appropriately and effectively?

7. What fruit of the Spirit (for example, love, joy, peace, patience, kindness, goodness, faithfulness, gentleness, self-control) do group members exhibit often? Which would you like to see members exhibit more frequently?

8. How do group members respond to the expectation that the group exists to carry out the congregation's mission and ministry?

9. To what extent do group members model Christian discipleship to one another?

10. Do you see any group members exhibiting spiritual leadership in the group? If so, how might their leadership be nurtured?

11. How actively do group members encourage one another to identify, develop, and use their spiritual gifts and talents?

12. How is the group helping each member to live out his or her faith in daily life?

When to Use Set B: Focus on the ChristCare Group's Distinctively Christian Nature

This set emphasizes:

- God's work in and through ChristCare Groups;
- the spiritual aspects of group life;
- group members' ability to communicate and share God's love with one another;
- group members' discovery, development, and use of spiritual gifts;
- connecting faith in group life with living out faith in daily life.

A SEA Group might use this set to:

- Help a ChristCare Group Leader see more clearly what God is doing—or could do—in the ChristCare Group.
- Gain insights into a group whose members are frustrated by what they see as a lack of Christian love among themselves.

- Understand why a group has lost sight of God's part in group life: for instance, why they are more self-centered than Christ-centered or why they care more about the group's survival than about its mission.
- Help a ChristCare Group Leader understand why group members seem to ignore one another's needs.
- Analyze why group members have difficulty discussing their faith experiences and spiritual struggles.
- Understand better why a group's members are not growing as disciples.

Set C: Focus on the ChristCare Group's Direction

1. How is your group changing? How do you expect it to change in the future?

2. What dreams or concerns for the group's future have you or group members expressed?

3. Has the group identified its own mission and ministry goals?

   a. What are those goals?

   b. How were those goals established?

   c. How are those goals in line with the congregation's overall vision for mission and ministry?

   d. If the group has not established any goals, how might you effectively lead the goal-setting process?

4. What is the group doing to carry out its mission and ministry goals?

5. How are you maintaining the balance between providing strong leadership and fostering the group's independence?

6. What stage of group development is your group currently in? What's happening to move the group to the next stage?

7. If your group's size is changing, how is that affecting the group's quality of relationships and communication? What does your group plan to do about these changes?

When to Use Set C: Focus on the ChristCare Group's Direction

This set emphasizes:

- the ChristCare Group's mission;
- the ChristCare Group's future;
- the ChristCare Group Leader's expectations and goals, and those of the group members;
- changes in the group.

A SEA Group might use this set to:

- Help a ChristCare Group Leader clarify where his or her group is headed.
- Explore why group members seem unsure about why they're a group or what they should be doing.

- Understand why ChristCare Group members think it's time to end their group.
- Assess why the group seems to have lost its purpose or direction.
- Encourage a ChristCare Group Leader to look to his or her group's future.
- Decide if a group has taken on too much.
- Determine if a ChristCare Group Leader has unrealistic expectations for his or her group.
- Find out if a group isn't committed to a mission.

Set D: Focus on Birthing

1. Identify and evaluate the factors influencing your group's numerical growth.
2. To what extent do group members seek out and invite visitors to the group?
3. What might be holding your group back from evangelism and outreach activities?
4. What might your group do to add members?
5. How effectively does the group welcome and assimilate new members? Illustrate how this process typically occurs.
6. How close is the group to birthing?
   a. In terms of group size?
   b. In terms of emotional readiness to take this step?
7. What might be holding your group back from birthing?
8. If your small group is preparing to birth, answer the following questions:
   a. Have you been praying regularly for the wisdom and guidance to lead the birthing process?
   b. How have you planned and prepared for this birth?
   c. Has your group been praying regularly for wisdom and guidance in the birthing process?
   d. How has your group prepared itself for this birth?
   e. What problems has the group anticipated, and how does the group plan to deal with them?
   f. What feelings do group members have about the coming change?
   g. What are you doing to help your group prepare emotionally for birthing?
   h. How has the group dealt with anticipatory grief?
   i. Who will lead the two groups once yours births?
   j. How has your group matured through the birthing process? How have you matured?

When to Use Set D: Focus on Birthing

This set emphasizes:
- the group's growth;
- the group's outreach;
- welcoming visitors and incorporating new group members;
- preparing for birthing.

A SEA Group might use this set to:
- Investigate why group members aren't interested in outreach.
- Support a ChristCare Group Leader in searching for ways to stimulate growth.
- Figure out why a group doesn't retain new members.
- Find out how a group has achieved significant growth.
- Help a ChristCare Group Leader prepare and plan for birthing.
- Encourage a ChristCare Group Leader to prepare more carefully for birthing.
- Learn from a ChristCare Group Leader whose group has birthed a new group so other members can be more effective in a similar situation.

Set E: Focus on the ChristCare Group's Major Activities

Apply these questions to any of the four major activities of ChristCare Group life: community building and care, Biblical Equipping, prayer and worship, and missional service.

1. Evaluate the leadership of this activity.

    a. Are any group members taking leadership for this activity?

    b. How effective is this leadership?

    c. How could you as a ChristCare Group Leader help people to exercise more effective leadership?

    d. What indications are there that a change in leadership would be appropriate?

    e. How could a change in leadership be accomplished in a sensitive and caring way?

2. Evaluate group members' participation in this activity.

    a. Describe the level of participation in this activity over a specific period of time.

    b. What factors influence the level of participation in this activity?

    c. To what extent do group members need education or training in order to participate more fully or more effectively in this activity?

3. To what extent does the activity carry out the group's purpose or mission? How does it do so?

4. To what extent does this activity meet group members' needs? What evidence leads you to this appraisal?

5. Evaluate the resources you are currently using to carry out this activity (songbooks, Bible study materials, course manuals or workbooks).

    a. How effective are these resources?

    b. Could using these resources differently improve their effectiveness?

    c. Could resources be rotated or alternated to meet the needs, likes, and desires of more group members?

    d. What other resources have you tried?

    e. What potential resources have you explored?

6. Examine the format of this activity.

    a. What is the current format of this activity?

    b. What prior formats for this activity have worked well?

    c. What formats have you tried and discarded as ineffective?

7. What is the biggest challenge when it comes to planning for this activity?

8. What growth have you observed in group members as they have participated in this activity?

9. What are your plans for the next step your group will take in this activity?

When to Use Set E: Focus on the ChristCare Group's Major Activities

This set emphasizes:

- leadership in the four main areas of group life
    o community building and care
    o Biblical Equipping
    o worship and prayer
    o missional service;
- group members' participation in these activities;
- resources used in these activities;
- planning for these activities.

A SEA Group might use this set to:

- Assist a ChristCare Group Leader in exploring why group members aren't taking leadership responsibility in these four activities.

- Assess why the group's interest in a particular activity has dropped off significantly.

- Determine how a group's practice of these activities relates to the way the group carries out the congregation's mission.

- Investigate concerns about how well these activities are meeting group members' needs.

- Support a ChristCare Group Leader who is frustrated with what was supposed to be a really good resource for one of the activities.

- Encourage a ChristCare Group Leader who is looking for more effective ways to carry out these activities.

Set F: Focus on ChristCare Group Members' Caring for One Another

Questions about a Specific Situation

1. Do you as ChristCare Group Leader need to take immediate and decisive action in this situation?

   a. What makes you say there is such a need?

   b. How do you plan to respond?

2. How well does the group understand the need for care in this situation? What, if anything, has made it difficult for the group to grasp the need for care?

3. How well does the group understand the best response to this situation?

   a. What, if anything, has made it difficult for the group to determine the best response?

   b. To what extent might group members be overly zealous in providing care?

   c. In what ways might group members' responses be an attempt to meet their own needs as well as the care receiver's needs?

   d. How might you help group members reassess their caring response?

4. How are group members currently providing the following types of support and care?

   a. Physical

   b. Emotional

   c. Spiritual

   d. Intellectual

   e. Social

How might group members provide these types of support and care in the future?

5. Is a referral to another caring resource needed?

   a. What are the indications of such a need?

   b. To what extent might the group be tempted to see referral as a quick fix or an easy way out of this situation?

   c. What are your plans for referral?

   d. How will the group relate to the person once the referral is made?

6. How is the heightened need for care affecting the group?

General Questions about Caring

7. How broadly are group members sharing caring responsibility? What might you do to involve more group members in caring?

8. Is group members' caring more process- or results-oriented?

   a. Give some examples that illustrate your assessment.

   b. How might you guide group members toward a more process-oriented approach?

9. How has the group grown as a result of providing caring ministry?

When to Use Set F: Focus on ChristCare Group Members' Caring for One Another

This set emphasizes:

- the ChristCare Group Leader's level of involvement in caring for group members;
- evaluating the need for care;
- the appropriateness of the group's caring responses.

A SEA Group might use this set to:

- Confirm SEA Group members' feelings that ChristCare Group members are overlooking opportunities to care for one another.
- Support a ChristCare Group Leader who wants to mobilize group members to care for one another.

- Point out to a ChristCare Group Leader that he or she should be more actively involved in caring for a group member.
- Help a ChristCare Group Leader assist his or her group in assessing a group member's needs.
- Find out if a group has gone overboard in its caring response to a member.
- Respond to a ChristCare Group Leader who reports that group members are far too results oriented in their care.
- Determine whether a situation warrants the recommendation of other caring resources.

Set G: Focus on the ChristCare Group Leader's Feelings

1. What painful feelings do you have as a part of being a ChristCare Group Leader?
2. How does being a ChristCare Group Leader evoke enjoyable feelings?
3. Describe and evaluate your emotional ties to your group:
   a. Are you becoming too emotionally involved to be an objective, effective ChristCare Group Leader? If so, explore your emotional involvement.
   b. Are you detaching and becoming too distant from your group? If so, what might have contributed to this?
4. How do you feel about your group's progress at this point?
5. Do you experience strong feelings before, during, or after group meetings?
   a. What feelings?
   b. What causes those feelings?
   c. Are you able to express those feelings appropriately?
   d. What impact might these feelings have on your ability to lead the group?
   e. What issues may your feelings be inviting you to explore?
   f. How do those feelings affect your ability to lead the group?
   g. If strong feelings make it difficult for you to lead a certain activity, should you consider delegating the leadership of this activity to someone else?
6. What feelings do group members' values, beliefs, or lifestyles evoke in you?

When to Use Set G: Focus on the ChristCare Group Leader's Feelings

This set emphasizes:

- exploring the ChristCare Group Leader's feelings;
- the effect of the ChristCare Group Leader's feelings on the group;
- the ChristCare Group Leader's ties to the group.

A SEA Group might use this set to:

- Allow a ChristCare Group Leader to let off steam about what's going on in the group.
- Invite a ChristCare Group Leader to express his or her intense feelings about what is going on in the group.
- Clarify why a ChristCare Group Leader is dissatisfied with his or her group.
- Explore why a ChristCare Group Leader's feelings about the group seem too intense or not intense enough.
- Figure out why a ChristCare Group Leader seems bored or disinterested.
- Respond to the SEA Group's concerns that a ChristCare Group Leader is becoming too emotionally involved to be objective or effective.
- Understand why a ChristCare Group Leader has difficulty leading a certain activity.

Set H: Focus on the ChristCare Group Leader's Skills

1. Evaluate yourself in one or more of the following ChristCare Group Leader skills:
   a. Listening
   b. Communicating your own thoughts and feelings
   c. Being assertive
   d. Leading Biblical Equipping
   e. Exerting appropriate control over group process
   f. Leading prayer, helping others learn to pray, and praying for your group
   g. Maintaining an atmosphere where people feel free to share
   h. Resolving conflict
   i. Modeling Christian discipleship
   j. Helping group members discover and nurture their gifts for ministry
   k. Sharing Christ's love and helping others share Christ's love
   l. Dealing with day-to-day, nuts and bolts concerns
   m. Keeping the group mission-oriented
   n. Identifying and nurturing new leaders

   How could the SEA Group help you develop your skills?

2. Evaluate your understanding of your group members':
   a. History
   b. Motivations
   c. Feelings
   d. Hopes and dreams
   e. Deep pain and frustration
   f. World view (frame of reference)

3. How well do you lead group members to a better understanding of their feelings through reflective listening, summarizing, or interpreting?
   a. Give examples.
   b. Discuss past and future growth in this area.

4. How effectively do you help the group maintain confidentiality?

5. How have you responded when a group member has experienced a crisis situation (e.g., hospitalization, grief, divorce)?
   a. How have you provided care?
   b. How have you mobilized group support?
   c. How effective have you been in identifying needs for care that exceed your and the group's capacity and then making an appropriate referral?
   d. What help do you need from the SEA Group in order to provide or find more effective care for this individual?

When to Use Set H: Focus on the ChristCare Group Leader's Skills

This set emphasizes:
- how well the ChristCare Group Leader is using his or her caring and leadership skills.

A SEA Group might use this set to:
- Affirm the ChristCare Group Leader for using leadership skills he or she may not be aware of.
- Respond to the SEA Group's feelings that a ChristCare Group Leader is not using certain skills or is not using them effectively.
- Look in depth at how a ChristCare Group Leader handled a certain situation.
- Analyze the skill development that would most benefit a ChristCare Group Leader.
- Help a ChristCare Group Leader assess areas in which growth is required.
- Assist a ChristCare Group Leader in remedying a suspected deficiency in a certain skill area.
- Deal with the SEA Group's concern about a ChristCare Group Leader's ability to handle crisis or caring situations in a group or with a group member.

Set I: Focus on the ChristCare Group Leader's Personal Growth

1. How is God renewing, transforming, changing, or challenging you through this ministry?

2. What attitudes or feelings is this ministry challenging you to acknowledge, express, and confront?

   a. Do any of these attitudes or feelings impede your ministry? (That is, do they make it difficult for you to understand others in your group or to see life as group members see it?)

   b. How are you doing at facing these attitudes and feelings, accepting them, and dealing with them?

   c. How might the SEA Group help you deal with them more effectively?

3. As you engage in this ministry, what insights are you gaining about yourself, about other people, about the human condition, about God?

4. Is your understanding of this ministry's purpose, goals, and techniques changing? If so, how?

5. Is your understanding of servant leadership changing? If so, how?

6. Is your trust and dependence upon God growing through this ministry?

   a. If so, how?

   b. How do you express heightened trust and dependence on God?

7. What needs of your own does being a ChristCare Group Leader meet?

8. What are you learning about your Spirit-given gifts and how to use them?

When to Use Set I: Focus on the ChristCare Group Leader's Personal Growth

This set emphasizes:

- what God is doing in the ChristCare Group Leader's life as a result of this ministry;
- how ChristCare Group Ministry is reshaping the ChristCare Group Leader;
- the effect of the ChristCare Group Leader's own attitudes, values, self-understanding, self-esteem, and relationship with God on his or her ability to lead the small group.

A SEA Group might use this set to:

- Help the ChristCare Group Leader figure out how the person he or she is affects his or her role as a ChristCare Group Leader.
- Point out how the ChristCare Group Leader's relationship with God affects his or her ability to lead the group.

- Respond to the SEA Group's suspicion or opinion that the ChristCare Group Leader is experiencing a crisis of personal growth.
- Encourage a ChristCare Group Leader who doesn't think God is at work in her or him.
- Affirm a ChristCare Group Leader by pointing out the growth the SEA Group has noticed.
- Call the ChristCare Group Leader to be more of a servant leader.
- Explore how being part of a small group is helping the ChristCare Group Leader to grow personally.

Set J: Focus on Developing Apprentice ChristCare Group Leaders

1. How comfortable are you with delegating leadership responsibilities?
2. What leadership tasks have you been delegating? How well have these delegated tasks been performed?
3. How well have you been delegating responsibilities?
   a. Do you give clear assignments?
   b. Do you let the delegatee know how you want the assignment done and by when?
   c. Do you check on the delegatee's progress at appropriate times?
   d. Do you take back the assignment by not allowing the delegatee the freedom to do it him- or herself?
4. Who in your group might make a good Apprentice ChristCare Group Leader? What makes you think so?
5. If you are considering asking a group member to be an Apprentice ChristCare Group Leader, answer the following questions:
   a. How does this person fit the characteristics of a ChristCare Group Leader?
   b. Are there any red flags indicating that this person might not be a good choice as a ChristCare Group Leader? If so, what are they?
6. Evaluate yourself in the following aspects of apprentice leadership development:
   a. Praying for wisdom and guidance

   b. Identifying potential leaders among group members
   c. Encouraging potential leaders to try out their leadership skills
   d. Choosing and assigning tasks that help your Apprentice ChristCare Group Leader take the next step in his or her leadership development
   e. Assertively coaching and guiding your Apprentice ChristCare Group Leader
   f. Assertively talking with your Apprentice ChristCare Group Leader about his or her performance
   g. Affirming, supporting, and encouraging your Apprentice ChristCare Group Leader
   h. Modeling Christian discipleship for your Apprentice ChristCare Group Leader
   i. Making good decisions about the Apprentice ChristCare Group Leader's potential to be a ChristCare Group Leader
   j. Praying regularly for your Apprentice ChristCare Group Leader
7. How ready is your Apprentice ChristCare Group Leader for ChristCare Group Leader Training?
8. How have you grown through the process of developing an Apprentice ChristCare Group Leader?
9. How has your work with your Apprentice ChristCare Group Leader eaten into your time for other leadership activities? How have you responded to this challenge?

When to Use Set J: Focus on Developing Apprentice ChristCare Group Leaders

This set emphasizes:
- shared leadership;
- delegation of responsibility;
- identification of Apprentice ChristCare Group Leaders.

A SEA Group might use this set to:
- Confirm the SEA Group's feelings that the ChristCare Group Leader is having difficulty sharing leadership responsibilities.
- Explore why a ChristCare Group Leader is having trouble delegating tasks.
- Figure out why a ChristCare Group Leader has not identified an apprentice for a long time.

- Support a ChristCare Group Leader in deciding whether a particular group member has leadership potential.
- Express the SEA Group's concerns about a ChristCare Group Leader's selection of an apprentice.
- Determine why a ChristCare Group Leader is having trouble coaching an Apprentice ChristCare Group Leader.
- Advise a ChristCare Group Leader, at the Leader's request, on the selection of an apprentice prior to asking that person to become an apprentice.

Questions for Regular SEA Group Assessment

ChrisＯare Series

Answer these questions quickly and then give this questionnaire to your SEA Group Facilitator. If you don't have answers for any of the questions, simply mark them "NA."

Assessing the Overall SEA Group Process

1. How did you feel about today's SEA Group session?

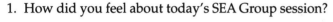

1	2	3	4	5	6	7	8	9	10

Terrible   Okay   Great

2. Rate the distinctively Christian nature of this SEA Group session.

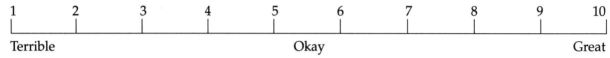

1	2	3	4	5	6	7	8	9	10

Not at all   Completely
centered on Christ   centered on Christ

3. How well focused was your SEA Group during this session?

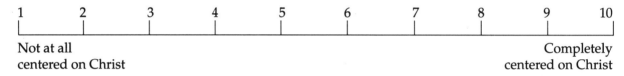

1	2	3	4	5	6	7	8	9	10

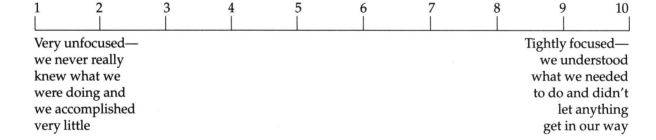

Very unfocused—   Tightly focused—
we never really   we understood
knew what we   what we needed
were doing and   to do and didn't
we accomplished   let anything
very little   get in our way

4. How do you rate the tempo of this SEA Group session?

```
1        2        3        4        5        6        7        8        9        10
|_____|_____|_____|_____|_____|_____|_____|_____|_____|
Too slow                            Just right                            Too fast
```

5. List any other comments or specific suggestions you'd like to make regarding the SEA Group:

Assessing Your Participation in the SEA Group Session

6. How actively did you participate in this SEA Group session?

```
1        2        3        4        5        6        7        8        9        10
|_____|_____|_____|_____|_____|_____|_____|_____|_____|
Not at all actively                                              Very actively
```

7. Did you find yourself wanting to say things, but not saying them?

❑ yes

❑ no

Questions for Periodic SEA Group Assessment

ChrisⒸare Series

This assessment of your SEA Group is designed to help you:

- examine your own SEA Group participation;

- gauge the quality of interaction among SEA Group members;

- monitor the effectiveness of your SEA Group experience; and

- discover areas of growth for you and the SEA Group.

I. Assessing Myself

A. My Feelings about My Participation in the SEA Group

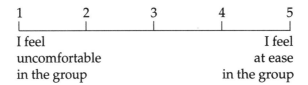

| 1 | 2 | 3 | 4 | 5 |

I feel
uncomfortable
in the group

I feel
at ease
in the group

Please be prepared to talk about your assessment. What specifically makes you feel at ease or uncomfortable in the group? Here are some ideas to prompt your thinking (you may indicate any that apply):

I'm at ease because . . .	I'm uncomfortable because . . .
"I feel welcome and included in the group."	"I feel left out in the group."
"I feel accepted as I am."	"I'm not sure I feel completely accepted by the group."
"I feel respected by group members."	"I wonder if group members respect me."

Thoughts to share with your SEA Group:

B. My Level of Participation in the SEA Group

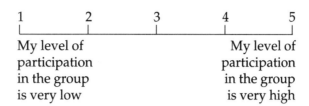

1	2	3	4	5

My level of
participation
in the group
is very low

My level of
participation
in the group
is very high

Please be prepared to talk about your assessment. Why do you think your participation in the group is very high or very low? Here are some ideas to prompt your thinking (you may indicate any that apply):

I participate because . . .	I don't participate much because . . .
"I am very trusting."	"Sometimes I have a hard time trusting people."
"I can really empathize with people."	"Sometimes I have a hard time empathizing with people."
"I tend to accept others' ideas and opinions unconditionally."	"I sometimes find myself being critical of others' ideas and opinions."
"I willingly praise and compliment others."	"I have a hard time praising and complimenting others."
"I freely express warmth and affection."	"Sometimes it is hard for me to be warm and affectionate."
"I'm a great listener."	"I sometimes have trouble paying attention to what others are saying."
"I enjoy sharing my thoughts and ideas in a group."	"I find it difficult to express myself in a group setting."
"I take others' suggestions and comments seriously."	"I don't like it when other people make suggestions about what I should do."
"I'm flexible and open to change and growth."	"I like the way I am and don't see why I need to grow."

Thoughts to share with your SEA Group:

II. Assessing My SEA Group

A. How Well the SEA Group Works Together

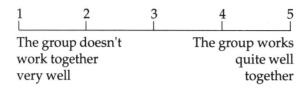

Please be prepared to talk about your assessment. Why do you think the group is working well together and/or not working well together? Here are some ideas to prompt your thinking (you may indicate any that apply):

The group works well because . . .	The group does not work well because . . .
"Everyone participates equally."	"A few tend to dominate the group."
"We listen carefully and understand one another's ideas."	"We have a hard time with listening and sometimes fail to understand one another."
"We share, recognize, and accept one another's feelings."	"We're uncomfortable with feelings and often withhold and ignore them."
"We often affirm one another."	"We're more critical than affirming."
"We are open and honest about ourselves."	"We tend to wear masks, hiding our real selves."
"We have a climate of mutual trust."	"We really don't trust one another very much yet."
"We support one another."	"We tend to be more competitive than supportive."
"We keep confidences."	"We aren't always willing to protect confidentiality."
"We keep on track and remain focused on our task."	"Our conversation often wanders and we lose our focus on our task."
"We use time wisely."	"We waste time in our SEA Group."

Thoughts to share with your SEA Group:

B. How Well the SEA Group Accomplishes Its Goal

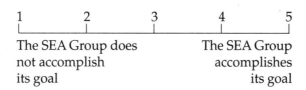

```
1           2           3           4           5
|_____|_____|_____|_____|
|                       |
The SEA Group does       The SEA Group
not accomplish             accomplishes
its goal                        its goal
```

Please be prepared to talk about your assessment. In what ways does the SEA Group accomplish or not accomplish its goal?

How much does the SEA Group help you provide quality leadership to your ChristCare Group in the following areas (rate only those areas that apply to you):

	Not Very Helpful				**Very Helpful**
Community building	1	2	3	4	5
Prayer and worship	1	2	3	4	5
Biblical Equipping	1	2	3	4	5
Missional service	1	2	3	4	5
Covenanting/recovenanting	1	2	3	4	5
Seeing that group members receive needed care	1	2	3	4	5
Group growth	1	2	3	4	5
Finding/working with an apprentice	1	2	3	4	5
Leading your group into/through birthing	1	2	3	4	5
Leading your group into/through closure	1	2	3	4	5

Thoughts to share with your SEA Group:

III. Where Do We Go from Here?

A. Identify one major area where the SEA Group needs to grow.

B. What might we do to help bring about that growth?

Group-Based Manual for ChristCare Group Leaders

How to Participate Effectively in a SEA Group

Outline and Focus Notes

Therefore encourage one another and build each other up, just as in fact you are doing.

1 Thessalonians 5:11

1. Watch the *SEA Group Live!* Video

2. SEA Group Practice—the Beginning

3. SEA Group Practice—the Middle

A. In-Depth Report

B. How to Choose Focus Questions

15-OFN.pmd C: 03/03/2004 R: 11/30/2004

The In-Depth Reporter Suggests

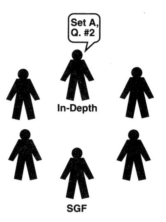

Other SEA Group Members Suggest

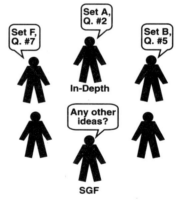

FOCUS NOTE 3

The SEA Group Facilitator Suggests

FOCUS NOTE 4

The SEA Group Agrees Together to Shift Focus Question Sets

C. Analysis

D. Possibilities

E. Action Plan

4. SEA Group Practice—the End

A. Summarize

B. Assess

5. Debriefing

In all my prayers for all of you, I always pray with joy because of your partnership in the gospel from the first day until now, being confident of this, that he who began a good work in you will carry it on to completion until the day of Christ Jesus.

Philippians 1:4–6

PRECLASS READING OUTLINE

I. What to Expect

You are about to begin the next step in your ChristCare Series adventure. This last session before you are commissioned and begin to lead your ChristCare Group marks the transition from the excitement of preparation to the joy of service.

In this Preclass Reading, you'll review or preview sections of ChristCare Group Leader training sessions that you need to have fresh in mind as you begin your ChristCare Group. If you haven't yet covered some sessions that you look at in this Preclass Reading, look forward to them in continuing education. The review or preview assignments are from the *Group-Based Manual for ChristCare Group Leaders* unless the assignment indicates differently. For this review you'll need both volumes of your *Group-Based Manual for ChristCare Group Leaders*, as well as *Beginnings: A ChristCare Group Experience Leader Guide* and *Group Member Guide* and *Biblical Equipping*.

During the in-class session, you'll receive your ministry assignment, learning about the ChristCare Group you are to lead. You'll have an opportunity to share your feelings about your training experience, your upcoming leadership, and the ending of the training ChristCare Group.

II. Get in Touch with Your Feelings

It's normal to experience strong feelings as you anticipate the challenge of leading a ChristCare Group and the closing of the training group. The following exercise will help you get in touch with your feelings.

On a blank piece of paper, write the following words in a circle at the center of the page: "My feelings as I plan to begin leading a ChristCare Group." Draw lines from that circle to other circles in which you write more feelings. Continue to draw lines and circles until you've finished identifying all your feelings.

Example of Feelings Diagram

Think and pray about your feelings. If some are especially difficult for you, take them to God, and maybe even find a friend, fellow trainee, or Equipper with whom to share your feelings. Bring this reflection with you to class. You'll have a chance to share your feelings with fellow trainees.

III. Review of Fundamental Principles

A. Process Orientation

Jim felt frustrated with his one-hour-old ChristCare Group. As members were covenanting, Rita expressed her dissatisfaction with the covenant promise "Attend group meetings faithfully, missing only when it is unavoidable." Rita felt that she should be able to attend group meetings when she felt like it because sometimes after a long day at work she didn't want to do anything but curl up in front of the television.

Jim's blood pressure rose as he recalled the sacrifices he'd made to attend training and the commitment he'd made to lead a group. Suddenly he felt the urge to tell her to find another group if she couldn't sign the covenant.

Jim bit his tongue and didn't say a thing. Within ten minutes the other members of the group had helped Rita see how important regular group attendance was and how much they would miss her if she missed a meeting. Rita signed the covenant, and Jim silently thanked God that he'd remembered to trust the process.

Process Orientation

"What is a process orientation? Simply put, you are process oriented when you focus on the relationship process itself instead of concentrating on the results you want to get. You focus on caring, listening, and accepting people as they are *right now*."[1]

- Review process orientation in session 11 by reading "Process versus Results" on pages 231–232 and "Helping ChristCare Group Members Be Process Oriented" on pages 234–236.
- Look through session 4, "Process-Oriented Caring," in the *Beginnings Leader Guide* and *Beginnings Group Member Guide*.

B. Confidentiality

"Sue won't be able to make the group tonight because she was arrested Tuesday for drunk driving. I'll tell the group and suggest that we pray for her." Kim, the ChristCare Group Leader, looked stunned by Jerry's revelation. "Jerry," she said, "I don't know where you learned about Sue's troubles, but I know for a fact that she doesn't want anyone else to know. That's confidential information, and we need to keep it to ourselves. The two of us can pray for Sue, but if anyone else asks about her, we can't share anything."

Confidentiality

"Breaking confidentiality can hurt individual group members, the ChristCare Group as a whole, a congregation's ChristCare Group Ministry, and even the congregation as a whole. Confidentiality is that important."[2]

- Review confidentiality in session 5 by reading "How You and Your Group Members Can Maintain Confidentiality in Your ChristCare Group" on pages 87–90.
- Confidentiality must be built into your group covenant from the beginning. Take a look at the group covenant in Appendix A of the *Beginnings Group Member Guide*. One of the promises involves the important issue of confidentiality.

IV. Review of Important ChristCare Group Leader Skills

A. Group Facilitation Skills

Don led the Biblical Equipping session. At the first Explore question, Alex jumped right in and began sharing what he'd learned about the passage. After a few minutes, Don said, "Thanks for that information, Alex. Let's see what others have to say. How about you, Lupe?" Lupe said, "I was wondering about the people this letter was written to . . ." Alex interrupted her, answered her question, and then said, "I did hours of research on this passage this week. Let me get my notes."

Don held up his hand and said, "Thanks, Alex, we appreciate your hard work, but we really want everyone to have a chance to share. Who else has a question or thought?"

FOCUS BOX 4

Facilitation

"For a ChristCare Group Leader to facilitate means to assist, encourage, foster, and support group members in order to make it easier for them to participate successfully in the group, care for one another, and grow as Jesus' followers."[3]

- Review facilitation skills by retaking the Facilitation Skills Quiz at the end of the Preclass Reading for session 12 on page 249. If you miss any questions on the quiz, review those sections in the Preclass Reading.

B. Listening

"My mother was just diagnosed with breast cancer," Joan said through tears. "I'd really appreciate your prayers for her and for our family." Barry said, "Of course we'll pray for your mother, Joan. First, though, would you like to tell us more about what happened?"

FOCUS BOX 5

Listening Skills

"Active listening is a way of fully understanding what others are communicating and also helping others understand themselves better. It is the act of listening fully—with your eyes, ears, intuition, and intelligence. Active listening means making sure you understand correctly what the speaker is trying to communicate.

It is using everything you know about listening to encourage the speaker to express his or her feelings and thoughts completely."[4]

- Review listening skills in session 4 by reading "Active Listening—Putting Theory into Practice" on pages 66–70.
- Take a look at the *Beginnings Group Member Guide*, session 2, "Listening as an Act of Love." You can use this session to help ChristCare Group members learn effective listening skills.

C. Caring

Tyrone called Helga, his group leader, and told her that his wife, Margarite, had just taken their three-month-old son to the hospital. "The whole side of his face is swollen and looks bruised," Tyrone said. Within two hours:

- Helga had called all the members of the group to ask them to pray.
- Alice and Felipe had arrived at the hospital to sit and wait with Margarite.
- Florence had arrived at Tyrone's house to take care of the other two children so Tyrone could go to the hospital.
- Isaac, a group member who worked with Margarite, had called the insurance company to find out what Margarite and Tyrone needed to do to make sure the hospital stay was covered.

FOCUS BOX 6

Definition of Care

"Care is responding to people's needs with God's love and with ours.

". . . As Christian caregivers, we can be sure that God is at work in and through our caring, and that the love we give to others is in fact God's love."[5]

- Review caring by reading session 3, section V, "How Do ChristCare Groups Meet People's Needs for Care?" on pages 43–46.
- Look through session 3 of the *Beginnings Group Member Guide*.

V. Review of the Four Group Activities

A. Community Building

"I've been attending this ChristCare Group for six months," Tracy said to her friend Cindy, "and I've made wonderful friends. When the group first started, I was pretty nervous. I don't make friends easily, and I was worried that I'd just sit there in the corner while everyone else got to know one another. But I can still remember the first meeting. We all shared about who we are and what our lives had been like. It was a little hard at first, but I really liked it—hearing about everyone else's lives, and also telling them about mine. Every meeting we shared more, and pretty soon, I really looked forward to it. Now, when I see others from the group at church, I have something to talk about with them. I really love the people in my group, and I know that they love me."

FOCUS BOX 7

Community Grows in Stages

"ChristCare Groups pass through several stages of development on their way to maturity. As groups go through these stages, the group members grow individually, learn to trust one another more, and start working together. Christian community develops."[6]

- Review community building in session 2 by reading section IV, "How to Build Christian Community in a ChristCare Group," on pages 24–25, and Supplement A, "Community-Building Activities," on pages 26–27.
- Each *Beginnings* course session has a section for community building and care. Look at those sections in all the *Leader Guide* sessions to see what community-building possibilities they offer.

B. Prayer and Worship

Felix excitedly told the group about his day. "I was doing what I usually do at work when a guy wearing a suit started asking me questions about what I was doing. I told him and he started taking notes. I got worried. He noticed and said, 'Let me explain. I'm trying to learn from you. No one in this company knows more about what you're doing than you. I want to learn from you.' A couple of guys I work with overheard, and they really kidded me after the guy in the suit left. But I felt kind of proud."

Barbara, the ChristCare Group Leader, said, "Felix, what a wonderful story. Let's take a moment and thank God for this surprising gift." After a few seconds of silence, Mike prayed, "Lord God, you give us such joy when we least expect it . . ."

FOCUS BOX 8

Prayer and Worship

"ChristCare Group prayer and worship can be exciting! Many group members find them to be some of the most meaningful experiences in their lives. They enjoy thanking and praising God in a community of people they know well and care about deeply."[7]

- Review prayer and worship in session 7 by reading "First Steps in Prayer and Worship" on pages 150–153 and "Moving Ahead in Prayer and Worship" on pages 153–160.
- Look through the Prayer and Worship section of each session in the *Beginnings Leader Guide*.

C. Biblical Equipping

Marsha's husband, Greg, greeted her as she arrived home from her ChristCare Group meeting. "Hi, Honey," he said. "What did you do in your ChristCare Group tonight?"

Marsha's face lit up. "We talked about this Bible passage, and it really made sense. It was about people who were in a really tough situation, and they had stopped hoping that God would help them. Then this prophet told them about all the ways God had helped his people in the past and told them to keep hoping that God would help them too. I was thinking that I had sort of given up on God recently, but when we started remembering all the ways God has helped us, I cheered up. I believe God hasn't given up on me."

FOCUS BOX 9

Biblical Equipping

"Biblical Equipping is a disciplined way of encountering the Bible—by yourself and with a small group—for the purpose of hearing and understanding God's Word more clearly, knowing and loving God and others more deeply, and living for and serving God more joyfully and obediently."[8]

- Review chapter 4, "The Biblical Equipping Cycle" in *Biblical Equipping: God's Word in Your World.*
- Review Biblical Equipping in session 9 by reading "How to Choose a Biblical Equipping Series" on pages 190–191.

D. Missional Service

Soon after her group began, Robin introduced the idea of missional service. "In our covenant, we agreed that we would reach out," she said. "I'd like to suggest that we start by praying for our pastor. Let's make a point at every meeting of asking God to bless and guide our pastor." The group agreed and prayed faithfully. A few months later the pastor preached about the importance of sharing Christ's love with others outside the congregation. John said at the next group meeting, "We've been praying for our pastor, and I've been thinking a lot about the sermon last Sunday. If we are really going to support our pastor, we need to find ways to reach out to people who aren't members of the church. How could we do that?"

FOCUS BOX 10

Missional Service

"Missional service means reaching out with Christ's love to meet the needs of people outside the group. There are three key aspects to this definition:

- **Reaching out with Christ's love.** Missional service is a way for groups to pass on to others the love they have received from God. The joy that group members find in loving Jesus and knowing of his love for them motivates them to serve. When groups reach out in missional service, they are being the body of Christ, touching others with his love.

- **Meeting needs.** ChristCare Groups can meet a wide variety of needs. God cares for people wholistically—physically, emotionally, spiritually, socially, and intellectually. ChristCare Groups also are called to care in some or all of these dimensions. ChristCare Groups serve Jesus by meeting the needs of those around them (see Matthew 25:31–46). . . .

- **Caring for those outside the group.** Missional service focuses on others' needs, not group members'. That certainly doesn't mean that group members don't provide care for one another. Yet they must also look beyond the group's boundary for service opportunities.

Otherwise, the group can become selfish and self-serving—certainly not obedient to Jesus or faithful to his example."[9]

Review missional service in session 8 by reading "Leading Your ChristCare Group into Missional Service" on pages 175–177.

VI. Future Group Needs That Require Attention from the Beginning

Eventually your group will close, perhaps birthing two new groups. You may choose and work with an Apprentice ChristCare Group Leader once your group is established. Though these aspects of group leadership may seem far off, there are important ideas to know and communicate and steps you need to take from the group's beginning.

A. Apprentices

Janet had suspected Pat would make a good group leader since the group began. When Pat agreed to serve as Apprentice, the group grew to a new level. Janet was very good at leading Biblical Equipping and helping group members get to know and care for one another. Pat had gifts in reaching out to include others in the group. By the time the group had grown to 12 members, Pat had completed ChristCare Group Leader training and was ready to lead one of the new groups that began as the old group gave birth.

FOCUS BOX 11

Apprentices

"Serving as Apprentices gives people the chance to find out what it is like to be a ChristCare Group Leader. It also gives you the opportunity to observe them in a leadership role and assess their gifts and commitment to this kind of ministry. Apprenticeship helps everyone make the best decision about whom to train as ChristCare Group Leaders."[10]

Preview apprenticeship in session 17 by reading "Identify Potential Apprentice ChristCare Group Leaders" on pages 342–344.

B. Birthing

Jerry summed up the group's feelings when he said, "This is really difficult, but I guess we knew it was coming. Dan told us from the beginning that we would eventually get so big we would have to end this group and birth two new ones." Pete said, "I guess the only thing harder than birthing new groups would be to try to keep meeting with this many people." "Things have changed since we've grown so big," Yolanda said; "the group we knew months ago has already ended." Amanda turned to Dan and said, "It looks like you were right."

FOCUS BOX 12

Birthing

"Birthing does not mean that one ChristCare Group sends some of its members off to form a new group and the original group continues. It means the original group comes to an end and two new groups form. As you will learn in session 21, How to Bring Closure to ChristCare Groups, all groups have a cycle: birth, life, and death. When your group reaches the point where it needs to birth, it will change so substantially that you will officially end it. Intentionally bringing it to a close will set free the two new groups. They will be able to begin their own lives without unresolved feelings about the old group."[11]

- Preview birthing in session 20 by reading "Reaching the Decision to Birth New Groups" on pages 383–387.

C. Closure

"Joann and Greg have been such an important part of our group, and now they have to move away and leave us," Ryan said. The group had just learned that Joann's employer had transferred her and the family was having to move. "It's very important that we take time to say good-bye to Greg and Joann and talk about how their leaving makes us feel. We've talked about how no group lasts forever, but it's still a big loss, knowing that we won't be seeing them at every meeting."

FOCUS BOX 13

Closure

"Closure is the process of bringing group life together to a productive, healthy end. You should bring your group to closure whenever your group disbands or divides to create new groups. . . . Groups also need some form of closure whenever a member leaves the group or before long breaks."[12]

Preview closure in session 21 by reading "Prepare for Closure from the Beginning of Your Group" on page 407.

VII. Preparing to Begin Your Group

Enrique arrived early for the first meeting of his ChristCare Group. He'd called all the group members to make sure they remembered the meeting. He'd prepared to lead the first session of *Beginnings* and had copies of the *Beginnings Group Member Guide* ready to hand out. He had prayed—a lot—for God's blessings on the group and especially on the first meeting. Enrique was ready. Now it was time to start the group, trusting God.

- Review your notes from session 1, How to Get Your ChristCare Group Off to a Great Start.

- Review the first section of the *Beginnings Leader Guide*.

VIII. Ready, Set, . . .

This is a time of excitement and joyful anticipation as you look forward to putting all your training to use leading a ChristCare Group. You're well trained and ready to lead. Continue praying, thanking God for the chance to serve, and counting on the Spirit to give you the guidance, faith, and love you need to serve Jesus well. Trust that "he who began a good work in you will carry it on to completion until the day of Christ Jesus" (Philippians 1:6).

To get ready for the in-class session, be sure to bring your feelings diagram and think more about your feelings as you prepare to begin group leadership and bring closure to this training ChristCare Group.

ENDNOTES

1. Session 11, Preclass Reading, page 231.

2. Session 5, Preclass Reading, page 87.

3. Session 12, Preclass Reading, pages 243–244.

4. Session 4, Preclass Reading, page 67.

5. Session 3, Preclass Reading, page 42.

6. Session 2, Preclass Reading, page 15.

7. Session 7, Preclass Reading, pages 145–146.

8. David A. Paap, *Biblical Equipping: God's Word in Your World* (St. Louis: Stephen Ministries, 1996), page 2.

9. Session 8, Preclass Reading, page 170.

10. Session 17, Preclass Reading, page 341.

11. Session 20, Preclass Reading, page 381.

12. Session 21, Preclass Reading, page 403.

Circles of Care with Christ at the Center

Outline and Focus Notes

In all my prayers for all of you, I always pray with joy because of your partnership in the gospel from the first day until now, being confident of this, that he who began a good work in you will carry it on to completion until the day of Christ Jesus.

Philippians 1:4–6

1. Class Member-Led Prayer and Worship

2. Community Building: Sharing Feelings at a Time of Change

A. Our Times Are in Your Hands

B. Sharing Feelings

FOCUS NOTE 1

Feelings You Might Share

1. You may want to share the feelings diagram you made as part of your Preclass Reading.
2. You may want to share other feelings about finishing ChristCare Group Leader training.
3. You may want to share your favorite memory from our time together as a training ChristCare Group.
4. You may want to share hopes, apprehensions, or excitement about leading a ChristCare Group.
5. You may want to say thank you to others in your group who were a blessing to you in some way during ChristCare Group Leader training.

16-OFN.pmd C: 03/03/2004 R: 12/08/2004

3. Biblical Equipping: Jesus Sends His Small Group Out to Make Disciples (Matthew 28:16–20)

FOCUS NOTE 2

Jesus Sends His Small Group Out to Make Disciples (Matthew 28:16–20)

[16] Then the eleven disciples went to Galilee, to the mountain where Jesus had told them to go. [17] When they saw him, they worshiped him; but some doubted. [18] Then Jesus came to them and said, "All authority in heaven and on earth has been given to me. [19] Therefore go and make disciples of all nations, baptizing them in the name of the Father and of the Son and of the Holy Spirit, [20] and teaching them to obey everything I have commanded you. And surely I am with you always, to the very end of the age."

FOCUS NOTE 3

Explore Questions

1. How would Jesus' disciples know how to fulfill his command to go and make disciples?

2. Jesus says that all authority has been given to him. What does that have to do with his disciples going out and making disciples?

3. Why do you think Jesus thought it important that new disciples be baptized and taught to obey everything he commanded?

4. Why is it important that Jesus promises to be with his disciples until the end?

FOCUS NOTE 4

Connect Questions

1. How do people become disciples: How do they reach the point where they obey everything Jesus has commanded them to do?

2. How can the members of your ChristCare Group help one another grow as disciples? How will you facilitate that growth in your ChristCare Group?

3. Jesus is with you in your work of making disciples. How do you sense his presence? In what additional ways do you need to sense his presence?

4. ChristCare Group Assignments

5. Go Forth to Lead

FOCUS NOTE 5

Go Forth to Lead, Go Forth to Serve

OPENING PRAYER

Worship Leader Let us pray.

Lord Jesus, thank you for the richness of this training ChristCare Group. We ask you to be with these new ChristCare Group Leaders as they go forth today to begin building circles of care with you, Lord, at the center. Bless each leader with the gifts that he or she needs for the ministry ahead. Send your Holy Spirit to comfort and encourage them, to give them the faith and courage they need to do the ministry you've called them to. Just as

Focus Note 5 is continued on page 340.

you assured the apostles that you would always be with them in their ministry, be with our new leaders as they build transformational ChristCare Groups that will bring glory to you.

All Amen.

LITANY

Worship Leader God has called each of you by name; he's given you gifts and a heart for this ministry.

All You have called us, Lord, and we follow.

Worship Leader Jesus, you said, "'Now that I, your Lord and Teacher, have washed your feet, you also should wash one another's feet. I have set you an example that you should do as I have done for you'" (John 13:14–15). Teach us all to be servant leaders in your service, Lord.

All You have called us, Lord, and we follow.

Worship Leader Be with each of these new leaders, Lord, as they go out, equipped to serve you. Work in and through them to accomplish your purposes. Help them build life-transforming groups that will bring members ever closer to you.

All You have called us, Lord, and we follow.

Worship Leader Let us pray.

All Lord Jesus, you have called us and we answer. We are ready. Send us out, as you did your own small group of disciples so long ago, to bring many others to you. Give us the faith, hope, and love we need to lead others into transforming encounters with you. In your name we pray. Amen.